ARCHITECTURAL ENGINEERING—NEW STRUCTURES

ARCHITECTURAL ENGINEERING

New Structures

Edited by

ROBERT E. FISCHER
SENIOR EDITOR (ENGINEERING)
Architectural Record

An Architectural Record Book

McGRAW-HILL BOOK COMPANY
New York   San Francisco   Toronto   London

PREFACE

More innovation has occurred in the design and construction of structures for buildings in the years since World War II than in any other period in this country's history. The influence of these innovations on the shape of architecture is perhaps less spectacular than was that of the steel skeleton frame, which spawned our skyscrapers; nonetheless, the range of materials and systems available to architects and structural engineers today offers limitless possibilities in span, height, and shape to suit any building purpose.

Many systems, while introduced to circumvent wartime shortage of materials, have had lasting values in economy and function, and thus have become part of the building lexicon. Other systems, stemming from the imaginations of mathematicians and structural theorists, had inherently high load-carrying efficiency, but caught the architect's eye because they suggested new architectural forms. More recently we have seen the reevaluation of such age-old concepts as the bearing wall, in an effort to make the structure a more integral part of the building, performing more functions and work. And not only are all the basic structural materials abundantly available, but as a result of growing competition, producers are offering materials of higher strengths and quality, and a larger variety of structural components. So now we have a plethora of new systems and techniques by virtue of improved materials and a growing sophistication in engineering analysis. On the negative side, this knowledge permits practically anything to be built, regardless of its architectural merit. On the positive side, structures can be designed to work with finesse, rather than by brute force, thus leading to better architectural solutions as well as engineering solutions.

This book, compiled from selected articles from the Architectural Engineering section of *Architectural Record*, covers new structural concepts, systems, and designs introduced during the past fifteen years. Subjects covered range from precast and prestressed concrete through thin shells; from composite construction through plastic design, suspension structures, and space frames in steel; from lamella roofs through stressed-skin panels in wood. Structural systems are discussed both in general terms and by means of specific case histories. Newly developed design theories and the personal design approaches of renowned engineers are included.

The structures are not considered as isolated entities, but in context with the total building design problem. Some of the design problems discussed are: how prestressing, composite construction, and suspension structures provide longer spans and freedom from column interference; how off-site construction offers greater economy; how structures can be designed to provide more space for and greater freedom in the location of mechanical services; how the trend toward greater efficiency in structural performance is manifested in the changing appearance of buildings; how unique structural systems have served as principal visual elements of important buildings. The purpose of the book is to give an orientation to what these new structural systems are, how they work, how they relate to architectural design, and how they are designed and built.

Robert E. Fischer

CONTENTS

Section 4 SUSPENSION STRUCTURES

Section 5 COMPONENT SYSTEMS

Section 6 DESIGN PHILOSOPHY, THEORY

Section 1

SPACE STRUCTURES

SPACE STRUCTURES IN STEEL

by Robert E. Rapp, Regional Engineer, American Institute of Steel Construction, Inc.

While grid and space frameworks are not new in concept, or even in practice, they have not been extensively used in this country.

But since the list of applications is beginning to grow, it is important that the architect and engineer be aware of the availability of information on the design of these frames, be able to distinguish types of systems, and be conscious of the considerations involved in their structural designs.

There are many types of space structures. These take the general form of the simple monolithic grid, double layer grid and coplanar systems (folded or curved structures).

GRID SYSTEMS

A grid framework can be described as a continuous monolithic plane system usually symmetrically tied together by a series of longitudinal and transverse members to resist all applied forces acting normal to the system's plane.

The most common of these grids are the rectangular and diagonal types. The diagonal arrangement is commonly referred to as a "diagrid." The diagrid is the most popular because of its greater rigidity as compared to the rectangular grid system. Figure 1 shows layouts of various grid patterns most frequently occuring in practice. It is apparent from the geometry of the different systems shown that the analysis and fabrication costs would be less for the rectangular or diagrid arrangements than for the other types illustrated.

John Hotchkiss, Senior Regional Engineer for the AISC, in a paper on lamellas, diagrids and arches has cited the following advantages of grid construction:

1) Considerable reduction in required structural depth,
2) Avoidance of main beams and girders,
3) Notable saving in steel,
4) Simplification of fabrication due to repetition of members.

He pointed out further that a hypothetical grid system measuring 45 by 75 ft with no internal column support weighed 20.3 tons as compared with a weight of 26.6 tons for a floor system of girder and beam design—a saving of 6.3 tons of steel. In addition the grid system had a required depth of 18 in. as compared to a 36 in. depth for the conventional design. With a depth difference of 18 in. the architect and engineer could imagine what the saving in height might be for multi-story buildings in which large column-free areas are required.

Grid systems are noted for their

TWO PROPOSED SPACE FRAME DESIGNS

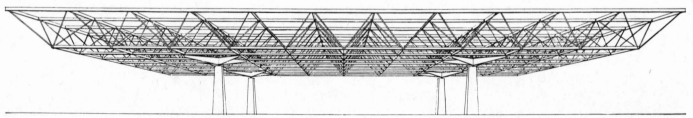

Structural steel space frame for a high school in Pekin, Illinois covers an area of 280 by 168 ft, has a 28-ft cantilever, and is 14-ft deep. Foley, Hackler, Thompson and Lee, Architects. The Engineers Collaborative, Structural Engineers

Ara Derderian

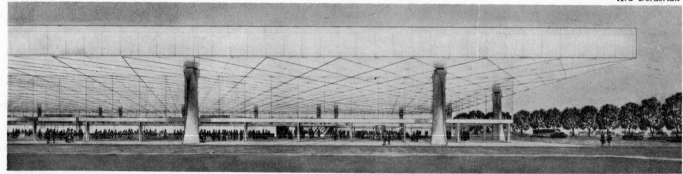

Competition winner for multi-airlines terminal at New York International Airport. Frame is 625 by 225 ft, spanning 200 ft between columns. Designed for pre-assembled steel tetrahedrons, the frame is tied together at the top by a reinforced concrete slab and at the bottom by tension cables in the central area, changing to steel compression members around columns. I.M. Pei & Associates, Architects; Ammann & Whitney, Structural Engineers

A RECTANGULAR DOUBLE-LAYER GRID

Roof structure of Cadet Dining Hall for Air Force Academy consists of 23 Warren trusses intersecting at right angles to cover an area 308 ft square. Skidmore, Owings & Merrill, Architects and Engineers

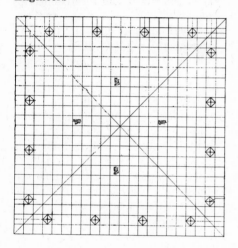

FOLDED-TRUSS ROOF

Folded roof for a high school gym in Littleton, Mass. is framed with structural steel shapes. The Architects Collaborative, Architects; Goldberg & LeMessurier, Structural Engineers

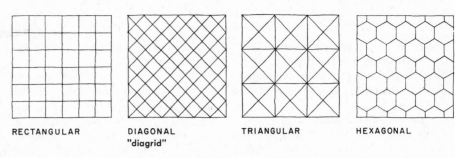

RECTANGULAR DIAGONAL "diagrid" TRIANGULAR HEXAGONAL

Figure 1. Grid Patterns Used in Structures

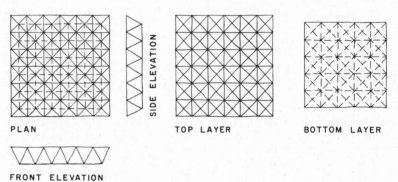

SIDE ELEVATION

PLAN TOP LAYER BOTTOM LAYER

FRONT ELEVATION

Figure 2. Typical Double Layer Grid System

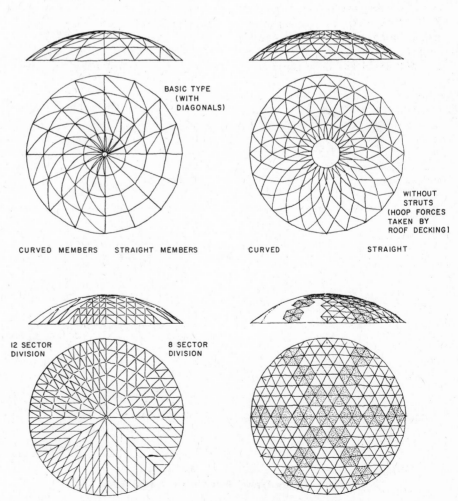

BASIC TYPE (WITH DIAGONALS)

WITHOUT STRUTS (HOOP FORCES TAKEN BY ROOF DECKING)

CURVED MEMBERS STRAIGHT MEMBERS   CURVED   STRAIGHT

12 SECTOR DIVISION   8 SECTOR DIVISION

Figure 3. Dome Designs Incorporating Grid Patterns

ability to distribute loads throughout their interconnecting members. It is distribution of stress which allows large areas to be covered without internal columns.

The monolithic plane grid framework is normally erected as a roof or floor system. Interconnecting members are commonly fabricated of uniform cross-section. Monolithic two-way grids form an ideal roof or floor frame for earthquake-resistant structures in which the floor and roof elements have to transmit horizontal forces. Such grids provide many paths for these forces.

As greater unsupported areas are required, it may be found that the monolithic grid system becomes too cumbersome. The designer may then resort to the double-layer grid. A typical double-layer grid is shown in Figure 2. These three-dimensional planar systems are designed in many geometric patterns and have many names describing them; however, this writer prefers to call these frames "double-layer grid structures" as they are referred to by Dr. Z. S. Makowski in his paper published by the *Architectural Association Journal*, March 1961 (London). Dr. Makowski has done considerable

research on many types of grid spatial structures.

These double layer systems are suited for structures under the action of heavy concentrated loads, and, like the monolithic grid systems, allow the engineer to take full advantage of repetition of members and prefabrication.

DOMES, ARCHES, FOLDED PLATES

The discussion thus far has been mainly about monolithic planar systems. Space structures often take the form of co-planar grid systems in the form of domes, arches, valley-ridge arrangements and other more complex spatial form.

From Figure 3, dome designs incorporating grid patterns can be classified as the following types:

1) Schwedler Dome.
2) Lattice or Lamella types.
3) Parallel Lamella systems.
4) Hexagonal systems.

This space frame is defined here as a multi-planar continuous framework which acts simultaneously in three dimensions to resist all applied forces. Space frames not only take the form of arches, and domes, but also can be constructed as spatial

grids and rigid frame bents in many different patterns.

Figure 4 shows some typical designs incorporating spatial grid arrangements.

Greater spans may be achieved with this folded plate, spatial grid method by utilizing what German engineers call a rhombic truss. The author prefers the term lattice girder. These girders are truss arrangements with interlaced, interconnecting members as shown in Figure 5 (a). Although these lattice sections are indeterminate, the idea is simply to provide a method for cutting down the l/r stiffness ratio of the truss chords and interconnecting members. This enables the engineer to design long span spatial truss arrangements constructed of relatively lightweight steel. Economical column-free spans up to 300 ft can be designed with lattice sections. For example, if lattice sections are laid in a simulated valley-ridge arrangement such as folded plates, one-story buildings can be made column free internally for widths up to 300 ft, and for lengths along the gable section to infinity. Figure 5 (b) shows typical double-layer spatial grid gable sections for long-span construc-

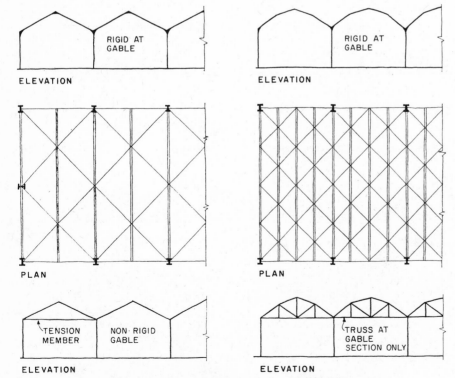

Figure 4. Two Typical Determinate Spatial Grids.

Definitions

GRID FRAMEWORK
A continuous monolithic plane system generally symmetrically tied together by a series of longitudinal and transverse members to resist all applied forces acting normal to the system's plane.

SPACE FRAME
A multi-planar continuous framework which acts simultaneously in three dimensions to resist all applied forces.

LATTICE GIRDER
An indeterminate truss system consisting of internal tension and compression members arranged in a grid pattern tying together the upper and lower chords so as to resist applied forces acting in line with the system's plane.

tion: valley ridge; barrel arches.

Spatial grids may be used for circular dome sections with the folded plate method. Figure 6 shows these members forming a valley-ridge, pie-shaped sectional arrangement terminating at a compression ring in the center of the structure. The individual truss sections may be designed as determinate members, or as lattice members where greater spans are required.

Axial forces are the prime concern in spatial grid arrangements. But in addition, the vertical loading conditions for bending must be investigated. Methods for determining axial and bending forces in determinate sections are covered in a very timely paper on a "Steel Frame Folded Plate Roof" by Oliver A. Baer shows the simplicity of designing these frames by statically determinate analysis. (American Society of Civil Engineers, *Journal of Structural Division Proceedings.*)

PLASTIC DESIGN

The author was asked recently if a ridged frame dome could be designed plastically. The structure in question was a circular shaped building divided into a 12-sided polygon with a diameter of 100 ft. The columns were 20 ft high. A typical section was analyzed. It was found that 14 WF 30 beams and columns were required to carry a uniform dead and live load of 70 lb per sq ft. Figure 7 shows the simple plastic analysis in algebraic-geometric form. Similar analysis may be performed for different dimensions and loading conditions.

A very good publication on the use of plastic analysis pertaining to grid frameworks is *Plastic Analysis of Structures*, Philip G. Hodge Jr., McGraw-Hill Book Co., Inc., 1959.

The most simple of the monolithic or co-planar grid-space systems are highly complex to analyze. If exact analysis is necessary, this complexity may be greatly reduced by assuming the joints as hinge-connected instead of rigid. Also, by ignoring the torsional forces the number of design calculations may be cut. Analysis of monolithic grids is discussed in "An

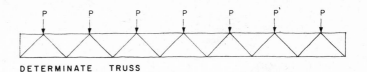

DETERMINATE TRUSS

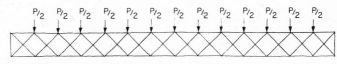

LATTICE OR RHOMBIC TRUSS

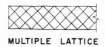

MULTIPLE LATTICE

ELEVATION

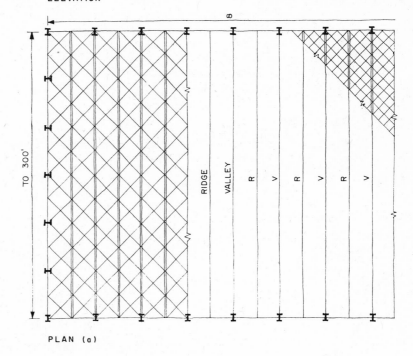

PLAN (a)

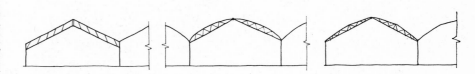

ELEVATION OF TYPICAL GABLE SECTIONS (b)

Figure 5. Typical Lattice Spatial Grid Arrangements

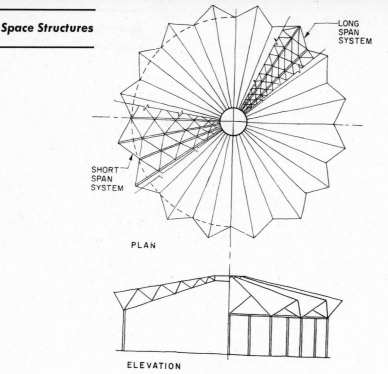

PLAN

ELEVATION

Figure 6. Rigid Frame Dome (Above)

Figure 7. Plastic Analysis (Below)

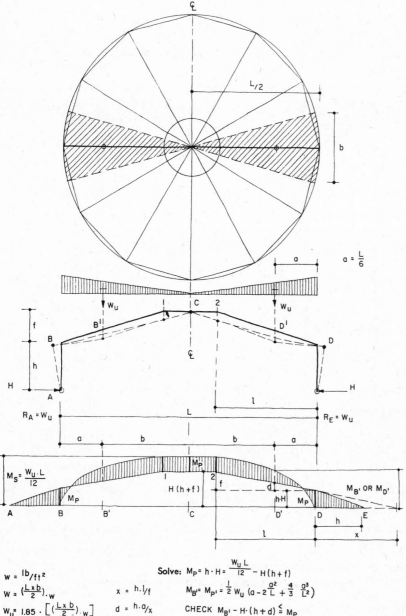

$w = {}^{lb}/_{ft^2}$

$W = \left(\frac{L \times b}{2}\right) \cdot w$

$W_u = 1.85 \cdot \left[\left(\frac{L \times b}{2}\right) \cdot w\right]$

$x = h.l/_f$

$d = h.a/_x$

Solve: $M_P = h \cdot H = \frac{W_u L}{12} - H(h+f)$

$M_{B'} = M_{P'} = \frac{1}{2} W_u \left(a - 2\frac{a^2}{L} + \frac{4}{3}\frac{a^3}{L^2}\right)$

CHECK $M_{B'} - H \cdot (h+d) \overset{\leq}{=} M_P$

Analysis of Open Grid Frameworks" by Dr. Makowski. His method permits the designer to solve a rectangular or diagrid frame in a matter of minutes. Dr. Makowski gives constants in chart form for determining moments, shears and deflections.

If the analysis is simplified by assuming the nodes hinge-connected, calculations will be on the conservative side. If lightness of the structure is the prime factor in design, however, the engineer must resort to more exact analysis. In this case the nodes would be assumed to be rigidly connected and all forces, moments and deflections would be considered. This analysis is highly redundant, especially with the co-planar or double layer systems. Where many contemplated complex designs are anticipated, it would probably be better for the designer to develop an electronic computer program. [Model analysis has been used where edge loading conditions were complicated and varying—Ed.]

The steel industry has made available new high-strength, low-alloy steels such as A440 and A441 which have yield strengths of 50,000 psi in rolled shapes and plate thicknesses to ¾ in. Another high-strength, heat-treated steel is now available in structural shapes with yields in excess of 100,000 psi.

Steel is available now with controlled properties and yield strengths ranging from 33,000 psi to over 100,000 psi.

Engineers can appreciate the structural advantages in conventional uses of these steels, let alone the advantages they may achieve with their use in space and grid frame design. And the architect can visualize the lightness in design possible.

Design tools are available to the engineer through a storehouse of reference material. It remains only for the architect and engineer to use these materials and apply these tools to open up space with structure.

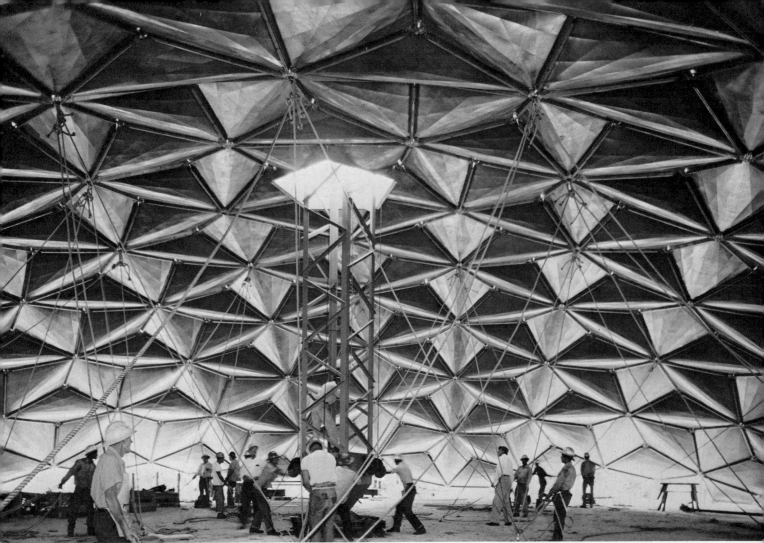

Werner Stoy

ALUMINUM PANELS PLEATED FOR STRENGTH

An aluminum dome built in 1957 at Hawaiian Village in Honolulu serves as a convention hall seating 2,000 people. Rising almost 50 ft at its highest point, it spans 145 ft with no interior columns. It is 1/16 in. thick.

TAKING A LEAF from the aerodynamicist's notebook, engineers of the Kaiser Aluminum & Chemical Corporation have fashioned thin aluminum sheets into rigid panels which combine to form a stressed-skin shell capable of resisting winds up to twice hurricane force. The diamond-shaped panels, proportioned in ten different sizes according to their position in the dome, are strengthened by six bends radiating from each end and intersecting in an intricate sunburst pattern. An aluminum strut, bridging the lengthwise valley created by this network of radial bends, makes each panel a strong structural unit, with loads equally divided between the panel and the strut.

These curved and stiffened aluminum segments are geometrically arranged and fit together jig-saw fashion to mold the spherical surface of the dome. Where the corners of the panels converge, they are connected with specially-designed castings that disperse the loads through the shell to aluminum pipe struts used to anchor the dome to its foundation. The dual use of the aluminum panels as skin and framing members produces a strong, lightweight shell in which a minimum of materials gives a maximum of usable space.

The repetition of the same easily-joined basic units throughout also made it possible for the erection crew to assemble the dome in a matter of hours, without benefit of previous experience with a similar structure. Only 20 hours after the first panel was placed, the dome was ready to be anchored to its foundation.

The dome components — panels, struts and castings — were fabricated at a Kaiser plant in California. Before being shipped to the Hawaiian Village site, the 575 aluminum panels, which vary in length from 106 to

140 in. and in width from 65 to 82 in., were color-coded with a dab of paint on each to assure proper positioning in the dome. The panels and struts were formed without special dies, on a standard press brake. The precision with which they were made, plus the inherent stiffness of the panels themselves, was demonstrated later, by a settlement of only ¾ in. in the completed dome.

Upon their arrival in Honolulu, the panels and struts were assembled, and trucked to the dome site where a demountable structural steel mast 96 ft tall had been set up in the center of the dome's concrete foundation.

Around this mast were assembled the panels which form the uppermost portion of the finished dome. When this section had been bolted together, it was raised high enough to allow another perimeter of panels to be installed. These in turn were bolted together, the larger section lifted, a third set of panels assembled — and so on until all the panels were in place.

For assembly, the dome was divided into five segments, with a five-man crew for each. Three of the men positioned the panels and joined them to the castings; the other two bolted adjacent panels together through

Werner Stoy

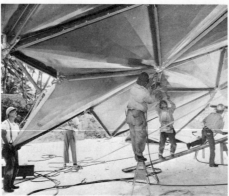

¾ in. flanges along their outer edges to form a rigid shell. At those points where six of the "diamonds" converged, their ends were slipped over the prongs of star-shaped gusset castings and held in place with drift pins until they were bolted, while at the obtuse-angle corners of the panels the hub castings used to fasten the struts to the panels were simply fitted together and joined. All connections were made with special aluminum lockbolts to obtain a permanent high-strength union.

When the dome had been completely assembled and lifted, it was lined up with concrete piers spaced at equal intervals round its circumference, and anchored to them with aluminum struts. These piers, from 18 to 65 in. high, reach down 6 ft to a coral base, providing firm anchorage for the dome. The 2½ in. pipe struts extending from each pier to the nearest gusset casting are connected at their base with pinned end connections to accommodate the 3 in. expansion and contraction of the dome. Rotary movement was prevented by placing the tips of the base panels in a track.

The anchorage of the dome completed, the portable

The stressed-skin aluminum dome of the Hawaiian Village convention hall was assembled in sections around a steel mast and hoisted with hand winches. Erection crews of the Terminal Steel Company of Honolulu fit the panels into place like a jigsaw puzzle, then bolted them to castings and adjacent panels. To anchor the completed dome, base struts extend from concrete piers to the nearest gusset casting. Erection time: 20 hours.

Werner Stoy

mast and rigging were removed and the exterior surface caulked along the joints between panels with a special sealing compound. A permanent overlapping cover of five aluminum panels was also placed over the 50 sq-ft opening left at the top of the dome. This elevated cap permits exhausting of air through the opening, forming what is in effect a built-in ventilating system.

Interior work on the convention hall involved only the construction of concrete walls at several of the openings to provide for a stage and other facilities, and the treatment for sound.

According to acoustical consultants Bolt, Beranek and Newman, the convention hall is expected to present no difficult acoustical problems. The large curved segments will in themselves provide better acoustics than would a smooth spherical surface, and the use of a sound amplifying system will further reduce the need for special sound control devices. Only $\frac{1}{3}$ of the interior surface will be treated, the acoustical material being applied directly to the panels to retain their geometric pattern while supplying alternate hard and soft sounding surfaces.

Aluminum hub castings (far left) fasten struts to panels, are bolted together during assembly. Star-shaped castings join tips of six converging panels.

GIANT BALLOONS HOIST
ALUMINUM STRESSED-SKIN DOME

A unique factory glistening on the plains of Kansas marks the first industrial use of Kaiser Aluminum's stressed-skin dome—and the first use of balloons as scaffolding for a metal building.

The dome, which will provide 16,-500 sq ft of manufacturing space for the Fi Fo Conveyor Company, is identical to the prototype dome built at Hawaiian Village, and shown in the preceeding article. However the steel mast that hoisted the Hawaiian Village dome onto its foundation was replaced in this instance by two rubber-coated nylon balloons, one 95 ft in diameter, the other 50 ft in diameter.

To hold the panels which form the dome's crown, two 10 ft high "A" frames were set on the concrete foundation with a ⅝ in. steel cable spanning some 50 ft between them. The pentagonal framework and sections which form the vent cover at the top of the dome were attached to a hook hung in the center of the cable span, and the first five panels fastened around it. The balloons were then laid on the foundation, the smaller atop the larger, and anchored in place with chain ties. As additional panels were bolted together about the perimeter of the shell, the balloons were gradually inflated by a high-capacity blower, permitting work crews to fasten all the panels at ground level. Inflation was controlled so that the balloons' diameters remained constant while they expanded vertically to a height of almost five stories—taking the shell with them as they went. When all the panels had been attached, the dome was anchored to 25 concrete piers about its circumference, and the supporting balloons removed.

The shell was erected in 22 hours by a 38-man crew under the direction of the Fi Fo Construction Company, originators of the balloon erection method. The completed dome is 145 ft in diameter, 49½ ft high.

Supporting balloons **expand**

Shell is lifted **gradually**

Panels are bolted **in place**

Balloons, shown during a test, expand vertically to a height of 5 stories

Completed dome is anchored **to base**

N. Bleeker Green

ADVANCED STRUCTURE FOR FLEXIBILITY

Put transistors and Texas together and you're bound to come up with something unusual in the way of a structure. To meet the swiftly changing patterns of the electronics market, production lines frequently must be expanded, deleted or built from scratch. So the owners wanted their building to be a versatile tool for adaptation to these needs.

This 310,000 sq ft building with its 37 hyperbolic paraboloids, and its space frame carrying 106 unit air conditioners, plus all pipes, ducts and wiring, not only anticipates rapid change—it says so to its employees and industry at large.

There are three levels in the new Texas Instruments Semiconductor-Components plant: (1) ground floor for administrative and engineering offices and laboratories, (2) the 8-ft, 3-in. space frame between the two main floors, containing air conditioning units and all pipes and ducts, and (3) the top floor for manufacturing.

The structure of the between floors mechanical area is comprised of a series of precast concrete, V-tetra-pods (four-footed diagonal members) which tie together the upper level floor slab and lower level ceiling slab into a rigid three-dimensional truss or space frame. The concrete space frame is supported by spiral-reinforced, square concrete columns on 63-ft centers, which is the bay dimension in both directions, and also the roofed over area covered by one hyperbolic paraboloid. On the manufacturing floor the column is divided into four smaller columns which support the roof. Each of these four carries one corner of a four-gable type hyperbolic parabolid shell. The columns are covered so as to form an air plenum and to enclose roof drainage pipes and sprinkler system plumbing. Each shell, 3 to 4 in. thick, is structurally

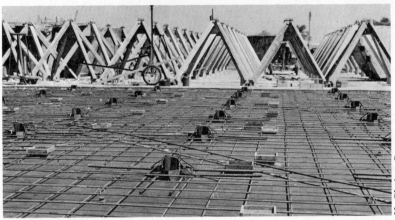

Space frame of precast concrete "tetrapods" is sandwiched between ground level office floor and manufacturing floor on top. It is supported by square concrete columns, 63-ft on center, except at the north and west perimeters where the frame cantilevers 32 ft to give a sheltered walkway. At these edges, columns are circular and smaller, and a column is added at midspan. Bottom slab of the space frame (shown directly above) which has prestressing cables acts as the bottom chord, slab of the manufacturing floor as the top chord. Webs in space frame at supports take heavy shear forces

Dust, and moisture as well, are enemies of transistor manufacture. Workers must don lint-free clothing, and pass through an air lock before going into the "Snow-White" area

1500 access holes at 10-½ ft centers in the manufacturing floor slab make available any service at any point. Services include natural gas, some rare gases, water, electricity, communications and comfort conditioned air

Extreme care in transistor assembly is exemplified by use of dry boxes in which humidity is limited to 12 per cent instead of 20 per cent as in room atmosphere itself

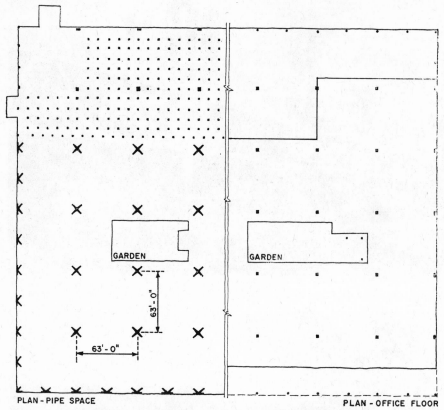

Where space frame cantilevers at west and north sides (bottom and left on plan), space frame diagonals have only two webs at 45 deg. angle in plan, but there are additional webs in the plane of the outside wall. Mechanical room was placed in one corner of building (upper left on plan) to hide cooling tower and give convenient shipping dock

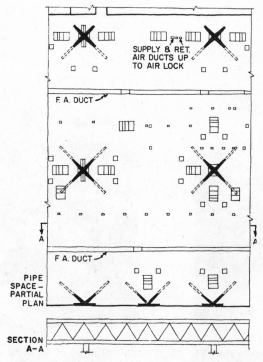

Blowup of manufacturing top floor plan indicates webbing in space frame (see photo previous page) and air conditioning units around columns

free from the adjacent one, and the space between is covered by precast wood-cement planks.

Air Conditioning

To give a high degree of air conditioning flexibility, 106 package units of 4000 and 2000 cfm nominal capacity were distributed throughout the space frame. They are grouped in threes around the columns, with air being fed to the manufacturing floor through the column "plenum" and to the office floor through the floor via metal ducts. High velocity drum outlets at the top of the columns provide distribution of large air volumes across the 63-ft bays. Air velocity in the column plenum is 4000 fpm, and discharge velocity is 2300 fpm. In this way there are no exposed ducts in the manufacturing area to be an eyesore and to collect dust.

Sixty thousand sq ft out of the 150,000 sq ft on the upper floor are devoted to a "Snow-White" area where the most critical of the manufacturing and assembly processes are performed. This calls for a dust free environment with temperature accurately controlled at 75 F and relative humidity at 20 per cent. This area is isolated from the remainder of the second floor, and access can be gained only through negative pressure "air locks". The second floor is windowless except for 10-ft high slits at 63 ft intervals.

The fresh air unit serving the "Snow-White" area incorporates both electrostatic and mechanical filtration and chemical dehumidification to maintain the stringent requirements. All return air is ducted from return air grilles in the floor to the units serving this space.

In the remainder of the building, the fresh air unit uses fiberglass filters constantly being replenished by driven rollers. Return air from these areas uses the whole space frame as a return plenum to the individual units. The lower floor has a luminous plastic ceiling in which are incorporated integral plastic diffusers of the same material.

In the non-Snow-White areas temperature is maintained at 78 F and humidity at 50 per cent.

Lighting on the manufacturing floor consists of concentric ring fixtures with reflectors containing 1000-watt, color-corrected mercury vapor lamps. The fixtures light the ceiling, giving an indirect source. They are mounted on a pendant mounted raceway which also conceals the wire-rope ties of the paraboloids.

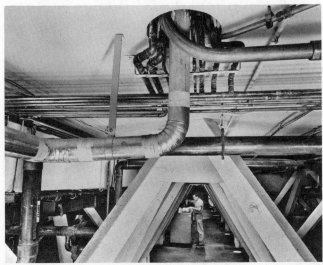

Above: As many as 16 different utilities are piped through one access hole. In a sense, space frame is a "basement" in the middle of the building. Openwork structure permits freedom of arrangement for equipment and accessibility for maintenance. At exterior, space frame has access doors to admit large equipment.

Right: Top photo shows air diffusers, directing vanes above them. The lower photograph indicates how the structurally independent shells are supported. Where four paraboloids come together in the interior, each of four columns supports one corner of a shell.

Texas Instruments, Inc., Semi-Conductor Building, Dallas, Texas. ARCHITECTS: O'Neil Ford and Richard Colley. ASSOCIATE ARCHITECTS: A. B. Swank and S. B. Zisman. CONSULTING ENGINEERING ON SHELLS: Felix Candela. CONSULTING ENGINEER, GENERAL STRUCTURE: Wallace Wilkerson. MECHANICAL ENGINEER: Thermotank, Inc. GENERAL CONTRACTOR: Robert McKie

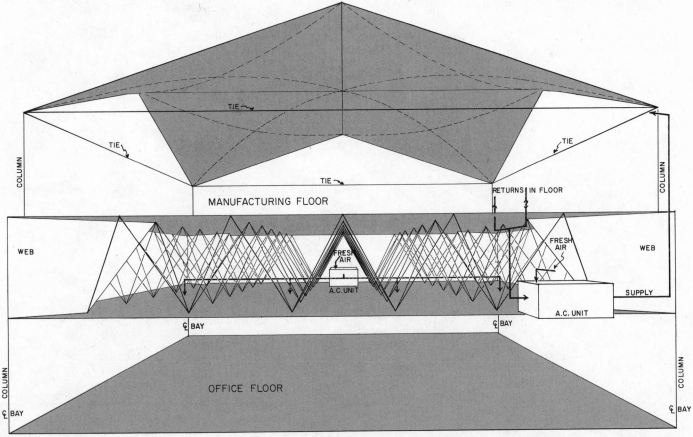

This perspective shows one bay and takes in the area circumscribed by column centerlines. The shells have edge stiffeners and are tied by wire rope cables across the bottom of each of the four gable triangles

THE STRUCTURE OF A SEA-SHELL ROOF

by Wayman C. Wing

United Church of Rowayton, Connecticut
ARCHITECT: *Joseph Salerno*
STRUCTURAL ENGINEER: *Wayman C. Wing*

P. E. Guerrero photos

The sculptured roof of this church resembles the shape of a sea shell, with its unique clerestory spiraling heavenward. Having conceived this shape as an appropriate one for the new sanctuary of the United Church of Rowayton, the architect's problem was how to get it built. Pooling their thoughts, the architect and engineer decided that a skeleton frame of wood with stressed-skin cover would suitably carry out the concept, while also meeting budget requirements. The result was a frame of 19 intricately-shaped, glued-laminated arch ribs, 13 springing from the floor line and the remaining six from the ground. They join at a ridge beam in the front, and a hub-and-spoke wheel at the back where the roof wraps around itself to form the opening for the clerestory.

The main engineering problem was design against horizontal thrust toward the front of the building. First, there is a continuous horizontal thrust due to the fact that several of the front arch ribs "lean" forward in varying degrees from the horizontal. Second, wind blowing from the back will also cause horizontal thrust forward which must be added to that caused by the "leaning" arches.

This force must be taken out in the sheathing and purlins, designed to work together as a stressed skin. The stresses from the thrust are carried back toward the rear of the building, and are gradually balanced by the anchorage of the rear arches.

After close study of the architect's model of the church building, it was evident to the engineers that a possible vertical plane of relative weakness existed between the front 50 ft of the building and the rear 40 ft, due to the complicated way that arches had to be framed and the problems in making the sheathing absolutely continuous.

They decided to make provisions in the structure so that if the shape were disconnected, or "the shell's back were to be broken," the structure would still be stable. In order to accomplish this, only the dead load of the rear portion was considered in resisting the wind forces. It was found that this portion of the building, with a spread of only 40 ft, would not be stable unless anchored down at the arch bases. In a similar fashion, the forward portion of the building was analyzed. All the arches

Norman R. C. McGrath

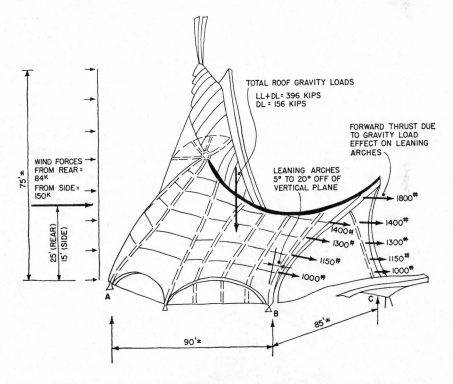

The engineer had to make sure the structure would resist overturning due to wind and forward thrust of front arches. Design loadings are given in the table below. Stability calculations are given on the following page

DESIGN LOADING ON ROOF					
Type	Live Load	Dead Load	Actual Area	Horiz. Area	Load (kips)
Gravity	30 lb/ft²			8000 ft²	240
Gravity		12 lb/ft²	13,000 ft²		156
Wind	30 lb/ft²		2800 ft² (rear)		84
Wind	30 lb/ft²		5000 ft² (side)		150

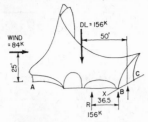

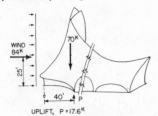

CHECK 1: Wind From Back

Moments about line B-C (Center of gravity 50 ft from line B-C):

50 ft $\times$ 156 kips $=$ 25 ft $\times$ 84 kips $+$ 156x

Then, $x = \dfrac{5700}{156} = 36.5$ ft (within middle

third, so stability exists)

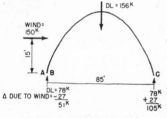

UPLIFT, P = 17.6^K

CHECK 2: Assume Roof Has Split

Dead load in rear portion:
45% $\times$ 156 kips $=$ 70 kips
Overturning moment:
25 ft $\times$ 84 kips $=$ 2100 ft-kips
Resisting moment:
40/2 $\times$ 70 kips $=$ 1400 ft-kips
Uplift resistance is required:

$$P = \frac{2100 - 1400}{40} = 17.6 \text{ kips}$$

(anchored at rear of building)

CHECK 3: Wind From Side

Moments about line A-B (Center Gravity 42.5 ft from line A-B):
Overturning moment:
15 ft $\times$ 150 kips $=$ 2250 ft-kips
Resisting moment (D. L. only):
42.5 $\times$ 156 kips $=$ 6620 ft-kips (roof is stable)

Norman R. C. McGrath

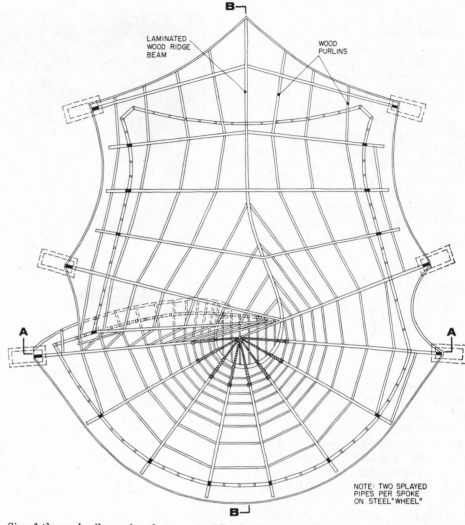

NOTE: TWO SPLAYED PIPES PER SPOKE ON STEEL "WHEEL"

Six of the arch ribs spring from ground-level abutments (see plan); the rest start perpendicularly at the first floor. Arch ribs meet at a ridge beam in front; are attached to 16 steel pipes of a spoked wheel at the back (eight spokes; two splayed pipes per spoke). Connections of purlins to arch ribs are shown below. Top is typical, bottom is at ridge

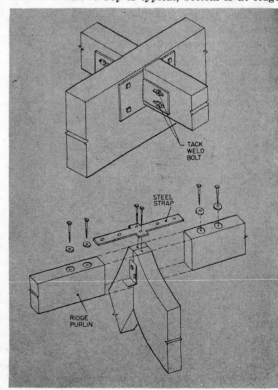

were detailed to resist possible uplift at their bases.

The glued-laminated arches vary in size between 5¼ by 21 in. and 9 by 37¼ in. Lengths were between 90 ft and 45 ft. A 1¼- by 6-in. tongue-and-groove wood decking was used, fastened with galvanized threaded nails. In order to insure necessary continuity of the 3¼- by 6⅜-in. glued-laminated purlins, all connections were detailed and specified to have sufficient strength in tension to resist the forward thrust of the roof.

All lumber is select structural West Coast Douglas Fir (allowable working stress, 2,200 psi; modulus of elasticity, 1,800,000.)

In the clerestory portion of the building, where nine laminated "sticks" come together, a complicated joining problem was resolved through the use of a hub-and-spoke assembly of steel pipes. (See plan and first-page photo.)

Three pairs of the ribs are supported by exterior concrete abutments for architectural reasons: the roof line reaches down to the ground. The remaining arches are supported on the first floor construction where a network of horizontal ties is fully continuous between the individual arches and welded to resist the horizontal thrust.

The first floor, which is the floor of the congregation seating area, was constructed in steel joists with a three-inch concrete slab poured on steel deck. This floor also serves as a horizontal diaphragm to resist the forces of the arches. Steel beams and pipe columns support the steel joists. Connections between the steel beams and columns were designed to resist a portion of the shear resulting from the wind forces on the roof above. The balance of these wind forces were resisted by the concrete walls around the perimeter of the building.

The approximate cost of the structural portion of the roof, excluding the wood shingles and furring strips, and the clerestory glass, was $55,000 or $6.85 per sq ft of floor area, or $4.25 per sq ft of actual roof area.

All the glued-laminated arches were provided by Rilco Engineered Wood Products Division, Weyerhaeuser Company. The general contractor, T. J. Riordan, was erector for the roof. James E. Flynn was in charge of the project for the structural engineer, and Richard Kasal for the architect.

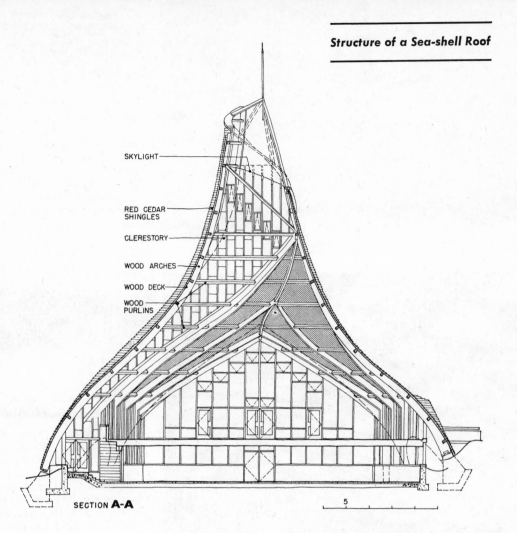

SKYLIGHT

RED CEDAR SHINGLES

CLERESTORY

WOOD ARCHES

WOOD DECK

WOOD PURLINS

SECTION **A-A**

5

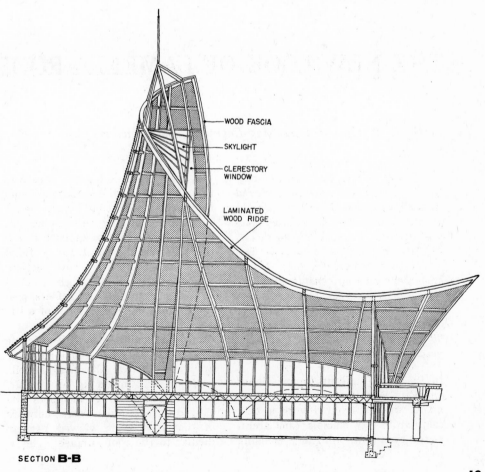

WOOD FASCIA

SKYLIGHT

CLERESTORY WINDOW

LAMINATED WOOD RIDGE

SECTION **B-B**

Piaget Studios

1. For the multi-purpose room of this elementary school, the architects called for ornamental short-span lamella arches between glued laminated beams 20 ft on center. Because of the short radius and short span required, the cut-off for the lamella curve became so excessive that it proved more economical to fabricate the lamellas of one-inch plywood than to use the customary short lengths of stock lumber. This also made it possible for the individual members to be curved top and bottom, using a centric joint, so that the resulting pattern of the barrels is unusually light and delicate

David R. Kitz

2. This bowling alley shows a new development in the lamella system: the projection of the gable ends of the lamella roofs, both along the side walls (above) and the end walls, along the lines of opposite skewed arches. In the small side roofs (34-ft spans), the sheathing was sufficient to take care of the longitudinal tension resulting from the skewing of the arches. However, on the large (109 ft) spans at left, the longitudinal tension is carried by tierods concealed in baffles at the joints. The light fixtures are also attached to these baffles, which act as glare shields for bowlers

THE NEW LOOK OF LAMELLA ROOFS

by Dr. G. R. Kiewitt, Consulting Engineer, Roof Structures, Inc.

For many years, the diamond-patterned lamella roof has been pictured in textbooks, and doubtless in most people's mind's eye, as an arch. Decorative, yes. Economical, no doubt. But still an arch, and as such limited in application. On these pages, however, a leading consultant on the lamella system presents its pros and cons, and with photos from his casebooks shows that lamella arches can be varied in form—and that they need not be arches at all.

In 1908, the Building Commissioner and City Architect of Dessau, Germany, was confronted with a task familiar to city officials (and architects) even now. Additional housing was needed; funds for new construction were not available. To compound the problem, existing houses defied expansion. Not only were their foundations inadequate to support an additional masonry wall for a third floor, but their roof construction, which consisted of high pitched trusses with purlins and rafters, precluded even the development of a livable attic.

At this point, necessity became the mother of invention, and Herr Zollinger devised the first lamella roof, an arch made up of similar, mutually supporting members arranged to form a decorative network of diamonds when viewed perpendicular to the roof surface.

Onto the existing walls went the arch. Into the crotches of its intersecting members went the ceiling joists for a new third floor. Up went the necessary housing within the city budget. And into the vocabulary of structural engineering went the lamella roof.

It was first imported to this country in 1925, and has since found ever wider use for hangars, exhibition halls, field houses, gymnasiums, auditoriums, and virtually any structure where wide clear spans are desired at relatively low cost and where a curved roof surface is more an asset than otherwise.

In its most familiar form, the lamella roof is still an arch. However,

3. This gymnasium is a further example of how the lamella roof may be adapted to achieve an architectural effect. The space is covered by twin barrels, this time of lightweight steel, supported at the center by a beam which leaves the floor unobstructed and also accommodates a folding partition

David R. Kitz

Thomas Korn

4. The parabolic cross section of the lamella roof for this small church was formed by using a short radius arch in the center section and longer radii for the sides. Since the lamella units for the very short radius would otherwise have required a considerable curved cut, this area was made just half that of the lower portions. This produced a visual division between "roof" and "walls," which was further marked by the installation of sound-absorbing insulation in the smaller ceiling panels

the system has also been used to construct spherical domes, parabolas, sections of cones, and hyperbolic paraboloids, and may theoretically be used to form almost any geometric surface.

Whatever its shape, the efficiency of the lamella roof stems largely from the fact that it takes full advantage of the triangle for stability in the pattern surface. The lamellas themselves are relatively short wood or steel members of uniform length, bolted or welded together at an angle so that each is intersected by two similar adjacent members at its mid-point. When the interlocking diamonds thus formed are triangulated by the decking or by purlins,

the stability requirements of the structure in the plane of the surface are complete.

Stress functions perpendicular to the plane of the surface are carried through the action of the lamella units as beam columns under combined axial and bending stresses. For this reason, the lamellas are oriented with their deeper section perpendicular to the surface of the structure.

As might be expected, the system is most efficient in compression. Since the lamellas brace each other at frequent intervals, concentrated or live loads are rapidly dispersed through the network of intersecting diamonds, so that loads seldom, if

ever, depend on one or two members for support, but are supported mutually by many members. Thus, if a few members fail because of fire, earthquake or excessive wind loading, adjacent lamellas assume the additional load and collapse is prevented. During the tornado in St. Louis last spring, for example, the twister scored a direct hit on the St. Louis Arena. A small segment of its lamella roof was ripped out and had to be replaced, but the rest of the roof was unscathed.

Moreover, since the singly or doubly curved surfaces of lamella structures maintain the neutral axis of the structure near the pressure line of the loads applied,

5. The 224-ft steel span for this civic auditorium was buttressed in the conventional way, using concrete struts with concrete distribution beams between them. The use of intermediate purlins permitted the steel deck to be run across the arch, forming a true curve which was highlighted by painting the undersides of the lamellas in a bright coral that contrast vividly with the brownish-gray painted decking

Sammy Gold

6. Though similar to the conventionally buttressed auditorium shown above, this exhibition hall represents an advance over it in that the need for buttress-type supports was eliminated by pulling the lamella barrel down almost to grade level and scalloping the frame between the low concrete piers. This proved to be doubly advantageous since the considerable reduction in the size of the buttresses cut expenses while the scalloping produced a pleasing esthetic effect

G. R. Kiewitt

7. The same buttressing system used for the exhibition hall above was repeated for the gymnasium shown here, although the span was increased to 252 ft. There were also other refinements, notably the emphasis of the scallops by building up sculptured "eyebrows" along their sides. The shape of the longer, lower abutments and of the eyebrows was established through collaboration with sculptor Hillis Arnold of St. Louis

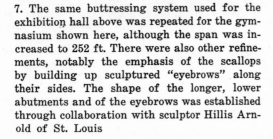

Piaget Studios

the predominant stresses are axial rather than bending stresses. This eliminates a mechanical disadvantage common to the straight prismatic beam or truss, and, combined with the interdependence of the individual lamella units, makes possible maximum efficiency in the use of material.

This material has traditionally been wood, and wood is still the predominant construction material for lamella roofs, but the recent trend toward longer spans has made the use of standard steel shapes increasingly important. Concrete has also been used, especially in Italy where Pier Luigi Nervi built two lamella-type hangars, one of poured-in-place concrete (1938) and one of precast concrete (1943). However, in the United States, concrete has so far been avoided for lamella roofs because of the high cost of the formwork involved.

In this country, development of lamella roofs has moved principally in the direction of applying the system to special shapes and improving conventional methods of support. Since lamella structures are, in effect, a series of intersecting diagonal arches, they exert a horizontal thrust which must be distributed to, and resisted by, thrust supports such as buttresses or tie rods.

The arch action of lamella structures also gives rise to other factors which must be considered in their design. To begin with, lamella arches, like all arches, are very sensitive to unsymmetrical loads. Some—wind and snow, for example—are natural and thus unavoidable, but imposed loads like those from mechanical equipment and hanging accessories can and should be located symmetrically if the arch is to perform efficiently. Uneven spring lines, which have basically the same effect as unsymmetrical loads, should also be avoided.

In addition, the lamella roof system is not easily adaptable to rapid

8. The roof of this community center is a conventional lamella pattern dome, which requires the same number of members in each concentric band. Since this crowds the members near the crown, with a resulting increase in dead weight in this area, the section of the lamella units was gradually decreased from 4 by 16 in. at the sill to 2¼ by 12 in. in the crown band. Similarly, the thickness of the sheathing membrane was reduced from two inches at the base to one inch over the crown

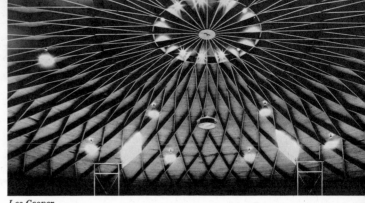

Les Cooper

Rohrabaugh & Millsap

9. The initial design for the fieldhouse dome shown above left employed three-hinged radial arches acting as load bearing ribs of a multi-sectored, spherical lamella roof. However, the designers soon noted a marked increase in dead weight toward the crown and, to maintain an even dead load distribution, instead divided the dome into twelve pie-shaped sectors with the lamella arches running parallel to the sector arches. This made the lamella size and spacing uniform throughout, and when the dome was analyzed as a pierced shell, resulted in a very lightweight structure. 10. Maintaining uniform lengths for the lamella units did not however permit the purlins to form a pleasing pattern of concentric rings, so this was remedied on subsequent domes. In the one shown above right, the bulb tees are also concentrically arranged and serve as stiffeners for the top chords. This lamella pattern, which has since been patented, has also been used for domes with fewer sectors, as well as for wood domes

changes in curvature except at points of support. If such changes are made, they cause high bending moment concentrations which substantially reduce the structure's efficiency.

In basically compressive structures like lamella roofs, the degree of curvature itself must be related to deformation in order to prevent buckling. If the point deformation becomes too large secondary stresses become excessive, bringing with them serious problems. These stresses can, however, be minimized by determining limiting curvatures—in the case of lamella arches and domes, a minimum rise to span ratio of about 1 to 7½.

In general, the circular segments used in the lamella system closely follow the parabola which represents the pressure line of a uniformly distributed load placed on an arch. The higher the rise required, the greater the deviation from this parabolic stress pattern, and the less efficient the structure. A rise to span ratio of 1 to 2 is still in the realm of practicality, but lower ratios are to be preferred.

Assuming that these requirements are considered in the design, the lamella system is competitive with more conventional framing methods for spans ranging from 40 to 1200 ft or even more. This is due not

only to the economy inherent in its efficient use of material, but also to the ease with which the lamellas can be fabricated and erected. Obviously, the high degree of repetition means that low cost mass production techniques can readily be adapted to lamella fabrication. But field erection is also quickly and easily accomplished, with a minimum of scaffolding.

Lamella arches, for example, are usually erected a bay at a time from a movable scaffold as wide as the roof. After the sill beams or spacers which distribute the horizontal thrust to the supports have been placed, the lamella network is simply

THIN SHELLS

1. STRUCTURAL BEHAVIOR AND FORMS

by Mario G. Salvadori, Professor of Civil Engineering and Professor of Architecture, Columbia University

Architects and engineers design structures principally to enclose space and span distances. Thin shells have been used successfully and in increasing numbers during the last 30 to 40 years for these two purposes. Constructed so far of reinforced concrete and, sometimes, in steel or aluminum, they offer new solutions to old problems with economy of materials and freedom of forms, and have revolutionized many structural conceptions in the mind of the designer.

The wide possibilities of thin shells have been only slightly tapped, particularly in the United States where, until recently, there has been little incentive for architects and engineers to get involved in their design and construction problems. But interest is growing. There's no doubt that they have esthetic appeal and create intellectual excitement. This would not mean much, though, if thin shells were not also competitive with other structures. So it behooves the American designer to get acquainted with this type of structure and its most efficient forms.

This can be done on a purely intuitive basis with the aid of simple arithmetic even though the detailed analysis of such structures is by its own nature highly mathematical. This survey on thin shells will take into account both the architectural aspects of form and the engineering problems of strength, and will endeavor to make shell behavior understood in the simple terms

while also discussing some of the fine points of theory and practice. It is hoped that the survey will encourage the reader to use this kind of structure in a variety of expressions where it has been shunned mostly because of lack of understanding of its inherent characteristics and possibilities.

STRUCTURAL BEHAVIOR

As soon as a structure is to be built, the designer is confronted with the age-long problem of carrying loads down to the earth. The earth is responsible for the pull of gravity and the earth is the agent eventually carrying the loads due to its own pull as well as other physical causes, like blowing winds or temperature changes. If we focus our attention on a vertical load — for example, the load due to the weight of a beam which is to be supported somewhere in space — we see that this load might be carried by resting the beam at its ends on two other beams. The weight of this composite element might then be carried by four columns, which could rest on two or more beams (if we wanted open space) and this process of load transfer could go on until the foundation were reached and the total weight carried to the ground.

One may challenge this load transfer for not being either the most efficient or the most logical way of doing the job: Dr. E. F. Masur of the Illinois Institute of Technology has aptly criticized this process for being "as eco-

nomical as if three men carrying a piano would perform their task by climbing on each other's shoulders with the top man actually holding up the piano."

But moreover one could, and perhaps should, even challenge the process by which a single beam carries loads to its supports. By projecting this thinking, one may find the fundamental reason behind the economy and efficiency of thin shell construction.

A beam is a tough resisting element which gives in only slightly under load and whose fibers are differently stressed. The bending stresses, which are maximum at the top and bottom of the beam, vanish at its axis, so that the beam material could well be said to be used at the most with a *local* efficiency of 50 per cent.

Now compare this kind of structural behavior with the way in which a cable carries its own weight. The cable, hanging from two fixed points, cannot carry its own weight if it must remain absolutely straight, since the stress in the cable would then be infinitely high and the cable would snap. But if the cable is allowed to give in and sag, it will support its own weight and additional loads, by means of tensile stresses identical at each point of a cross-section. The material is thus utilized with what might be called 100 per cent *local* efficiency. It is well known that the shape assumed by the cable under the action of its own weight is a curve called a catenary, and that the stress in the

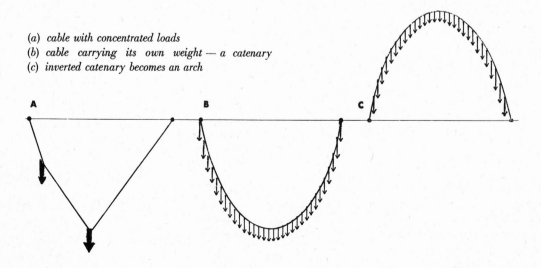

(a) cable with concentrated loads
(b) cable carrying its own weight — a catenary
(c) inverted catenary becomes an arch

cable can be computed easily at any cross-section. Of course, it should also be noticed that the stress in the catenary changes from point to point — being minimum at the lowest point and highest at the supports — so that the *over-all* efficiency of the catenary cannot be said to be 100 per cent.

Let us now imagine that the cable is frozen in a catenary shape, so that its form cannot change, and turn the cable upside down, keeping the loads unchanged and the point supports fixed. The cable shape is called in this case an "inverted catenary," and it is easy to realize that the stresses in the inverted cable are of the same magnitude as before, but are now *compressive* instead of tensile. Apart from the freezing of the cable, such a structure capable of sustaining its own weight in the form of an inverted catenary, or of sustaining given concentrated loads in the shape of a polygon (called an *anti-funicular*), can be actually realized by means of a very thin arch capable of withstanding compressive stresses, provided the structure be made stable by supporting it laterally so that it will not buckle out of its vertical plane.

The essential point about the behavior of the cable or of the inverted catenary arch is that its strength does not depend so much on thickness or depth as on shape. The straight beam needs depth to withstand the loads; the curved cable or arch resists the loads because of its form. Thus *purely geometrical form may be used to create strength:* a form well adapted to the loads to be carried will constitute the most efficient solution of the structural problem with the least amount of material.

The preceding analysis arises from the knowledge of the local inefficiency of the beam behavior and shows one of the many ways in which this handicap can be met. The following analysis will now show how an answer may be found to the challenge of the load transfer process inherent in a beam-column structure.

The beam, the cable and the thin arch are one-dimensional structures, ideally represented by a line — their geometrical axis. Most structures built in the recent past were of this kind and a "one-dimensional" mentality has pervaded structural and architectural design, essentially because of the "handbook" easiness with which such structures can be analyzed. But the advent of the airplane has pushed into the limelight

so-called stressed-skin structures and it is in this direction that we must point to grasp the behavior of a thin shell.

The two-dimensional equivalent of the beam is the flat slab, a structural element resisting loads mainly by bending and twisting, and whose *local* efficiency is again 50 per cent. But the *over-all* efficiency of a slab is far superior to that of a grid of beams covering the same area because of two new essential factors:

1) The two-dimensional behavior of the slab introduces twisting, and hence participation of a large portion of a slab in supporting concentrated loads;

2) As soon as the flat slab deflects, its middle surface stretches and the material in its middle surface tries to resist the deflection and becomes stressed. (It is only in particular cases that this increase of stiffness does not occur; for example, if a slab is bent by the applied loads into a cylindrical shape, its middle surface is not stretched, in which case its stiffness is practically identical with the stiffness of a series of beams set one parallel to the other.)

In flat slabs under common loads, bending stresses are much higher than stresses due to stretching and hence the local slab efficiency is, to all practical purposes, the same as the efficiency of a series of beams, although its over-all efficiency is higher. But if the slab is made thinner and thinner, its flexibility increases and the stretching of its middle surface becomes the essential phenomenon. In this case we say that the flat slab becomes a membrane and that its membrane stresses become high as compared to its bending or plate stresses. In the limit — that is, for a very thin sheet of material — the plate stresses vanish and the slab becomes a pure membrane. A physical membrane can be obtained by attaching a piece of cloth to a frame, as in a camping tent or an umbrella. An extremely thin membrane often used to perform experiments on membrane stresses is obtained by stretching a soap solution (or soap bubble) over a hole cut out of a plate.

It is intuitive that just as the cable could not carry loads, not even its own weight, unless allowed to sag, the thin membrane can only carry its own weight or additional loads *if it is either allowed to sag naturally or if it is stretched,* before the loads are applied. Both principles may be theoretically used in a membrane structure. Pretensioning could be applied to a metal membrane, for exam-

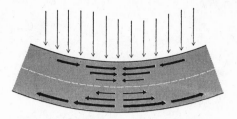

Bending stresses in a beam—maximum at top and bottom, zero at neutral axis

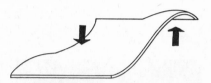

Flat slab resists loads mainly by bending and twisting action

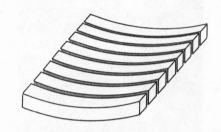

A slab bent into cylindrical shape is practically the same as a series of beams

An umbrella is a "stiffened" membrane which takes loads upright or inverted

Curvature gives a piece of paper structural strength enabling it to support its own weight

This paper shell, only 1/100-in. thick, has a ratio of span to thickness = 1200

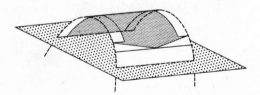

A horizontal line sliding along a vertical curve forms a cylinder

Half-cylinders form corrugated shells

ple. But, the most commonly encountered procedure is to allow the membrane to sag, thus creating strength in the membrane by means of form. But now the two-dimensionality of the structure brings a new state of affairs, as far as stresses are concerned. While the catenary was entirely under tension, the membrane could under certain loads develop tensile stresses in one direction and compressive stresses in another, at the same point. If we assume, as is often the case, that the membrane will be in tension in all directions over most of its area, and if the membrane material is well suited to tensile stresses, the local efficiency of the membrane may now be said to be 100 per cent, although the stress will change from point to point in the membrane and hence its over-all efficiency, in general, will be less than that.

Let us now do to the membrane, assumed to be mostly in tension, what we did to the all-tension cable. The membrane is frozen under the given loads and turned upside down, while the loads on the membrane keep acting in the same direction, as is necessarily the case for its dead load. It is obvious that the stresses in the membrane, while remaining identical in magnitude, will change from tensile to compressive and from compressive to tensile. A two-dimensional equivalent of the inverted catenary is thus obtained and, if the membrane material is well suited to sustain compressive as well as tensile stresses, we have created a structure with a 100 per cent local efficiency capable of carrying loads by means of membrane stresses, which are mostly compressive, if the stresses in the original membrane were mostly tensile.

An inverted membrane is a *thin shell*: a structure capable of supporting loads, including its own weight, by means of direct stresses, tensile or compressive, but incapable of developing bending or twisting moments, i.e., plate stresses because of its extremely small thickness. In practice, of course, whether the material used be steel sheet, reinforced concrete or a plastic, it is impossible to build a structural shell so thin as not to have bending or twisting stresses at all; but as soon as the thickness of a shell is less that 1/50 to 1/100 of its span, the ratio of plate to membrane stresses becomes so small that plate stresses may be neglected everywhere, *provided the shell is loaded and supported so that membrane stresses are balanced and displacements developed by the applied loads are allowed to occur.* The stresses

arising from an inconsistency between actual and "membrane required" conditions will be discussed in detail later.

It is easy to realize that a very thin *curved* sheet can carry loads because of its curvature and that, once more, form rather than amount of material may create strength. An elementary experiment can be performed to get a physical grasp of this result. A thin sheet of paper, grabbed by the short side, bends limply and is incapable of carrying its own weight, but if, by a light pressure of the hand, one gives the sheet of paper a slight curvature upwards, the sheet can be cantilevered out and is stiff enough to sustain additional loads plus its own weight. From the viewpoint of strength of materials, one could well expect this result by noticing that the curved sheet can now behave as a beam of curved cross-section with a greatly increased moment of inertia over the flat sheet. An application of this principle is shown in the photograph where a thin shell built with a piece of creased paper only 1/100 in. thick and spanning 12 in. (ratio of span to thickness = 1200) is shown loaded with a heavy stack of books. Apart from the interesting forms obtainable by this method, the figure shows the tremendous strength obtainable by means of form and illustrates a type of corrugated construction which has been successfully applied to very large shells by the famous Italian engineer Pier Luigi Nervi.

The transfer of loads from plate to beams, from beams to columns, from columns to other beams and so on to the foundation is totally absent in pure thin shell construction: the loads are channeled through the shell directly and by means of lines of tension and compression are carried to the ground. In mixed types of shell construction the thin shell is used as an element channeling the loads to other structural elements, usually arches or trusses or walls, which in turn carry the loads to the ground. But it is important to realize that in most cases even these other elements are mostly under direct stress; for example, the stresses in arches carrying a thin cylindrical shell can be almost entirely direct stresses, thus giving a high efficiency to the complete structural system.

This high efficiency, coupled with the freedom of form inherent in a spatial, continuous structure makes a thin shell one of the most interesting and practical solutions to the modern challenge of large spans.

The essential influence of form on the

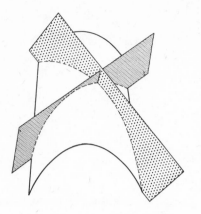

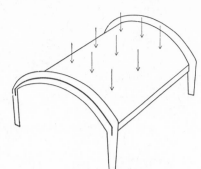

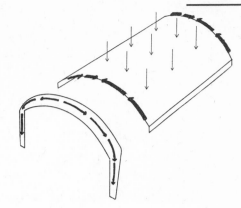

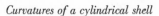

Curvatures of a cylindrical shell

Cylindrical shell channels loads to end stiffeners

strength of thin shells indicates the importance of familiarity with the shapes currently employed in shell construction and with those that could be profitably used. Therefore, it is practical to divide shells into various categories, mainly according to their curvatures, in order to have a clear idea of the various types of behavior to be expected structurally.

FORMS

Cylindrical shells. Cylindrical surfaces may be obtained by sliding a horizontal straight line (generator) along a vertical curve (directrix) at right angles to it. The sliding curve is often a circle, but may be an ellipse, a parabola or any other kind of curve, having in most cases a downward curvature. Moreover, cylinders with curvatures up and down may be joined by the edges to obtain corrugated shells, and cylinders with curvatures up only are used at times.

If a cylinder is cut by planes with different orientations, but all passing through the normal (perpendicular) to the surface at the same point, it will be found that the curvature of the sections thus obtained vary between a minimum (equal to zero) in the direction of the axis of the cylinder, and a maximum curvature at right angles to it, that is, in the plane of the directrix. The maximum and minimum curvatures of a surface at a point are called its *principal curvatures* at that point. In the case of the cylinder it is seen that the curvature

of any cut has the same sign (is in the same direction) as that of the directrix, except for the curvature in the direction of the generator, which equals zero.

Cylindrical shells can be supported in a variety of ways and their behavior varies depending upon their support conditions. If a cylindrical shell is supported directly on the ground it will behave like a "frozen inverted catenary" only for a given set of loads, for example, its own weight; but it will not be capable of sustaining other loads without developing a certain amount of bending and twisting stresses. In fact, a cylindrical shell supported directly on the ground behaves very much like a series of arches, one parallel to the other, and hence develops large bending stresses for all loads except the particular loading condition for which it is originally designed. For this reason, thin cylindrical shells are not usually supported directly on the ground.

If instead, a cylindrical shell is *hung* from two end arches, usually called "stiffeners," it is capable of supporting a variety of loads by means of membrane stresses only. This means that the loads are channeled by the shell to the end stiffeners, and that the stiffeners transfer the loads to the ground by means of direct and bending stresses. A typical example of this kind of behavior is found in the covered wagon of pioneer days, where the hoops act as stiffeners, and the cover, although made of thin cloth incapable of taking bending, can

resist very high wind loads by means of purely tensile stresses. It is, therefore, important to realize that a cylindrical shell with stiffeners does not act as an arch, but *as a thin piece of material hanging from stiffeners.* A cylindrical shell of reinforced concrete or steel is capable of taking both tensile and compressive stresses. Differing in this from the wagon cover, it can sustain, as a membrane, loads of different character, like dead, live and wind loads. It is only in the neighborhood of the longitudinal edges and at the intersection with the stiffeners that direct stresses may not be capable of sustaining the load, as will be seen in detail in Article 2 in which the influence of the boundary conditions will be taken into account.

Interesting cylindrical shells are obtained by intersecting cylinders at right angles: these roofs were classical in the middle ages, but a renewed interest in them is now apparent. Modern intersection roofs are typified by their low rise and could not be built except in reinforced concrete in view of the high stresses developed in them and of the high value of their thrust which must be taken by tensile ties, or buttresses.

Shells of revolution. These surfaces are obtained by rotating a plane curve of given shape (a meridian) around a fixed vertical axis. When the meridian is a half-circle and is rotated about its vertical diameter, the classical spherical dome results, but a variety of forms can be obtained by rotating around the

*Meridian turned around a vertical axis forms
a shell of revolution*

Principal curvatures of an elliptical rotational shell

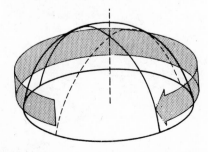

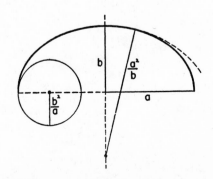

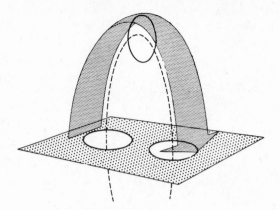

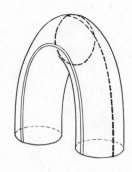

Formation of a torus

Principal curvatures of a torus

vertical axis a circular arch subtending less than 180°, a half-ellipse, a parabolic sector or any other kind of curve. Because their horizontal sections are all circles (parallels) these shells are often referred to as circular shells. Usually the meridian curve has a curvature downward (variable or constant), so that the rotational surface has downward curvature whatever the direction of plane with which the surface is cut. In surfaces of revolution it is found that one of the principal curvatures at a point lies in the meridional plane, i.e., is the curvature of the meridian at that point, while the other principal curvature is in a plane at right angles to the meridian. The principal radius of curvature at right angles to the meridian is thus the distance from the point of the shell to the axis of rotation measured along the perpendicular to the meridian. For example, in an elliptical rotational shell, whose meridian has semiaxes a and b, the two principal radii of curvature at the equator are respectively b^2/a in the meridian plane and a at right angles to it, and at the top of the shell a^2/b in both the meridian plane and at right angles to it.

Surfaces of revolution have been used for centuries to cover big halls and temples, but in view of the materials employed they were necessarily thick shells. With the type of materials available today it is possible instead to consider extremely thin shells which will support all kinds of loads by means of direct stresses only, provided suitable supports are provided. If the supports are not of the right kind, bending stresses will again unavoidably appear, as is the case for domes stiffened by a ring at the equator and supported by masonry, or for shells of revolution supported by vertical cylinders into which they merge. In most cases such shells will develop both tensile and compressive stresses, and must therefore be built of materials capable of resisting both types of stress. The domes built by the Romans were limited in shape since these masonry structures could only resist very small tensile stresses and had to be subjected essentially to compression.

When the meridian curve is rotated around an axis either tangent to it or outside it, we obtain a torus which presents interesting possibilities of application.

When the curve describing the rotational shell is a straight line, the shell becomes a cone. Cones can be used structurally in a variety of ways. With a vertical axis they may be used as roofs, when their vertex is up, or as bottoms of storage tanks when the vertex is down. Half cones with a horizontal axis may be used as cantilever roofs, and, when coupled so as to have curvatures in opposite direction, create an interesting circular corrugated roof that can be supported either by a central column or by an external wall.

Just as the cylinder can be used as a structural element to channel loads to other structural elements, portions of rotational shells can be used to transfer loads to arches or trusses. The umbrella is a classical example of a shell of revolution stiffened by arches. The vault of a gothic cathedral is a shell carrying loads to stiffening ribs and constituting in this manner a complex structural system whose components are mostly under direct stress.

Translational surfaces. A translational surface is obtained by moving a vertical curve parallel to itself along another vertical curve, usually in a plane at right angles to the plane of the sliding curve. This kind of surface, often used in Europe to cover a rectangular area, may be obtained by sliding a vertical arc of circle of radius a along another vertical arc of circle of radius b. The cylinder is a translational surface in which one of the curves, the generator, is a straight line.

One of the forms best adapted for a variety of reasons to thin shell use is a translational surface called the *hyperbolic paraboloid*. This surface is obtained by sliding a vertical parabola with upward curvature on another parabola with downward curvature in a plane at right angles to the plane of the first.

In the hyperbolic paraboloid, curvatures of two sections at right angles are in opposite directions, up in one and down in the other, and the surface is often called a "saddle surface" because in a horse saddle the curvature along

Section of a cone — often used as a cantilever roof when the axis is horizontal

A vertical curve sliding on another curve forms a translational surface

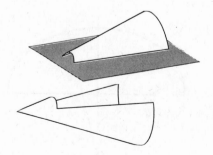

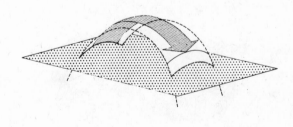

the axis of the horse is up, while it is down across the middle of the horse.

Another saddle surface can simply be obtained by sliding an arc of circle with curvature up on another arc of circle at right angles with curvature down, but such a surface is actually more difficult to build in practice than a hyperbolic paraboloid. It will be noticed later in Article 2 that saddle surfaces, in general, have extremely interesting structural properties, which have made them most popular in thin shell construction.

Saddle surfaces can be supported in a variety of ways and are usually designed with small rises, so as to produce fairly flat roofs. If cut by planes parallel to the sliding and fixed parabolas, the edges of the hyperboloid are parabolas and hence its supporting elements must be parabolic arches. It is most interesting to notice that the hyperbolic paraboloid is capable of transmitting its own dead load to the parabolic arches by direct stresses lying in their plane so that the arches are only subjected to forces lying in their own plane and not to normal forces, tending to tip them over.

Ruled surfaces. A ruled surface is described by a straight line segment which moves so that its ends lie on two fixed curves. The cylinder is a lined surface described by a horizontal line segment whose ends slide on two identical vertical curves (the directrices) and which remains always at right angles to them. Consider now the lined surface obtained by having one end of a line segment slide on a vertical curve while the other slides on a horizontal line. Most often the curve is a half circle (or a smaller arc of circle) and the horizontal line is parallel to the circle's diameter. Such surfaces are called "conoids" and have curvatures of opposite sign, i.e., are saddle surfaces.

The cone is the limiting case of a conoid in which one end of the segment is kept at a fixed point rather than being slid on a line segment.

Amazing as this may seem, the hyperbolic paraboloid is also a lined surface; in fact, it may also be described by a straight line segment one of whose ends moves along a horizontal line while the other moves along an inclined straight line.

Hyperbolic paraboloid surfaces may be used to cover a rectangular area and may be supported on four vertical boundary trusses; only forces in a vertical plane are produced in the trusses. This fact and the fact that forms for the erection of such shells can be built of straight planks make ruled surfaces very practical in thin shell design. Of course, any combination of surfaces may also be used to create new shell forms.

Only the most elementary forms have been used, so far, in the design of thin shell structures. Even within the limited field of shapes mentioned above, a wide variety of applications is possible if one keeps in mind on one hand composite shells and on the other methods of support. It would be difficult to conceive all the new forms that could be evolved in the future if the modern architect should decide to explore this field.

It must be pointed out that, although the mathematical difficulties inherent to the stress analysis of thin shells may appear at first staggering whenever a rigorous solution is required, approximate methods can always be employed to find out whether a form is well adapted to the solution of a given structural problem. In fact, the architect should not feel limited by the existing mathematical solutions and should rely essentially on his imagination and physical intuition in designing new forms. The engineer who is familiar with shell behavior will always find it possible to investigate the strength of a proposed form. It might be wise to point out that it is not always possible to do the engineering design through theoretical analysis alone. For example, the Saarinen shell at M.I.T. is simply a section of spherical shell, but the existence of wide cut-outs on three sides makes the analysis of this structure arduous by standard mathematical methods; it was only by means of a combination of mathematical analysis, model experiments, and physical intuition that such an unusual structure could be designed.

On the other hand the more commonly encountered types of shells can be easily studied by standard procedures which are not inherently more difficult than the procedures used in arch or frame design. In fact, quite often shell analysis is simpler than the analysis of other types of commonly encountered structures and it is only their novelty that, in certain cases, prevents their adoption on the part of designing engineering offices. As shall be apparent from the material in the next article, enough tested knowledge is available in the field of shell design to warrant for this type of structure the same popularity afforded any other type of standard structure.

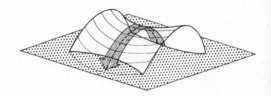

A vertical parabola with curvature up following a vertical parabola with curvature down, and at right angles to it, forms a hyperbolic paraboloid

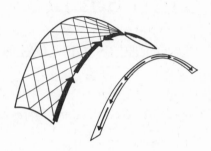

Loads on a hyperbolic paraboloid surface are transferred to end stiffners through stresses in the plane of the stiffner

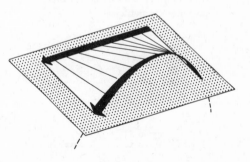

A conoid is a ruled surface formed by one end of a line sliding on a vertical curve while the other end slides on a horizontal line

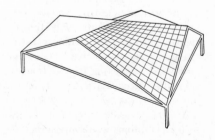

Hyperbolic paraboloids may be used to cover rectangular areas

THIN SHELLS

2. EFFECTS OF LOADS AND FORCES

by Mario G. Salvadori, Professor of Civil Engineering and Professor of Architecture, Columbia University

THIN SHELLS are usually employed to cover wide floor areas and must be designed to support: (1) their own dead load; (2) a live load, commonly due to snow; (3) pressures and suctions due to wind; and (4) concentrated loads due to special equipment.

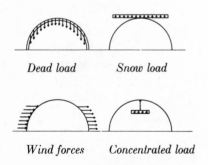

Dead load   *Snow load*

Wind forces   *Concentrated load*

Moreover, so-called "secondary stresses" are often induced in thin shells by shrinkage of the concrete, uneven settlements of foundations, temperature differentials between various elements of the structure, and by continuity between the shell and its supporting elements. Although these loading and stress conditions are considered in all structures, it is interesting to note from the outset that *secondary stresses are in most cases the determining factor in shell design.*

Rigorous consideration of all the preceding conditions would make shell design an almost insurmountable mathematical problem, and the reader may wonder whether it is possible at all to consider thin shells for moderately large buildings, without incurring prohibitive engineering design expenses. But such difficulties need not be feared. Although the design of a large hangar, spanning hundreds of feet, is a major engineering task, to be entrusted only to a designer familiar with its theoretical and practical difficulties, it cannot be overemphasized that the *fundamental principles of shell design are simple* and that *shells of moderate dimensions can and should be designed by the average engineer without any more caution than required by any other structure of the same dimensions.*

SHELL LOADS

In what follows, the dead load will be considered specifically for a thin curved

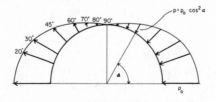

Wind forces

slab of reinforced concrete, since for this material it is, usually, the most important load, but of course the analysis applies to other materials as well.

The live load is usually a snow load of intensity specified by local codes. It is commonly assumed as a uniform load per unit area of horizontal shell projection, while the dead load is a load per unit area of sloping shell.

The wind load is important for very large shells, but can be neglected usually in small buildings, particularly if the shell is relatively flat. When it is not flat, the wind pressure is customarily assumed to vary in relation to the angle between the tangent to the shell and the horizontal (more exactly as the cosine or square of the cosine of the angle, see above). Thus, for purposes of calculation, the wind becomes a perpendicular pressure on the windward side and a perpendicular suction on the lee side.

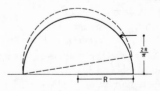

Tipping wind force

Many codes allow the wind to be neglected by lowering the allowable stress, but for simple shell shapes it is not difficult to determine the maximum stresses due to the wind. It should not be forgotten that the complete building must be checked against the tipping

Wind underpressure

force of the wind, and that the shell, if very large and subjected to strong winds, should be designed for the under pressure due to a wind capable of blowing out the windows. Wind pressure from below can be considered as an upward uniform load and the corresponding stresses can be determined by the formulas for snow loads.

Quite often the shell is flat enough to allow dead load and snow load to be combined so that the total stresses can be checked by means of a simple set of formulas. Although approximations are thus introduced in the computations, the uncertainties of concrete design usually justify this kind of simplification. Moreover, shell stresses are usually checked just at a few critical points, since only a very complex job would justify the evaluation of stresses all over the shell.

Very seldom are shells designed for specific concentrated loads. Not only do concentrated loads rarely occur, but also a well designed shell, in which the reinforcement required for temperature changes and shrinkage is sufficient, will easily sustain additional concentrated loads. Such loads and also holes are taken care of by additional reinforcement, and this can be done on the basis of flat slab practice, since in a small area the curvature of the shell can be ignored.

Foundation settlements are not usually considered in an elementary design,

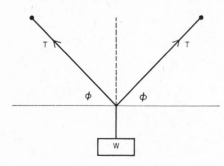

Thin wire carrying concentrated load

since thin shells are particularly resistant to this exceptional type of disturbance, as will be seen later.

The loading conditions discussed

above determine in almost all cases a minimum thickness that may have to be increased for practical construction reasons, or because of secondary stresses. Regulations concerning temperature and shrinkage usually determine the minimum amounts of steel, and this also may have to be increased near the edge of the shell because of secondary stresses. These stresses will be discussed later after it is shown how the thin shell carries principal loads.

SHELL STRESSES

In order to picture how the internal stresses of a thin shell may carry loads, we will consider the equilibrium of a thin wire, attached to two fixed points and carrying a concentrated load. The wire deflects under load and the load is carried by tension in the wire. The tensile forces in the segments of wire adjoining the load are equal, and the vertical components of the tensile forces must equal the load for equilibrium. Similarly shown above is a small length of cable Δl, in equilibrium under its own weight, w lb/ft. From the figure it can be easily

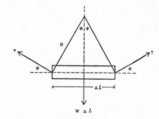

$$2T \sin \phi = w \, \Delta l$$

$$T = w \left(\frac{\Delta l}{2} \right) \frac{1}{\sin \phi}$$

$$\sin \phi = \frac{\Delta l}{2} \Big/ R$$

$$T = w \left(\frac{\Delta l}{2} \right) \left(R \Big/ \frac{\Delta l}{2} \right) = wR$$

Thin wire carrying own weight

seen that the tension is directly proportional to the radius of curvature R of the cable: the larger R, the larger the tension; the smaller R, the smaller the tension.

Membrane Stresses

In a small rectangle of sides Δx and Δy cut out of a membrane and loaded with a pressure p per unit area (below), the internal forces per unit length acting on the sides of the rectangle can only be tension or compression stresses T_x and

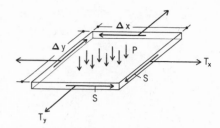

Membrane stresses

T_y perpendicular to the sides, and shears S parallel to the sides. (A membrane can only develop direct stresses; bending is impossible.) The stress analysis of the membrane consists in determining at each point of the membrane the three internal stresses T_x, T_y and S capable of carrying the load. This can be done *in all cases* by means of three equations of statics, so that membrane stresses are "statically determinate," and their mathematical analysis is not difficult.

Stresses in Cylindrical Shells

Assume that a small element cut out of a cylindrical shell has sides parallel and perpendicular to the cylinder axis, and consider the load applied to the element split into two components, one Z lb/ft² perpendicular to the shell surface, and the other Y lb/ft² tangent to the shell cross section.

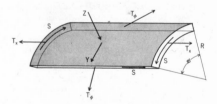

Membrane stresses in cylindrical shell

The component Z must be balanced by the stresses T_ϕ in the transverse direction on the cuts parallel to the cylinder axis. The situation is identical with the equilibrium of the cable under its own weight, and the equation giving the stress T_ϕ per unit length is:

$$T_\phi = - Z \cdot R \qquad (1)$$

where R is the radius of the cylinder at the point considered. If Z acts into the cylinder, as is the case for dead and live loads, the stress T_ϕ will always be compressive (conventionally given a negative sign), while it will be tensile (positive sign) for loads directed outward.

The other two equations of equilibrium which determine stress in the longitudinal direction T_x and shear S are not elementary, and are derived by mathematics beyond the scope of this article. In order to indicate the kind of stress distribution obtained by the three equations of equilibrium, the values of the stresses T_ϕ, T_x, and S are given below for circular cylinders under a uniform snow load, p. These values may be used with sufficient approximation for dead load as well.

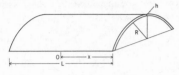

$$T_\phi = - pR \cos^2 \phi \qquad (2)$$

$$T_x = - \tfrac{3}{2} pR \left(\frac{L}{R}\right)^2 \qquad (3)$$

$$\left[\tfrac{1}{4} - \left(\frac{x}{L}\right)^2 \right] \cos 2\phi$$

$$S = - \tfrac{3}{2} pR \left(\frac{x}{R}\right) \sin 2\phi \qquad (4)$$

$$T_{\phi \, max} = - pR$$

$$T_{x \, max} = \pm \tfrac{3}{8} pR \left(\frac{L}{R}\right)^2$$

$$S_{max} = \pm \tfrac{3}{2} pL$$

Membrane stresses for cylindrical shells under snow loads (all values in lb/in.)

By means of the formulas of the table, the stresses at any point in the shell can be determined by simple arithmetic.

It can be seen from the formulas that the maximum value of the longitudinal stress, T_x, occurs at the middle of the

Diagrams of maximum stresses due to snow load

shell and is compressive at the top and tensile at the edge. The transverse stress T_ϕ is independent of the location along the axis, is maximum at the top and zero at the edge, and is always compressive. The shear S is maximum at the shell ends at an angle of 45° measured from the top.

But a simpler way of checking the thickness and the reinforcement in the cylindrical shell is available. This can be done by considering the shell as a

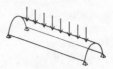

Cylindrical shell under vertical loads

simple beam of semi-circular cross section, weighted by snow load p, and determining the maximum longitudinal stresses and the shear by simple beam theory. The stresses T_x and S thus obtained at the top of the shell and at its edge are identical with the values given in the table. Once these stresses are checked, the T_ϕ stress may be obtained by Eq. (1) and a rough evaluation of the required shell thickness and reinforcement can be obtained very quickly. This beam behavior holds for other loads and support conditions provided the shell length is more than five times its radius.

In order to have a rough idea of the stresses produced in a cylindrical shell by wind forces, one may use the same principle discussed above for dead and

Cylindrical shell under wind loads

live loads. The formula for a beam of semi-circular cross section gives the following maximum stresses due to wind:

$$T_{x \, max} = \pm \frac{1}{4\pi} p_w \frac{L^2}{R} \qquad (5)$$

$$S_{max} = + \frac{2}{\pi} p_w L$$

where p_w is the wind pressure required code. It will be noticed that these stresses are usually very small, and can be neglected.

Convenient tabulations of membrane stresses in circular cylindrical shells under a variety of loads appear in a recently published manual of the American Society of Civil Engineers on *Design of Cylindrical Concrete Shell Roofs (Manual of Engineering Practice No. 31)*.

The analysis of short shells is not difficult, since the essential stress T_ϕ can always be checked by Eq. (1), while the longitudinal stresses are of minor importance. Very flat and short shells tend

to behave very much like flat slabs and develop high "plate" stresses; hence their membrane stresses are minor and evaluation is unimportant.

In all cases, secondary stresses must be added to membrane stresses since they are critical in determining thickness and reinforcement near the boundary.

Stresses in Circular Domes

If a shell of rotation (circular dome) is loaded by its own weight or by a symmetrical snow load, no shear stress will be developed in any meridional section because of symmetry, so that a piece of shell cut by two adjoining meridians and two adjoining parallels will be maintained in equilibrium by only two internal forces, the meridional force T_ϕ and the parallel or *hoop* stress T_θ. In the drawing below the radius of curva-

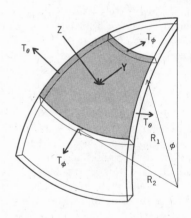

Membrane stresses in circular dome

ture of the meridian is R_1, the radius of the parallel is $R_2 \sin \phi$, and the normal component of the vertical load is Z. Equilibrium of the shell in the direction perpendicular to its surface requires that:

$$T_\phi/R_1 + T_\theta/R_2 + Z = 0 \qquad (6)$$

For the case of spherical domes, where $R_1 = R_2 = R$ (radius of the sphere), this equation reduces to:

$$T_\phi + T_\theta + RZ = 0 \qquad (7)$$

(This equation is the equivalent of Eq. (1) when the surface of the shell is doubly curved.) It can be shown also that:

$$T_\phi = - W/(2\pi R_2 \sin^2 \phi), \qquad (8)$$

where W = resultant of all loads from top of shell to the parallel considered.

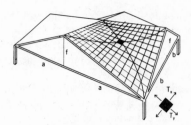

Hyperbolic paraboloid shell

Once T_ϕ is obtained from this last equation, T_θ can always be derived from Eq. (6).

To get an idea of the nature of dome stresses, let us see what they are in a half-sphere whose weight per unit area is w. We find from Eq. (8) that:

$$T_\phi = -2\pi \, wR^2 \, (1 - \cos \phi)/2\pi \, R \sin^2 \phi$$
$$= -wR \text{ at the boundary (where}$$
$$\phi = 90°; \sin \phi = 1) \qquad (9)$$

The meridional stress is compressive since it is negative in sign.

To find T_ϕ we use Eq. (7). Since the Z component of the weight w equals $w \cos \phi$, we obtain:

$$T_\theta = -RZ - T_\phi$$
$$= -Rw \cos \phi - [-Rw \, (1 - \cos \phi)/$$
$$\sin^2 \phi] \qquad (10)$$
$$= wR \text{ at the boundary (where } \phi = 90°;$$
$$\cos \phi = 0)$$

The hoop stress T_θ is tensile at the boundary, since it is positive, and reinforcement will have to be provided at the boundary.

If the same stress analysis is carried out for a parallel at an angle ϕ, it will be found that the meridional stress T_ϕ is always compressive while the hoop stress is compressive up to an angle equal to 52° from the top, and is tensile below this angle. This indicates that spherical shells will develop only compressive stresses if their angle is less than 52°, while tensile hoop stresses will appear when the angle is over 52°.

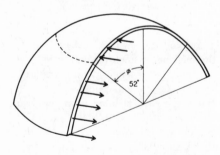

Hoop stresses due to weight

Similar results are found for the case of a uniform snow load on a semi-spherical shell. The meridional stress is always compressive and equals $- wR/2$ at the boundary. The hoop stress is compressive from the top down to 45°, and becomés tensile from then on, reaching a maximum value equal to $+ wR/2$ at the boundary.

Values for stresses in shells of revolution can be found in *Design of Circular*

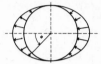

Wind forces

Domes by the Portland Cement Assoc.

The evaluation of wind stresses is theoretically more complicated, but the only result of practical importance is very simple. A wind of intensity p_w psi creates no perpendicular stresses at the boundary of a semi-spherical dome, but only shear stresses S, whose maximum value in the direction of the wind equals:

$$S_{w \, \text{max}} = \tfrac{2}{3} \, p_w R \qquad (11)$$

Apart from the boundary conditions to be taken up later, it is seen that the stress analysis of a circular shell is extremely simple.

Stresses in Saddle Shells

The stress distribution in saddle shells cannot be written easily in general terms, but it is extremely simple for the shape most commonly used, the hyperbolic paraboloid, which is ideally suited to cover rectangular areas. A roof having four paraboloid sections is shown at top right. Calling $2a$ and $2b$ the sides of the rectangle to be covered, and f the rise at the center of the area, the principal stresses T_x and T_y due to dead load act along the center diagonals of the rectangles and at right angles to them. They are given by:

$$T_x = wab/2f; \; T_y = -wab/2f \qquad (12)$$

These equations demonstrate the most important structural property of the hyperbolic paraboloid: *this surface develops, under its own weight, stresses which have the same value all over the surface.* Since membrane stresses were already found to have 100 per cent *local* efficiency, and since we now find that every point of the paraboloid is under the same state of stress, it may well be said that this surface has also an *over-all* efficiency of 100 per cent.

The typical way in which a saddle shell balances the load is clearly illustrated by Eq. (12). The two principal stresses T_y are compressions, while the other two, T_x, are tensions. Hence the shell acts in the y-direction as an inverted cable or thin arch, while in the

x-direction the shell behaves like a tension cable. This also explains the great stiffness of such shells: as the shell deflects and tries to buckle under compressive stresses in one direction, it is prevented from doing so by an increase in the tensile stresses in the other direction.

Moreover, it can be proved that the stresses in the direction of the sides of the rectangles are pure shears:

$$S = wab/2f \qquad (13)$$

These shears, independent of location, are balanced on the shell boundary by trusses whose elements are under direct stress only.

Since the hyperbolic paraboloid is usually built with a small rise, the formulas given above can be used also for determining stresses due to snow load; in view of the flat shape of these roofs, wind stresses can usually be neglected.

Their perfect stress efficiency, the simplicity of their stress analysis, the ease with which the stresses can be balanced on the boundary, and the fact that forms for hyperbolic paraboloids can be built of straight planks, make this surface ideal for shell use.

Boundary Disturbances

It was noticed in this and the preceding article that membrane stresses may not be capable of sustaining the load in the vicinity of the shell edge because of the conditions of support and restraint. It is easy to see why this is so in a particular case.

Take a semi-spherical dome under the action of its own weight, supported on a circular wall. Since the T_ϕ stress at the boundary is vertical, the wall reaction (assumed vertical) will balance the stress, and, if the shell boundary is allowed to move freely outward due to the load, stresses will be of the membrane type everywhere.

If instead, the shell has an angle ϕ less than 90°, although resting on a wall capable of vertical reactions only, it is seen that the horizontal component of

T_ϕ cannot be balanced by the wall reaction. An additional set of stresses must be added to the membrane stresses to wipe out the horizontal component of T_ϕ. Unavoidably this will introduce bending stresses in the shell.

But even if the shell is semi-spherical, in most cases bending stresses will exist around its boundary. In fact, under its own weight, the shell will expand, and points on its boundary will move outwards. If this motion is prevented either by friction of the supporting wall or by a ring beam (usually built around the boundary of a shell) a force Q_0 toward

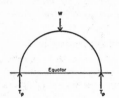

Boundary reaction in half-sphere

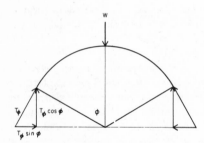

Boundary reaction in dome

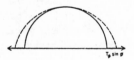

Additional boundary stresses wiping out $T_\phi \sin \phi$

Boundary bending due to restraint

the center of the shell will act all around its boundary and produce bending stresses in its neighborhood.

It is thus seen that bending stresses in the shell may be due either to the direction of the boundary reaction or to the prevention of motion of the boundary. *These bending stresses do not penetrate deeply into the shell, but are localized to the immediate neighborhood of its boundary. For this reason they are called "boundary disturbances."*

A study of the transverse shears created in the shell by boundary forces Q_0 shows that these shears peter out rapidly and that, moreover, *their distribution into the shell is oscillatory and damped. This type of behavior is typical of all boundary disturbances in curved shells.*

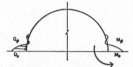

Boundary disturbances

If the boundary of a semi-spherical shell is compelled to remain vertical by means of a stiff ring, bending moments will be applied by the ring to the shell boundary. These bending moments also die out quickly and have a "damped" oscillatory behavior.

While evaluation of boundary forces, moments, and of the bending stresses caused by them is somewhat complicated, tabular results have recently been obtained by the writer and his students for circular shells under conditions encountered most often.

In the extreme case of a semi-spherical shell whose boundary is completely fixed, the bending moment per unit of length at the boundary can be proved to equal

$$M = 0.1443\, phR \quad \text{(in.–lb/in.)} \quad (14)$$

where p is the uniform load (psi), h the thickness of the shell, and R its radius. Since for most other cases the boundary moment is smaller than given above, a rough check may be obtained by Eq. (14); the dead load may be included in the value of p.

Boundary forces of the same type may be due to temperature differentials and shrinkage. For example, if the concrete shrinkage is prevented by a stiff boundary ring, bending moments will be created around the boundary. Calling d the movement of the shell boundary due to shrinkage or temperature differential, the boundary moment per unit length is given by:

$$M = 0.2886\, Eh^2 d/R \quad \text{(in.–lb/in.)} \quad (15)$$

where E is the modulus of elasticity of concrete.

The behavior of boundary forces and moments is typical not only of uniform distributions around the boundary; even if the forces and moments vary from point to point of the boundary, they die out rapidly into the shell and will not affect more than a small portion of it. The quantity which indicates how rapidly

the bending stresses vanish is directly proportional to the square root of the radius times the thickness. Thus if $\sqrt{Rh}$ is small, the stresses vanish rapidly. A simple formula for the approximate evaluation of stress penetration s is:

$$s = 1.8 \sqrt{Rh} \quad (16)$$

For a shell thickness of $\frac{1}{100}$ of the radius, this gives a penetration s of the order of $0.18R$; for a shell thickness equal to $\frac{1}{500}$ of the radius the penetration is reduced to $0.08R$ (see graph).

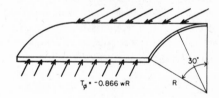

Stress penetration

The same phenomena observed at the boundary of spherical shells occur at the boundary of cylindrical shells, whenever the reactions or displacements are not identical with those produced by membrane stresses. For example, consider the membrane stresses for the case

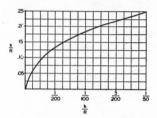

Boundary reactions in cylinder

of a cylindrical shell under dead load. If the shell has an angle ϕ equal to 30°, the T_ϕ stress on the longitudinal boundaries of the shell would equal $-0.866wR$. When the shell is hung from two end stiffeners, its longitudinal boundaries are free and there is no way of balancing the T_ϕ there. Therefore, bending stresses will be developed capable of producing forces equal and opposite to $-0.866wR$ on the boundary. These forces, in turn, produce shears and moments penetrating the shell, but only to a limited extent. No elementary formulas for the evaluation of boundary forces and bending stresses in cylindrical shells can be given, but the designer may figure them out easily by means of the tables contained in the ASCE manual, *Design of Cylindrical Concrete Shell Roofs.*

Bending stresses may occur for other reasons and at other than longitudinal boundaries in cylindrical shells. They should always be checked, and are easy to evaluate. For example, a difference in shrinkage between the thin shell and the thick rib is almost always to be considered: if the differential radial displacement at the worst point in the shell due to this cause is d, the corresponding maximum bending moment may be computed by Eq. (15).

Two additional causes of bending stresses in cylindrical shells will be mentioned here. The end stiffeners or arches, which actually support the shell, deflect under the loads transmitted to them by the shell and carry these loads down to the foundation by means of direct and bending stresses. In computing the bending stresses in the stiffeners it must be realized that any bending of the stiffeners will be accompanied by bending of a

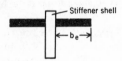

Effective shell width

portion of shell attached to them. The stiffener acts as if it were somewhat "stiffened" by the shell. The minimum width of shell participating in this bending action is called the "effective width" b_e of the shell and is:

$$b_e = 0.38 \sqrt{Rh} \qquad (17)$$

Indicating now by f_ϕ the bending stress in the stiffener with participating shell, the maximum bending moment in the shell may be proved to equal at the most:

$$M = 0.28h^2 f_\phi \quad \text{(in.–lb/in.)} \quad (18)$$

Bending stresses are also caused by the contraction of the shell due to the transverse force T_ϕ. This is prevented at the stiffener by the rigidity of the stiffener in its own plane. The bending moment can be calculated by Eq. (18) by taking f_ϕ equal to T_ϕ/h.

The simple results on the interaction of shell and stiffening elements given above cover only a few of the cases that may be encountered in practice. But the designer should be aware of bending stresses and should provide for them by suitable increases in thickness and by suitable reinforcement. As shown above, elementary formulas are available to determine bending stresses, and the mystery shrouding thin shell design should vanish rapidly, even when these refined points are taken into account.

Buckling

Whenever a very thin structure is acted upon by compressive stresses, the danger of "buckling" is present. Buckling is the phenomenon by which a thin element will deflect laterally under the action of purely compressive and centered forces.

The danger of buckling cannot be studied by assuming the existence in the shell of membrane stresses only. Hence, a complete solution assuming the shell to develop both membrane and bending stresses is necessary and this presents great mathematical difficulties. Luckily, it is possible to give simple formulas for a rough check of buckling in shells. Their use is imperative, since a buckling shell will collapse inward under the applied loads and will in most cases become a tension membrane. Unless the material the shell is made of can take locally a complete reversal of stress, the shell will certainly be destroyed.

For the case of spherical shells or shells of revolution the value of the uniform compressive stress capable of producing local buckling equals

$$f_{cr} = 0.58Eh/R \quad \text{(psi)}$$

If the maximum compression in the shell is less than one-third of this value, the shell may be considered safe. Hence a safe compressive stress for buckling is:

$$f_{cr} = 0.2Eh/R \qquad (19)$$

For non-spherical shells R should be taken to be the radius of the sphere tangent to the shell at the point considered.

For long cylindrical shells the longitudinal compression at the top may be critical and should be not more than:

$$f_{cr} = 0.2\ Eh/R \quad \text{(psi)} \qquad (20)$$

For short cylinders the transverse compression $f_\phi = T_\phi/h$ may become critical and should be checked against the Lundgreen formula:

$$f_{\phi\ cr} = f_T / \left[1 + \frac{2840 + f_T}{7,100,000} \left(\frac{L}{h}\right) \sqrt{\frac{R}{h}} \right]$$
$$\text{(psi)} \qquad (21)$$

where f_T is the concrete 28-day strength in psi, L the distance between stiffeners, and all lengths are in inches. A factor of safety of three should be sufficient.

The Lundgreen formula may be used to check the buckling strength of other types of shells, including saddle shells, by ignoring the curvature in the direction of tensile stresses. In this last case

it should be remembered that the shell strength is actually much higher than indicated by the Lundgreen formula and smaller factors of safety should be used.

Inherent Shell Strength

It is hard, if at all possible, to take care scientifically of the stresses set up in a shell by a settling of the supports. But one more essential property of shell structures comes again to our help in this case. It is well known that if a one-dimensional structural element, as a beam or a column, is overstressed locally and starts failing, it will collapse in almost all cases. This is because the stresses in the element have no way of being redistributed. On the other hand, if a two-dimensional structure is overstressed locally, it can still sustain loads. This is because overstressing produces yield and yield produces in turn a redistribution of stress. Consider a shell under load in which we pierce a hole: the lines of stress that went through the material in the hole will now swerve around the hole, channeling more load to the regions about the hole and permitting the same total load to be successfully carried to the ground.

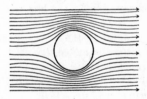

Stress redistribution

The possibility of stress redistribution makes thin shells much stronger than is shown by theoretical calculations. During the war a thin cylindrical shell sustained on columns was "shelled" and a projectile cut through one of the supports: the shell adapted itself to this new situation, by cantilever action from the remaining supports, and did not fail.

The simplicity of the design formulas gathered in this article and the really amazing reserve of strength typical of thin shells should give the architect complete confidence in their design, whether the material used be reinforced concrete, steel, plastic or wood. The next article will show how architects the world over have already found this confidence and have built some of the most extraordinary structures of the modern age by means of thin shells.

THIN SHELLS

3. EXAMPLES HERE AND ABROAD

by Mario G. Salvadori, Professor of Civil Engineering and Professor of Architecture, Columbia University

THE FIRST APPLICATION of thin shell construction to reinforced concrete goes back to 1910. But it was only in the 1920's when Carl Zeiss of the Zeiss Works in Jena, Germany built a small barrel roof on 4 columns, that construction of this type began to expand rapidly under the guidance of U. Finsterwalder and F. Dischinger. Their studies led to the Zeiss-Dywidag patents on thin shell barrels, in which the reinforcing bars were placed along the theoretical lines of principal stress. The Dywidag patent rights for the United States were acquired by Roberts and Schaefer, who were responsible for the first reinforced concrete barrel shell hangars built in the United States in the 1930's. Ammann and Whitney promoted thin shell design independently in the United States and have produced a large number of original shell designs since 1930.

The original development of *saddle surfaces* is mainly due to the studies of French and Italian engineers (among them Aimond in Paris and Baroni in Milan), who popularized this type of shell starting in the late 1920's in France and in the early 1930's in Italy. Torraja has used them in Spain and Candela in Mexico since 1940.

Prestressed concrete was used in thin shell design by Professor Magnel of Belgium and popularized in the United States by the Preload Corporation.

Tile roofs of the thin shell type are extremely popular in European countries, particularly in Italy and Germany, and have been built in a variety of forms since 1920.

Steel shells have been commonly used in tank construction the world over for the last 50 years and *wooden roofs* are popular both in Great Britain and the United States.

This brief historical survey shows that thin shells are anything but new, and

that a wider use of this method of construction is justified not only on theoretical grounds but on the basis of past performance. In what follows we shall concentrate our attention on reinforced concrete roofs, and give only a few examples of the use of other materials.

Barrels

The first shells built of reinforced concrete were of the barrel type, and for many years this shape was virtually the exclusive form adopted for shell roofs.

Cylindrical shells are classified as short or long barrels since these two types differ essentially in structural behavior. Short barrels have a length L not greater than their radius R and quite often much less than this (down to $R/5$ or $R/10$). They hang from arches (or ribs) in the form of circles, ellipses, parabolas, or in the shape of the "funicular line" of the dead load of the roof. (This shape minimizes bending stresses in the arches.) They have been used frequently for hangar construction in the United States with spans up to 340 ft, and ribs spaced at about 30 ft. Their thickness varies with the span but is usually $3\frac{1}{2}$ in. for spans up to 280 ft with increase in thickness to 5 or 6 in. near the ribs. The same type of short repeated barrel has also been used successfully to cover large halls and arenas. An interesting variation of the short ribbed barrel consists in cantilevering the shell outward from two consecutive stiffeners, creating an element which is separated by expansion joints from adjoining identical elements.

In an original application of ribbed barrels, the Onondaga County War Memorial, Syracuse, N. Y., the arches are supported by "gallows" in order to increase their span while reducing their thrust. The short barrel shell with stiffeners may also be used to cover non-

rectangular areas as in the Livestock Coliseum at Montgomery, Alabama.

The twin hangar built in Marseilles, France, in 1952, which is of the short barrel type, has barrels arched in the short direction so that stiffening ribs are unnecessary. The shells span 305 ft and have a thickness of about 2.4 in. This design appears to be an improvement over the usual, ribbed short barrel, which inefficiently utilizes the potential structural properties of shells: the short shell acts more like a flat slab supported by the arches, because of the small span and the large curvature.

The long barrel shell, which also hangs from stiffeners, behaves like a beam of curved cross-section and can be used to cover large areas. Spans of up to 328 ft in length with a radius of 41 ft have been employed. There are also barrels of intermediate size. For example, a hangar in Münich, Germany, has a barrel 236 ft long with a radius of 65 ft.

"Funicular curves" are most common in large short barrels, while long barrels usually have circular cross-sections, although elliptical cross-sections are adopted at times to increase the enclosed volume.

A particular type of barrel developed in Germany combining somewhat the advantages of shell construction with simplicity of forms is the polygonal "hipped plate" barrel. These barrels develop fairly large bending stresses and, therefore, cannot be classified as pure membranes. In a hangar now being planned the "hipped plate" barrels are combined so as to create a corrugated surface which cantilevers out from the structure and is supported by means of tension cables. This combination of thin shell, hipped plate, steel cable construction presents most interesting possibilities structurally and economically.

In the applications presented so far,

1 2

3

1. Small barrel roof built in the 1920's by Carl Zeiss in Jena, Germany. 2. Hockey arena in City of Quebec; Caron and Rinfret, Architects; Roberts & Schaefer Co., Consultants for shell roof. 3. Short barrel roofs for twin hangars in Marseilles, before being jacked up into place. 4. Airport Terminal Building, St. Louis, Mo.; Hellmuth, Yamasaki & Leinweber, Architects; William C. E. Becker, Structural Engineer; Roberts & Schaefer Co., Consultants for shell. 5. Alabama State Coliseum, Montgomery; Sherlock, Smith & Adams, Architects & Engineers; Ammann & Whitney, Structural Engineers. 6. House in Mexico, Félix Candela, Architect. 7. Factory in Mexico; Félix Candela and Raul Fernandez, Architects. 8. Garage in Nüremberg, Germany.

4

5

6

8

7

half-cylinders are often the standard roof element, but interesting structures have been built by means of portions of cylinders combined in a variety of ways. Cylindrical shells with considerable rise, meeting at right angles have been adopted at the St. Louis, Mo. airport.

The "butterfly shell" consists of two cylindrical sectors cantilevered from a row of central supports. It is a standard element in railroad platform roofs. It can also be successfully used to build hangars, in which the central portion is for services and the cantilevered roof provides airplane shelter area. Moreover a butterfly roof built by means of repeated elements permits the introduction of large glass areas and hence the easy daylighting of large buildings. The problem of daylighting has also been brilliantly solved by cutting the barrel with a vertical plane, which is completely covered with glass or which is left open, as in the Nervi shell at Chianciano.

In Mexico Candela employed a large, unsymmetrical cylindrical sector to roof a private house. For a factory he combined half-cylinders at different heights and placed glass surfaces at the ends of the cylinders.

The same problem may be solved also by means of inclined cylinders generated by a half-circle sliding along an inclined line. It is possible in this manner to obtain a shed type structure of the multiple barrel type, although this solution does not seem the most economical.

The direct inclusion of glass in barrels, which is permissible in view of the low shell stresses, is currently accepted, and in some cases up to 50 per cent of the shell area consists of glass. In all shell regions where stresses are compressive, glass bricks can be incorporated in the shell without difficulty, giving freedom of light patterns in daytime and at night, since concealed lights are also easily incorporated in the shell. This can be said, of course, of any shell and not only of cylindrical roofs.

Shells of Revolution

Domes of circular or polygonal shape, in which a thin shell is carried by meridional arches, are typical of church construction and are also used to cover large halls up to 400-ft diameter. In at least one structure of this type the dome is supported by "gallows" rather than by columns to create the necessary hoop force around the boundary of the shell without relying exclusively on tensile steel. But it is in industrial tank construction that spherical domes have become most popular. Diameters of up to 150 ft with rises of $\frac{1}{5}$ in. to $\frac{1}{10}$ in. and thicknesses of 2 in. at the top increasing to 5 in. at the boundary are quite common.

The unribbed dome of revolution, circular or elliptical in cross-section, has been recently adopted by two outstanding architects. Saarinen conceived the M.I.T. building as a spherical sector, cut by a triangular vertical prism, obtaining an elegant form of monumental appearance: the diameter of the shell is 170 ft and its thickness is $3\frac{1}{2}$ in. for 80 per cent of the dome area and 24 in. at the supports. The shell is thicker than might be anticipated since the cuts disturb the membrane stresses, introducing bending stresses throughout most of the shell.

Noyes has adopted an elliptical shell of revolution with either two or four inclined cuts in his design of houses and campus type schools which have diameters up to 45 ft with a thickness of 2 in.

Special Shapes

Hyperbolic paraboloids for covering large factory areas were built by Baroni in Milan, Italy in the 1930's with great economy of forms. In his applications, Baroni, following the French approach, coupled four very flat hyperbolic paraboloid sectors, obtaining a structure limited by triangles at the boundaries. These triangles are trusses capable of taking the shear forces of the shell and of transmitting them to the columns by means of direct stresses.

The hyperbolic paraboloid sectors used by Baroni can also be turned upside down and supported on a single central column, or combined in a variety of ways.

In contrast, the hyperbolic paraboloids built by Candela to cover the Cosmic Ray Laboratory of the Ciudad Universitaria in Mexico City have a very high rise and are limited by parabolic arches 16 ft apart, with a span of 33 ft. Their thickness of $\frac{5}{8}$ in. required for the penetration of cosmic rays perhaps makes this the thinnest shell built of reinforced concrete. Flat, single, complete conoids have been recently built by Candela, but the sector of conoid is ideal for shed roof construction and has been extremely popular in France and Italy during the last three decades.

It is also possible for a sector of hyperbolic paraboloid (of the type used by Candela) to be cantilevered out and supported on one of its bounding parabolas. A solution of this type was adopted by Torraja in the Madrid race track roof.

Although in this article thin shells have been referred to exclusively as roofs, it is interesting to notice that perhaps the most daring application of thin shells occurs in dam construction. A new type of double curvature dam has been developed in recent years by engineers Oberti and Rocha on the basis of mathematical and model studies. Its dramatic applications in the Alps show heights of up to 883 ft, spans of up to 500 ft and thicknesses varying from 10 ft at the top to 50 ft at the bottom. Such structures are considered thin in view of the tremendous pressure supported. Another "hydraulic" application of concrete thin shells, by now very well known the world over, is the lovely ketch built by Mr. Nervi with a shell only $\frac{1}{2}$ in. thick.

Materials

Concrete. The use of reinforced concrete is standard for large shells. The reinforcement consists usually of steel bars, but welded steel net of mesh sizes varying between 2 and 4 in. is becoming more and more popular in view of the ease with which it is put in place. The complicated arrangement of reinforcement along the lines of principal stress, typical of the early Zeiss-Dywidag patents, has been practically abandoned. For relatively small shells and even for large shells of small thickness (up to 3 in.), pneumatically applied concrete is gaining popularity over poured concrete. It results in a more homogeneous, stronger, monolithic construction, which allows smaller thicknesses and a reduction of the dead load of the shell, in most cases the most important load on the roof. Pneumatically applied concrete can be placed rapidly and sets rapidly, with the additional advantage of freeing the forms for re-use. Quite often it is possible to lower the forms 36 hours after spraying a 1-in. thickness of concrete, and to use the 1-in. shell as a form on which to spray the additional concrete required by the final design.

Prestressing is widely used in this country for the construction of thin shell concrete tanks for liquid storage since complete impermeability is essential in this type of structure. It is interesting to notice that almost all of the structures recently built by Dyckerhoff and Widmann in Germany and elsewhere combine thin shells with prestressing.

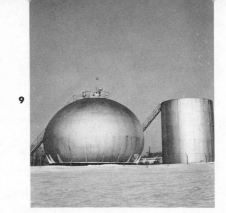

10

Courtesy Standard Oil Co., N. J.

Courtesy G. Baroni, Milan, Italy

11

12

9. Steel storage tanks for an oil company in Maine. **10.** Conoids for a transportation building in Rome provide day-lighting; G. Baroni, Structural Engineer. **11, 12.** Hyperbolic paraboloids for a factory roof in Milan; G. Baroni, Structural Engineer. **13.** Model of a proposed classroom; Eliot Noyes and Associates, Architects. **14.** Hyperbolic paraboloids cover Cosmic Ray Laboratory at University of Mexico City; Félix Candela and Jorge Gonzalez Reyna, Architects. **15.** Doubly curved thin shell for dam in the Alps; G. Oberti, Structural Engineer. **16.** Olympic Hall, Berlin, built in 1936, has shell roof with ribs from foundation to skylight; Professor W. March, Architect; Dyckerhoff & Widmann, Structural Engineers.

13

E. J. Cyr

14

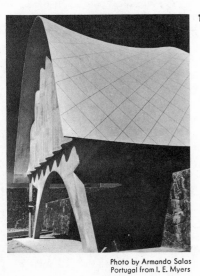

Photo by Armando Salas
Portugal from I. E. Myers

15

Courtesy G. Oberti, Milan, Italy

16

Concrete really will be used to its best capacity and in its most rational manner when prefabricated, prestressed elements will become standard in the construction of thin shells.

Tile. Flat slabs combining tiles with reinforced concrete, in which the reinforcement is reduced to steel wires (diameter less than 0.1 in) and the concrete ribs are poured in forms created by the tiles, have been used in Europe for the last 40 years. During the last 20 years this method of construction has been adapted to shells in Germany, Italy and France.

Sheds of the conoidal type, incomplete cylinders, multiple barrel roofs, and spherical domes spanning 25 to 50 ft have been economically built with hollow tiles less than 6 in. thick. The amount of steel for a flat dome covering a water tank 59.5 ft in diameter with a rise of 7 ft is only 0.48 lb per sq ft.

One of the most interesting applications of a tile thin shell roof is the flower market built in 1953 in Pescia, Italy, a flat barrel with large cuts, supported by arches forming buttresses. The span is 90 ft, the hollow tile thickness 8 in.

Steel and Aluminum. Tanks of steel sheet are commonly used in industry in the shape of cylinders with spherical or elliptical heads, of complete or incomplete spheres, and of "drops," presenting the interesting property of a constant stress under static hydraulic pressure. But steel shells were used also in France in 1929 for movable hangars in the form of barrels hanging from stiffeners. (The interesting saddle roof designed by Nowicki for the North Carolina State Fair Pavilion is a metal structure in which cables constitute the essential structural elements and thus cannot be classified as a thin shell.) The recently built LeTourneau semisphere, 310 ft in diameter and 85 ft high, capable of covering an area of 71,000 ft and seating 12,000 people, is made out of aluminum sheet $\frac{1}{8}$ in. thick. It is probably the thinnest shell in the world to-day.

Wood. Although wood lacks the continuity typical of concrete or metal, curved surfaces can be easily built out of this material, particularly if they are of the ruled type. Outstanding wooden structures are in existence which cover large areas with spans of hundreds of feet, but none is of the "membrane stress" type, since numerous ribs stiffen the shell. (Lamella construction, not considered here, is of this type.)

Plastics. The writer is unaware of large shells in which plastics are used as structural materials, but would like to call the attention of the architect to the possibilities presented by these materials in the field of shell construction. Plastics with the strength of steel are at present available which can be molded into the most complicated shapes, welded and attached to other materials. They can be transparent or opaque. Plastics used in airplane construction are typical. While it may be uneconomical at the present time to build a complete structure of these materials, large plastic surfaces could be incorporated wherever the lighting problem or the shape problem becomes important. It is easy to predict that the increased production of plastics well adapted to construction purposes will add interesting possibilities to thin shell design.

Construction Problems

The greatest single obstacle to the expansion of reinforced concrete shell construction is the high cost of building forms. In the case of large barrels, complex scaffolding made out of wood or steel tubing must be erected and supported on jacks. Once a pour is completed, the heavy scaffolding is lowered by the jacks, shifted to a new location and jacked up again. This complicated operation must be repeated for each pour and it is rarely that the scaffolding can be used more than four to six times on the same job. The form structure must then be dismantled and shipped to a new site, if made of steel tubing, or disposed of if made of timber. The surface on which the concrete is poured is always made out of disposable timber.

The cost of materials and labor involved in building, shifting and dismantling the forms may be as much as one third of the total cost of the concrete structure even when the forms are used many times over on the same job. When the forms are used only once, this ratio may be higher.

The cost of forms for large shells of the barrel type, spanning 250 to 300 ft, varies between $4.00 and $6.00 per sq ft. Using the forms an average of six times, this gives a minimum cost of 67 cents per sq ft. In multiple barrel factory roofs, in which simple forms are used a great number of times, this cost is said to be at least 30 cents per sq ft. Hence any solution lowering the cost of forms is to be welcomed.

In one of the solutions successfully adopted by Dyckerhoff and Widmann (Germany) the heavy reinforcement of the shell is erected without scaffolding, and the concrete is poured against small movable forms which hang from the reinforcement.

For the 1952 Marseilles hangars, the numerous short, arched barrels were poured on the ground using the same form, and the barrels were then lifted in place. This combination of thin shell construction with prefabrication of the shell *as a whole* has economic advantages where labor costs are high and material costs low. Monolithic shells are easily transportable without danger of damage, while their pouring as a whole at ground level is practical and structurally wise.

A series of barrels designed for use by the U. S. Army (15 by 30 ft) and the school shells by Eliot Noyes (45 ft in diameter) are designed so that they can be picked up and moved. The common use of heavy equipment in the United States should add further attraction of this method of construction, particularly in view of the popularity recently gained by the "lift-slab" system.

Prefabrication of small elements which are then assembled to create a thin shell has been perfected by Nervi in Italy. The Nervi element is itself a corrugated shell reinforced by layers of thin mesh and precast on the ground; the various elements are then put together on light forms, by welding the steel reinforcement and by pouring the joints. This method has the obvious advantages of prefabrication of standard elements at ground level and the elimination of heavy forms. On the other hand, it may require welding of the reinforcement and always requires local pouring of the joints. It is currently under study in the United States. Nervi's procedure is well adapted to an economy of low labor and high material costs.

Another entirely different solution of the form problem called the "Airform" method was initiated in the 1940's by the West Coast architect Wallace Neff and has been successfully applied to a variety of shells. A balloon of neoprene-nylon fabric in the shape of the shell inner surface is inflated by compressed air to a pressure of 6 lb per sq in. The steel reinforcement, usually welded mesh, is set on the balloon and concrete is shot against the neoprene form, completely engulfing the steel. Door and window frames are incorporated into the shell, by attaching them to the reinforcement.

17

18

19

20

17. Platform and shell roof, which cantilever out about 50 ft, utilize pre-stressing in this demonstration structure for a German Fair (1951); Dyckerhoff & Widmann, Structural Engineers. **18.** Placing section of "ferro-concrete," a system patented by Nervi in which corrugated elements are precast, steel reinforcement is welded and joints are poured to join them. **19.** Roof of Tramway and Bus Depot, Turin, Italy, designed by Nervi and built by means of precast triangular elements of "ferro-concrete." **20.** "Airform" balloon used for building concrete shell house designed by Eliot Noyes; pneumatically applied concrete is sprayed over mesh. **21.** Beginning of formwork for M.I.T. auditorium by Eero Saarinen; Ammann & Whitney, Structural Engineers; George A. Fuller Co., Builders. **22.** Formwork for Onondaga County War Memorial, Syracuse, N. Y.; Edgarton & Edgarton, Architects; Ammann & Whitney, Structural Engineers. **23.** Dyckerhoff & Widmann method in Germany has reinforcement erected without scaffolding; concrete is then poured against small movable forms.

21

23

22

Once the concrete is set, the balloon is deflated and taken out of a door or window opening, and the shell is finished by increasing its thickness, if necessary. A variety of technical problems had to be solved before the "Airform" method became practical. For example, the lowering of temperature due to a passing cloud could decrease the air pressure in the balloon, changing its shape. To avoid this an electronic pressure gage, controlled by a thermostat, is attached to the air compressor and puts into, or takes out of the form the amount of air necessary to maintain the pressure constant within very strict limits. One-family houses, grain storage tanks, ammunition huts and other types of structures have been built by the "Airform" method, all involving thin shells of reinforced concrete. Spans of up to 100 ft have been reached with thicknesses of 2 in. of concrete. Shells built by this method have been in existence for the last 20 years.

Conclusion

When nature decided to shelter its most precious particle, the embryo, it created the egg shell, a shape of great resistance realizable with a small amount of material. A chicken egg shell will withstand a pressure of 75 lb; its diameter is approximately 1 in., its thickness about 15/1000 of an in.; its span to thickness ratio is 66 to one. A concrete barrel spanning 340 ft with a thickness of 5 in. sustains a greater unit load with a span to thickness ratio of 825 to one. The LeTourneau semisphere with a diameter of 318 ft and a thickness of $1/8$ in. has a span to thickness ratio of 30,600 to one. Man has outdone nature in daring, and has produced securer shelters, since our shells are not as fragile as an egg.

The technical possibilities are here. The mathematician, the engineer, the builder have done their lot. But no building technique can be successful, even in our predominantly technical civilization, unless it is used to create a living structure, filling the deeply felt needs of the human beings who are to dwell or work in it. This is why, although the fundamentals of shell theory have existed since 1828, shells are only today being integrated into our lives.

The mission of the architect is indeed a difficult one. Artist by nature, he must become a master craftsman before his dreams materialize. Craftsman by trade, he must become a technician in order to understand and make his own the achievements of the engineer. In order to design shells he must think three-dimensionally, and be a master, not a slave of geometry. He must know materials and their strength, be aware of stresses flowing in steel and concrete, be able to channel these stresses economically. He must have an eye for color and adapt his shell to its surroundings, while making sure that rain will not penetrate it, heat will not crack it, ice will not break it. He is aware of life inside his shell: he worries about acoustical responses and heat insulation. Can a single man encompass all this knowledge?

The present dichotomy between architecture and engineering is absurd and must vanish before long if we are to get the utmost out of our creations. In the statement of a leading architect, "architects are so outdistanced by engineers in inventiveness and resourcefulness that the engineers may soon take over their profession." A leading engineer objected to this remark; he felt that "engineering was potentially ahead of architecture, but that engineers were often, in his opinion, far behind architects."

There is a simple solution of this puzzling situation and it can be found at the roots of modern society. Today no one is "independent;" we all rely on each other for survival. The architect is just like any other modern man: he needs help. His main difficulty is to know *at least* the kind of help he needs. The engineer is ready to help, but on one hand his training is often so unimaginative that he does not understand the creative expressions of the architect, and on the other he is such an "exact," scientific person as to dislike problems that cannot be rigorously solved. Leaving aside the "handbook" engineer interested only in routine problems, and the "handbook" architect, who can only copy a preordained scheme, modern architecture needs the architect capable of grasping the fundamentals of structural design and the engineer willing to tackle new and unsolved architectural problems. Such persons exist, but only by rare chance do they come together. In the field of construction touched upon by these articles there is a crying need for more getting together of the brilliant architect with the daring engineer. A horizon of infinite possibilities is now open: the stay-at-home will be scared, the pioneer will feel attracted by it. The future is the pioneer's.

Bibliography

1. S. Timoshenko, "Theory of Plates and Shells," McGraw-Hill Book Co., New York, 1940.
2. W. Flügge, "Statik und Dynamic der Schalen," Julius Springer Verlag, Berlin, 1934. In German. The most complete book on shell theory.
3. "Calcul des Voiles Minces en Béton Armé." L. Issermann-Pilarsky, Dunoud, Paris, 1935. In French. Particularly important for the theory of hyperbolic paraboloids and conoids due to F. Aimond.
4. "Design of Cylindrical Concrete Shell Roofs," ASCE Manual of Engineering Practice No. 31, Am. Soc. of Civil Engineers, 29 W. 39th St., New York 18, N. Y.
5. "Design of Circular Domes" Concrete Information circular of the Portland Cement Association. Membrane stresses for domes under dead load and snow load.
6. "Circular Concrete Tanks without Prestressing." Concrete Information circular of the Portland Cement Association. Bending stresses and membrane stresses in circular cylindrical tanks under a variety of loads.
7. "Transactions of the American Society of Civil Engineers." Articles on shells starting in the 30's.
8. "Journal of the American Concrete Institute." Numerous articles on theory and practice of thin shell construction during the last 15 years.

The author acknowledges the assistance of Mr. Ali Raafat in assembling the illustrations for the three sections of the article.

Church San Antonio de las Huertas, Mexico, D.F. Shows first of three groined vaults completed. No edge beams; bars at borders carry windows. With Enrique de la Mora, Architect.

UNDERSTANDING THE HYPERBOLIC PARABOLOID

by Felix Candela

"Of all the shapes we can give to a shell, the easiest and most practical to build is the hyperbolic paraboloid." With this as his thesis, Candela decrys the use of arbitrary shapes for structure and examines the logic of the h.p. in terms of "proper" structural behavior, simplicity of stress analysis and ease of construction.

The hyperbolic paraboloid is now a project type in design offices and school workshops across the world. It finds great favor with the architect, who sees it as an "exciting" new form. Too often, however, the projects using this shape are quite unbuildable. This is because of the prevalent conviction that absolutely any structure is possible. Nothing could be falser than this.* The modern architect is seldom able to undertake structural invention, based on mathematical and engineering considera-

*These statements might be considered contradictory to some of my earlier writings. But I must explain again that my attacks against the excess of mathematical field trips referred mainly to the over-emphasis on elaborate "elastic" calculations, that is to the indiscriminate use of shadily based elastic hypotheses. I was not attacking a clear understanding of the play of stresses in a structure which can sometimes be pictured with accuracy by pure statics only.

tions, and it is not likely that he will become so, as building problems get even more subdivided and complex.

We might ask why the modern architect (heir to hundreds of years' tradition of utter disinterest in structural problems) should be so absorbed of late in constructive forms and their plastic expressiveness. Is he intrigued by the forces acting inside a structure, by the urge to discover what prevents it from collapsing? No, his enthusiasm has a more emotional basis. Space frames, hanging roofs and concrete shells are all legitimate prey in what is pronounced a move to humanize the arid, primitive idiom left to us by the pioneers. "Structuralism" is originality's new escape-valve.

The hyperbolic paraboloid has not escaped this climate of sensationalism. Its use in a few buildings of

rare and unusual shape has helped to encourage a kind of collective fury to design extravagant and pseudo-structural forms. This naturally places the poor people whose mission is to calculate such structures in a very unhappy position.

It is forgotten that the paraboloid stemmed from purely functional and economic reasoning. I doubt very much that it can be the answer to any stylistic problems. But after the novelty of its shape has subsided perhaps it will be realized that the thin shell paraboloid has qualities as a building form that are far more persuasive than just esthetic considerations. I believe it is more practical to build than other concrete shells and much less rigid in its requirements. I am speaking of concrete shells since for the moment reinforced concrete is the basic construction material: it is cheap, easy to manipulate and available at nearly any location in the world.

My purpose in this article is to try to explain the hyperbolic paraboloid, and by explaining, perhaps to defend it. For the architect or engineer who wishes to build the paraboloid must know the general conditions a shell structure has to satisfy, and he must

Figure 1: Membrane and Flexural Stresses

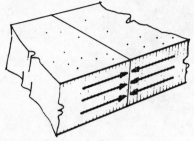

Compressive membrane stresses

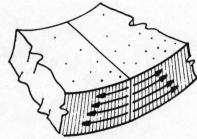

Flexural stresses in pure bending

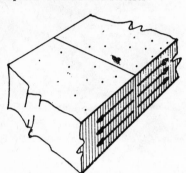

Tensile membrane stresses

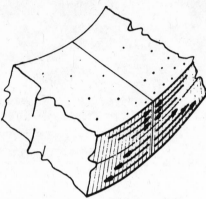

Flexural stresses in combined bending

know how to calculate it, not only because building regulations may demand this, but for his own personal assurance. As far as can be ascertained, this information is not readily available to him now.

It might be wise now to define a shell structure. The word shell is commonly used to describe practically any kind of laminar structure, but a line must be drawn between *"proper"* and *"improper"* shells. The distinction is not only geometrical but directly relates to their structural behaviour. The designer of shell forms is restricted if he cannot see this distinction.

A laminar structure is one whose thickness is of a much smaller order of magnitude than its other two dimensions, but it cannot be considered a "proper" shell unless it is doubly-curved. The criterion of a "proper"

shell is the avoidance of bending stresses. A "proper" shell is a laminar structure which acts mainly by means of membrane or direct stresses. Membrane stresses are those equally distributed in the thickness of the slab and parallel to the tangential plane to the surface (Fig. 1). They can of course be tensile or compressive stresses.

An "improper" shell is a laminar structure in which an important part of the structural action is performed by bending of the slab. The limiting case of this is the ordinary flat slab which works exclusively in bending. A folded or prismatic slab is another "improper" shell in which part of the load is carried to the supports by direct stresses, but important bending moments exist nevertheless. In the barrel (or long cylindrical) vault the proportion of loads trans-

mitted by direct stresses is greater than in the folded slab, but transverse bending cannot be avoided. In both cases substantial thickness must be given to the slab in order to resist bending. The common (or short cylindrical) vault can work exclusively with direct stresses under certain distributions of loads whose pressure-line coincides with the form of the directrix or cross-section. This means it must be shaped to the funicular or pressure line of the permanent loads (Fig. 2). But with the intervention of accidental live loads the vault develops bending which must be taken at short intervals by means of stiffening ribs or substantial arches. In brief all these examples are *developable* or simply-curved surfaces which can only oppose change of shape or curvature by the bending resistance of the lamina itself. They are "improper" shells.

But compound surfaces, as most of nature's shells are shaped, can work (when properly supported) by direct stresses only, regardless of the distribution of loads upon them. Bending cannot appear until direct stresses reach a value very much in excess of the elastic limit. This is obvious when we try to crush a small dome of any practically non-extensible material such as concrete and compare the type of rupture with that resulting from pressure applied to a non-compound surface of similar material (Fig. 3).

There are two kinds of compound surfaces, synclastic and anticlastic. *Synclastic* or elliptical surfaces have both main curvatures in the same direction (as a dome). They are called elliptical for the type of equation representing them. They are "proper" shells which can and should be built as thin as practically possible, but they are expensive to form by ordinary methods since they require a considerable number of arches and the boards must be bent on top of these (Fig. 4, top). *Anticlastic* or hyperbolic surfaces have both main curvatures in an opposite direction (as a saddle) (Fig. 4, bottom). There are some anticlastic surfaces which can be generated by straight lines and which at the same time have a clear geometrical definition. They are called rule or warped surfaces, and are namely the conoid (which has only one system of straight generators), and the hyperboloid and the hyperbolic paraboloid (which each have two systems of straight generators) (Fig. 5). All three types are simpler to build than synclastic surfaces because they may be formed with straight boards and they share in common the mark of a

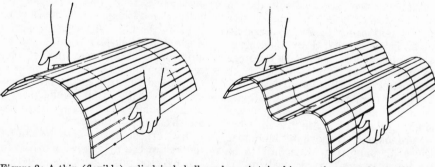

Figure 2: A thin (flexible) cylindrical shell can be maintained in a rather unstable equilibrium as long as its cross-section conforms to the pressure line of the external loads (left). Any slight changes in their distribution or in the shape of the cross-section of the lamina produces rupture by bending due to instability or buckling (right). To prevent this the cylinder must be stiffened by rigid arches or diaphragms

SHORT CYLINDRICAL SHELL: Mexico City Customs Warehouse. Short shells, span 66 ft; 20 ft cantilever wing; ties above roof. With Carlos Recamier, Architect.

"proper" shell—the ability to avoid bending stresses. The conoid is the hardest to form of the three, since it requires a series of arches of differing rise before the boards can be placed. Besides, the conoid and the hyperboloid are restricted because of their difficult analysis.

But of all the shapes we can give to a shell, the easiest and most practical to build is the hyperbolic paraboloid. Like the conoid and the hyperboloid it is a doubly-curved or *non-developable* surface (and so can work with membrane stresses only), but it is the *only* warped surface with an equation simple enough to allow the calculation of its membrane stresses by plain, elementary mathematics.

This feature of the paraboloid, the comparative simplicity of its analysis, is most important. Resolving partial differential equations which are not directly integrable is still a very lengthy and cumbersome mathematical process. The average structural office finds this outside its range. Electronic computers and analogical machines are still not in popular use, and cost of their use for average projects is prohibitive. The construction industry itself is still quite unstandardized. The production lines of the automobile and aircraft industries enable them to spend huge sums on research and analysis of prototypes; but in building we keep on trying to work a different solution for each project, while knowing that the cost of analytical investigation must not exceed

LONG CYLINDRICAL SHELL: Sawtooth arrangement over dining hall at Toyoda Factory, Irolo, Mexico; span 62 ft. With Masso Watanabe, Architect.

Figure 3

Rupture by bending of a non-compound laminar structure

Rupture by tension of a doubly-curved shell

CONOID: Factory in Mexico, D.F. With Raul Fernandez, Architect.

HYPERBOLIC PARABOLOID (Vertical axes): "El Leon" Confectionery Factory, Mexico, D.F. "Half-umbrellas" spanning 66 ft in sawtooth. Ties are necessary to take lateral thrusts

HYPERBOLIC PARABOLOID (Vertical axes): Herdez Factory, Mexico, D.F. Rectangular domes formed by 4 h. ps. Catwalk carries lighting and conceals ties. Span 52 by 52 ft. Vertical axis; limited by straight generators

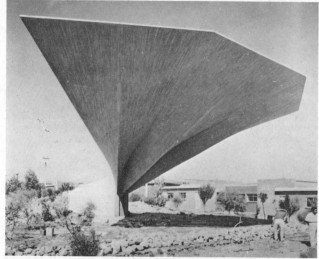

HYPERBOLIC PARABOLOID (Non-vertical axes): Bandshell, Santa Fe, Mexico, D.F. Six h. ps coupled at base to form 40 ft cantilever. Upper edges in tension, lower common edges forming groins in compression. With Mario Pani, Architect.

HYPERBOLIC PARABOLOID (Arbitrary curved boundary): Mexican Stock Exchange, Mexico, D.F. Groined vault on a rectangular plan. Edges are inclined for daylighting. Span 85 by 50 ft. With Enrique de la Mora, Architect.

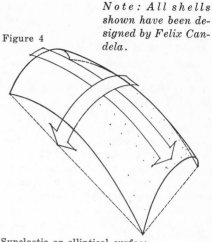

Note: All shells shown have been designed by Felix Candela.

Figure 4

Synclastic or elliptical surface

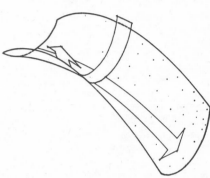

Anticlastic or hyperbolic surface

a small percentage of the total cost of the structure. Moreover as our reward for inventing a "Theory of Structures" we are now obliged to calculate everything we build and to justify it with numbers. This can be really discouraging to the adventurous mind. If we wish to surpass the pedantic pace of the building codes, we must defend our audacity with a formidable array of figures and equations.

Although the extent to which we can assess numerically the *real* behavior of a structure is rather hypo-

Figure 5

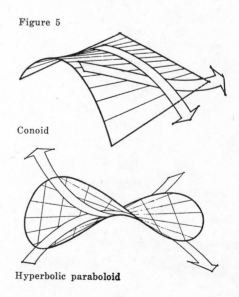

Conoid

Hyperbolic paraboloid

thetical, our mathematical elaborations have a certain value. They can give us a rough assurance that the structure will stand, after we have called on our experience and common sense to determine its form and dimensions.

Moreover when we analyze membrane stresses we are only using statics, and we do not have to assume anything about the elastic properties of the material. When the results of this analysis give us comparatively low value for the stresses, these will produce only negligible elongation or shrinking in the structure and we can be sure that the change of shape of the structure after such deformations will also be negligible. Therefore the theoretical investigation and the actual behavior of the structure must agree satisfactorily in our case, since the former is based on the abstract truths of logical statics, and not on any hypothetical simplifications of the material's physical properties.

The first requisite in understanding the behavior of the hyperbolic paraboloid is to define its surface. It is surprising how many designers are deficient in this primary consideration.

Surface Definition: Assume two straight nonparallel, nonintersecting lines H O D and A B C (Fig. 6) in space which will be provisionally named directrixes. Straight lines h_n that intersect both directrixes, being at the same time parallel to one plane xOz named *director plane,* define the surface. They will be called the *first system of generators.* The two directrixes determine in their turn a second director plane yOz, parallel to them. The surface may also be considered as created by a *second system of generators* in parallel to this plane and intersecting every generator h_n of the first system.

The hyperbolic paraboloid contains, therefore, two systems of straight lines h_n and i_n, each system being parallel to a director plane and both planes forming an arbitrary angle ω. Every point of the surface is the intersection of two straight lines contained in the surface.

It is convenient to take as coordinate axes the two generators passing by the crown of the paraboloid and the paraboloid axis or intersection of both director planes, which is always normal to the plane of the other two axes. In these birectangular coordinates, the equation of the paraboloid will be

$$z = kxy$$

k being a constant which represents *the unitary slope or warping* of the paraboloid (in **Fig. 6,**

$$k = AA\ (OB \cdot OH));$$

xOy can be any angle; xOz and yOz are right angles.

This is the *simplest possible equation* of second degree tying together the three coordinates of each point. When the director planes form a right angle (x = 90°) the paraboloid is *equilateral* or *rectangular.* When ω is any other angle, the paraboloid is *oblique.* Plane sections parallel to the bisecting planes of the director dihedral angle xOy are parabolic. They are named *principal parabolas,* and are respectively curved upward (G O C) and downward (A O E); hence the surface is *anticlastic* or inversely doubly-curved. All other plane sections are hyperbolas, except those parallel to the z axis which are also parabolas and, of course, those parallel to the director planes which give the straight generators.

As a translation surface (Fig. 7) the paraboloid may be considered as generated by a principal parabola A B C that moves parallel to itself along an inverse principal parabola B O F. Therefore the surface has two systems of parabolic generators. Each system is composed of *identical* parabolas situated in parallel planes. All these well-known properties are very useful in the erection of forms.

Sometimes the designer may wish to arrange the surface in such a way that the z axis is not vertical. In this case the xy plane will not coincide with the horizontal plane and so the horizontal projections of the generators will not be parallel. The loads will have components along the three axes of the paraboloid. The analysis of this general case has never been published in a workable form. But no designer who wishes to venture beyond the limited cases of paraboloids with vertical axes and very flat surfaces can afford to be ignorant of it.

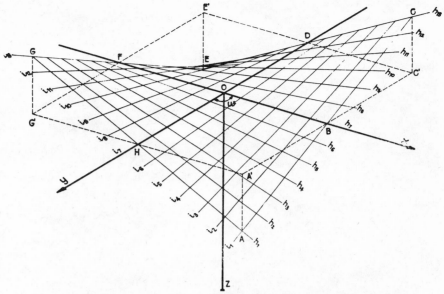

Figure 6: Hyperbolic paraboloid as formed by two systems of line generators

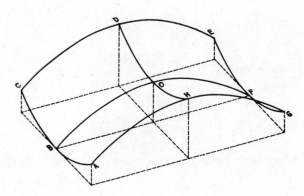

Figure 7: Hyperbolic paraboloid as limited by two principal parabolas

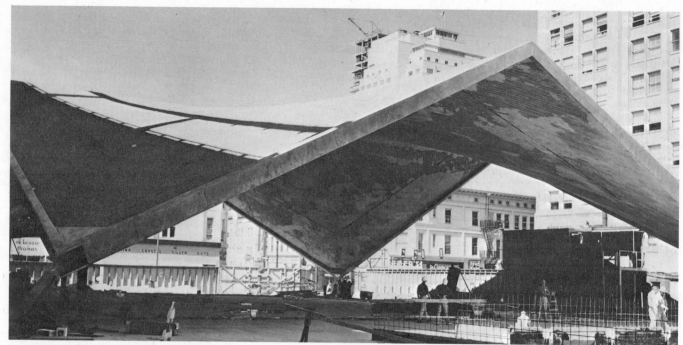

Mammoth (112 by 131½ ft) hyperbolic paraboloid houses specialty shop of adjacent department store in Denver's Court House Square

HUGE THIN SHELL ROOFS SHOP

Wire-reinforced shell is poured in place

One of the largest hyperbolic paraboloids yet constructed in this country hovers at the base of a seven-story department store in Denver, Colorado's $35 million Court House Square development. Designed to house the store's specialty shop, the structure spans an area of approximately 112 by 131½ ft without interior supports, and rises to an elevation of 32½ ft. Its four supporting steel buttresses are hinged to the shell with stainless steel pins, and tied diagonally with 1 by 12 in. tension plates made up of three or four sections bolted together.

Ranging in thickness from 3 in. for the skin proper to 6 in. at the ridges, the concrete shell is reinforced with 6 by 6 in., 4/4 welded wire fabric, augmented by strips of 4 by 4 in. mesh in the center of the slab and by No. 3 bars placed diagonally on 8 in. centers. It is surfaced with a built up roofing over a layer of fiberglass insulation.

The formwork, which was constructed of 1 by 8 in. tongue and groove hemlock, was supported on 290 jacks, each capable of being lowered 4 in. Upon completion of the shell, the roof was "de-centered" by lowering these jacks a turn or two at a time, starting at the center and working outward concentrically.

The shell was built by Webb & Knapp Construction Company, with Ketchum, Gina & Sharp, associate architects; William B. Tabler, consulting architect. Roberts & Schaefer Company were consulting engineers for the shell.

Edge beams (forms above) meet at supports

Soaring to a height of 32½ ft without interior supports, giant shell dwarfs man at center

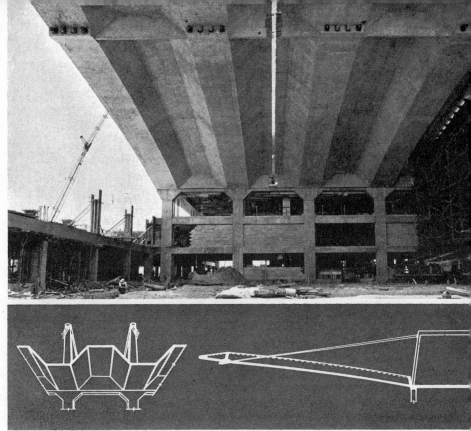

Pan-American World Airways hangar, New York International Airport: Chester L. Churchill, Architect; Ammann & Whitney, Structural Engineers

Trans World Airlines hangar, New York International Airport: Ammann & Whitney, Engineers

National Airlines hangar, Miami International Airport: Weed, Russell & Johnson, Architects; Ammann & Whitney, Engineers

Charles Payne

FOLDED PLATES ROOF NEW HANGARS

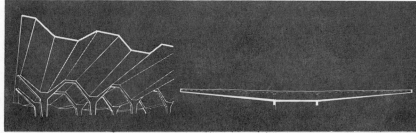

The rapid evolution of the flying machine from the frail mechanized box kite of the Wright brothers' day to the sleek skyborne giants of today has demanded equally rapid progress in the design of structure to house them. Converted barns long ago gave way to the more elaborate hangars currently prominent in our airport-scapes. Now, with jets on their way into commercial use and who-knows-what to follow, these too are being waved aside to make room for such mammoth symbols of the coming Jet Age as the hangars shown here.

For all the simplicity of these structures, the problem is a complex one. Its most critical aspect from the hangar designer's point of view is the size of the new aircraft. Hangars to shelter them must be large. To accommodate varying sizes and shapes of planes—they must be free of space-stealing supports. And because hangars are still essentially utility structures, they must be economical.

Within the last few years, a new type of hangar has appeared which seems to offer maximum clear spans at minimum cost. Developed by New York structural engineers Ammann & Whitney for a Trans-World Airlines hangar at Kansas City, the scheme is being used for four other hangars.

The Kansas City hangar consists, basically, of a cantilever span cable—suspended on both sides of a central

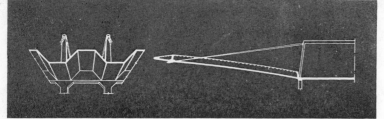

Before slabs are poured, cables are pin-attached to each end of anchor walls. Stresses go through walls via heavy plates welded to tension bars at top

When concrete reaches a compressive strength of 2500 psi, hydraulic jacks are set up to tension the cables to an average stress of 176 kips in each

Outer ends of cables, with sockets attached, are drawn through sleeves in the valleys of the roof. Sixteen cables, 8 on each side, are tensioned at a time

As cables tighten, slabs are lifted to final position. Lateral ties prevent sag before construction joints are poured between adjacent sections

Photos by Charles Payne

office core. Two of the hangars now completed—one for National Airlines at Miami, the other for Mohawk Airlines at Utica, N.Y.—have departed from the original model in that their corrugated roofs are pure cantilevers. Shorter required spans made it possible to omit the suspension cables; nose pockets in the center section and canopy-type sliding hangar doors added enough depth to accommodate even large planes.

At New York International Airport, however, the Kansas City scheme has been borrowed intact for two hangar-office buildings which sit side-by-side just off the approach road to the main terminal area. Although the buildings for TWA and Pan-American World Airways differ slightly in size and shape, and in the arrangement of administrative facilities, they both closely follow the structural pattern set by the Kansas City prototype. Their cantilever roofs are suspended with the 6 ft deep corrugations running 30 ft on center perpendicular to the long axis of the building so that the beam action of the folded section supports loads parallel to the direction of suspension. To increase the strength which the corrugations give to the thin (4¾ in.) concrete deck, the cables are anchored in the valleys. The horizontal component of their thrust thus produces a negative moment which helps to counteract the positive moment from loads on the folded slab. At the other end, the cables are anchored to walls at 30 ft on center.

At Kansas City, where two floors of the center section were hung from these anchor walls, the combined loads from cable, roof and suspended floors were used to counter-balance each other. The unbalanced moments possible under certain conditions of loading (e.g. when the floors are not carrying a full load) were taken care of by reinforcing bars in the bottom of the wall, and a combination of reinforcing bars and post-tensioning wires at the top. At Idlewild, the floors—except in a part of the PAA hangar—are supported from below. The anchorage assembly was modified to include a tension tie made up of 24 square bars welded to steel plates which receive the four suspension cables at each end of the wall. Thus when the cables are tensioned, their horizontal force is carried through the wall.

To give access to the whole length of the hangars, the horizontal sliding doors along the sides roll on several tracks, stacking to leave about two-thirds of the hangar open if desired. Their design was complicated by the inherent flexibility of the roof and the deflection of its free edge under variations in temperature and loading. (Before the construction joints between adjacent sections were poured, it "gave" noticeably even under the weight of a single man.) To prevent the door leaves from restraining the vertical motion of the roof edge, the doors were made in two sections joined by a horizontal hinge. The lower vertical section is set out 10 ft from the roof edge; a short sloping upper section spans the gap between it and the roof. The roller assembly at the top, the wheels at the base, and the hinge at the break form a three-hinged arrangement which permits free vertical deflection —and adds 10 ft to the usable span.

Once the hangars were out for bid, the contractors took over where the engineers left off. Their problem was the same: The size of the buildings demanded the use of some sort of traveler rather than rigid falsework to support the forms; the folded plate roofs demanded the use of forms that could be lowered to clear the corrugations, raised for pouring. They came up with solutions as different as the hangars themselves are similar.

The roof for Pan-American's hangar was formed with a "piggy-back" traveler devised by Corbetta Construction Co.'s vice president, Charles J. Prokop. Made up of two sections of timber falsework with an inclined rail system between, the traveler is big (two bays wide), awkward and complex in appearance. Actually it is as simple and efficient as the wedge principle on which it operates. The bottom wedge, 75 ft wide, is topped by heavy timbers which carry the sloping rails. To raise or lower the upper section, double flanged wheels at four "carrying trusses" along its length are rolled up or down the inclined plane.

When the form is in pouring position, the lower section is secured by sills wedged under vertical jacking posts. Similar jacking posts in the upper section line up with those below, and screw jacks set along the plane of movement between the posts of upper and lower wedges lift the top section clear of the rail. By adjusting the jacks, the forms are brought to the exact height required.

Using four of these travelers, the roof for the Pan-American job was concreted in double 60-ft sections, one on each side of the center core, starting at both ends and working toward the middle. After the slabs were cured, they were loaded by tensioning the cables in both sections simultaneously, thus lifting the outer edge of the roof about 6½ in. off the form. This started the stripping,

"Piggy-back" traveler for PAA hangar at Idlewild is made up of two sections of timber falsework with an inclined rail between. To lower forms, bottom wedge is allowed to slide forward under downward thrust of top section. Its primary advantage: lumber can be salvaged

Similar hangar for TWA was formed using travelers made up of laminated timber trusses on eight posts braced by cross beams and steel rods. Hydraulic jacks at each column raise forms and lower them 6 ft to clear corrugations; sand jacks support them during pouring

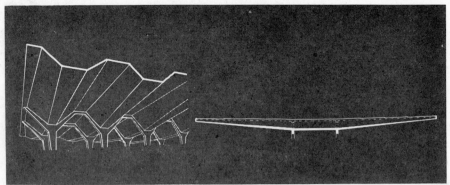

Tapered folded plate for National Airlines hangar at Miami is cantilevered—sans cables—from a 2-story center core. Offices are on top level; shops in open nose pockets below

Wall at end of hangar (far left in photo below) indicates outset of hinged, canopy-type sliding doors which enclose two of six hangar positions, add 20 ft to their total usable depth

Giant "earthworks" shows scale of double span. Total hangar width is 270 ft; cantilevers extend 110 ft on each side of 50 ft center core, taper from 12 ft at roof to 3 ft at free end

National Airlines

which was helped along by driving wedges under the slab at its outer edge and along the sides. At the hinged end, where the tensioning lifted the concrete very little, the forms had to be stripped by removing the screw jacks that supported the upper sections.

To prevent movement when the wheels came in contact with the inclined rail, the top wedge was first anchored to a deadman in the ground. The bottom wedge was then released and allowed to slide forward under the downward thrust of the top section until the form had dropped enough to clear the valleys of the roof slab. When the upper and lower wedges had been locked to prevent further relative movement, the traveler was hitched over 60 ft to the next position, the top section re-anchored, and the bottom section pulled back until the jacking posts on both sections were again lined up. The form was then jacked up to a pouring position and the forming cycle repeated. Joints between sections were poured after the cables had been tensioned.

Although the forming method used by Grove, Shepherd, Wilson & Kruge for the TWA hangar was essentially the same as that used by Corbetta, the travelers themselves were not. In this case, the double wedge was replaced by laminated timber trusses supported on columns and braced in both directions by ¾ in. diagonal rods. Single-acting hydraulic jacks mounted on each column were used to raise and lower the forms; tripod sand jacks supported the concrete loads. Once the travelers were rolled into position, they were lifted clear of the rails by the hydraulic jacks, which also supported them while sand jacks were slipped under each vertical post. The hydraulic jacks were then retracted, and the form was allowed to settle onto the sand jacks during pouring.

When the slabs had set and had been raised to their final position by tightening the cables, the hydraulic jacks were again lowered onto chairs on each side of the rails and used to lift the traveler enough to permit removal of the sand jacks. They were then released slowly until the wheels at the base of the column had come to rest on the rails and the traveler could be moved to its next position.

A variation on the same theme, the nose hangar for National Airlines at Miami International Airport is similar to the pair at Idlewild in approach —different in detail.

In this case the largest plane to be housed was the 140 ft DC-8. Because engine overhaul facilities were to remain in an adjacent building, the 50 ft wide, single-story office core could be lifted to second floor level, leaving the shops below and freeing enough ground space to provide a nose pocket 25 ft deep on each side of the hangar. With this added usable depth, the necessary roof span could be reduced to 110 ft. Thus while column free space along the entire 630 ft length remained a design criterion, the hangar depth became a less critical problem, and the folded plate roof—which had been proved economical for spans of 120 ft or less—was used as a pure cantilever on both sides of the two-story center section, giving a total hangar width of 270 ft and a usable depth of 135 ft on each side.

Although enclosed hangars are not necessary in Miami's mild climate, two of the six hangar positions were fitted with hinged canopy-type doors to form a sheltered area for certain maintenance operations and for storing disabled planes during hurricanes. The outset doors add 20 ft to these sections, making them 15 ft longer than the longest planes. In consultation with the engineers, the architects' original design for a simple folded plate with points at top and bottom evolved into a tapered folded plate with the ridges flattened to give a more efficient section at the lightly-loaded outer end. Because of the absence of supporting cables, the depth of the corrugations was increased to 12 ft at the roof of the cantilever, tapering to about 3 ft at its outer edge.

Fred Howland, Inc. contractors for the Miami job, escaped the problem of suspending the cantilevers, but forming was complicated by the extra depth of the corrugations, which made it necessary to raise and lower the forms in two stages. The laminated truss-type travelers, similar to those used for the TWA hangar in New York, were supported on vertical timber posts over steel jacking chairs made up of four perforated steel posts connected by cross braces on two sides. Two more steel beams placed crossways over the first two braces seated the sand jacks on which the traveler post rested; a third brace along one side of the frame seated a double-acting hydraulic jack which met a jacking seat on the post. When the traveler was being lifted, the hydraulic jacks raised it 6 ft and held it in place while cribbing and sand jacks were moved up and pinned to the perforated posts. The traveler load was then transferred to the sand jacks while the hydraulic jacks were moved up on cribbing and used to lift the forms another 6 ft. At this point, the sand jacks were again moved up to support the load during pouring.

Traveler for nose hangar at Miami closely resembles that used for TWA hangar, but extra depth of corrugations made two-lift jacking necessary. Hydraulic jacks were used to lift and lower; sand jacks supported traveler between 6 ft lifts and during pour

National Airlines

STOCK LUMBER BUILDS BUDGET SHELLS

1. MASSENA COUNTRY CLUB

Associated Architects: Victor Prus; Norval White

Consulting Engineers: Robert P. Levien (Structural); Sidney Barbanel (Mechanical)

Although the Messrs. Prus and White admit that geometry is a favorite subject, the hyperbolic paraboloidal roof over the Massena Coun-

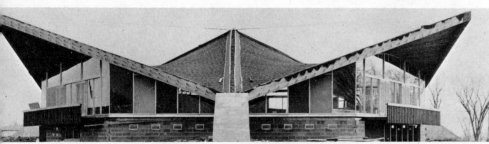

Two-story Massena Country Club is roofed by three hyperbolic paraboloids aranged in a hexagon and supported on concrete piers. Lower walls are masonry; upper walls glass with brightly colored aluminum panels. Sharp definition of each level helps to establish scale

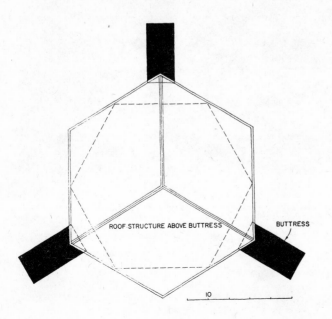

ROOF STRUCTURE ABOVE BUTTRESS

BUTTRESS

10

Photos courtesy of National Lumber Manufacturers Association

try Club is no structural tour de force—unless building hyperbolic paraboloids with two by four's and without scaffolding can be so considered. The tour de force, if any, lies in the cost figures. An exact per-square-foot price for the roof is difficult to sift from the general contract, but all parties concerned agree that it cost substantially less than a similar span built by conventional methods.

The initial choice of the hyperbolic paraboloidal roof stemmed primarily from two factors. The site, surrounded on all sides by the golf course, called for a centric building that would capitalize on the view; the members of the club, serious golfers all, called for a simple, informal nineteenth hole that would house such necessary facilities as locker rooms and a bar. (A kitchen was later added to their program.) So the architects emerged from their preliminary studies with a pavilion-like structure roofed by three hyperbolic paraboloids arranged in a scalloped hexagon. This choice was confirmed when they hit on a method by which the roof could be formed with almost do-it-yourself simplicity by local carpenters using stock lumber.

According to White, the use of two by four's for the warped surfaces of

the hyperbolic paraboloids was "obvious"—although it has not, to his knowledge, been done before. Wood, a native material, was appropriate to the site. Two by four's were cheap and readily available. But more important, the long, thin strips of lumber could be laid so that they themselves conformed to the basic straight line geometry of the hyperbolic paraboloid, forming the warped surfaces directly rather than by the usual procedure of fitting a wood membrane over an elaborate—and costly—scaffold.

The roof framing began with the erection of the laminated edge beams, each 19 in. deep, 7½ in. wide and some 53 ft long. The three pairs of edge beams along the inner edges of the adjacent "saddles" of course formed a stable tripod, meeting the ground via welded shoe connections attached to heavy concrete piers, and rising to a 30 ft peak at the apex. The outer edge beams, however, were supported on a scaffolding until they were stabilized by temporary cables stretching from the center peak to the high points along the perimeter.

The membrane was then formed by simply stacking the 2 by 4's on edge, parallel to one of the outer edge beams in each "saddle," and gluing them together with an epoxy resin. (Nails were used only to clamp the members together while the glue set.) Since the lumber came from the yard in standard short lengths, it was glued end-to-end as well as lengthwise across the span. The members at the ends of each row were also glued and bolted to the edge beams.

Because the "sides" of each panel slope in opposite directions, the 2 by 4's rotate enough to reduce the effective membrane depth to just under three inches—half an inch less than the actual depth of the lumber. The same rotation produces a slightly serrated surface, which was left exposed on the interior. On the exterior, the roof was covered with a protective compound consisting of tiny flecks of aluminum foil suspended in a base of highly-refined asphalt and non-drying oils. Two coats were applied, the first directly onto the roof and the second over an intermediate layer of cotton cloth.

This one-story addition to the Henry Strub house in suburban Montreal, Canada, was designed by Victor Prus to provide general living quarters for a large family so that the adjacent two-story house could be converted to a "dormitory." Its roof was built in substantially the same way as the one for the Massena Country Club, with intersecting hyperbolic paraboloids made up of short strips of stock lumber. However, there is one unique difference. Since 2-by 3-in. members, the smallest size practical, gave a membrane depth greater than the short spans required, some of them could be left out of every other row. This was done in the three panels over the living room and the resulting lacy pattern emphasized by covering this section of the roof with a translucent polyester glass fiber resin instead of the opaque roofing used elsewhere

Prefabricated segments of stressed skin plywood are bolted together on the site to form a fanciful four-pointed star that is also strong, lightweight—and economical

2. CHILDREN'S THEATER

Arroyo Viejo Recreation Center
Oakland, California

Architect: Irwin Luckman

Consulting Engineer: Allen McKay,
Berkeley Plywood Company

The bilaterally symmetrical star that roofs this children's theater is the result of architect Luckman's attempt to devise a form that would appeal to pintsize theater-goers without being representational. (Tudor castles, he feels, are appropriate for knights and ladies—but not for children.)

It is also the result of the application of one of the newer techniques of wood fabrication: stressed skin construction. The most obvious advantage of a roof built along the lines of an airplane wing is that the hollow sections can be shop fabricated, thus eliminating scaffolding and other costly impedimenta of building in place. But, equally important, stressed skin construction is also a relatively simple way of producing complex shapes with maximum strength and minimum weight.

In this case, minimum weight was of more than ordinary importance because the theater was built on the site of an existing amphitheater which featured, among other things, a running creek where the stage should be. The use of a lightweight structural system greatly simplified the problem of building the theater across the 16½ ft gap without reinforcing the existing retaining walls.

The eight roof sections, each pair of which forms one point of the star, were framed of 2 by 3's and 2 by 4's with plywood gussets. Three-eighths inch fir plywood was also used to panel the top and the underside. After the sections had been assembled at the Berkeley Plywood Company's local plant, they were set up on the ground and temporarily bolted together for final fitting. The roof was then trimmed and disassembled into four double sections, each measuring about 22 by 38 ft and weighing close to a ton. These were moved to the site with the help of a police escort and flat bed trucks.

There they were hoisted onto eight 3½ in. o.d. steel pipe columns—four at the inner hub of the star and four midway out beneath the bottom ridges of the double V'd roof. Bolted together, the sections formed a rigid, lightweight, four-winged structure which was topped with a plywood cupola "for fun." The building was then enclosed by freestanding, redwood-paneled stud walls. At the corners, the walls also serve as shear panels, reinforced by a plywood diaphragm under the siding.

So that its lines would not be marred by ridges of built-up felt roofing, the top of the star was covered with glass cloth embedded in an asphalt emulsion. The underside was painted with textured paint.

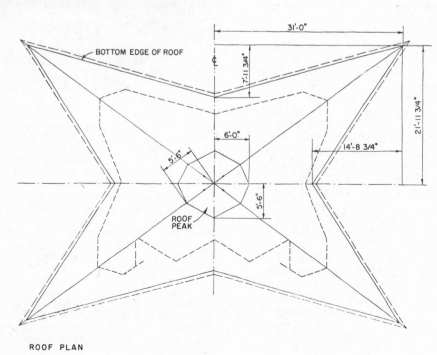

ROOF PLAN

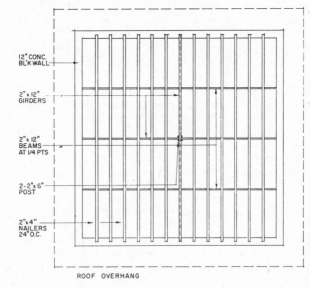

ROOF OVERHANG

3. A LUMBER STOREHOUSE

New Hope, Pennsylvania

Designer: George Nakashima
Consulting Engineer: Paul Wiedlinger

A storage shed would seem an unlikely candidate for architectural innovation, but this one became the guinea pig for (another) new method of constructing a hyperbolic paraboloid; this time of three layers of ⅜ in. plywood laid over two by four nailers. Designer-owner Nakashima calls the system "perhaps the easiest and cheapest way to roof a clear span of this size (31 ft square) or bigger."

The twelve-inch concrete block walls that enclose the shed also support the hyperbolic paraboloid, with an 8-ft rise on each side following the reverse twist of the roof. The triangular gaps in the stepped block walls are filled in with reinforced concrete "beams," warped to follow the contour of the roof. When capped with a 3- by 8-in. plate, these beams provided a smooth slope to which the membrane could be attached.

The membrane itself was formed over a scaffold of 2- by 12-in. girders that divided the building into quadrants, with beams at the quarter points in one direction only. This framework was supported on a post in the center and on simple props at the walls. (Since it carried only its own weight after the roof was in place, it was taken down as easily as

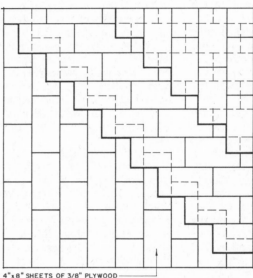

4"x 8" SHEETS OF 3/8" PLYWOOD

The extremely thin (1⅛ in.) hyperbolic paraboloidal roof on the storage shed shown above is notable for its economy and ease of construction. Made up of three layers of plywood joined in a continuous membrane, it was formed over the minimal scaffolding diagrammed at left. The roof is nailed to a plate along the tops of the sloping walls, which serve as both supports and edge beams. Since the block walls were designed for shear, with mesh reinforcing laid in every other course and vertical rods grouted in at the corners, no tie rods were necessary. The finished membrane was topped with a 20 year built-up roof with white chips and aluminum flashing

it was put up—by simply knocking out the center support.)

Over it went the 2- by 4-in. nailers, laid flat on 2-ft centers perpendicular to the beams, and the three layers of plywood. The first layer was laid parallel to the nailers; the second in the opposite direction, with all joints broken; and the third in the same direction as the first—again with all joints broken. Each successive layer was screw nailed to the two by four's and to the plate along the top of the walls with 8d galvanized nails on three-inch centers; and, in addition, the joints in the second and third layers were screwed to the sheets of plywood immediately below.

The extreme rigidity of the thin (1⅛ in. thick) roof is attributed to this method of overlapping and joining the layers of plywood so that they form, in effect, a continuous membrane. To maintain a straight roof line, the membrane was stiffened with a 2- by 3-in. strip nailed under its edge where they overhang some 18 in. from the walls.

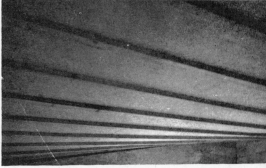

PREFAB REINFORCING CUTS SHELL COSTS

The thin shell-roofed, glass-enclosed library constructed on the Bronx (N.Y.) campus of Hunter College marked the first major use of the hyperbolic paraboloid in the eastern United States, and the first major use anywhere of welded wire fabric instead of individually placed reinforcing bars.

The structural system devised by architect Marcel Breuer, F.A.I.A., consultant Eduardo Catalano, and structural engineers Farkas and Barron consists of six 60-ft-square inverted concrete umbrellas supported on central columns and joined at the edges to form a roof 120 ft wide by 180 ft long. Each umbrella is divided into four hyperbolic-paraboloidal quadrants whose thin concrete membranes transmit stresses to heavy ribs which in turn carry them to the supporting columns.

The hyperbolic paraboloid shape used has several inherent economic advantages: it requires less concrete for a given area than is needed for conventional roof construction, and, since its compound curves actually consist of straight lines, it can be formed relatively easily of stock lumber. However, in the case of the Hunter College library, the savings in manpower and money—and particularly in time—were greatly increased by the contractor's choice of an alternate which called for heavy wire mesh reinforcement (½-in. wires on 6-in. centers) to replace the usual shaped, detailed bars. When the concrete work had been completed, it was found that, while the higher per ton cost of the prefabricated steel fabric kept actual savings in labor and materials down to about $600, construction time had been cut by about six days.

The four tons plus of reinforcing steel required for each of the umbrellas was supplied in the form of 31 by 10½ ft mats, which were placed three to a quadrant. A crane was used to hoist them from the stock-pile one at a time and ease them into position, guided by a four man lather crew. They were then overlapped at least two wire spacings (one foot), and nested so that there were only three thicknesses of wire at the lap. Thus, with one inch chairs under the mats, the 3½ in. depth of the shell provided at least a one inch cover of concrete at top and bottom of the steel.

All the mats were made the length required at the center of the umbrellas (the point of deepest drape), and, in order to permit nesting at the overlaps, were placed as nearly parallel to one another as possible. For continuity of reinforcement, they were tied securely at regular intervals, beginning at the center of the umbrella and working out to the edges, where the excess fabric was trimmed.

According to the general contractor, Leon D. de Matteis & Sons, Inc., and Dic Concrete Corp., the subcontractor for the concrete work, the steel fabric adjusted readily to the compound curves of the hyperbolic paraboloids, fitting "like a glove," in spite of the thickness of the wires and a difference in elevation of as much as 4 ft between opposite corners of the mats. This confirmed the results of experiments that engineer Maurice Barron had conducted previously to determine the "drape-ability" of the wire mesh.

The reinforcing work was completed by placing standard bars for the stiffener ribs that divide the shells into quadrants and for the tension edges or perimeters of the membranes. The concrete was then poured at the outer edge, worked down to the center, vibrated and rough screeded.

Architect's rendering shows completed library with accompanying classroom structure

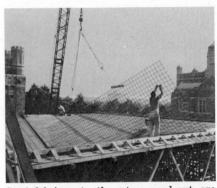

Steel fabric mats, three to a quadrant, are hoisted in place on mushroom-shaped forms

Parallel reinforcing mats are nested to assure adequate concrete cover for steel

THIN SHELLS CUT FROM A TORUS

SHELL 1: DIFFICULT TO ANALYZE

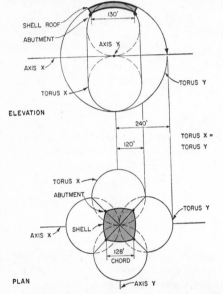

This large doubly-curved dome for a supermarket near Honolulu is known as a double torus (a torus is doughnut-shaped). It departs from conventional practice in shell design in that it has no edge beams (to get a thin edge), no stiffening ribs, no hinges at the abutments. Richard Bradshaw, the structural engineer says, "I have little patience with engineers who place hinges and other gadgetry in buildings which actually weaken the structure." The shell is thickened in the proper areas to manage the stresses and to channel forces to the ground. The unusual design made analysis a rather complicated affair (Bradshaw's theory is explained on the following page). The shell rises and falls with a change of temperature and window mullions telescope to accommodate shell movement. *Wimberly and Cook, Architects; Nordic Construction Co., Contractor.*

R. Wenkham photos

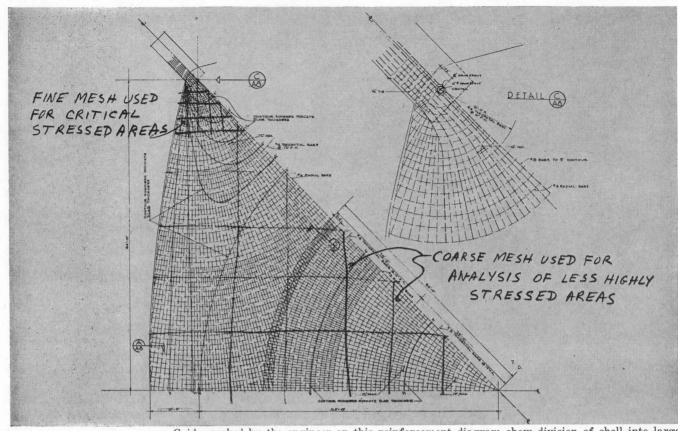

FINE MESH USED FOR CRITICAL STRESSED AREAS

COARSE MESH USED FOR ANALYSIS OF LESS HIGHLY STRESSED AREAS

DETAIL

Grids marked by the engineer on this reinforcement diagram show division of shell into large sections for analysis where stresses are not so critical and small sections where stresses are large

ENGINEERING ANALYSIS   *by Richard R. Bradshaw*

The method of analysis is unusual. To my knowledge, no shell has ever been analyzed in this same way. The three general differential equations of a thin shell were solved, including terms for bending. These equations consist of three linear, partial differential, simultaneous equations, two of the second order and one of the fourth. It should be mentioned at this point that no two authorities ever use quite the same identical equations for shell theory. This is because certain terms are always dropped out. The terms to be dropped are decided upon by the geometry of the shell. In my case, I dropped out certain terms and then substituted them back in after obtaining an answer. From this it was possible to determine that the terms could be omitted. My actual choice of equations were the ones derived by Donnell in 1933. Since these were derived for cylindrical shells only, it became necessary to extend them for the case of double curvature. This was done under the assumption that cross-product terms, employing both radii of curvature, would be small in comparison to those employing single radii curvature. In this way, perfectly general equations for any shell were obtained. If one radius goes to infinity, equations for a cylindrical shell are obtained. If both radii go to infinity, the general equation of a flat plate is obtained. If the width of the plate is decreased to unity, the general differential equation of a beam is obtained. Hence, it might be said that the equations solved for this shell were the general equations of almost all structures.

The equations were cast in a finite difference form.

The shell was divided into imaginary pieces on a coarse grid. These pieces were imagined to be held in position by various moments, shears, axial loads and twisting moments. As these were released one by one, a sort of three dimensional moment distribution was employed. By proceeding around and around the shell from piece to piece, it was possible eventually to get convergence and thus get the deflection pattern of the shell about all three coordinate axes. Upon completion of the analysis on a coarse grid, the critical areas near the abutments were divided into a finer grid and convergence obtained again. This system of analysis is known as Southwell's Relaxation. Moment distribution is a very simplified special case of Southwell's General Method of Relaxation. The mathematical method used to obtain convergence is known as "Liquidation of the Residuals." This is obtained by pushing the unbalanced forces across the borders. To my knowledge, this method has never been used for the solution of these particular equations. The method was exceedingly tedious and laborious and I do not recommend it for general usage. In fact, I have not used it since. However, as a pioneering step I believe it to be noteworthy. Engineers still have found no convenient way of analyzing a general shell.

The shell was checked for buckling in the upper flat region. The classical elastic buckling formula was used with a reduction to allow for plasticity, initial roughness, and the generally low stresses occurring during buckling of a doubly curved surface under radial compression load.

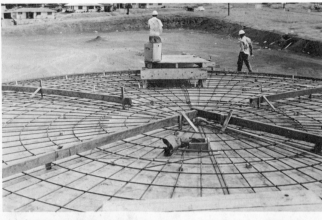

Conventional formwork was built for the shell and, while not an engineering requirement, the contractor elected to pour it in one piece. In the first few weeks after removal of the forms the center deflected approximately 2 in. The discontinuous edge deflected about 3 in. downward at the center of its span, and rose 1 in. at the quarter point

All photos by R. Wenkam

To avoid edge beams, which would have made the shell appear heavy, the 130-ft unsupported edges were made slightly thicker than the center portion. The dome ranges from 3- to 4-in. thick 40 ft from the center; the edges go from 4 in. at the perimeter to 5 in. at 10 ft inside; the shell at the abutment is about 9-in. thick, tapering to 5½ in. on an arc 23 ft toward the center of the dome. The corrugated shells seen at left above span 20 by 20 ft, are 2-in. thick and ribless. The slab is thickened slightly over column heads to take concentrated loads at these points

SHELL 2: INEXPENSIVE TO BUILD

Interest in this shell for a Los Angeles ice skating rink is the reverse of the previous one: problem was complications of construction rather than theoretical analysis. Construction method, taken together with the shape of the shell (geometrically, its sections are cut from a corrugated torus), yielded the low cost of $2 per sq ft of projected floor area. The shell, whose ridge line is slightly curved, spans 100 ft and is 180-ft long. It is 3½-in. thick to meet a 1-hr fire rating; a shell this thick might span twice as far. Sections toward the ends tip slightly forward so that the end sections provide a 10-ft overhang. An earth form was used for precasting the 36 sections in piles of nine each. The forms were dug in a pit to avoid using a crane for pouring. (The mathematics get involved for casting doubly curved pieces on top of one another.) The pieces were picked up two at a time and set in slots cast in the footings; steel in the upper ends was then welded. Due to fire restrictions glass was not permitted in openings, so these were gunited. *Carl Matson, Architect; Richard R. Bradshaw, Structural Engineer; Raines-McClellan, Contractor*

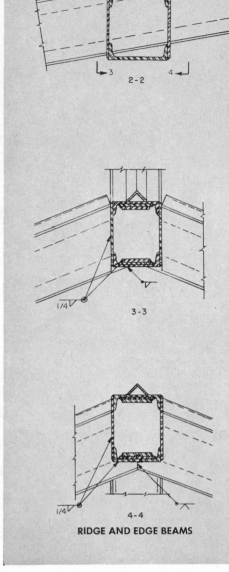

2-2

3-3

4-4

RIDGE AND EDGE BEAMS

NEW WAY TO BUILD A SHELL: ROOF IS WELDED STEEL DECK

Two layers of metal decking are crisscrossed
to form a four-quadrant hyperbolic paraboloid

by Harry T. Graham, Truman P. Young Associates, Cincinnati

A top award winner in the 1961 James F. Lincoln Arc Welding Foundation competition was this structure for a Cincinnati restaurant. Program requirements called for striking appearance, square-shaped floor plan, and reasonable cost. A metal-deck hyperbolic paraboloid easily matched these requirements.

Size and Shape
The structure consists of four paraboloids, each 33 ft 6 in. square, having a common column in the center of the structure and four exterior corner columns, giving a basic building 67 ft sq. For the sake of appearance overhangs were added on each of the four sides in the form of triangles. Since the basic paraboloid is square, this overhang complicated the design. The analysis considered first the basic square paraboloid, and then the overhang as a simple span supported on the outside edge beam and the fascia member. The edge beam is a straight line, thus the fascia member necessarily is a curve.

Roof Membrane
The main problem in using a membrane of laminated sheet metal was

fastening the two sheets together. Riveting and bolting as well as welding were considered. Of the three methods, only welding with the semiautomatic gun gave a reliable connection that was economically feasible.

The dead load was 22 psf and the live load was assumed to be 25 psf for a total load of 47 psf. Using 20 ga deck for both top and bottom sheets, the stresses were all within the allowable range. However, for ease in welding it was decided to use an 18 ga lower layer and 20 ga upper layer with flutes at right angles to each other, and the panels of decking parallel to the edge members. This made all lines of stress at 45 degrees to the decking, but it was felt that using two layers at right angles would make for easier and faster erection, as each sheet would be essentially a straight line between members with only a slight warp in the 2-ft width. The top and bottom layers were welded at each intersection by a series of plugwelds, having a maximum stress of 1190 lb per weld.

The pattern of welds is shown at top of the page along with the special

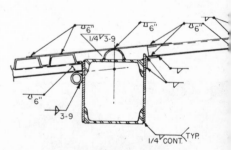

EDGE BEAM WELDING

Edge beams are straight. Roof cantile
fascia. Ridge beams slope down to 10½

66

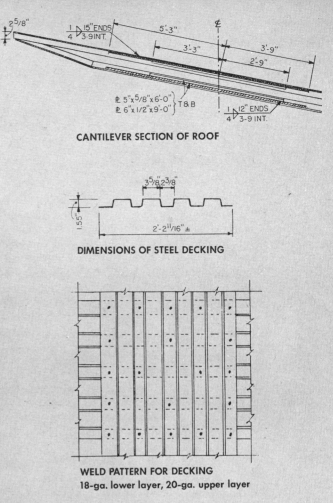

CANTILEVER SECTION OF ROOF

2 5/8"
1/4 △ 15" ENDS
3-9 INT.
5'-3"
3'-3"
3'-9"
2'-9"
℄
ℙ 5"x5/8"x6'-0"
ℙ 6"x1/2"x9'-0" } T&B
1/4 △ 12" ENDS
3-9 INT.

DIMENSIONS OF STEEL DECKING

1.55"
3 5/8", 2 3/8"
2'-2 11/16" ±

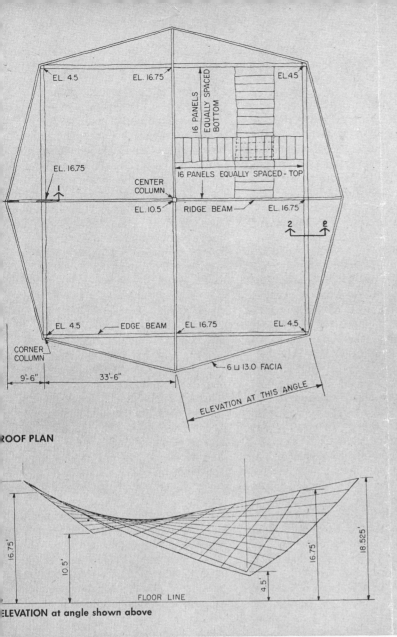

ROOF PLAN

EL. 4.5
EL. 16.75
EL. 4.5
16 PANELS EQUALLY SPACED BOTTOM
EL. 16.75
16 PANELS EQUALLY SPACED - TOP
CENTER COLUMN
EL. 10.5
RIDGE BEAM
EL. 16.75
2
℄
EL. 4.5
EDGE BEAM
EL. 16.75
EL. 4.5
CORNER COLUMN
6 ⊏ 13.0 FACIA
9'-6"
33'-6"
ELEVATION AT THIS ANGLE

ELEVATION at angle shown above

16.75'
10.5'
4.5
16.75'
18.525'
FLOOR LINE

WELD PATTERN FOR DECKING
18-ga. lower layer, 20-ga. upper layer

The doubly-curved hyperbolic paraboloid can be constructed geometrically by means of straight lines. Thus it was possible to build a steel-surfaced hyperbolic paraboloid using 2-ft. wide sheets of fluted metal decking; there is only slight warping across each sheet. The shape of one quadrant of the hyperbolic paraboloid is shown in the elevation, left.

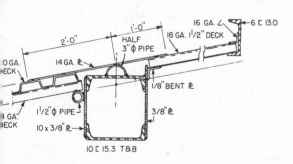

2'-0"
1'-0"
16 GA. ∠
6 ⊏ 13.0
18 GA. 1½" DECK
HALF 3" φ PIPE
0 GA. DECK
14 GA. ℙ
1/8" BENT ℙ
8 GA. DECK
1½" φ PIPE
3/8" ℙ
10 x 3/8" ℙ
10 ⊏ 15.3 T&B

EDGE BEAM DIMENSIONS

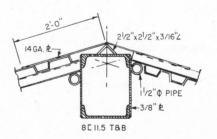

2'-0"
2½"x2½"x3/16" ∠
14 GA. ℙ
1½" φ PIPE
3/8" ℙ
8 ⊏ 11.5 T&B

RIDGE BEAM

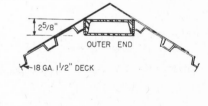

2 5/8"
OUTER END
18 GA. 1½" DECK

RIDGE BEAM AT CANTILEVER

a curving ...ter column

"Warp" of roof can be seen in this photo. Note plugwelds which fasten upper 20-ga. sheets to lower 18-ga. sheets

Peak is 18½-ft high sloping down to 4½ ft at corners. Interior is free except for center column which is 10½-ft high

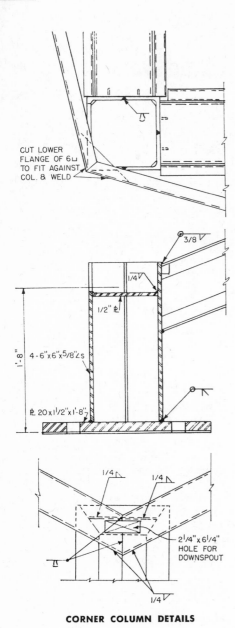

CUT LOWER FLANGE OF 6⊔ TO FIT AGAINST COL. & WELD

3/8

1/4

1/2" ℄

1'-8"

4 - 6"x6"x⅝"s

℄ 20 x 1½"x 1'-8"

1/4   1/4

2¼"x 6¼" HOLE FOR DOWNSPOUT

1/4

CORNER COLUMN DETAILS

STRUCTURAL ENGINEERS: *Hanly and Young (now Truman P. Young & Associates)*

ARCHITECTS: *Woodie Garber & Associates*

roof deck section used. This section is a standard shape without the edge bends, made by lifting the rolls that form the edges. The flat edges then overlapped by varying amounts and were practically unnoticable.

Edge Beams
The basic stress in the edge members is compression and for that reason a box section was used giving the best "r" (radius of gyration) for the amount of metal used. The approximate sizes were dictated by architectural reasons, so a section composed of channels and plates was chosen. In addition to the compression and horizontal bending in the edge members, the overhang introduces vertical bending.

The most difficult problem was the method of connecting the membrane to the edge beams. After much experimentation on the drawing board, it was decided to use a small pipe for the bottom and a half pipe for the top. By using these shapes, a contact for welding was always made, regardless of the angle of the deck. The fascia member, being on a parabolic curve, became a catenary. The member could have been a bar which would have draped very readily. However, to obtain a fascia, a 6 in.-channel was used; and, to get enough web thickness to prevent buckling, a heavy 13 lb section was needed. The corner columns were quite short, so presented little difficulty in taking the 100,000 lb horizontal thrust. These steel columns rest on heavy concrete piers, which are tied diagonally across the building just below the floor with four No. 11 reinforcing rods in concrete. Since the center forms a pocket, a roof drain had to

be placed at this point. The drain was located directly over the column, a copper downspout was placed down through the boxed angle column and out the side of the footing. Details of the columns are shown at left.

An unusual cut was required on the ends of the edge beams to connect them to ridge beams. This was made very well in the shop, and as a result there was perfect fit in the field. The metal deck was placed following the erection of the beams. Three lines of wooden shores were used at quarter points of the 33-ft span. These consisted of a 2 by 8 full length of a quadrant supported on single 2 by 4 posts. The lower layer of deck was placed on the edge members and the wooden supports. The sixteen sheets were equally spaced allowing the side laps to vary across the span. The ends of the sheets were trimmed as necessary and welded to the pipe on the side of the edge members. After the entire lower layer was in place, the upper layer was laid at right angles. The ends were welded to the edge beams as each sheet was placed. After all top sheets were laid, the interior spot welds were made by one man, using a welding gun. After one quadrant was completed, the procedure was repeated on the diagonally opposite.

Cost
Cost of completed roof structure, deck, insulation and roofing (built-up with marble chips) ran slightly over $3.00 per sq ft.

Following this project, three other structures were built, similar in principle but somewhat different in shape. Cost of these has been reduced to just above two dollars per sq ft.

Steel skeleton for the h.p. Posts under edge beams are for shoring purposes

The stub corner columns are cut off at an angle to receive drain scuppers

Half-round pipes on edge beams are used for welding attachment of roof

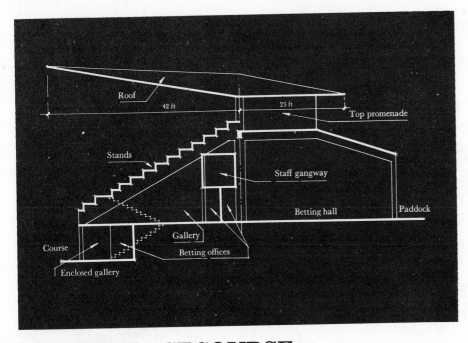

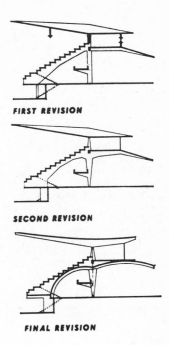

FIRST REVISION

SECOND REVISION

FINAL REVISION

MADRID RACECOURSE

by Eduardo Torroja

Seldom do our great engineers trace in retrospect the creative process which produces their finest work. Here Torroja offers just such an insight into the thought sequence by which the famed Zarzuela Hippodrome evolved from initial concept to final form—and a rare opportunity to view the building in all its aspects, from the construction and testing of the model to the soaring drama of the completed structure

Excerpts from *The Structures of Eduardo Torroja: An Autobiography of Engineering Accomplishment* by Eduardo Torroja, with a foreword by Mario Salvadori, McGraw-Hill Book Company, New York, 1958.

The functional requirements of the Zarzuela Hippodrome may be ascertained from the large cross section above: but, quite obviously, the first pattern was not very satisfactory. It is clear that the weight of the cantilevered roof over the stands will be greater than that of the counterweight over the top promenade. As the rear support will consequently be

in tension it has to be a tie rather than a strut. The other support, which has to take the whole weight of the roof plus the load applied by the tie member, must thus serve as the main one. Because this support must be massive, there will be no difficulty in supporting the gangway on a structure cantilevered from it.

The weight of the roof over the betting hall will be largely offset by the tie member, and the load on its supporting columns will be slight. Therefore these columns can be omitted. On the race track side, supports are also

unnecessary because the height between the track and the underside of the stands will accommodate a cantilevered beam.

Thus the initial plan developed into the first revision. On close inspection it becomes clear that a rigid attachment of the roof at the main support is not very useful because the roof has good stability under the vertical forces provided by the main support and the tie. On the other hand it is essential that the main support be rigidly fixed at the promenade level.

The cantilever roof of the betting

1

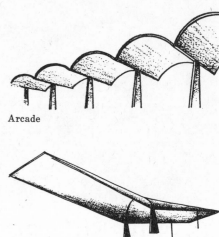

Arcade

Conoid

Hyperboloid

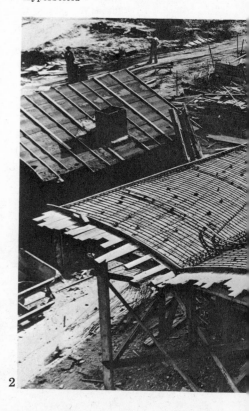

2

hall must be flat over the central portion to provide a floor for the promenade. Also its depth has to increase toward the main support where bending moments are highest.

The main support, in turn, must resist these moments. Its full section could be extended to and fixed rigidly in the foundation in order to resist wind forces. However in such a structure the existence of two very rigid supports (the main one plus the bottom part of the stands) could restrain too severely the thermal expansion or shrinkage of the portal frame. Hence it seemed advisable to reduce the over-all rigidity of the main support without impairing its capacity to transmit horizontal shear to the promenade level. The provision of a flexible joint at the bottom of the support consequently seemed a natural, if not an essential, step.

Finally the scant height between the staff gangway and the structure supporting the stands made it necessary to reduce the depth of the latter as much as possible.

At this point the design (see second revision) was allowed to rest for a while. In the end, it was given a certain curvature of outline, which seemed so straightforward and suitable to the purpose that the imagination resisted any attempt at further improvements.

After having adopted curved outlines for the lower part of the structure, it seemed reasonable to give a curved form to the roof also. More was involved, however, than the mere running of an arch or vault from one support to the next as shown above. The main structural function of such vaults is that of arched cantilevers. And to meet the strength requirements, it is necessary that the height-span ratio of the vaults be greatest over the main supports and decrease towards the free edges. The resulting surface could well have been a conoid but for the objection that the conoid is not very attractive. It seemed preferable to choose some other form of curvature. Among the better known ones, none seemed more adaptable than the hyperboloid; hence the cantilevered vaults have the shape of hyperboloidal sectors.

And now the question arises: Is the invention of an especially adapted form to solve a specific problem strictly an imaginative process, or is it the result of logical reasoning based on technical training? I do not think it is either of the two, but rather both together. To me it seems clear that the imagination can operate successfully only in conjunction with the basic principles that a long experience of technical creative work leaves in our personality so that these may later subconsciously condition our intuitive thought. But basic principles are not enough in themselves to create, critically and deductively, a new form. For this to emerge, a spark of imagination is required.

3

4

5

(1) A full-scale model built to test structural properties and construction procedures for the cantilevered vaults proved to be three times stronger than was necessary to meet predicted loads. *(2)* Reinforced echoes lines of stress in curved shell. To avoid danger of water seepage, joints occur along crown of lobes. *(3)* and *(4)* Interior views of gallery show main supports, stairs leading to stands. *(5)* and *(6)* Shells vary in thickness from 2 in. at the free edge to 5½ in. at the crown of the vaults over the main supports. Lower vaults are 2 in. thick throughout. Arcade which now appears to support lower part of stands (photo page 69) is false, was later added to the basic structure shown in these photos

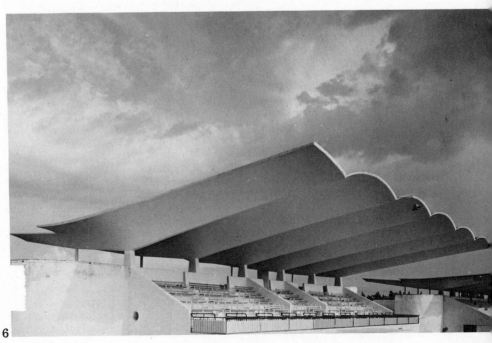

6

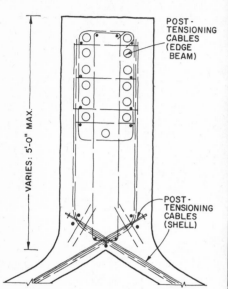

POST-
TENSIONING
CABLES
(EDGE
BEAM)

VARIES: 5'-0" MAX.

POST-
TENSIONING
CABLES
(SHELL)

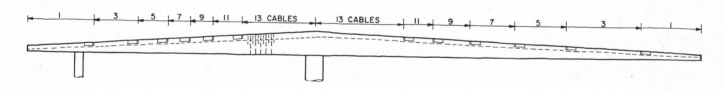

1   3   5   7   9   11   13 CABLES   13 CABLES   11   9   7   5   3   1

THREE-INCH SHELL CANTILEVERS NINETY FEET

Three grandstands at Venezuela's new racetrack project, the Hipodromo Nacional in Caracas, are roofed by thin (3 in.) concrete shells which straddle a longitudinal support, cantilevering 90 ft out over the grandstand seating, and extending back 60 ft to a row of anchor columns at the rear of stands. From the front the roof appears as a series of concave scallops with a catenary sag varying from 2½ ft at the tip of the cantilevers to 6½ ft at the supports. The side elevation reveals the tapered edge beams which occur at the intersections of the 30 ft wide scallops. The dual action of these two elements —both of which are prestressed—is largely responsible for the efficiency and economy of the structure.

The design was based on the effort to prevent deflection of the cantilever, which would then act as a horizontal column subject only to direct stresses. This could have been accomplished by using exposed cables. However, for the sake of appearance and structural rigidity, edge beams were built to house the prestressing cables that run in the direction of the cantilever. When the cables, which are of varying lengths (detail above), were post-tensioned, the tip of the cantilever was lifted 1 in. above its falsework. Loss of prestress due to creep and shrinkage is expected to cancel this initial camber in time, leaving the roof structure level.

To minimize cracks and deflections in the shells themselves, and to add to the economy of the structure, the spans between the edge beams were also prestressed. Post-tensioning cables follow the catenary curve at mid-depth of the shells—which are 3 in. thick over most of their length, 5 in. thick near the columns—and anchor on either side of the beams. Nominal reinforcing reduces shrinkage.

The anchor columns were also prestressed to insure their elastic behavior under the action of the uplift force produced by the design load.

Arthur Froehlich was the architect for the project; Henry Layne was the structural engineer, with T.Y. Lin & Associates as special consultants on the design and construction of the prestressed, cantilevered roof shells.

Section 3

RECTILINEAR FRAMES

PRESTRESSED CONCRETE
EARLY HISTORY AND TECHNIQUES

by H. Vandervoort Walsh, Architect, and Anselm Cefola, Civil Engineer

Editor's note: When this article was published in 1949, very little prestressed concrete had been used in this country — and then only for cylindrical water tanks. In fifteen years' time prestressing has become a very familiar technique in the United States. This article has been included here because the basic principles still apply, and consequently much of the article remains valid.

SUCH delicate bridges as these could not have been built with ordinary reinforced concrete; such long, straight, shallow spans could not be strongly enough reinforced. Only through the use of a revolutionary technique in reinforced concrete construction, *prestressing*, could they have been produced. Prestressing has been practiced for some 35 years in Europe where costs of materials are high, and of labor, low; it is beginning to gain considerable interest in this country.

Actually, circular tanks of prestressed concrete have been built in this country for at least 35 years, and the manufacture of large-diameter prestressed concrete pipe has been common. Through the application of new techniques introduced about 20 years ago, the architect and engineer can now utilize the advantages of prestressed concrete in most types of circular structures. On the other hand, practically nothing has been done in this country with prestressed concrete bridges, beams, slabs, etc., which are in evidence in Europe.

Examples of such bridges and buildings in France and Belgium have emphasized to alert American engineers the system's many advantages for exploitation in this country. Shortage of steel was one economic factor in Europe which abetted the development of prestressed concrete, which requires less steel than ordinary reinforced concrete; for the same reason its use in the U. S. may have a sound practical value. Probably one of the most important features to American architects, however, is the possibility of obtaining *crackless* concrete by prestressing.

How Prestressed Concrete Works

What happens when any beam carries a load? It bends and its center sags lower than its ends. Thus the bottom fibers are stretched while the top fibers are compressed. Since concrete resists compression well, the designer puts enough of it in the top to absorb all the compression safely. On the other hand, since the concrete has very little tensile strength — but steel has a lot — he inserts steel bars to take care of tensile stresses.

The trouble is that concrete shrinks as it hardens. The reinforcing bars, however, do not shorten much and consequently offer resistance to the concrete shrinkage, actually putting the bars in compression. When the concrete is loaded, the load causes considerable tension in the reinforcement. Since this reinforcement started out with a slight compression, and then in turn is subjected to considerable tension, it is obvious that its change in length is of such magnitude that the concrete cannot usually follow; it cracks.

In prestressing, concrete's virtue of high compressive strength is used to compensate for its lack of tensile strength through a very different concept in the use of reinforcing steel.

Steel wires are strung through a concrete beam, for example, are stretched and then anchored at the ends of the beam when the concrete is hard, to put a "squeeze" on the beam. The wires either are strung through a hole in the beam provided by a mold, and are tensioned against the end of the beam (we shall call this process post-tensioning), or else they are stretched first and held by some anchorage, after which the concrete is poured around them. When the concrete is hard, the wires are cut and the ends of the wires return to their original shape outside the beam — because the stress is relieved there — and act as wedges to help hold the wires bonded to the concrete in tension (this

Drawing courtesy of The Preload Corp.

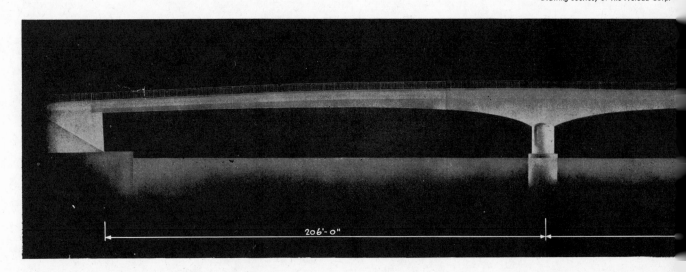

206'-0"

1   Photos by H. Baranger, courtesy of Raymond Concrete Pile Co.

is called pre-tensioning, and is explained more fully later in the article).

In prestressing, the concrete in the beam is squeezed so that it is always in compression, and any tensile stresses that might appear due to loading, and cause cracks, are automatically canceled out. The application of stresses before the beam is loaded is the basis for the name "prestressed concrete."

A simple analogy of the workings of prestressed concrete is illustrated in Fig. 8. A man is holding a stack of books horizontally by pressing against the ends. The books held by the man correspond to slices of concrete that are squeezed together by the prestressing forces illustrated by the arrows and hands and arms. Obviously if the forces are large enough, there can be no cracking tendency since all the joints between the books, or concrete slices, are in heavy compression.

In prestressed concrete the full potentialities of high-strength steels are utilized because the wires can be tensioned in excess of 140,000 psi. Compression in concrete, however, is not much more than 2000 psi at any point because the dead and live loads work to cancel the great squeeze put on the

2

3

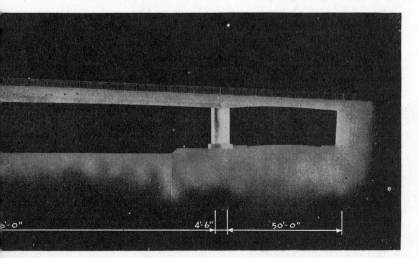

1. Bridge over Marne at Luzancy, France, span 182 ft. Designed by Freyssinet, the bridge has depth to span ratio of 1 to 45. 2, 3. Another Freyssinet bridge, this one at Esbly, has 240 ft. span. These bridges were assembled from precast sections. 4. First continuous bridge to be built with prestressed concrete, going up over Meuse at Sclayn, Belgium; supervising the project is Prof Gustave Magnel. Shape at the center pier is completely functional

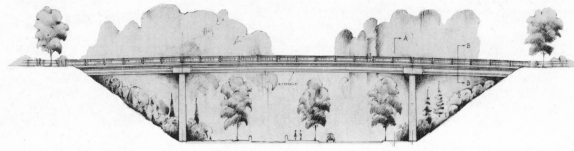

74' 0"   160' 0"   74' 0"

B-B

A-A

Walnut Lane bridge to be built of pre-stressed concrete at Philadelphia will be first of its type on this continent. High strength steel wires stressed to 125,000 psi put girders in compression (max. 2000 psi) to cancel out tensile stresses that tend to appear due to dead and live load, thus preventing any cracking

5

beam. Since the allowable stresses in a prestressed beam are much higher than they can be in an ordinary reinforced beam (about twice as much compression in the concrete and more than seven times as much tension in the steel) this suggests, in itself, the possible savings in materials.

As an example, a comparison has been made by Herman Schorer using a rectangular beam or slab to carry a live load of 200 lb. per sq. ft.* The prestressed

*Journal of the American Concrete Institute, Sept., 1946

concrete beam design was based on using steel wires with an ultimate tensile stress of 200,000 psi and on concrete having an ultimate compressive stress of 6000 psi with an ultimate safety factor of 2.5. As a result of calculations, the beam was designed to be 12 by 16 in. and had in it only 0.725 sq. in. of steel wire per ft. of slab width.

By contrast, design of ordinary reinforced concrete for the identical load resulted in a beam 12 by 32 in.; area of steel reinforcing rods was 3.64 sq. in.

per ft. of slab. This design was based on 1000 psi compression for concrete and 20,000 psi tension for the steel.

Advantages

All this leads to the following conclusions as to the advantages of prestressed concrete:

(a) It is economical of materials due to the use of higher steel and concrete stresses. (It is impossible to generalize much about building costs until more work is done in this country. However,

6. Shows effect of load on ordinary reinforced concrete beam; concrete can't stretch so under side begins to crack. 7. In prestressed beam wires are tensioned to put beam in permanent compression (gives slight arch); under load beam bends but does not crack. 8. Prestressing is explained simply by this analogy — the more squeeze the man puts on the books, the more he can hold

6

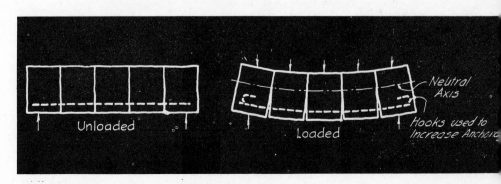

Unloaded   Loaded   Neutral Axis   Hooks used to increase Anchor

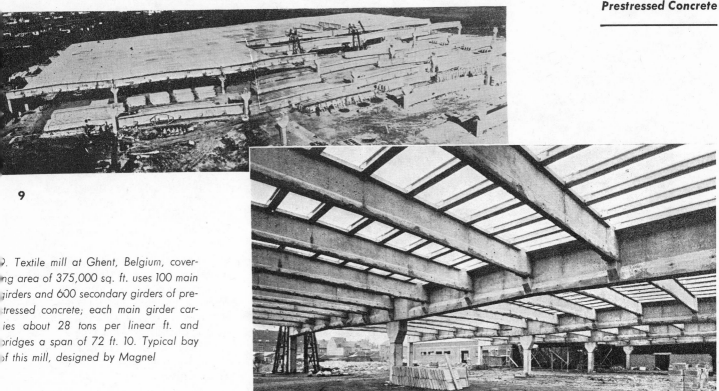

9

10

9. Textile mill at Ghent, Belgium, covering area of 375,000 sq. ft. uses 100 main girders and 600 secondary girders of prestressed concrete; each main girder carries about 28 tons per linear ft. and bridges a span of 72 ft. 10. Typical bay of this mill, designed by Magnel

Photos and rendering courtesy of The Preload Corp.

it is known that for large spans, as in bridges, great economies can be effected. The same holds for circular prestressing. Smaller units such as building framing would undoubtedly have to be mass-produced to achieve economy, but not enough is known to make a conjecture on this score.)

(b) It eliminates cracks because the concrete is always in compression.

(c) It permits less depth of beam as related to the span, and hence gives more headroom (this is especially important with bridges and airplane hangars).

(d) It has remarkable elastic properties. For example, tests were made on a floor slab only 1⅝ in. thick, reinforced with not more than 1 per cent of steel. Although the span was only 10 ft., the slab deflected 3 in. under a concentrated load of 1070 lb. at its center. When the

load was removed it returned to its original level, undamaged.

(e) Beams do not have to be cast at the site in one form, but may be cast in small sections or blocks at the factory with reinforcing wires threaded through them. When the wires are stressed, the small units are brought together like one large beam.

(f) It develops remarkable resistance to shear stresses. In one case a 4-in.-thick slab was tested by a 6-in. punch. Its resistance to this shearing action was 800 lb. per sq. in.

The items which contribute most to the higher cost of making prestressed concrete in comparison with regular reinforced concrete are the special form-work and devices required to anchor the prestressing steel on the ends of the beam, and the cost of the actual prestressing operation in the field.

Development and Applications

As long ago as 1888, Doehring, in Germany, secured a patent for a mortar slab that was to be reinforced with metal that had tension stresses applied to it before the slab was loaded. Test failures here were said to have resulted from a poor quality of concrete. Early attempts at prestressing failed principally, however, because the designers did not take into account either the shrinkage and plastic flow of concrete or, to a lesser extent, the creep of steel which soon canceled the low prestress applied.

In 1923 R. S. Dill of Alexandria, Nebraska, recognized the need for high tensile steel and carried out the prestressing after the greater part of the shrinkage had taken place.

First to appreciate the full significance

7

8

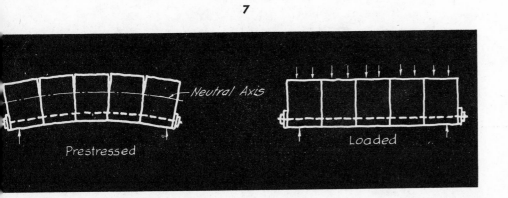

11

Main building of proposed shopping center for Beverly, Mass., has a circular prestressed dome 220 ft. in diameter, freeing interior space of columns. It is possible to design such a large dome by stretching wires around its edge, putting it in high compression

cable and jack method of prestressing concrete, wherein a cable embedded in the concrete is prevented from bonding by means of a steel sheet tube or a wrapping of impregnated paper. In his work, before the concrete was placed, concrete drums were set at opposite ends of the form, and the ends of the reinforcing wires were threaded through conical holes in the drums. Used as anchor plates, the drums transferred the stress in the wires to the concrete. After the concrete had been poured and had attained sufficient strength, the wires were secured to one drum by means of a conical plug which acted as a wedge. The wires were then attached to a double-acting jack at the other end, were tensioned and then secured by ramming another conical plug into the drum at that end. The original procedure has been refined, but the principles are basic.

A method similar to this was developed by Prof. Gustave Magnel of Belgium. After the concrete hardens, Magnel prestresses the wires with jacks. When tensioned sufficiently the reinforcing wires are locked against a cast steel distribution plate by using a sandwich plate and wedges (see Figs. 12, 13, 14, 15).

In addition to many successful bridges, Freyssinet has designed and built another prestressed wonder, the airstrip at Orly airfield, near Paris. It is only 6⅜ in. thick, but has strength equal to that of a conventional strip 24 in. thick. When heavy planes land, the elasticity of the prestressed concrete

12

of plastic flow and creep, and to measure them, was Eugene Freyssinet of France, who is frequently called the father of prestressed concrete. In 1928 he did the first practical prestressing with a high-grade, vibrated concrete heated almost to boiling temperature, and high-tensile steel.

Reinforcing Not Bonded

In 1939 Freyssinet introduced the

12, 13, 14, 15. Prestressing as done by the Belgian method. 12. End of girder before it is prestressed; cables are strung through beam after concrete is hard. 13. End of girder after wires have been tensioned by a hydraulic jack (14) and anchored by means of sandwich plates; pipes sticking out are for injecting grout after girder is prestressed

13

14

Photos and rendering courtesy of The Preload Corp.

16   **17**   **18**

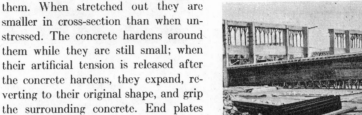

allows it to crack under impact, but the cracks heal as soon as the load is removed.

In Brussels, Belgium, under the direction of Prof. Magnel, an airplane hangar recently was completed which is noteworthy for its shallow prestressed concrete roof beams. These have a span of 168 ft. and are only 9 ft. 6 in. deep at the center. They are spaced 32 ft. 6 in. center-to-center and have a clear height, even at the ends, of 32 ft. To solve the same problem with ordinary reinforced concrete would have called for arches having a rise of 30 ft. Magnel has prepared a motion picture on prestressed concrete that has been shown frequently in this country; he has also written an authoritative textbook on the subject.

Bonded Prestressing

Bonded prestressing was suggested by E. Hoyer in Germany and has been used much in prefabrication shops in England. Piano wire is used so that the surface that contacts and bonds with the concrete is large in proportion to the total cross-sectional area of the steel. The wires are placed in forms and put under tension before the concrete is poured and vibrated into position around

them. When stretched out they are smaller in cross-section than when unstressed. The concrete hardens around them while they are still small; when their artificial tension is released after the concrete hardens, they expand, reverting to their original shape, and grip the surrounding concrete. End plates are not necessary since the bond between concrete and wires is sufficient to create compression in the concrete. Two-inch concrete exterior wall panels have been similarly made in casting beds up to 100 ft. long. It is possible to box out window and door openings in these panels, letting the wires run through the openings, and to cut the wires here at the same time the others are being cut. In this manner, two-story panels have been produced and raised from a horizontal to a vertical position without any sign of cracking. Similar panels of ordinary reinforced concrete usually require at least 4 in. thickness to resist the lifting stresses.

Another method, suggested by H. Shorer, involves the use of prestressed units which can be laid in the forms just as reinforcing bars are laid in ordinary concrete. The unit consists of a core rod with end disks to which are attached

16. Hangar at Melsbroek, airport of Brussels; one prestressed beam carries load of 3,500 tons. 17, 18. Use of 168 ft. beams of prestressed concrete allowed a clear height of 32 ft. from floor to beams

the wires that are to be prestressed. These wires are strung around the core in spirals and kept in place by intermediate disks spaced equally along the core. When the wires are stressed, the core acts as a column, and the intermediate disks keep it from buckling. After the wires are stressed sufficiently they are locked at the end disks; and the core bar, now acting as a compression member, maintains the tensile stresses

Method of anchoring the tensioned wires to the end of a beam. Sandwich plates hold wires by wedge action and transfer stress of wires to distributing plate and thus to beam, placing the beam in compression; each wedge holds two wires. In early applications cable was placed in sheath to prevent bonding during concreting; now, steel or rubber cores, later removed, leave holes for introducing cables

15

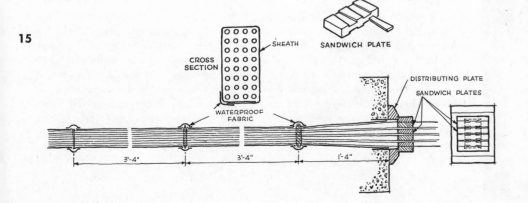

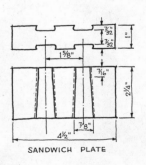

19

20

19. In manufacture of prestressed concrete tanks, machine stresses high strength wire by pulling it through a die as it is spiralled around the tank; the wire is later covered with gunite. 20. This prestressed water tank in Miami, Fla., has a diameter of 128 ft., depth of liquid 27 ft. 8 in., and capacity 2,700,000 gal.

in the wires. In this condition the reinforcing is laid in the forms and the concrete is poured. Since the rod is covered by a paper tube, the concrete does not bond with it, but it does bond with the wires. After the concrete is hard, the core rod is pulled out and the tension in the wires now sets up the needed compression in the beam.

Present Applications in the U. S.

The most direct application of prestressed concrete in the U. S. at present

Manufacture of large diameter prestressed pipe. In contrast to tank construction, the pipe itself rotates on a turntable, tensioning the wire as it is spiralled

Photos courtesy of The Preload Corp.

21

is the making of concrete tanks, pipes and tubular concrete piles. The internal or hydrostatic pressures in the pipes and tanks cause tensile stresses in the walls. By prestressing the steel wire spiralled around the concrete, the tension set up by internal pressures is more than canceled out; thus walls of prestressed concrete require much less steel and concrete than conventional designs.

A water tank built for Kansas City, Kansas has a diameter of 180 ft. and a liquid depth of 19 ft. 6 in. Quite comparable is the circular prestressed structure proposed for a shopping center at Beverly, Mass., with a dome 220 ft. in diameter, which frees the interior of columns.

In building prestressed concrete tanks, the walls are first poured, then high tensile wire is machine-stressed around the outside, after which the wire is covered with gunite. It is possible to have very thin domes because of the tremendous squeezing force around the top. The dome can be thinner with respect to its volume than the thickness of an egg shell in relation to the volume of the egg.

A prestressed concrete bridge, the Walnut Lane Bridge, is soon to be built over Paper Mill Creek Valley at Philadelphia, Pa. It will have a main span of 160 ft. Depth of the girders will be 6 ft. 7 in.; distance between them will be 4 ft. 4 in. Maximum unit stress in the concrete will be 2000 psi and working stress in the steel wires will be approximately 125,000 psi.

Conclusion

Architects who become familiar with the remarkable properties of prestressed concrete can exploit its possibilities in graceful and delicate structures. It is essentially an engineering material as compared to ordinary concrete because the calculation of internal stresses is more positive, resulting in economies of steel and concrete. Most ordinary concrete buildings are over-designed in parts and under-designed in others.

In addition to prestressed concrete bridges, factory construction, airplane landing strips, top blankets for old roads, crackproof floor slabs, pipes and tanks, we probably shall see its application to retaining walls, crackproof exterior walls for buildings of all kinds, precast floor slabs, precast tubular piles and prefabricated building parts for dwellings. Nor are all these developments going to wait for a purely economic impetus, although figures show in certain types of construction, prestressed concrete offers substantial savings in cost over conventional designs. In any event, prestressed concrete will find its place in the architecture of the United States in the near future. Already there exists a great deal of interest in it, and we shall see more and more engineers and architects collaborating to find new release for their imaginations in its unique properties of lightness and elasticity, in its possibilities for prefabrication and its freedom from cracking.

PRECAST FRAMING GROWS TALLER

1. MEDICAL BUILDING

New Haven, Connecticut

ARCHITECTS AND ENGINEERS: *Westcott & Mapes, Inc.*

PRESTRESSING CONSULTANTS: *C. W. Blakeslee & Sons, Inc.*

Welded wire fabric reinforces structural topping cast over floor tees

Welder making top moment connection between column tee and floor tee

Basically the same type of structural member, a precast-prestressed single tee, works both for the wall-columns and the floor structure of this five-story, fully precast building.

Approximately 75 per cent of the exterior area is enclosed by exposed precast members, continuous from foundation to roof. The remainder of the wall is a combination of exposed aggregate precast concrete panels and a metal and glass curtain wall. Even the two cores containing stairs and elevators are of precast wall and column construction.

The prestressed floor tees span 41 ft from the exterior wall-column tees to an inverted T-shaped girder at the center of the building which is a rectangle 83 ft wide and 148 ft long. Smaller, 32-ft prestressed tees span between the exterior and the precast core.

Vertical and horizontal joints in the precast core are cast-in-place to tie precast core panels to columns and to the floor, providing a rigid, monolithic structure to resist the lateral force of winds.

A moment and shear connection between floor tees and column tees is made by welding two steel connection plates in the floor member to an inverted structural tee cast in the exterior column. A top moment connection between the floor tees and the columns is made by welding threaded rods attached to the columns to plates set in the top surface of the floor tees.

Ducts and pipes for this air-conditioned building are run through holes provided in the stems of the floor tees.

A 14-in. space between floor tees is filled by a 5-in. cast-in-place slab to prevent rocking of the panels and provide lateral stability.

Wall-column tees are prestressed to withstand handling and wind loads.

Precast walls and columns become monolithic by casting in place horizontal and vertical joints

Floor tees span 41 ft between exterior wall-columns and interior inverted T-girders. Holes in web are for duct and pipe penetrations

Webs of the wall-column tees, extended at the top to engage future two-story column extensions, make interesting pattern

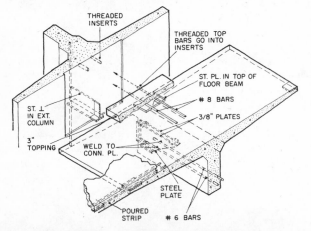

Lash Bauman photos

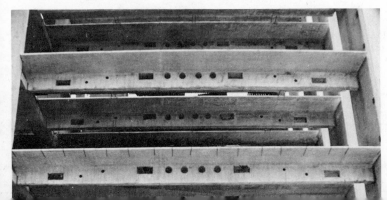

2. TECHNICAL TOWER

Boulder, Colorado

ARCHITECT: *Hobart D. Wagener, A.I.A.*

STRUCTURAL ENGINEERS: *Ketchum & Konkel*

Since the tenant of this building, Ball Brothers Research Corporation, specializes in space exploration, electronics and materials research, the architect felt that an exposed precast concrete structure of advanced design would appropriately mirror these technological activities.

A multistory building was chosen because it saved land, provided more daylight for scientists' offices, provided good identification for the company, gave greater access to the striking mountain scenery of Boulder and permitted fast construction.

The structural system consists of a one-way, composite precast-prestressed and cast-in-place floor slab carried on composite beams and girders to precast "ladder" columns, founded on spread footings which have sockets to receive the columns.

The "ladder" columns were constructed and erected in one piece at the exterior and two floors at a time

at interior locations. Precast-prestressed girders 8 in. deep and 24 in. wide, and beam soffits 6 in. deep and 16 in. wide were then erected and shored at midspan. Next precast floor planks 5 ft 8 in. by 9 ft by 2½ in. thick were laid over the girders. Finally, the upper portions of beams and girders and top of the floor slab were poured in place.

The structure was designed for continuity in both directions. Positive bending moments in the beams and girders are carried by prestressing strands; negative moments are taken by mild steel reinforcing in the cast-in-place portions. Horizontal shear is resisted by stirrups in the beam and girder soffits extending into the cast-in-place sections. While there is no mechanical anchorage between the precast and poured portions of the floor slabs, welded wire fabric provides negative moment restraint and control of cracking.

Above and right: Exposed precast "ladder" columns, projecting girders and precast spandrel panels, plus an infilling of concrete block, establish the architectural expression of this five-story building to house space and electronics experts.

Below: The skeletal components stand out against mountain scenery: exterior "ladder" columns, girders and beam soffits (stirrups projecting) and interior square columns. After precast floor planks are laid cast-in-place concrete finishes off beams, girders and floor slab system (see detail).

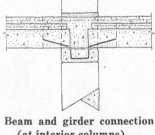

Beam and girder connection
(at interior columns)

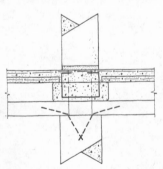

Girder to interior column connection

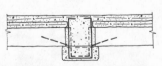

Beam to girder connection
(between columns)

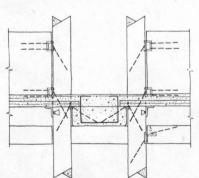

Girder to "ladder" column connection

Cast-in-place concrete ties the whole structure together for continuity

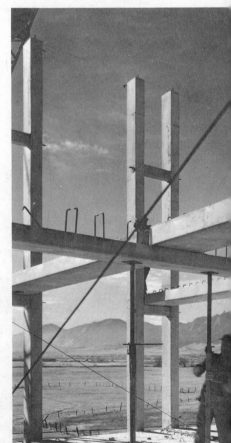

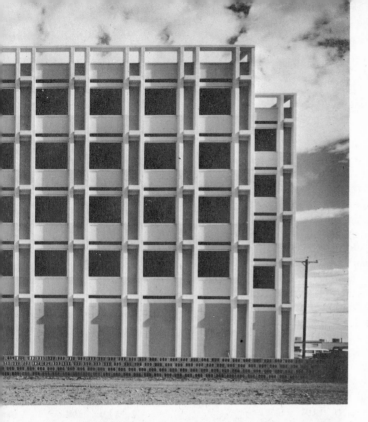

Above: Crane hoisting precast floor plank to an upper story. Some of the precast spandrels are installed. Space above the spandrels is clear glass; slot below is of tinted glass, which helps give a lighter feeling to the structure inside and out. *Below:* Several floor planks have been laid on beams

3. NINE-STORY OFFICE BUILDING

University of California at Davis

ARCHITECTS: *Gardner A. Dailey, F.A.I.A., and Associates*

STRUCTURAL CONSULTANT: *T. Y. Lin and Associates International*

The most noteworthy structural feature of this prefabricated concrete building is the nine-story height of its precast-prestressed columns, a record height for the United States.

All columns, each precast in one piece, are exterior with precast-prestressed floor channels spanning 36 ft between them. This gives a 36- by 127-ft area of open space on each floor.

The two-story-high wall panels, spanning between columns, are pretensioned to withstand handling stresses and also to minimize possibility of cracking. Since the wall panels are two stories high, the floor channels butt against the wall panels on one floor and project over them at the next.

A 3-in., cast-in-place structural topping over the channel slabs provides a horizontal diaphragm to transmit earthquake and wind loads to the cast-in-place stair and elevator towers at the ends of the building.

Support for ends of the floor channels is provided by tee-shaped seats of steel plate cast into the columns.

Columns are tied to the structural floor system by dowels which pass through the tee seat and extend into the cast-in-place topping. Where required, the doweled connections are supplemented by the welding of metal clips cast into the precast units.

Exposed aggregate for the wall panels is of a warm gray granite from the Sierra foothills. The column members use a light gray cement which will be stained with a warm gray waterproofing compound.

The underside of the floor channels will be left exposed except in the corridors where a suspended ceiling will be hung to cover utilities.

Panel-column joints and panel-slab joints are sealed with a drypack grout followed by a bead of polysulfide mastic.

Cranes hoist 86-ft-long precast column; will be braced against elevator tower at le

Basalt Rock Co., Inc.

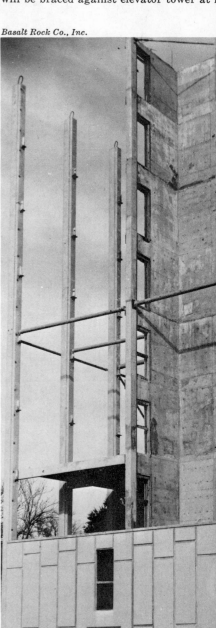

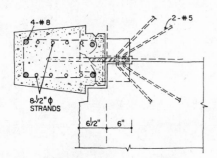

Section: Channel-column connection

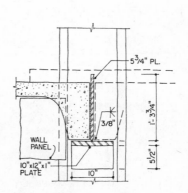

Section: Channel seat

Plan: Channel-column connection

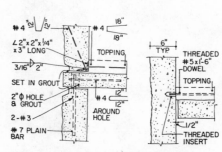

Wall-floor channel connections

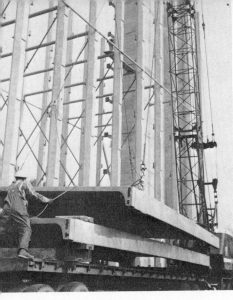

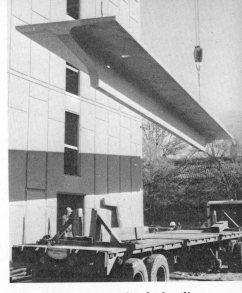

stressed channels span 36 ft; are supported by inverted T's set columns. Pipes and straps temporarily brace columns

Two-story-high wall panels have grooves to provide shadow-line pattern. Roof structure consists of sculptured T-beams

Basalt Rock Co., Inc.

HIGH-RISE STRUCTURES IN HAWAII COMBINE PRECAST, POURED CONCRETE

by Alfred A. Yee, Alfred A. Yee & Associates, Inc., Structural Engineers, Honolulu, Hawaii

1. TEAMING PRECAST, POURED CONCRETE EFFICIENTLY

Our experience has shown that simplicity of erection and handling of utilities can be achieved by utilizing a combination of precast units and cast-in-place concrete in a composite system. Framing for a typical floor in this system requires precast, prestressed joists and beams cast with stirrups in the top flange to develop composite structural action with the cast-in-place floor slabs. On the job, the units are individually hoisted into position.

To achieve the highest efficiency, all connections between precast units should develop full bearing and continuity (detail below and page 87). The connecting ends can either rest on, or butt against, intersecting units, with mild steel reinforcing added in the poured slab portion to serve as continuity ties. In this situation no steel bearing plates, bolts or weld points are required.

Tolerances. Precast concrete units cannot be manufactured with the same degree of precision as machine-shop-produced steel units. Some dimensional deviations from specified alignment, camber and length will exist in precast units. Fortunately, however, under the composite method all of these dimensional inconsistencies can be easily absorbed by the cast-in-place concrete with no sacrifice in structural strength. Cast-in-place concrete forming the spandrels and slab also completes the jointing media between precast units; thus

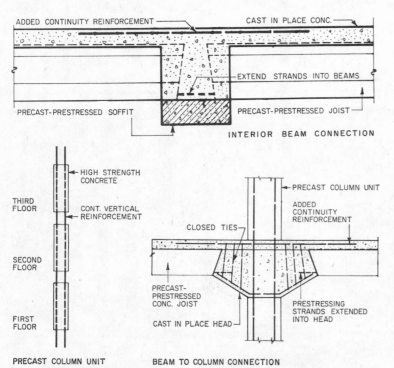

Top: In this composite connection between precast, prestressed joists and a poured-in-place interior beam, the joists rest on a precast, prestressed "soffitt." Bottom: Several floors of columns may be precast as one unit, with spaces in the column at each floor for continuity reinforcement. Column head is poured-in-place

The prestressed "soffitt" becomes part of the beam through use of stirrups pre-embedded in the unit. The "soffitts" are connected to columns by poured-in-place corbels. The "soffitt" units may range in length from 15 to 45 ft

the entire deck frame is compositely "glued" together to resist both lateral and vertical forces.

Precast Columns. One of the most encouraging of recent cost saving developments has been in the field of precast concrete columns or combination column-beam units which are adaptable for use in either low- or high-rise buildings.

One of these methods permits the precasting of several floors of columns in one unit (page 86). In the multiple-column units, vertical reinforcing steel is continuous throughout, but spaces are left in the concrete portion of the column at each floor level to accept continuity bars for the intersecting beams. The joint between beams and column can be completed with a cast-in-place column head.

There are several advantages in using precast columns. Where the building site is located in a congested area, and there is little room to store materials and equipment, columns can be precast at a central plant and hauled to the site for erection. Because of the nature of precast work, these columns can be made with a high quality architectural finish. Precasting saves much formwork and shoring, and the construction can progress much faster. However, where buildings are higher than 10 stories, the column sizes usually become quite large for handling and, therefore, must be spliced often. There may be difficulty in developing the full load transfer at these splices because of the greater amount of vertical reinforcing steel necessary in these heavily loaded columns.

In general, for buildings below 10 floors, columns can be precast, and above 10 floors should be poured. When buildings have about eight or nine floors, it is open to question whether they should be poured-in-place or precast, and the answer depends upon structural and architectural considerations.

Beam Ends. Ends of the beam units are tapered to develop more favorable bearing stress patterns and the beam's prestressing tendons are extended into the cast-in-place portion for additional tie. Spalling at this joint is prevented by the use of small diameter mild steel reinforcing cages in the corbel area near the ends of the beams. Full continuity is assured by adding mild steel in the composite deck slab.

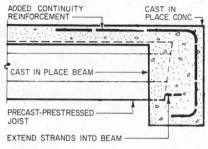

ADDED CONTINUITY REINFORCEMENT

CAST IN PLACE CONC.

CAST IN PLACE BEAM

PRECAST-PRESTRESSED JOIST

EXTEND STRANDS INTO BEAM

EXTERIOR BEAM CONNECTION

Composite connection of prestressed concrete joists to spandrel beams is shown in the detail. This system was used in the 25-story structure below. Beams were moved into position on rolling tripods whose vertical posts telescope to lower beam. 1441 Kapiolani Boulevard Office Building, Honolulu; Architects & Engineers: John Graham and Co.; Contractor: Hawaiian Dredging Construction Co., Ltd.

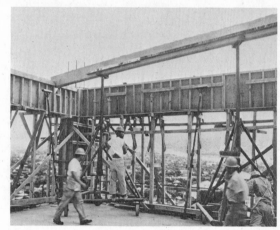

Ben Ranada Photos

64-ft prestressed concrete girders are hoisted by boom of conventional crane on lower floors

The girders are shown in place ready to receive slab form work. Columns are poured-in-place

Forming and pouring of the floor slab is accomplished through use of a climbing crane

2. ACCOMMODATING UTILITIES

For maximum economy in the use of mass-produced precast units, the variety of beams and joists should be held to a minimum. If unusual loads or other irregular conditions occur in the deck framing, it is possible in most cases to use the same kind of components throughout by simply doubling them up for additional strength or altering the spacing to meet the situation.

In the 19-story building shown here, a traffic jam of air conditioning ducts leading into the main air conditioning shaft created a headroom problem. Precast, prestressed joists, which had been evenly spaced for the rest of the deck frame, were doubled up adjacent to the congested area and thickness of the cast-in-place slab was increased. This left the area near the shaft free of joists, thus providing the required head room while maintaining adequate structural strength. Air conditioning ducts, wiring and plumbing were accommodated with no loss of head room throughout the remainder of the floor area by casting the joists with holes in the webs.

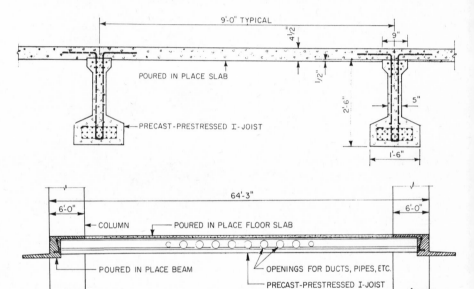

Prestressed girders are tied compositely to the floor slab by stirrups in the 19-story First National Bank of Hawaii. Openings in joist web accommodate services. Joists are doubled near air conditioning shaft to get more head room for ducts. Architects: Lemmon, Freeth, Haines & Jones; Structural Engineers: Alfred A. Yee & Associates, Inc.; Contractor: E. E. Black, Ltd.

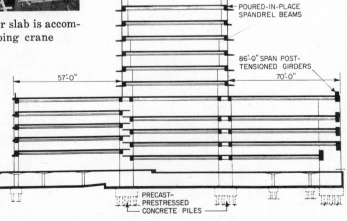

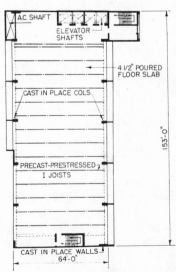

3. THE PRECAST "COLUMN TREE" CONCEPT

Photo-Craft Co.

Photo of apartment building which utilizes the "column tree" concept. The four-story "trees" are precast in one piece. (Details of the structural system are on the following page.) Towers Corporation Apartment Building, Waikiki, Honolulu. Architects: Bassetti, Morse & Tatom; Structural Engineers: Alfred A. Yee & Associates, Inc.; Contractor: T. Takahashi, Ltd.

Erection sequence of the "column-tree" apartment building. Top, left: "Column trees" were cast in a five-layer sandwich; note how they were staggered to save space in the contractor's yard. Top, right: First column is lifted at the site. Below, left: "Column trees" in place after eight hours' time. The units have been plumbed, positioned and placed to final dimensions. Below, right: All "column trees" and precast, prestressed beams for the second and third floors are up after 16 hours' time

One of the most recent developments in multi-story framing is the so-called "column tree" concept. Principal components of this system are combination column-beam units and precast, prestressed joists. We have employed "column trees" successfully in a number of multi-story buildings. The tallest thus far is nine floors, now under construction.

A typical "column tree" unit consists of a precast column with contiguous, branch-like beams projecting out at the various floor levels. The joists rest on these "branches" of the tree. The first three floors of the column-beams are normally cast as a single unit, with all "trees" for the upper floors cast individually for ease of handling and placing.

The base of the column fits into a concrete socket in the footing which is cast to a dimension somewhat larger than the column. First a grout pad is put down into the bottom of the socket to exact elevation. When the grout pad hardens, after a day or so, the column is set on the pad at the exact vertical elevation. Then the column is adjusted laterally in either direction or rotated clockwise or counterclockwise as necessary. This oversized concrete socket has permitted all of these adjustments, even though the footing or column may not have been cast to exact dimension. Finally, the gap between the socket and the precast column is filled with expansion grout for permanent anchorage.

The space between the "branch" ends of adjacent "column trees" offers a decided advantage since it can be utilized for running air conditioning ducts, plumbing and other utilities close up against the deck slab with a resulting savings of head room. At the same time, "column tree" units can be designed so that they closely follow stress lines, making reinforcement placing simple and effective. In the completed structure, lateral forces are resisted by shear walls and the cast-in-place floor slab acts as a shear diaphragm tying together all precast components at each floor level.

89

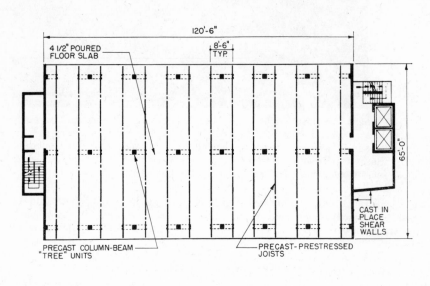

120'-6"

4 1/2" POURED
FLOOR SLAB

8'-6"
TYP.

65'-0"

CAST IN
PLACE
SHEAR
WALLS

"PRECAST COLUMN-BEAM
"TREE" UNITS

PRECAST-PRESTRESSED
JOISTS

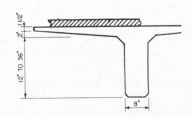

UPPER FLOOR
"TREE" UNITS

4th

3rd

2nd

PRECAST CONC.
COL. "TREE" UNIT
FOR LOWER FL'RS

1st

FOOTING
SOCKET

EXPANDING
GROUT

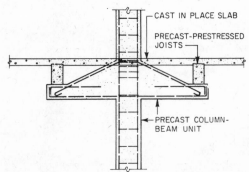

CAST IN PLACE SLAB

PRECAST-PRESTRESSED
JOISTS

PRECAST COLUMN-
BEAM UNIT

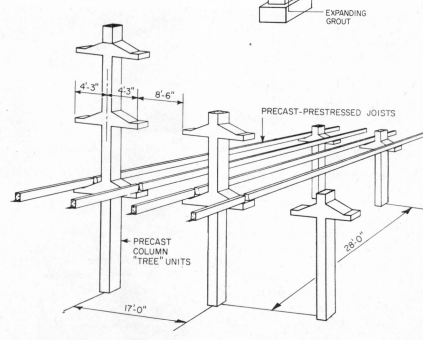

4'-3"   4'-3"   8'-6"

PRECAST-PRESTRESSED JOISTS

PRECAST
COLUMN
"TREE" UNITS

28'-0"

17'-0"

Prestressed joists are supported by the "branches" of columns. Dimensions in the sketch right are for a building under construction. The first three levels of "column trees" are precast in one piece; upper floor "trees" are precast in single-floor units for ease of handling. Precast units are tied together with a cast-in-place floor, which acts as a shear diaphragm to transmit lateral forces to shear walls. Detail above shows reinforcing pattern (follows stress lines) of a "tree"

Ben Ranada photos

1 1/2"
2"
12" TO 36"
8"

A two-story warehouse and laboratory uses "column trees," but in this case precast Lin-Tees form the floors (detail right gives general dimensions for this type of unit). This technique permitted construction of a two-story addition over an existing warehouse. Architect: George W. McLaughlin; Structural Engineers: Alfred A. Yee & Associates, Inc.; Contractor: Rothwell Construction Co., Ltd.

4. PRECAST PILES ECONOMICAL IN VOLCANIC SOIL

If Hawaii's builders have made significant advances in the use of precast, prestressed components for high-rise structures, it has been possible only because they first solved a variety of perplexing foundation problems. The island's basic volcanic substrata are literally interlaced with erratic deposits of sand, clay, boulders and coral reef. It is not uncommon to have a difference of as much as 50 ft in the driven length of piles which are only 3 ft apart.

Precast, prestressed concrete pilings have proven to be the most satisfactory solution thus far. Because of the prestressing action, the concrete will take a great deal of punishment from the driving hammer which permits the piles to be driven to extremely high bearing capacities. This, of course, means considerable savings can be realized through a reduction in the number of piles required for a given column load and a consequent reduction in the size of concrete pile cape and reinforcement.

Equally important is the relatively low initial cost. Eighteen-inch, octagonal, prestressed piles have been sold at the plant for as little as $5.23 per lineal foot, and driven at the construction site to carry a design load of 200 tons each.

To meet the inconsistent ground conditions mentioned earlier, it has been imperative to develop a simple and economical method of pile splicing. A dowel splice has been used extensively with 18-inch octagonal piling. Experience, however, has shown that the dowel connecting the two pile sections can occasionally cause severe damage. Chipping at the splice point may cause the pile contact points to disintegrate, with the result that the dowel begins acing like a driving wedge which eventually destroys the connecting units.

Elimination of the dowel has provided a simple solution. Recent tests have shown that the "steel-can" splice collar by itself is capable of developing all the strength needed to resist the bending movement of connecting piles under actual driving conditions. On a recent job a pile driving rig with the hammer resting on the top pile toppled over shortly after making a splice. The upper of the two connecting piles broke off just above the splice joint, which was still exposed above ground. Despite its inconvenience, the accident offered solid proof that the "can" splice was stronger than the piles it connected.

Lightweight Concrete

One other recent development that must be included in any discussion of multi-story construction in Hawaii is lightweight concrete. Commercial operations have now begun on two deposits of lightweight pumice aggregate. This material is giving designers a new opportunity for reducing building weight, a critical factor in high-rise construction.

These aggregates can easily produce 3000 to 4000 psi concrete weighing about 105 pounds per cubic ft. This concrete is being used for cast-in-place composite slabs, walls, spandrels and columns. With these basic structural elements reduced in weight, pile footing costs are saved, and additional savings are realized through a significant reduction in the amount of concrete and reinforcing steel required in the structure.

This article is derived from a talk given at the Western Conferences on Prestressed Concrete Buildings sponsored by the Engineering and Sciences Extension of the University of California

Splicing an 18-in. octagonal prestressed, precast concrete pile

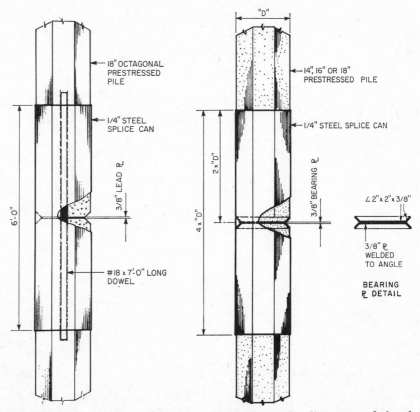

Left: Pile splice detail showing use of both the steel splice can and dowel
Right: Pile splice detail with dowel eliminated

PRECAST,
PRESTRESSED WALLS
FOR A HIGHWAY HOTEL

1.

The Treadway Inn, St. Davids, Pa.

Architects: Wise · Burke · Scipione, A.I.A.; *Structural Engineers:* Garfinkel & Marenberg; *Mechanical Engineers:* Garber & Cohen; *General Contractor:* Fleming Co.

In the course of precast concrete's development from a new import to a structural staple, many attempts have been made to venture away from the tried and true column-girder systems in which precast units simply replace more conventional framing members, and to move toward systems in which large precast panels are themselves the columns and girders.

A recent and promising step in this direction was made in the design of the highway hotel shown on these pages. The precast floor and wall panels that serve as both framing and enclosure for its 145 bedrooms were assembled in much the same way as a giant house of cards, by stacking the floor slabs and wall panels. However, to prevent the structure's succumbing to wind loads as a card house would succumb to a sneeze, the walls were stiffened and made continuous by post-tensioning (see details page 94).

Although the Treadway Inn, an L-shaped building with all of a three-story wing and two floors of a four-story wing made up of identical-size rooms, must in any case have offered a tempting opportunity for prefabrication, the real impetus for the development of the "honeycomb" framing system was provided by the owner's insistence on better-than-adequate soundproofing. After studying the relative costs of several alternate ways of meeting this requirement, the structural engineers concluded that, since the common means of soundproofing is sheer mass, 6-in. load-bearing walls of solid concrete would perform this function and give the added advantage of built-in fire resistance.

Moreover, although the precast panels were used only for the bedroom floors, the irregular bays in the public and service areas being conventionally framed of reinforced concrete, they made possible substantial savings in overall construction time and costs. The guest rooms were framed in about two months; the precast walls eliminated the need for additional soundproofing and fireproofing; and the concrete surfaces needed no finish treatment other than painting. It was also possible to extend the precast slabs at each floor to provide a horizontal sunshade over the room windows and to extend every other wall to the edge of this sunshade to provide fixed vertical louvers, thus forming at very little added cost the shadow-box facades that are a principal feature of the building exterior.

The precast floor slabs and wall panels used for the guest room floors in both wings of the Treadway Inn were precast on the site in stacks of as many as twelve units (1), a procedure that saved on formwork and time, and also assisted in proper curing since the stacks formed ready-made curing rooms with slabs sealed at top and bottom. Although all the panels are not identical (the plans show, for instance, nineteen different types of wall panels), the variations in dimensions and detailing—openings, conduit, and so forth—were minor enough to be taken care of by modifying the forms between pours.

Essentially, there are only two types of wall panels—the full-length prestressed walls that define each two-room bay, and the shorter intermediate panels; and only two types of floor slabs (2)—solid slabs along the outer rims of each floor, and a center strip of pierced slabs that per-

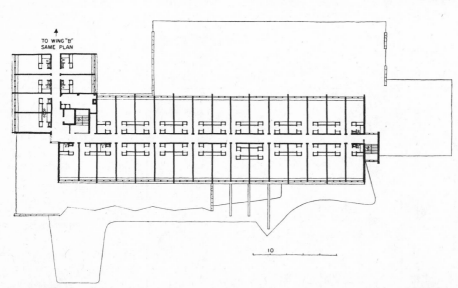

TO WING "B"
SAME PLAN

10

2.

3.

Photos by Michael P. Marcelli

4.

mit passage of service piping for the baths along the corridor.

The floor slabs, which were hoisted flat by means of cables that, spread by I-beams, ran from the crane to eye-bolts screwed into threaded inserts in the concrete, were simply laid across the walls, meeting at the center line of the long walls and resting on the shorter walls at midpoint in each bay. The wall panels, though handled in much the same way, were lifted vertically (3) and set one atop the other at the joints and midpoints of the slabs. To brace them until they were capped by the floor slabs of the next story (4), the contractor used the corridor stud walls, which he pre-assembled on the site (5). Those that braced the outer ends of the walls were removed once the slabs had been placed, and set up elsewhere in the building, either again as bracing or in their final position as corridor partitions. As shown (6), the outer ends of the walls were alternately pierced and cut out to permit passage of the piping for fan-coil air conditioning units in each room.

After the wall and floor panels had been placed (7), the "house of cards" was made stable by threading continuous high-strength prestressing rods through galvanized tubes embedded in the long walls, and stressing them with a jacking load of some 20 tons. According to the engineers, it was both quicker and less costly to achieve continuity by post-tensioning than by field welding conventional reinforcement. The rods were inserted through the walls and jacked in less than half an hour each.

Another time-saver, not so easy to calculate, was the technique of erecting the wall and floor panels on steel shims which left a ¼-in. joint, later grouted with a very dry mix, between the concrete units. This not only assured uniform bearing over the full length of the walls, but also made it possible to take up small tolerances at the joints, so that time-consuming precision in forming and erection was unnecessary.

5.

6.

7.

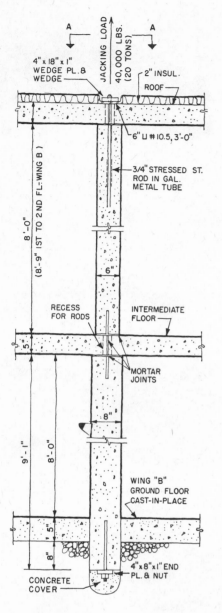

JACKING LOAD
40,000 LBS. (20 TONS)

4" x 18" x 1" WEDGE PL. 8 WEDGE

2" INSUL.
ROOF

6" U # 10.5, 3'-0"

3/4" STRESSED ST. ROD IN GAL. METAL TUBE

8'-0"
(8'-9" IST TO 2ND FL-WING B)

6"

RECESS FOR RODS

INTERMEDIATE FLOOR

5"

MORTAR JOINTS

8"

9'-1"
8'-0"

WING "B" GROUND FLOOR CAST-IN-PLACE

5"

8"

CONCRETE COVER

4"x 8"x1" END PL. 8 NUT

TYPICAL SECTION PRECAST CONCRETE WALLS 8 SLABS

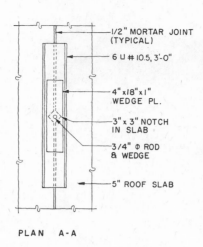

1/2" MORTAR JOINT (TYPICAL)

6 U # 10.5, 3'-0"

4"x18"x1" WEDGE PL.

3" x 3" NOTCH IN SLAB

3/4" Φ ROD 8 WEDGE

5" ROOF SLAB

PLAN A-A

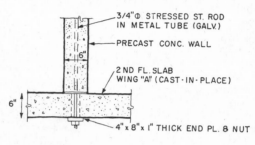

3/4" Φ STRESSED ST. ROD IN METAL TUBE (GALV.)

PRECAST CONC. WALL

6"

2 ND FL. SLAB WING "A" (CAST-IN-PLACE)

6"

4" x 8" x 1" THICK END PL. 8 NUT

BEARING WALL ANCHORAGE

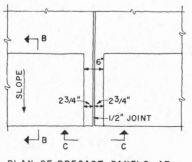

As shown in the details above, the method of anchoring the prestressing rods varied slightly from Wing B, where all the walls were precast, to Wing A, where the two lower floors were framed of reinforced concrete. Note that only the intermediate floors, one in Wing A and two in Wing B, and the roof were precast, and that the first floor walls in Wing B are 8 in. rather than 6 in. thick. The photos show the upper anchorage used for the three rods in each prestressed wall (see also Plan A-A) as well as the process of inserting and jacking them

PLAN OF PRECAST PANELS AT EXTERIOR JOINTS

SLOPE

6"

2 3/4"   2 3/4"

1/2" JOINT

B   B
C   C

2'-0" TYPICAL
1'-8" ROOF

1 1/2"
1"
3 1/2"
5"

SECTION B-B

6" PRECAST WALLS

3 1/2" EDGE THICKNESS

5"

SECTION C-C

To prevent water's collecting on the horizontal slab projections outside the room windows, the slabs were cast with a downward slope from the spandrels to their slim outer edges. These details of the exterior joints between the slabs and the walls show how this was done without the need for a corresponding slope in the wall panels

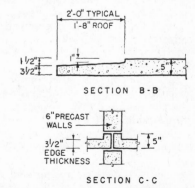

PRECAST CONCRETE JOINERY

1. DESIGN PRINCIPLES

by Kenneth C. Naslund, Partner, The Engineers Collaborative, Consulting Structural Engineers, Chicago

Design considerations for precast concrete connections include the following: 1) feasibility, 2) practicality, 3) serviceability, 4) appearance, 5) fireproofing of the construction in some cases, and 6) the stress analysis of very localized conditions.

Feasibility of a precast concrete joint is determined by checking it for load carrying capacity, or, more simply, determining if the joint can be used for the intended load at the desired location.

The *practicality* of a joint is determined by considering the amount and kind of material used, the cost of its fabrication and placement and the speed and ease it imparts to erection.

Serviceability can be determined by consideration of how the joint will stand up under repeated loadings, exposure to climatic or chemical conditions, and possible overloadings.

Appearance of a precast concrete joint is what many of us are interested in, having blithely assumed that anything can be made feasible, practical, fireproof and serviceable. In an architectural sense, it seems most logical that precast joints be expressed as joints rather than being disguised to look like cast-in-place concrete.

Fireproofing of joints requires consideration of the type of protection required for specific hourly ratings and the method of applying the fire resistive covering.

Stress analysis of very localized conditions is the least written about aspect in the design of precast concrete joints, even though it is the most important design consideration. With this the case, this article will deal exclusively with the types of loadings on joints and the requirements of the various connections used to resist those loadings.

TYPES OF LOADINGS

In the design of a precast joint it is very desirable to consider each type of loading separately and then the combined loadings of the structure being studied. This procedure will help prevent overlooking any one type of loading. There are five basic types of loadings: *Tension (Axial)*, *Compression (Axial)*, *Shear*, *Moment* and *Torsion*. It is entirely possible to have as many as four of these present in a single joint.

In the design of connections it is necessary to 1) consider each type of loading and 2) to establish criteria for each of the loadings and each of the types of connections.

TYPES OF CONNECTIONS

Tension (Axial). This type of loading (experienced, for example, in a truss) requires a connection which will transmit the entire tensile force without any reliance on the tensile strength of concrete. The design should be checked for the effects of possible eccentricities.

Tension may be transmitted by reinforcing steel (Fig. 2a), embedded structural steel shapes (Fig. 2b), by prestressing forces (Fig. 2c) and by anchored steel plates (Fig. 2d). When reinforcing steel is used to transfer tension, the design should be checked to make sure that the stresses in the reinforcing bars are fully developed either by bond or some form of mechanical anchorage. Also, sufficient welding or lapping of bars should be provided to transfer the load across the joint. Reinforcing steel should also be arranged symmetrically in the section to eliminate the effects of localized eccentricities.

When embedded structural steel shapes are used to transfer tension, the same criteria used for reinforcing steel is applied. That is, stresses in the structural shapes must be fully developed by bond producing devices attached to the shapes, or by sufficient welding to the mild steel reinforcement used in the member.

Structural steel shapes also should be arranged symmetrically in the section to eliminate the effects of localized eccentricities.

Tension can be transferred across a joint by having that joint precompressed or prestressed by a force which exceeds the design tensile force (multiplied by the appropriate load factors). The design criteria for such a joint involves: (a) the bearing stresses created by one member on another with only the prestressing force being applied (maximum

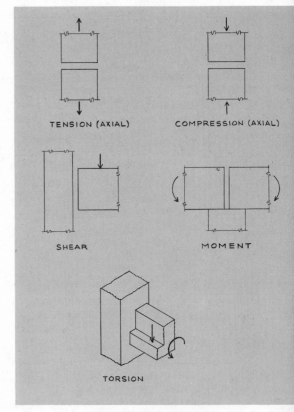

Figure 1   TYPES OF LOADS

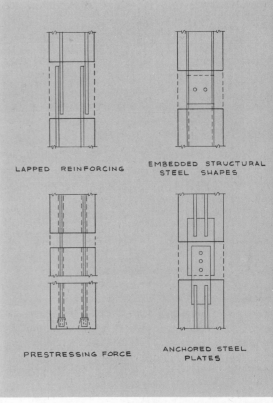

Figure 2   TENSION CONNECTIONS

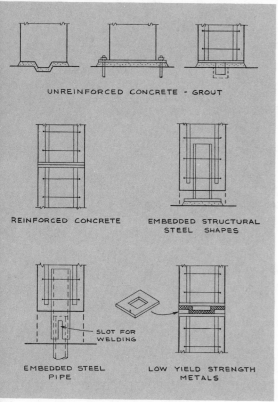

Figure 3   COMPRESSION CONNECTIONS

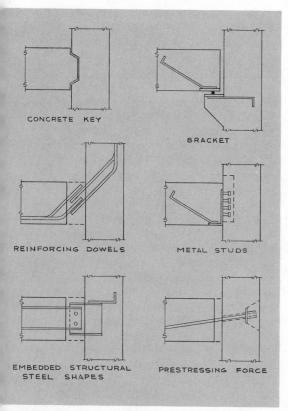

Figure 4   SHEAR CONNECTIONS

concrete stress); and (b) the bearing stresses created when the prestressing force and the maximum tensile force are applied simultaneously (minimum concrete stress). Positive means, such as grouting, should be employed to insure uniform contact between members. The joint should also have provisions for preventing lateral movement. Prestress losses should be carefully studied and provisions made for their effects in this type of joint.

Compression (Axial). For this type of loading, the joint is required to transmit the entire compressive force while keeping within the allowable stresses for the materials involved.

Compression may be transmitted by unreinforced concrete (Fig. 3a), reinforced concrete (Fig 3b), structural steel shapes (Fig. 3c) or steel pipe (Fig. 3d) and by low yield strength alloys (Fig. 3e).

When compression is transmitted by unreinforced concrete (grout) the design consists only of going through the same procedure used when checking bearing stresses under column base plates. This type of joint should also have provisions for preventing lateral movement.

The transfer of compression across a joint by reinforced concrete consists of designing the joint in the same manner used for the design of the member, taking into account bond length requirements of reinforcing when bars are lapped or butted and welded. Most important is the placement of structural concrete which is intended to complete the joint. The concrete must be carefully compacted and cured, and attention should be given to the transfer of stress by bond between the reinforcement and the concrete.

The joint used to transfer compression by means of structural steel shapes has the same general requirements as a joint used to transmit tension with structural steel shapes.

Use of low yield strength alloys to transmit compression across a joint requires careful attention due to the general lack of information of the properties of these alloys, and the problem in determining the possible range of loads they will be required to transmit.

These alloys are extremely useful in compression connections because of their ability to redistribute very localized stress concentrations that occur when one member bears on another. Low yield strength alloys should be of the type that will not "flow" under sustained loads. Those of the "Babbitt Metal" family have proven satisfactory.

Shear. This connection must be capable of transmitting the entire shear by only one means. In other words, you cannot assign 50 per cent of the total shear to a concrete keyway and 50 per cent to another device (such as a structural steel shape). The designer must select one or the other to carry 100 per cent of the shear, just as he would if he were designing a structural steel connection where bolts and weldment are both present.

Shear may be transmitted by concrete keys (Fig. 4a), reinforcing steel (Fig. 4b), brackets (Fig. 4c), embedded structural steel shapes (Fig. 4d), metal studs (Fig. 4e) and by prestressing (Fig. 4f).

The use of concrete keys for the transfer of shear is a very familiar method. The criteria for their use in precast concrete joints is the same as that for poured-in-place concrete work. Specifically, it is recommended that the unit stresses in either the key itself or the area in the member where the connection is being made do not exceed the following: bearing $0.08f'_c$; shear $0.02f'_c$ (which are less than the values permitted in ACI-318, the *American Concrete Institute Building Code*). Also, the joint should be constructed so that the contact sufaces remain in contact during the life of the structure with adequate provisions against possible tension between the surfaces.

The use of reinforcing steel for the transfer of shear from one member to another through a joint requires that the bearing stresses and tensile stresses of reinforcing bars be carefully considered along with the anchorage of the bars so used in the members, and the lapping or welding of these bars in the joint.

Brackets are frequently used for shear transfer. When they connect precast concrete members, certain practices ought to be followed. Some of these are: The distance from the leading edge of the bracket to the point where the load is acting should not be less than one third of the bracket depth; the brackets must be designed for flexure, shear, bearing area, splitting and other tensile stresses in the bracket; flexure and shear computations should be done in accordance with the requirements of ACI-318, the *American Concrete Institute Building Code.*

Bearing calculations should be made to suit the particular seating arrangement of the member on a bracket. For uniform bearing, a maximum stress of $0.3f'_c$ should not be exceeded. Provisions such as chamfered edges or well anchored corner angles should be employed to prevent spalling. Bearing plates on the member and bracket should be used either with or without bearing pads.

Concrete to concrete connections should be avoided except where the designer has other requirements which make this type of contact desirable. Splitting, or the tensile stresses resulting from bearing, should be guarded against by using reinforcement parallel to the bearing surface in both directions. A maximum of $1\frac{1}{2}$ in. of cover is recommended. Reinforcing for splitting should be in addition to that required for flexure and other design stresses.

Extreme care is necessary in the detailing of member-to-bracket connections to eliminate, or take into account, the effects of member length changes due to shrinkage, creep or thermal expansion or contraction.

The use of embedded structural steel shapes for the transfer of shear requires that positive anchorage of these shapes be provided. With a given load on a projecting element, such as a steel wide flange projecting from the end of a beam, local bending, bearing and tensile stresses are produced in the end of the member as well as shear in the web of the wide flange. Therefore the designer should check the following:
a) The fiber stresses in the projecting element resulting from its section modulus and the moment produced by the shear force.
b) The bearing stresses produced where the projecting element is in contact with the concrete of the member.
c) The tensile stresses produced on planes perpendicular to shear force, i.e. the plane on the bottom of the projecting element which lies above the rest of the depth of the precast member.

Use of prestressing force to transfer shear requires that the designer familiarize himself with the results of combining moment, shear and compression at such a joint. The designer must determine through mathematical means the angle and magnitude of the principal stresses, and then satisfy these localized stress conditions. The stresses produced should not exceed those permitted by ASCE-ACI Committee 323 —Tentative Recommendations for the Design of Prestressed Concrete —for segmental elements.

Moment. In the transfer of moment through a precast concrete joint, the entire moment must be taken by one type of device, as in the transfer of shear, even though more than one such device may be available at the connection. Moment may be transferred by reinforcing steel (Fig. 5a), mechanical devices (Fig. 5b), and by prestressing forces (Fig. 5c).

When reinforcing steel is used to transfer moment, the designer must check the joint so that the full yield strength of the bar may be developed, if required, by bond or by welding. Where welding is used, care should be taken to prevent excessive heat from damaging the concrete. The detailing of such a joint should provide for the necessary protection of the reinforcing, and should provide means for limiting rotation at the joint to that assumed in the original design. This is accomplished by giving special attention to the erection and loading sequences and the condition at the time the joint is to be completed. The completion of the joint with concrete requires careful attention to compaction and curing, and the effects of shrinkage, creep and temperature changes.

It is very common to use mechanical devices to transfer moment in precast joints. Mechanical devices include structural steel shapes, welded plates and couplings—to mention a few. The main criteria for their use is that they be fully developed and are anchored adequately in the members. They are designed by checking net areas available, unit stresses in tension or compression, weld sizes and similar design conditions.

Prestressing force employed to transfer moment through a joint can be designed by following the recommendations for the design of segmental members in the ASCE-ACI Committee 323 Report. In the joint

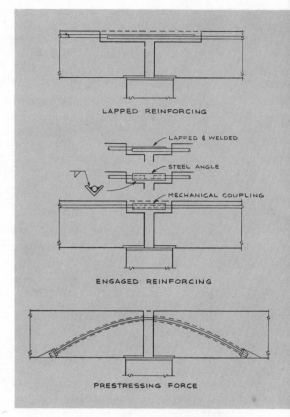

Figure 5 MOMENT CONNECTIONS

design, means must be provided for distributing the force over the contact surfaces without creating local stress concentrations. Grouting is one of the most satisfactory methods.

Torsion. This is the most difficult of all connections to design and detail. It is also a loading condition that should be avoided whenever possible. Some designers have avoided the problem by simply ignoring it; but this is a very unscientific attitude and could cause serious legal difficulties if failure of a structure occurs.

Torsion may be transferred by concrete keys, reinforcing steel, mechanical devices, embedded structural steel shapes, and prestressing force. With any of these devices the designer must combine the effects of torsion with the other loadings present. This means that if a joint has been designed for shear it must also be checked for the effects of any applied torsion.

2. JOB-PROVEN DETAILS

A series of connections developed and used by Arthur R. Anderson, Partner, Anderson, Birkeland & Anderson, Consulting Structural Engineers, Tacoma, Washington

National Bank of Washington, Tacoma
Architect: Robert B. Price
Contractor: Concrete Engineering

Series of rigid frame bents made from precast columns and a prestressed roof beam comprise the structure. The connection detail at the corners is shown in Figure 4. The column to footing connection is shown in Figure 2

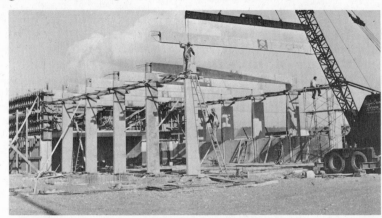

Woodrow Wilson High School, Tacoma
Architects: Lea, Pearson and Richards
Contractor: Nelsen Construction Company

Prestressed concrete I-beams span 105 ft over the swimming pool. These beams are 48-in. deep with 18-in. flanges and a 4-in. web. Since the structure is exposed, a clean, simple connection between beam and column is desirable; a bearing seat or corbel projecting from the column must be avoided. The connection in Figure 5 makes this possible

Office Building and Carport, Tacoma
Designer and Builder: Concrete Engineering Co.

In this two-story rigid frame of precast columns and prestressed beams, the second floor beam is joined to the columns in accordance with the detail in Figure 5 and the roof beams as in Figure 4. Precast channel slabs are carried on the beams with the negative steel being welded prior to casting concrete into space over the beams (Figure 8)

Ala Moana Shopping Center, Honolulu, Hawaii
Architect: John Graham and Company
Contractor: Hawaiian Construction & Dredging Co.

Two-level parking structure of precast and prestressed concrete is designed composite with a cast-in-place deck slab. Prestressed piles also serve as columns. Upper ends of columns are joined to girders by connecting steel projecting from the column and the two girders and filling in the space surrounding the steel with concrete. Prestressed beams are carried on the lower flange of the girder as shown in Figures 7 and 8

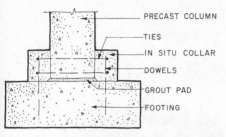

Figure 1

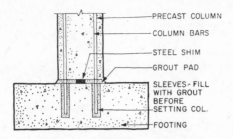

Figure 2

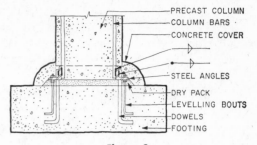

Figure 3

One-story columns may be set on footings with the simple connection shown in *Figure 1*. Footing is cast rough with accurately placed grout pad added later. A row of dowels around the column set in the footing anchors the cast-in-place collar. *Figure 2* shows a simple and inexpensive, moment-resisting, column-to-footing connection. The footing has sleeves to receive column bars. The steel shim near the center of the column provides temporary support. Prior to setting of the column, the sleeves are filled with a thick grout paste. Space between column and footing is grouted last. When columns must develop high bending moments at the base, the connection in *Figure 3* is used. In this case an angle bar collar is welded to the column bars. Small leveling bolts are convenient for setting the column. After the column is positioned, by these bolts, the dowels are welded to the angle bar

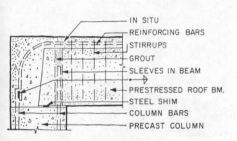

Figure 4

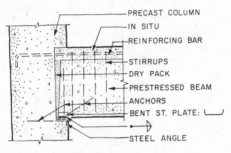

Figure 5

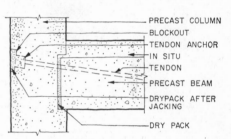

Figure 6

Figure 4 is a simple but effective detail for a roof beam-to-column connection in which the interior column bars project upward into sleeves of the beam, and the sleeves are filled with grout. Bent reinforcing bars placed over the ends of the beams are welded to the exterior column bars. Space over the beam and column is filled with in-situ concrete. The roof slab may be cast-in-place or precast. *Figure 5* shows connection for floor beams in multi-story buildings. Beam seat is a steel angle anchored in the column. Steel plate in the beam is welded to the angle bar after beam is erected. Reinforcing bar in column projects inward over the beam to develop a negative bending moment in the joint. Careful analysis is required for concentrated bearing stresses and moments and shears in the members. *Figure 6* shows the beam joined to the column by post-tensioning. This method is particularly effective for beam spans up to 70 or 80 ft. Space at the end of the beam is drypack grouted

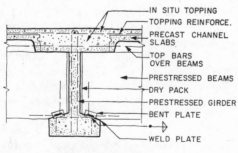

Figure 7

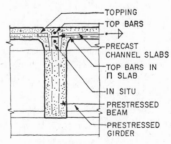

Figure 8

Economical framing for large bays is possible by using precast girders, beams and slabs, particularly when the precast members are prestressed. Girders of inverted T section may be used so that the bottom flange serves as a seat for the beams as is shown in *Figures 7* and *8*. The connection between the beam and girder is made by welding embedded steel plates. The precast channel slabs are composite with the in-situ topping. The precast slabs over the girder may be omitted, allowing a substantial in-situ section to be cast as a composite top flange for the girder and for placing negative reinforcing bars over beams and girders. Figure 8 is a section through the detail of Figure 7 and shows negative bars projecting from the ends of the precast channel slabs which are welded together; space over the beam is filled with in-situ concrete

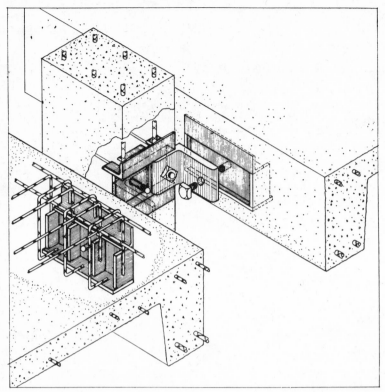

R. M. Gensert Associates

PRECAST APARTMENT STRUCTURE SAVES COST, SHOWS ITS DESIGN

Assembly of four-story columns and channel slabs is speeded by a special connection detail

How to join precast elements efficiently is a difficult problem for the engineer. How to join them in a way that makes sense spatially and visually is a difficult problem for the architect. Here is how architect Tasso Katselas and engineer R. M. Gensert view their participation in design of this Pittsburgh apartment building:

ARCHITECT'S REMARKS:

In speculative housing, the strongest design drive is economy of construction. This calls for a straight forward approach to get as much space and thermal comfort as the budget will allow.

The structural frame of this building, ready to receive exterior facing and mechanicals, cost well below

$3.00 per sq ft. Without this economy the project couldn't have been built.

Next came the problem of how to express this method architecturally. Since the floor slabs could be run past the columns, it was possible to make this read on the exterior by extending the slabs as hooded covers for each apartment unit.

Since rooms are oriented in this direction, the canopy cover gives a sense of privacy and enclosure to apartment occupants.

Beams become strong directional members from the inside, defining each space.

At the roof level, a stronger expression is gained by making the canopy overhang even larger. This serves the same function as a period

at the end of a sentence: it terminates the simple geometric pattern which otherwise might seem endless.

The same structural system is used also to frame the canopy and bridge members that lead into the building, as well as the enclosed individual garages at the lower level.

With garages on the lower level, it was possible to separate pedestrian and vehicular traffic. The building is on a corner lot, so it made sense to use one street for approach by auto, and the other more residential street for approach directly by foot from shopping areas.

Architecturally, one of the big problems with any precast system is how joining of the diverse parts takes place. In this case, the voids

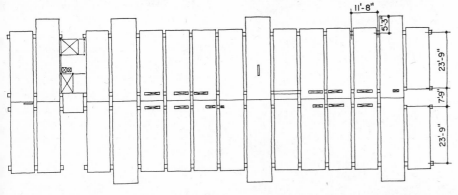

11'-8"

5'-3"

23'-9"

7'-9"

23'-9"

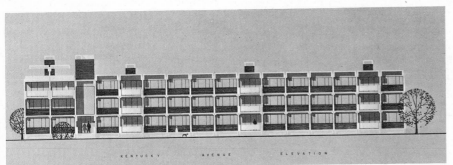

KENTUCKY   AVENUE   ELEVATION

Building consists of three apartment floors and a basement garage. Only two basic structural components, columns and channel slabs, are used throughout. Slabs provide canopies for windows and are cantilevered to make balconies at three points on the elevation. Framing plan is of the third floor. Open space on plan is above lobby, which has elevator in center and stairs at back

Kentucky Negley Apartments, Pittsburgh, Pennsylvania
ARCHITECT: *Tasso Katselas*
STRUCTURAL ENGINEER:
R. M. Gensert, Associates
GENERAL CONTRACTOR: *John R. Hess*

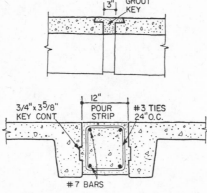

Spaces between channel slabs in the longitudinal direction are filled in by pour strips which are reinforced and tied to interior columns to form portal frames. Spaces between slabs in corridor (see photo) have a grout key. No topping is necessary

Precast columns are precision plumbed by bolting to steel plates set in the pile caps. Columns and ordinary reinforced slabs are precast on a vacant lot near the site

between slabs were simply filled in for required wind bracing after the mechanicals were installed.

The design for this apartment building proves that a simple direct approach to precasting is possible in speculative housing. Here is one solution to economical fire-resistive construction with endless possibilities for expression.

—*Tasso Katselas*

ENGINEER'S REMARKS:
We feel that this is an interesting application of precast concrete from both architectural and structural viewpoints.

As an architectural concept, it expresses the simple relationship of horizontal and vertical elements without interruptions in either one.

The structural concept is one of maximum continuity of columns for stability, and minimum number of floor elements for ease and economy in erection. The single type of floor element with joints occurring only at column lines made it possible to eliminate concrete topping.

The beams or stems of the channels are designed as L-shaped members; the slabs are considered for continuity with these integral supporting beams.

The construction method was oriented toward site precasting, which was performed by Hufschmidt Engineering Company of Menomonee Falls, Wisconsin. Precasting was done on a vacant plot of land across the street from the building site. A rapid schedule required stripping of forms within 24 hours.

Connections are always a problem in precast concrete, and they were the most difficult design problem on this project. Columns were one piece and connected to pile caps with four anchor bolts and eight nuts. Double nuts per bolt permitted precision plumbing of columns.

Columns and slabs contained welded steel boxes that were cast within the concrete. Large steel angles were used to transfer the load from slab box to column box. Purpose of these boxes was to accommodate high shear and bearing stresses within the concrete.

The cast-in-place strips between the slabs were reinforced and attached to the interior columns via reinforcement to resist wind moments.

—*R. M. Gensert*

LOGIC AND ART IN PRECAST CONCRETE

MEDICAL RESEARCH LABORATORY *University of Pennsylvania, Philadelphia, Pa.*
Architect: Louis I. Kahn, F.A.I.A.
Structural Consultant: Dr. August E. Komendant
Consulting Engineers: Keast and Hood
Prefabricator: Atlantic Prestressed Concrete Co.
General Contractor: Joseph R. Farrell, Inc.

Louis Kahn's comment on the precast shapes shown on these pages is that they convey the spirit of the building —just as a few battered columns can still convey the spirit of ancient Greece. The comparison is an apt one. For the shapes themselves, like the structure they form, evolved so logically from the architectural requirements that "structure" and "building" cannot be separated: the one evokes the other.

In the beginning, however, Kahn had neither. He started with just two premises: that for students and researchers, as for architects, the studio is the best environment; and that the extensive services needed for their work should not interfere with it. From these premises, he devised a plan not essentially different from the standard one of distributing offices and laboratories along service corridors. But the corridors are vertical, the "studios" are stacked on top of one another, and the Laboratory is four buildings instead of one.

The central building in the complex is a poured-in-place utility tower with two-way slabs supported on the load-bearing walls that enclose elevators, stairs, lavatories, quarters for laboratory animals, and other facilities shared by the three, eight-story studio towers distributed swastika-style around it. Each of the three studio towers is in turn flanked on four sides by slender brick sub-towers which rise some 25 ft above the main buildings. Three of the sub-towers link their respective buildings to the central core; the others enclose fire exits, vertical service lines, and exhaust stacks.

With all vertical circulation of services and people thus confined to the sub-towers or the central utility tower, each laboratory floor becomes a self-contained studio, unencumbered by permanent verticals of any kind. To leave the corners light and open, the two columns on each side of the studio towers were moved in to the third points. The 47-ft clear spans are bridged by precast Vierendeel trusses which allow free horizontal circulation of the complex network of services for each floor.

The framing system for the studio towers consists of four basic precast shapes. But the four are standard only in the sense that they are repeated. Each was tailored to meet the particular requirements of this particular building; and each was carefully detailed to meet variations in field conditions through modifications in the members themselves rather than in the connections. As a result, the elements lie somewhere between the stock members (channels, T's and so forth) that are used primarily for economy, and the intricate geometric forms that are used primarily for visual expression. Perhaps they also point the way to a more logical use of precast concrete: one that takes full advantage of factory techniques without resorting to assembly line engineering.

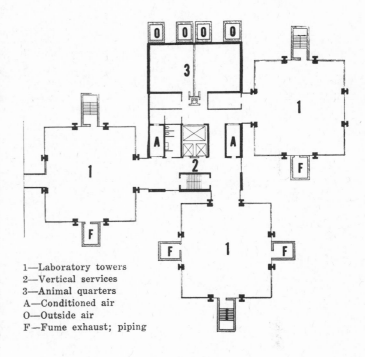

1—Laboratory towers
2—Vertical services
3—Animal quarters
A—Conditioned air
O—Outside air
F—Fume exhaust; piping

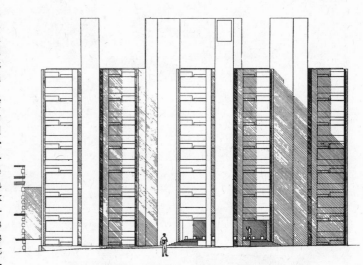

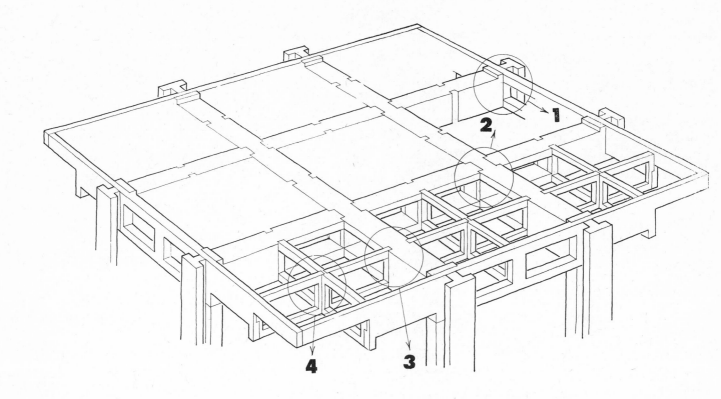

Basically the structure for the studio towers (top floor shown above) is an eight-story rigid frame whose 45-ft-square clear spans are bridged by heavy Vierendeel trusses supported on H-columns at both ends. Stepped spandrel beams cantilever outward from the columns, while slim secondary trusses span between the main trusses and spandrels. The horizontal framing members of each floor thus form a 3-ft-deep open web which supports floor loads and the network of pipes, conduits, ducts and hood exhausts within the confines of the structure.

Although the extensive services and the heavy laboratory equipment brought the design live load up to about 100 psf, prestressing kept the columns and girders down to manageable size and linked them into a fully continuous, and highly efficient, structure—reportedly the highest precast frame of its type ever built

All photographs by Ronald C. Binks

Although the columns and spandrels are "architectural," they are not arbitrarily so. For example, the web-deep separation between the column's outer flanges and the face of the building does lighten the columns visually. But the H-section was chosen for maximum efficiency under the eccentric loads. The deep truss section that permits passage of service lines through the center of the spandrel also supports its cantilevered ends; and the stepped cantilevers themselves take advantage of the gradually decreasing stresses in the span without making it necessary to frame the glazing into a sloping member. As shown, the inner flange at one end of each column is cut short to form a niche for the spandrel and truss which rest on the column below. To preserve the continuity of the columns at the joints, the prestressing rods in their inner flanges are also run through the spandrel and truss, tying them in place with a prestress force of 90 tons

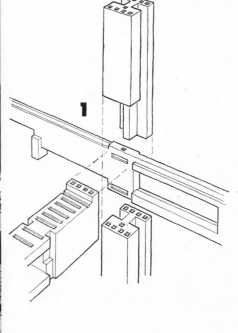

1

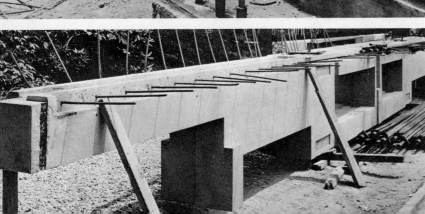

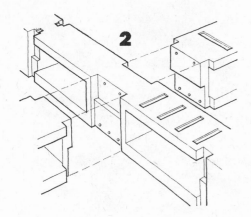

Two of the four Vierendeel trusses on each floor were cast in three parts which slip in between the columns and the two one-piece pretensioned trusses running in the other direction. Both ends of the middle truss section (above right) and the inner ends of the sections on either side of it (right) are notched to match seats cut into the pretensioned trusses. The outside ends are seated on the columns. Once in place, the three sections are joined by post-tensioning to form a continuous member that duplicates the pretensioned truss. The vertical joints were filled in with ¼-in. steel plates instead of grout so that the sections could be post-stressed as soon as they were seated; the grouting was done after post-tensioning

The one-piece main trusses (right) were pretensioned slightly higher than the final loads required so that they could carry the extra weight of the three-part trusses until the latter had been post-tensioned. Field tests on the main trusses have shown an almost exact correlation between their actual and theoretical behavior under various conditions of loading.

The one-part trusses are prestressed by ⅜-in. strands: 12 in the top flange and 26 in the bottom flange. The post-tensioned trusses have three 1¼-in. rods stressed to a total of 200 tons in the bottom flange, and two 1-in. rods with a 70-ton prestress force in the top flange. They camber about ⅛ in. after post-tensioning

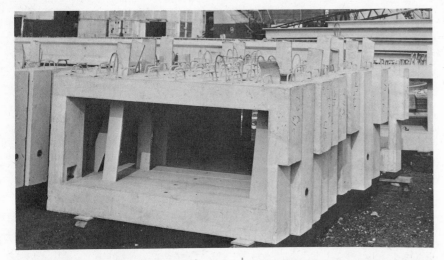

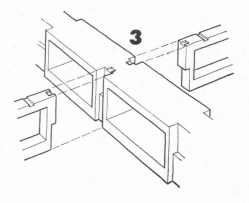

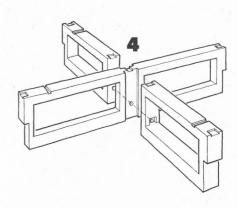

The slim (8 in. thick, 38 in. deep) secondary trusses at left above were also notched to match seats on the Vierendeel trusses, which they join as shown in detail 3. One of the two in each bay was cast in two parts and bolted together through the one-piece truss perpendicular to it (see detail 4).

Since they could be omitted altogether without seriously affecting the basic structure, the primary purpose of the secondary trusses is to provide intermediate supports for the pipes and ducts. (They cost no more than hangers would.) However, they also provide convenient locations for partitions, and help to lighten the floor slabs

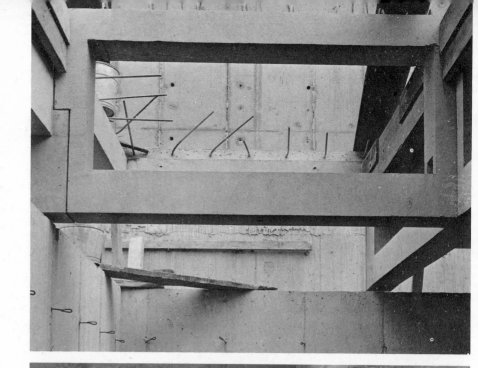

At this stage of construction, as the photos here show, one of the most striking features of the Medical Research Laboratory is the precision with which the elements were assembled into a monolithic whole. Kahn insisted on craftsmanship—and he got it: the exposed members fit together with a deceptive simplicity more typical of fine cabinetwork than of concrete construction.

To begin with, they were detailed to expedite a carefully worked out erection procedure. They were then cast to extremely close tolerances and steamcured to obtain smooth, durable lime-packed surfaces. As a result, the laboratory floors are being put together at the rate of three a week; the joints are so precise that they will be emphasized by tooling out the grout to a depth of ¼ in.; and it is difficult to find a flaw in the finish.

The speed of field operations is attributed to the joining system, which provides seats for all members, thus assuring faster and more accurate placement than would be possible if welded plates or cast-in-place sections were used at the joints

PRECAST JOINERY: MANY LESSONS TO LEARN

by Laurence Cazaly, Cazaly Associates, Toronto

Grosvenor House in Winnipeg is one of the tallest precast structures in North America. On these grounds it may be thought by some to be newsworthy, and by others to contain some worthwhile ideas. The lessons to be learned from this structure, however, have little to do with statistics of this nature.

Lesson 1: *Classic and romantic schools have as much place in engineering as architecture*

Each building material has engineering characteristics which change the principles of design. For example, aluminum is used for light structures and is therefore usually present in the form of thin sections. Since it has also a low modulus of elasticity compared to its strength, the skill in designing aluminum lies in overcoming buckling, excessive deflections and fatigue. Thus a highly theoretical understanding of structural form is desirable.

In contrast, reinforced concrete is comparatively cheap and heavy, and since it is a composite material its behavior cannot be deduced directly from the theory of elasticity. Concrete is most likely to fail in ways which can be guessed but not analyzed. Concrete design, particularly precast concrete design, is therefore largely a matter of detail.

The emotional impact of a material on an engineer is therefore quite different from its impact on an architect.

Sizing the members of Grosvenor House took but a few hours. Connecting the pieces took weeks of grumbling, sweating and the highest professional discipline. The discipline lay in the necessity of working for greater and greater simplicity long after the problem became tedious. Of all aspects of structural engineering this is the least glamourous.

(There is a paradox here. Concrete

attracts glamour-seeking student engineers because of the striking forms in which the material can be cast. Only the most determined retain their ideals after a few years of practice.)

Lesson 2: *Never experiment with everything at once*

The main difference between the professional and the amateur is experience and discipline. The professional gradually acquires a library of solutions which work. The most original designers may be defined as those who keep building their library. The fact that original designs can be recognized as characteristic of their designers shows how much of the tried has been retained.

In Grosvenor House there were many new problems because of the size and shape of the building. The methods used were therefore old methods with which we were completely familiar. All connections are made of mild steel components, bolted and welded. As an example of this school, Grosvenor House is extremely sophisticated. The following details will show, however, that even the most complex connection can be described in terms of the simple basic components.

Lesson 3: *"Structure" is not a visual phenomenon akin to "form"*

The increasing use of exposed structural members for architectural effect has led to the practice of using structure to rationalize what is basically

an architectural feature. It is quite common to read descriptions of buildings, which should be judged on their architectural merit alone, in which the designer has explained his creation in terms of structural "economy" and "logic." In many cases a qualified observer can detect immediately that the structure is neither economical nor logical. Some designs still possess architectural value but for reasons disassociated from engineering.

In the case of Grosvenor House it can be seen from the plan that the frame is made up of lapping rectangular pieces of constant cross section. While this is a natural way to build in wood it does not follow that precast concrete should be designed this way.

The architects, who selected the "seen" details of Grosvenor House, should not be criticized because these details generated awkward structural problems. An architect has the right to expect his engineer to solve such problems and to present him with an opinion for making a decision.

Lesson 4: *Building codes are a prop for the incompetent, a protection against the dishonest, but a restriction placed on good design*

The Grosvenor House structure is a classic example of one in which no significant feature is covered by a building code. This is because no code writing committee visualized the type of construction used and could therefore say nothing about it. There are,

however, numerous regulations and formulas which must be satisfied even though the conditions under which they apply have been limited by special considerations of the design. In effect, a building code relates to three phases of knowledge. There is the part wherein it agrees with the designer's own decision and need not have been referred to; there is the part wherein general rules put unnecessary restrictions on the particular case the designer has in mind; and there is the part wherein nothing is said and yet design limits are necessary. Apart from the irritation and cost of complying with unnecessary restrictions there is also the danger that a designer may feel that having complied with the code he has made a safe design.

It should be appreciated that a building code is a list of instructions made by a committee. The instructions are limited to those which can be put in writing without becoming too long or too complicated and are limited also to those that the committee consider necessary. Since they are to be used by a man they have never met on a job of which they know none of the details, it is unlikely that the instructions will be wholly correct. At best they can be a reasonable approximation. On these grounds a competent design should always be preferred to a code-based design, except in cases of dispute when the code becomes a useful legal weapon to enforce minimum standards.

How the frame of Grosvenor House was put together

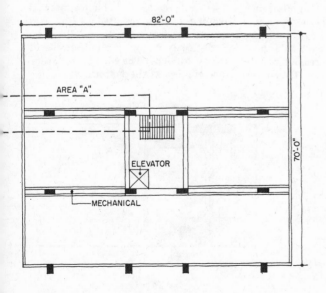

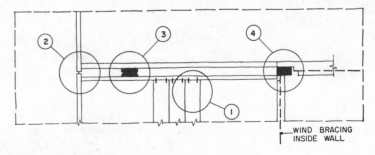

The four most important connection details, identified in the drawing above (Area "A"), are illustrated and discussed on the following two pages. Detail 1: precast double tees hung from main beams. Detail 2: edge beams hung from main beams. Detail 3: attachment of double-cantilevered main beams to columns. Detail 4: interior column connection and steel-strap cross-bracing system

Detail 1: The hung floor slabs

The floors are made from standard double tees with topping and a suspended ceiling. To utilize the full available depth and width for the main beams, these tees are hung from the top of each web with a simple hanger. In its basic form this consists of a rectangular steel bar cantilevered from the end of the concrete to which is welded a vertical U strap. The U is used principally to carry the reaction to the bottom of the web, but serves a secondary purpose in containing bursting forces from the prestressing strands, and generally binding the end of the unit. The forces on the cantilevered bar are shown in the equilibrium diagram. We have made a practice of designing these hangers for ultimate load with a load factor of four. This figure allows abuse of the unit during manufacture and erection.

The horizontal reinforcing bars in the detail are simply to hold the hanger in the concrete. They should be more than nominal size if high shrinkage and temperature restraints are expected. The seat for the hanger is usually an isolated frame. However, in this application the small reaction per hanger and the close and varied spacing of the webs suggested a continuous angle as the best form of seat

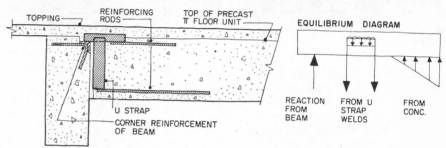

Detail 2: The edge beam

The edge beams of Grosvenor House form a continuous ribband on the exterior. These beams are also exposed (with plaster finish) on the front and back interior walls. They are required, therefore, to have the same depth as the interior beams supporting them, and must show an unbroken face with clean vertical joints. A hanger similar in principle to detail 1 is used but with certain variations. Since the edge beam is 7 ⅛ in. wide, a flat U strap would cut too deeply into the face, reducing the shear strength of the beam. This has been replaced by a 3- by ⅝-in. flat with a shelf at the bottom to transfer the reaction to the concrete. The hanger seat consists of an angle to distribute the bearing pressure and to reinforce the corner of the supporting beam. It is held in, and also prevented from rotating, by the 2- by ⅜-in. flats, which are in turn anchored by small reinforcing bars.

Since the hanger is side mounted, the bending moment created by the cantilevered bar cannot be taken by the unit itself (except by an undesirable degree of torsion). The edge beam is therefore clipped at the bottom

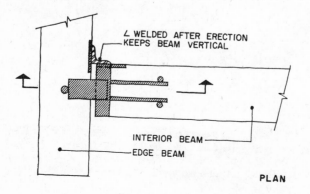

PLAN

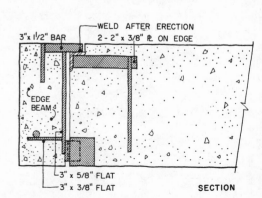

SECTION

Detail 3: The double-cantilevered beams

In designing the connection of the double cantilevers to the column, a number of complications had to be allowed for: (1) the cantilever distance is short compared to the interior span, and under a fully fixed condition the interior fixed end moment would apply bending to the column. The column size, however, is such that under full vertical load no bending (other than wind) may exist. This bending was eliminated by shimming the exterior, X_1/X_2 connection only, for part of the dead load. When the right proportion of the structure was on, the interior connection Y_1/Y_2 was made and the connection then became fixed under the action of the couple, Y/X. The proportions are such that under full live load Y_1 and X_1 reactions are equal; (2) the size of the double cantilevers is such that the stresses are high in bending and shear at the section near the column. The connection had to be such that no excessive weakening was induced at this point; (3) the lower halves of these beams are exposed (with plaster finish) and no haunches or brackets could appear under them.

The solution again used side-mounted hangers. These were located below the negative reinforcement. The twin U straps present the maximum amount of length for welding to the cantilever plate, and also allow better compaction of the concrete than a single large plate. To help these straps distribute their load quickly, reinforcing dowels were welded to them. (All but one of these has been omitted from the diagram for clarity.) The fabricated channels in the column have heavy dowels welded to the back. These lie inside the main reinforcing cage and are capable of carrying all the load by bond if necessary. The angle ledge to the channels, however, will restrain the face concrete sufficiently to take the load in bearing unless it is removed by fire. In addition the channels also play a part in taking the connection load. After erection, both flanges of X_1 are welded to X_2 so that X_1 is able to take both negative moment induced by X_2 and positive moment induced by the U straps. The net result is an oversafe connection capable of yielding in several of its parts before collapse of the whole will result

Detail 4: Interior column connection

Most complex of all, this connection transfers the load from four concrete beams and four wind bracing ties to the column. The Area "A" drawing on the second page illustrates this situation. There is, in addition, a steel stair supporting beam (not shown).

Although it has many parts Detail 4 is still composed of basic plates, ties and angles which bear on the concrete in tried and tested ways. The method of carrying load is the same in principle as the basic hanger.

Our instructions for this job were that the complete structural frame was to be supplied by the precast concrete producer, and that erection would continue

if necessary through 10 or 20 degrees below zero weather. This eliminated a slip-formed shaft for the central core as a possibility, and left as possibilities the cross-braced system actually used, or post-tensioned precast panels. These were eliminated because of the cold weather problem. The wind forces on the core are high due to the several openings and its general proportions.

The use of steel tension members was an inexpensive way of taking force, and since the owner-builder was accustomed to making 2-in. leaf block walls, everyone was happy with the solution to the esthetic, financial and technical variables that had been established before we started the design

Grosvenor House, Winnipeg, Manitoba

ARCHITECTS: *Libling, Michener and Associates*

STRUCTURAL ENGINEERS: *Cazaly Associates*

OWNER AND GENERAL CONTRACTOR: *G. Mida*

PRECAST CONCRETE CONTRACTOR: *Preco Ltd.*

ASSOCIATE STRUCTURAL ENGINEER: *John Glanville*

PARTITIONS FUNCTION AS COLUMNS

Olgyay and Olgyay, Architects

Bela Kiss, Structural Engineer, Budapest

Comments by Paul Weidlinger

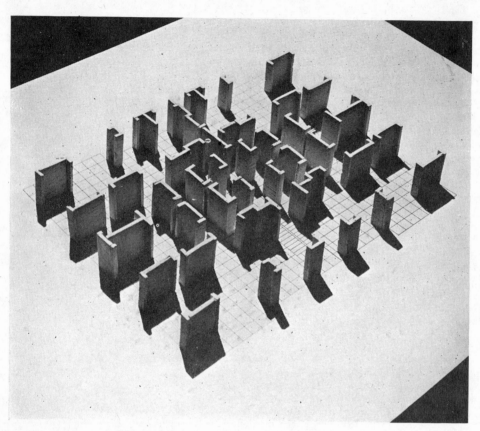

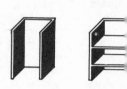

Various types of partiti

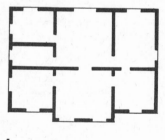

1.

Model of floor in walk-up-type apartment pictures how concrete partitions work as columns

THERE is a growing tendency in some phases of building, just as there has been in the aviation and automotive industries, to depart from "frame and enclosure" types of structures—that is, those structures which separate load-bearing elements from the rest of the construction. For example, "stressed skin" type of construction employed in airplanes also has found application in load-bearing plywood walls for prefabricated houses.

Architects, Olgyay, and engineer, Bela Kiss, have encouraged this tendency with their system of multi-story construction: *reinforced concrete partition walls become the supporting elements, eliminating separate columns.* Broken shaped partitions, especially suitable for apartments, and two-way ribbed floors work together to carry imposed loads.

Efficiency of building construction often is expressed on the basis of ratio of total dead load to utilizable live load — efficiency varying inversely with this ratio. The system of construction presented here, called *cellular* by the architects, is aimed at reducing this ratio to a practical minimum.

Partitions, by virtue of their shape, obtain maximum utilization of strength of materials, following somewhat the idea of light gage steel construction. The partitions are functional otherwise in that horizontal ribs used to stiffen the vertical sections can serve as shelves.

System Originated in Europe

This method of construction is one of the many advanced methods which have

come to us from Europe, where the importance of saving materials has given the impulse to a number of new developments. Innovations, based on an economic system and material and labor cost relationship which are quite different from ours, often are not suitable to adaptation here.

Of many such ideas, only those which represent fundamentally new and sound structural concepts are destined for application in the U. S. The recent successful "Americanization" of prestressed concrete is an example of this. *Cellular* construction, if introduced here, might become the next contender.

What's New About It

It is in many respects a basic development in the spirit of advanced building technology. These are as follows.

1. It is the next logical step in development of the flat slab, which represented the transition from linear column-girder construction into the three dimensional rigid frame.

With *cellular* construction, the linear, one-dimensional column is replaced by the two-dimensional wall. (It is interesting to note the reappearance of the "load-bearing" partition in its new form.)

2. In the quest for elimination of all unnecessary weight from structures, full utilization of new building materials of high strength and uniformity has become a problem. Structural elements are now reduced to critical cross-sectional areas; and instead of strength, elastic stability (i.e. the over-all or local buckling of the members) becomes the controlling factor in design. This is clearly expressed, at present, in structural elements and shapes developed for light gage steel, aluminum and also plywood.

The very same problem is faced and solved now in this new method of construction in reinforced concrete. Load-bearing elements are thin-walled concrete shapes, stiffened to avoid local buckling through stiffening flanges very similar to those of light gage steel studs (see top drawings on this page).

3. Structurally, this system is one which only a decade ago would have been nearly impossible to analyze. Even today, the design of a flat slab with irregularly placed supports requires a complex and time consuming analysis. The design of a slab supported and restrained by irregularly placed thin wall sections is even more complex.

Similarly, the design of concrete wall sections to avoid over-all torsional and local buckling is no simple task. However, the challenge presented by these problems can be met today with advanced methods of engineering analysis, but would not have been practicable a short time ago.

4. Finally, because of the complexity of the engineering analysis, successful application of this system requires the disciplined approach and structural understanding of the contemporary architect. It is a structural system which requires honest architecture.

All these are sure signs that one is faced here with a fundamental innovation which is bound to have beneficial influence on our building technology, if it is given a chance for application in this country. The advantages to be gained are clearly shown in the two apartment house designs that follow: one, an elevator-type and the other, a walk-up type. These buildings were projected originally for the rebuilding program of Budapest, Hungary. The apartments actually built were modified because of the urgency for residential construction and the economic situation abroad.

How Apartments Are Built

Concrete partitions are poured in forms (or molds) which remain in the construction; molds serve as internal insulation and outside finish. Before concrete is poured, vertical and horizontal reinforcing is inserted in the molds. The molds are expanded gypsum and lime. Concrete in contact with the molds loses its water content and gets rigid immediately, shrinkage being less than in normal concrete construction. Molds are prefabricated in various shapes to permit precise and easy placement of the reinforcing.

Floors are grids of two-way beams with the open spaces being filled by

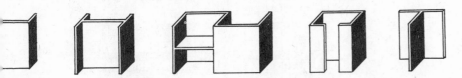

...signed to get high strength and consequent thinness of section using reinforced concrete

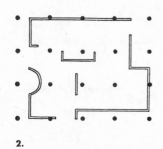

2.

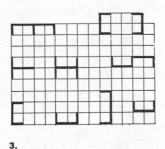

3.

Comparison of conventional framing with cellular construction

1. *The load-bearing wall system utilizes all faculties of the material: bearing capacity, space enclosure and insulation value. Between limits it is still the most economical. But above a certain height, it becomes impractical because of necessary wall thickness. At the same time, its cumbersome nature makes free planning quite difficult*

2. *Skeleton framing yields the essential advantages of economy in floor space, flexible planning and light structure. However, walls function only for space enclosure and insulation. Structurally they are only dead loads*

3. *Scheme of cellular construction. Vertical concrete slabs in various shapes act both as load-bearing elements and walls. They can be shaped, within a certain discipline to the grid, to fit a desired plan. Floors are two-way beams poured monolithically with the partitions. Structure thus works in all three dimensions. Forms may be permanent, providing both insulation and facing*

hollow-core gypsum blocks. First these blocks are laid on formwork, and then concrete for the beams is poured in between. Where partitions are located, the beams are poured monolithically with them.

In a six-storied apartment in Budapest, the load-bearing partitions were built 2 to $3\frac{1}{2}$ in. thick. Spans of the floor grid varied, with 24 ft as maximum.

Care has to be taken in design that the load-bearing partitions are placed in more or less equal "density." Due to the two-way floor grid it is not necessary that they line up. The amount of reinforcing necessary depends on how close partitions are spaced.

Implications for U. S.

Material saving aspects of *cellular* construction should gain added importance in the present economic situation. The feasibility of low cost walk-up apartment buildings in fire-resistant construction should be welcomed by all, including city planners and insurance companies. Elimination of all columns means increased floor area. Reduced depth of floor construction means reduced building height. Lightness of structure means smaller footings. All these spell more economical construction.

Many details of this system need modification and simplification to reduce the amount of hand labor required in its present form. The floor could be designed and built like our present "flat plate" construction or like the two-way concrete joist systems, such as the so-called "Grid System."

Wall sections possibly could be precast in standardized sections, or special steel forms might be developed. The European method of using permanent forms which serve as a finished wall surface could also be well adapted to our needs.

Simplified Design Method

Before general application can be attempted, a simplified method of design acceptable to building codes needs to be developed. This should not be too difficult, with present methods of experimental stress analysis. Recent commercial availability of the photo reflective stress analysis (*Presan*), developed especially for flat slab design, would seem to be adaptable to this type of work. As a matter of fact, it seems very likely that an adapted form of the *cellular* construction should bring about quite a few simplifications in both design and building in reinforced concrete.

ARCHITECTS' DESIGN FOR ELEVATOR-TYPE APARTMENTS

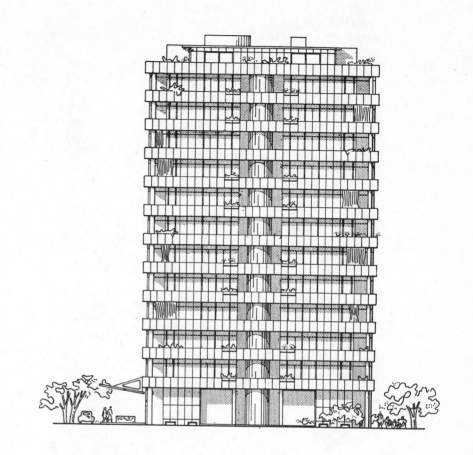

ARCHITECTS' DESIGN FOR WALK-UP-TYPE APARTMENTS

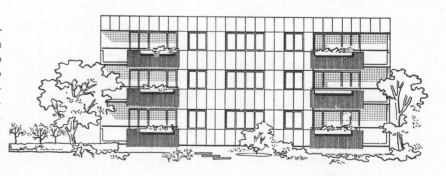

Elevator-type building designed with 12 floors. Four apartments on each floor are symmetrically arranged around the elevator lobby. The fire stairs are located outside the building itself, being accessible from terraces off the kitchens. There are four mechanical cores going through the building, ventilated by a central fan at the top

One module equals 2½ ft

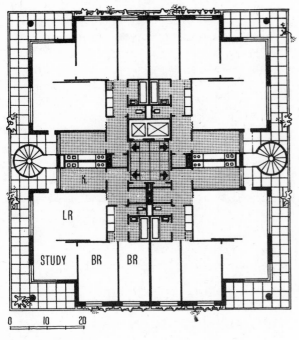

Typical Floor Plan

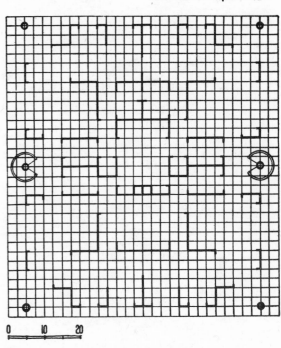

Plan of Load-bearing Partitions Only

Walk-up-type building with three floors. Each floor has two, 2-bedroom type, and two, 1-bedroom type apartments. Service areas are in the interior, and living areas around the edge; mechanical equipment is in two cores. Outside wall area is only 65 per cent of floor area

One module equals 2½ ft

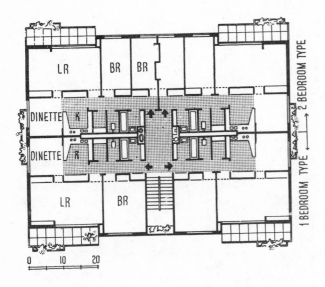

Typical Floor Plan

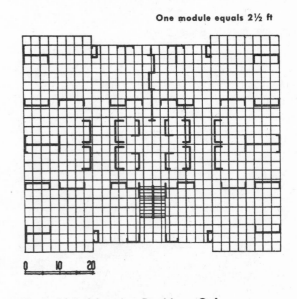

Plan of Load-bearing Partitions Only

ARCHITECTS' DESIGN FOR ELEVATOR-TYPE APARTMENTS

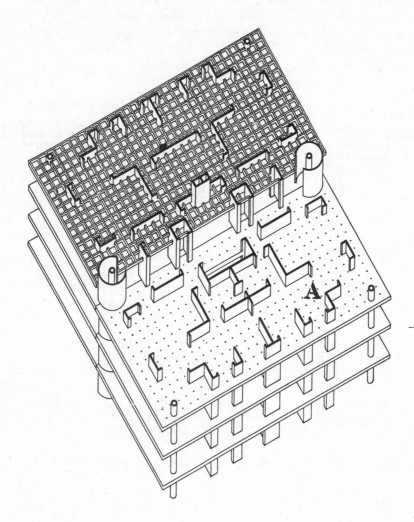

Upper floor in this structural sketch shows the two-way beam grid and how the load-bearing partitions lace through it. In the system as proposed for use in Europe, hollow core gypsum blocks fill in the spaces between the beams. These blocks may be left out to provide space for lighting fixtures. Ceilings are plastered and various types of flooring materials may be placed on top of the blocks. Partition "A" is shown enlarged at right

ARCHITECTS' DESIGN FOR WALK-UP-TYPE APARTMENTS

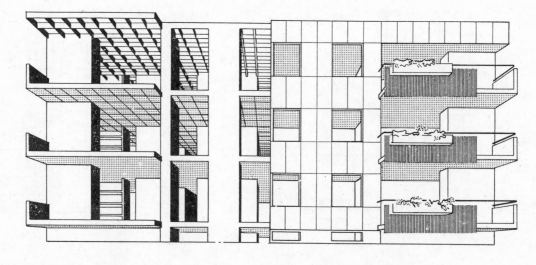

Perspective showing structural and facing elements of construction

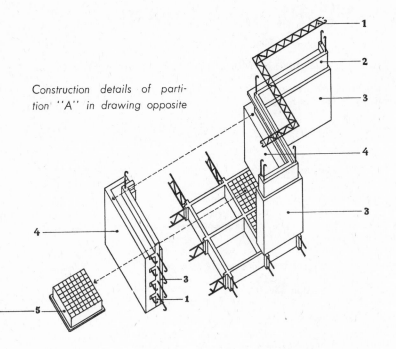

Construction details of partition "A" in drawing opposite

LEGEND

1. reinforcing in the horizontal stiffening rib

2. concrete slab

3. precast exterior form serving as final finish

4. precast interior form serving as insulation

5. hollow core gypsum blocks

Top photo: apartment similar to ones illustrated on foregoing pages, but designed with fewer amenities for lower cost. Middle load-bearing walls are "U" shaped, with horizontal ribs being used as book shelves. Note glazed lighting strips which are easily formed in hollow spaces left in the ceiling. Bottom photo: here the load-bearing walls form cupboards. Spaces between them are filled with movable glass panes; glazed tile is underneath. Outside walls have one row of glass block at top

THIN BRICK WALLS ARE THE ONLY SUPPORT
IN A DESIGN FOR MULTI-STORY BUILDINGS

by Robert L. Davison, Howard T. Fisher & Associates and Clarence B. Monk, Armour Research Foundation

An Architectural Record report on Housing and Home Finance Agency
Research Project No. 1-T-99 with Illinois Institute of Technology

Editors Note: The idea of 6-in. brick walls holding up the concrete floors of a building 10 stories high, or even higher, rather staggers the imagination, but that is the gist of the design presented here. It's not just supposition because much study has been devoted to the principles involved. The ways in which the authors feel such a daring structure will behave under the effects of wind, gravity and earthquake forces are outlined here.

It is beyond the scope of this article to substantiate every premise with a host of formulas and data as would be required for presentation in a technical paper. This is contemplated for the future. Its purpose is to get the core of an idea before you so that the researchers may have the benefit of your thinking.

It is too early to guess just how far reaching this scheme could be. It is not impossible that it might rival the development of the steel skeleton frame. The system is efficient in the use of materials — the walls are used structurally as well as for space separation and sound isolation; but they are, of course, fixed once and for all, and they should be directly in line, one over the other.

In an engineering sense, the system is a reversal in the trend toward more complicated structural systems and methods of analysis. It takes the old fashioned bearing wall and puts it within the structure in such a way that it need not get increasingly thicker the closer it is to the foundation, but remains 6 in. thick for the whole height of the building. Actually the engineering problems of a 10-story building are reduced to those posed by a stack of ten one-story buildings.

"SCR Multi-Story Construction," developed by Structural Clay Products Research Foundation, is based upon the use of the new SCR brick, a modular clay unit with nominal dimensions 6 by 12 in. and three courses to 8 in. (see sketch this page; also see ARCHITECTURAL RECORD, May 1952, p. 214). However, the engineering principles could be applied also to buildings using other types of masonry materials.

FEATURES OF THIS NEW STRUCTURAL SYSTEM:

- Dispenses with the conventional skeleton frame of steel or reinforced concrete

- Employs thin partition walls as the sole vertical structural elements, wholly without the use of steel or other reinforcement

- Takes advantage of the inherent prestressing provided by gravity

- Improves sound isolation within the building

- Permits use of inexpensive spread foundations

- Simplifies construction and eliminates costly engineering and detailing

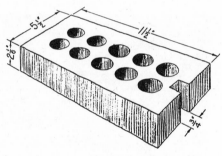

Supporting walls are composed of this new SCR brick having a nominal depth of 6 in.

SIX-INCH THICK partition walls of brick, without any added columns, girders, or reinforcing, can theoretically hold up the floors of an apartment building 10 or more stories high. This is accomplished by setting brick walls between rigid, continuous floor slabs to form a discontinuous stack of stories which are held together by the downward pull of gravity. Wind loads are transmitted from exterior walls to the floor slabs, which in turn transfer them by friction to the bearing partition walls.

Thus, "SCR Multi-Story Construction" will be limited in its use to those types of buildings where repetitive bearing walls occur: apartment buildings, for example, and offices, hospitals and hotels. Plan requirements in buildings such as these can allow the weight of the structure to be sustained on the wall lines, instead of on columns, as in skeleton framing.

This structural system is one of a number being analyzed on a comparative basis by Illinois Institute of Technology under the Housing and Home Finance Agency contract in an effort to improve residential design and construction in multi-story dwellings.

For demonstration purposes we have taken a typical apartment house floor plan (actually the "basic" plan used in the HHFA Research Project described in ARCHITECTURAL RECORD, December, 1951). This plan might be anywhere from 25 to 55 ft wide overall.

To simplify mathematical calculations, the partition walls in the plan have been reduced to a series of transverse bearing partitions (the space between them could range from 9 to 27 ft) buttressed by wing walls which represent corridor, closet and other longitudinal partitions. Although a simple rectangular structure has been assumed, the construction system is not limited to rectangular buildings, and buildings without continuous corridors would prove much stronger.

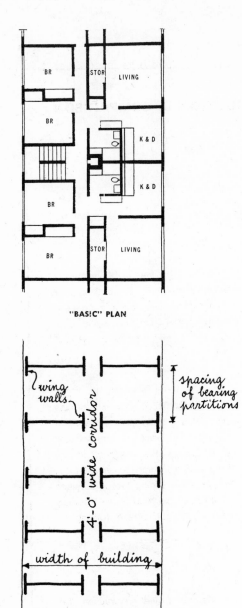

"BASIC" PLAN

wing walls

spacing of bearing partitions

4'-0" wide corridor

width of building

SIMPLIFIED VERSION

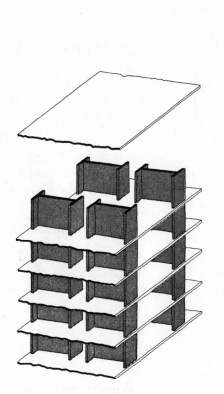

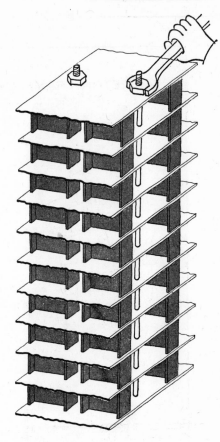

To simplify understanding and analysis of this brick construction system, the "basic" apartment plan used in this research (top left) is idealized into the repetitive series of bearing partitions and wind walls shown at left. In a multi-story building these masonry bearing partitions are interlayered with rigid floor slabs of reinforced concrete (above). Gravity pulls together this stack of floors and bearing walls, so that when subjected to horizontal wind pressure, this structure is analogous to a cantilevered beam prestressed by a long bolt. Below are four types of possible failure investigated

Investigating the building design becomes analogous to investigating a prestressed cantilever beam made up of blocks, gravity being the prestressing force in this case, and wind the load on the beam. It will be necessary to guard against (1) excessive compression within, and bearing between, the walls and floors; (2) opening of the joints between walls and floors; (3) sliding of walls and floors relative to one another; (4) excessive diagonal tension or shearing stress within the walls and floors.

Since the vertically discontinuous brick wall has little strength in tension, it cannot be designed to resist bending forces, but it must resist overturning through dead weight. The deflection in a multi-story building of this type would be due largely to racking (or shear) and would tend to produce a deflection curve the reverse of that normal in skeleton framing (see sketches p.122). The relative horizontal displacement of one story with respect to another is prevented in a

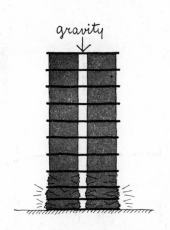

1. excessive compression or bearing

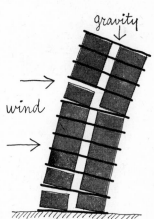

2. opening between walls and floors

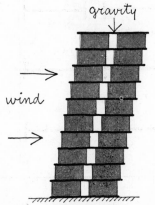

3. sliding of walls and floors

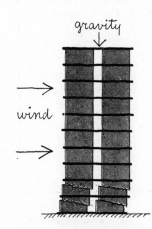

4. excessive diagonal tension

SKELETON FRAME AND BRICK MULTI-STORY CONSTRUCTION: A COMPARISON

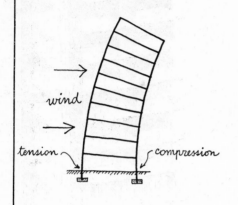

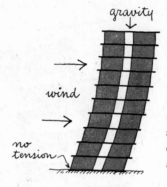

Deflection in the brick multi-story building will be in racking (or shear), and will tend to produce a deflection curve the reverse of that normal in skeleton frame construction

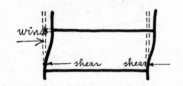

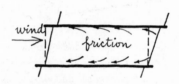

The horizontal displacement of one story relative to the next is prevented in skeleton frame construction by shear across the columns. In the brick wall multi-story construction it is prevented by sliding friction between wall and floors, and by the capacity of the wall itself to resist racking

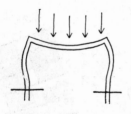

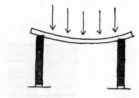

In skeleton frame construction, because of the continuity of horizontal and vertical elements, the columns must participate in bending. In the brick construction, the floors rest on the brick walls but are not tied into them. So the brick walls do not then have to resist bending

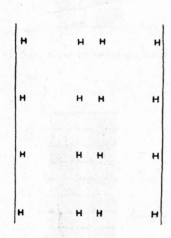

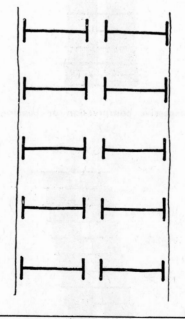

Instead of the point loading typical of skeleton frame construction, the brick walls with their line loading already have their reactions semi-distributed to the soil. In poor soil conditions it would be economical and advisable to use a continuous mat foundation

skeleton frame by shear across the columns; in the brick construction it is prevented by sliding friction between wall and floor, and by the racking capacity of the wall within itself.

Since the resistance of unreinforced masonry walls to bending is limited, it is wise to have the floor system rest on the walls but not tied into them, so that deflections in the floor will not cause the walls to participate in flexure. Theoretically, floors not continuous with the vertical building elements should be thicker than those that are. But because of code requirements or constructional limitations, floors generally are approximately 4 in. thick, in spite of thinner theoretical requirements. In practice, then, the advantages of continuity between horizontal and vertical elements may not be realized.

How far the ponderous weight of the superstructure will clamp the ends of the floor slab to the walls in the lower stories, remains to be investigated. It is important that parts bearing on the walls should not introduce bending into them.

Strength properties and analysis of SCR brick walls

Development of the construction system described in this article has been founded on the strength characteristics of SCR brick walls for home construction. Initially, predictions of wall strength were based on tests of 8 in. solid masonry walls performed at the National Bureau of Standards and reported in *Building Materials and Structures, Report No. 109.* Recommended allowable loads on such walls are summarized in the table at right.

At present, static tests as prescribed by ASTM are being conducted at the Armour Research Foundation to determine experimentally the strength of SCR brick walls for home construction. Indications to date are that the results agree favorably with the allowable loads asumed above.

What factors will determine whether non-reinforced brick walls will be used in multi-story construction as the structural framework? They appear to have a sizable bearing capacity, a useful amount of resistance to racking, and a dead weight which can be turned to advantage. The limitation of non-reinforced brick walls in bending must be faced frankly, and the bearing walls so positioned in the structure that their bending participation will be small.

The bearing capacity of 6-in. brick walls is sufficient to sustain apartment

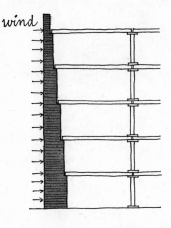
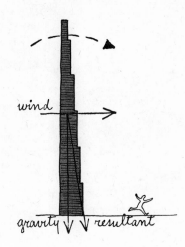

GRAVITY BRICK WALL CONSTRUCTION

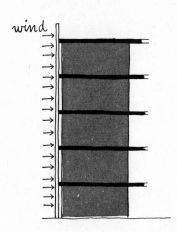

SCR BRICK WALL MULTI-STORY CONSTRUCTION

In old-style gravity brick wall construction (which reached its peak in 1891 in the Monadnock Building, Chicago) the exterior wall is designed to resist wind the whole height of the building. The exterior wall also helps to carry the floor load, but the floors give the wall little help in resisting wind load. In the brick wall system of multi-story construction, the exterior walls deliver wind load directly to the floor system at 8 ft intervals, thus minimizing any horizontal loading of the exterior walls

Wall	Compressive Load (height 8'-0") kips/ft	Transverse Load (span 7'-6") lbs/ft	Racking Load (8'-0" by 8'-0" spec.) kips/ft	Wt. lb/ft
AA, high strength brick; cement mortar; excellent workmanship	99.6	46	2.50	96.00
AB, medium-strength brick; cement-lime mortar; commercial workmanship	21.0	15	2.50	73.90
AC, medium-strength brick; cement-lime mortar; excellent workmanship	36.2	32	2.50	78.90
From these tests and other published experiments the following predicted strength was prognósticated:				
SCR brick	40.0	20.0 (8'-0" span)	2.0	45.00

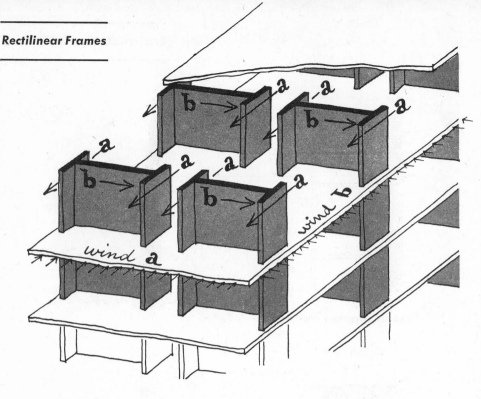

Horizontal loading due to wind, from whatever direction it may come, is always transformed, in this construction system, into a racking load (which brick walls can well resist) on the bearing partitions (shown resisting wind b), or on the wing walls (shown resisting wind a) which also add useful buttressing

The curtain wall pilasters become identified with the wing walls of the brick bearing partitions. To provide lateral support and prevent buckling, these pilaster walls should be tied into each floor slab. Three additional ties, between one floor slab and the next, would be preferable for help in resisting wind suction or outward acceleration from earthquake

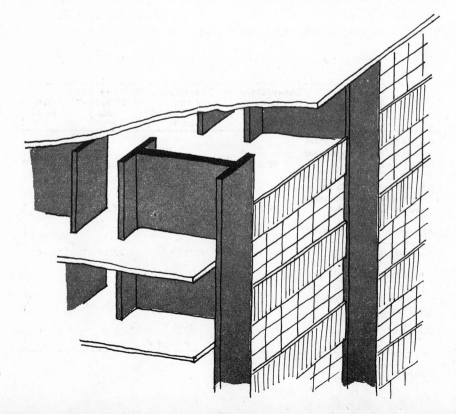

buildings as high as 15 stories even when the increase in pressure, caused by wind, on the leeward side of the building is taken into account. While 40 kips per ft may seem like a tremendous load for such a slender wall, tests indicate that in heights up to 8 ft, there is no tendency for the wall to buckle — failure is a matter of crushing. Naturally, a 6 in. wall, 15 stories high would buckle under its own weight; however, in the proposed structure the floor provides lateral support every 8 feet.

Assuming that SCR brick walls can sustain an allowable bending force of 20 lb per sq ft over a span of 8 ft, they would appear to be suited for use as curtain walls. Theoretically, they could sustain a 75–80 mph wind with a safety factor of $2\frac{1}{2}$.

Instead of the whole exterior wall being designed to resist wind the full height of the building, as in old-style gravity wall construction, the exterior walls deliver their wind reactions directly to the floor system at 8 ft intervals, thus minimizing horizontal loading on the brick wall.

The floor system must deliver its edge forces from wind loading to the transverse bearing walls which are to be the major structural masonry. It is assumed that friction between floor and wall will be sufficient to transfer this load; for multi-story structures such as we are discussing here, the coefficient of friction of masonry on concrete (assumed to be 0.50) is sufficient to prevent sliding.

Actually, the horizontal loading from wind has been introduced into the major structural masonry as a racking load. SCR brick walls are assumed qualified to resist racking loads of 2 kips per ft.* They can therefore resist the accumulated horizontal load that occurs on the bottom story from wind reactions introduced at each story level above. Since horizontal loads from any direction must be allowed for, longitudinal walls (idealized here as wing walls) must also participate in racking resistance. The buttressing action of these longitudinal walls is especially important for earthquake resistance.

Since this scheme consists of a discontinuous stacking of floor and wall elements, is there any danger that the upper stories would tip, or the whole building overturn? In the case of uniform wind pressure, static forces upon the structure are such that the whole

* The racking test for walls used in home construction under ASTM specifications doesn't simulate accurately the behavior in a multistory building. Further verification of this figure is planned.

building would overturn before the upper stories would tip over to the leeward side. Resistance to overturning is achieved through dead weight. Provided there is sufficient dead weight to prevent any tension at the base of the building on the windward side, there will be no danger of overturning.

As shown above, loads are delivered to the main transverse bearing partitions through the floor slab. Dead and live loads are transmitted through bearing. Horizontal wind and earthquake loads are transmitted through friction and racking.

Exterior Walls

Before considering the interior walls, something should be said about structural action of the exterior walls. The wind reaction of the curtain wall is delivered to the floor slab.

The curtain wall sustains its own weight. This is carried through pilaster walls to the foundation. Where windows puncture a curtain wall, the spandrel from window head to window sill may be considered as an integral spandrel beam if the lower courses of masonry are reinforced, making a reinforced brick masonry beam. The spandrel from window head to window sill is deep enough — when reinforced — for spans up to 27 ft. The curtain wall should be securely enough tied into the floor slab to withstand outward suction pressure of at least 10 lb per sq ft and, in earthquake areas outward accelerations of at least 15 lb per sq ft.

The reactions of the integral spandrel beam within the curtain wall are to be sustained by the pilaster wall. Since the accumulated dead weight of curtain walls is relatively light, a minimum pilaster width of 3 ft will be sufficient for buildings up to fifteen stories with spandrel spans up to 27 ft. The pilaster wall should be tied at least every 8 ft (at the floor slab) to provide lateral support against buckling. Three additional ties attaching the pilaster to the partition walls (between each floor slab and the next) would be preferable, to help in resisting wind suction or outward accelerations due to earthquake.

Floor Slabs

While floors are not our primary concern here, they must of necessity be discussed since their weight must be sustained by the walls. To predict the loads on the bearing walls, the dead weight of the floor system as a function of the span has been computed. Designs to date indicate that relatively long reinforced concrete slabs will resist stress requirements.

Engineers, however, are reluctant to design slabs solely on the basis of stress considerations. In addition to normal deflection there is experimental evidence to indicate that long, thin, reinforced concrete slabs will creep measurably under long sustained loads.

To guard against this possibility an arbitrary limitation of an L/D ratio of 40 was imposed on this design. The minimum weight (as determined by stress) was used to compute frictional and stability limitations; the maximum weight (determined by deflection) was used to compute bearing or equivalent static earthquake loading. In other words, that floor slab weight was used which most severely limited the design.

A live load of 40 lb per sq ft has been assumed in all calculations. Requirements for corridor spaces, dead weight of non-load-bearing partitions, storage areas, etc., have been assumed allowed for in the following manner: Because it is improbable that all floors will be loaded simultaneously, it is customary under most building codes to reduce the live load on vertical elements; therefore, based on the New York, Chicago and San Francisco building codes, our calculations use a reduction factor of 65 per cent for all stories.

Ideally the floor slabs should be so designed as to behave as rigid plates. Where breaks at corridors or doorways occur through the main transverse partitions, the floor plate or slab must not be so flexible that the building acts in resisting horizontal loads as two separate parallel structures, separated by the gap at the opening. The floor must be stiff enough to ensure the full building width will act as a whole in resisting lateral load. This assumption has been made in the graphical forecast of story heights to follow. If the floor is not sufficiently stiff, then in the extreme case of continuous corridors on each floor the predicted story heights may be reduced to roughly 50 per cent.

How Tall Can the Building Be?

A statical analysis of the 6-in. brick walls was made to predict how many of the 8 ft-6 in. stories could be stacked up safely, depending on the spacing of the main transverse bearing partitions and the depth of the building. This prediction was based on the following investigations:

1. The maximum bearing or compressive load on the bottom story.
2. The stabilizing effect of the dead weight against tipping of the building from wind.
3. The frictional force under each story.
4. The racking load on the bottom story due to wind.

The bearing capacity of the brick walls must resist both the vertical dead and live loads plus the additional stresses resulting from wind or other horizontal loading. The limiting condition for stability has been set by permitting no tension at the windward base. Since the total wind load increases in the same proportion as the dead load, progressing from top to bottom of a building, the coefficient of friction required under each story is theoretically the same; that is, the frictional resistance does not depend on the number of stories. Racking was assumed to be a function only of the wind load and depth of building.

Results of the above investigation have been summarized in the graphs on page 126. All graphs allow for an arbitrary choice of building width and spacing of transverse bearing partitions. On the extreme left of the large graph is the boundary of the region of insufficient friction. Choices falling into this region should not be allowed because the statical friction under each story would be exceeded, allowing it to slide. Fortunately, this region is small and away from the usual building proportion.

Bays ranging from 9 to 27 ft have been considered and building widths ranging from 25 to 55 ft. Each curve is the limit of height for a particular set of dimensions, in terms of 8 ft-6 in. stories, to which the building may go before exceeding (1) the bearing capacity of the walls, (2) the stability of the building, or (3) the racking strength of the bearing partitions. Ideally, the most efficient use of material would be when all three curves coincide, so that the limiting conditions are reached simultaneously. However, based on the assumptions made above, bearing and stability are the two controlling factors. It appears that racking does not govern story heights within the building proportions considered here.

The large graph, therefore, is a composite of bearing and stability curves. The stability and bearing surface intersect along line "I". To the left and below this line stability controls; to the right and above this line bearing controls. As an example, if a building were 32 ft deep, with transverse bearing partitions spaced 12 ft on center, then the maximum height of the building would be about 15 stories. It would be 15 stories as controlled by stability, but 18

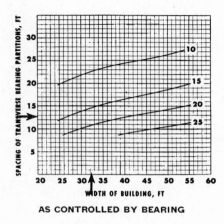

AS CONTROLLED BY BEARING

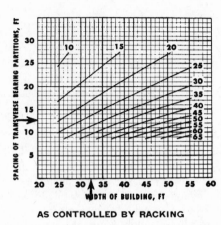

AS CONTROLLED BY RACKING

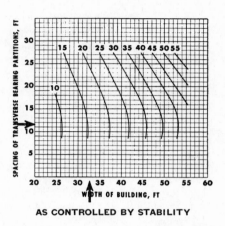

AS CONTROLLED BY STABILITY

Statical analysis of the brick wall multi-story construction system is summarized in the large graph at right (a combination of the smaller ones above). It will be seen that, for a building 32 ft deep, with transverse bearing partitions 12 ft on center, the maximum permissible height would be about 15 stories. If bearing alone controlled, the limit would be 18 stories, if racking controlled, it would be 27 stories.

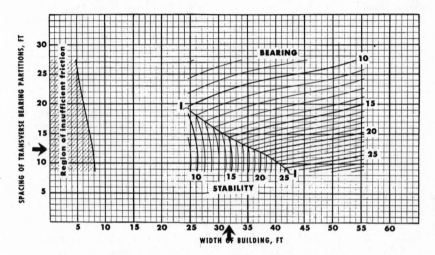

ALLOWABLE NUMBER OF 8 FT 6 IN. STORIES IN TYPICAL MULTI-STORY APARTMENT

stories as controlled by bearing, or 27 stories as controlled by racking.

While exact dynamic analyses are most tedious and difficult, West Coast building codes provide the designers with a method for computing horizontal loads which may be applied to the structure statically to produce equivalent seismic effects. Based on the San Francisco Building Code, 1952, and the Uniform Building Code, 1943, an equivalent static analysis was made similar to the above procedure for the 32 ft deep building with bearing partitions 12 ft on center. At the bottom of this page is a tabular summary of results showing the allowable number of 8 ft 6 in. stories:

The unusually high value for racking under the San Francisco code is due to the decidedly lower accelerations provided for in the lower stories. Since earthquake accelerations are more severe in the top stories, the minimum width of building must be 10.6 ft (San Francisco Code) in order to prevent the top story from sliding, as compared to 7.9 ft under static wind load. Vibrations

of the walls themselves are a matter of future study.

Foundations Simplified

This multi-story system simplifies foundation problems where soils do not have much bearing capacity. Instead of the point loading typical of skeleton frame construction, the load is distributed along the partition wall line.

Since continuous footings underneath the main bearing partitions are required, and since, in most apartment buildings, partition walls will be spaced 10–15 ft apart, it is calculated that, with poor soil conditions, the footing of one wall would spread almost half way toward

the adjoining wall. In such cases it would seem advisable to use a continuous mat foundation. This would also provide bearing for the longitudinal walls which, although not receiving gravity loads, must resist horizontal loading from any direction.

Calculations indicate that if a continuous mat is placed underneath a 10-story SCR building, the load intensity on the soil varies between 1000 and 2000 lb per sq ft. Any but the most adverse soil conditions would be satisfactory for this load.

Historical Perspective

The use of load-bearing masonry in

Limiting Condition	Static Loading	NUMBER OF STORIES Earthquake Loading	
		San Francisco Code	Uniform Building Code
Bearing	18	18	13
Stability	15	15	8
Racking	27	71	11

high multi-story buildings, has been practically abandoned since 1891, completion date of the Monadnock Building in Chicago. The exterior masonry bearing walls in this 16-story building were proportioned by a rule of thumb dating back to the Renaissance: a minimum wall thickness of 12 in., with an increase of 4 in. for every story below the top. The result was that the walls of this building measure 72 in. at the base.

No wonder that the skeleton frame — launched to fame in 1883 by William Jenny's Home Insurance Building in Chicago framed in cast and wrought iron — seemed the ideal structural system for building owners who were already sensitive to the amount of expensive real estate occupied by the structural frame, the square feet that paid no rent.

Jenny's creation was made possible by the contemporary development of iron and steel. The application of this new material was aided by the work of bridge engineers whose experience in building metal structures dated back at least 100 years. Laboratory material testing was now possible. Steel fashioned into strong machines tested itself.

The greatest impetus to structural engineering in recent years has been given by the aircraft industry, where the weight-strength ratio is a maddening challenge for precise structural analysis and efficient structural systems. Complete dependence on the beam, strut, and truss soon gave way to the monocoque system, i.e. the skin, or fuselage of the structure, was called upon to be force-resistant. Creators of automobile bodies are aware of this monocoque principle.

Is the building industry going in this same direction? Rumblings are heard. We speak of rigid diaphragm floors (the flat plate). Cellular, or box-frame, construction of walls — though limited — is a reality. Theoretical tools for analyzing plates, shells, membranes — though tedious at times — are available. Will the contemporary skeleton frame give way to a technique of integrated walls and floors? This multi-story system is a step in this direction.

Masonry construction need no longer be shackled by unreasonable factors of safety. Professor I. O. Baker's "Treatise on Masonry Construction", which had a profound influence on the Chicago Building Code during the reconstruction period after the Great Fire of 1871, recommended a safety factor of ten. This extreme caution was representative of masonry practice throughout the coun-

try at the time when the skeleton steel frame was evolving. This position is not tenable today. The minimum safety factor suggested for unreinforced masonry by the National Bureau of Standards is two and one-half.

Application to Apartments

Almost any common type of apartment plan is well suited to this construction system. The strip plan, typical of walk-up apartments, was selected for our research study because it permitted simple analysis and comparison of different materials and construction methods. Such a plan could be used for three-story garden apartments, or, by piling three such garden apartment units one on top of the other and connecting them with a skip-stop elevator, an efficient high-rise building results (see ARCHITECTURAL RECORD, December 1951, page 138).

Construction Details

Construction details for bearing partitions, exterior walls, insulation, windows, doors, etc. are identical for 1, 3, 10 and 15-story buildings. The reason is that the thickness of all bearing walls is constant throughout the height of the structure.

In cooperation with the Structural Clay Products Institute and the Structural Clay Products Research Foundation, Howard T. Fisher & Associates have developed comprehensive details for use of SCR brick for single-story residences. These details take care of corners, windows, doors, lintels, sills, insulation, through-wall flashing, wiring, lath and plaster, or dry wall finish, etc. and are fully applicable to this multi-story system.

Additional details, especially those required for fireproof floors, stair wells, and fireproof doors to public halls, are now being developed.

Exterior Walls

In contrast to traditional masonry construction, the exterior walls do not carry any floor loads. (The end walls are the single exception; they may be considered as insulated bearing partitions, with window openings kept to a minimum.) The exterior walls are not true curtain walls because they are not supported by the floors.

In some earlier versions of this construction system, the exterior walls were recessed between the floor slabs. However, the pilaster sections were designed to carry the exterior wall load. The dominant reason for setting the exterior wall outside the floor slabs was to reduce the heat loss caused by through-

conduction from floors and bearing partitions.

The space between the edge of the floor slab and the exterior wall is filled with a non-combustible insulating material, which will also prevent the passage of sound and fire.

It is suggested that the inside face of the exterior walls be furred out on 2 by 2 in. wood strips. This prevents moisture penetration, facilitates installation of electric wiring, and allows for 1 in. blanket insulation if this is desired. The furring strips are quickly and easily attached by impaling them on special staples in furring clips which are installed by the mason when laying the wall.

There is a wide choice of insulating materials and plaster finishes for use on such a furred wall. The completed wall may have a U-factor ranging from .15 Btu (1 in. blanket insulation, plus $\frac{3}{8}$ in. gypsum lath, plus $\frac{3}{4}$ in. vermiculite plaster) to .25 Btu. ($\frac{1}{2}$ in. gypsum board with aluminum foil back).

Exposed Brick Interior Walls

How far it might be desirable to leave the brick partition walls exposed will probably depend upon the location of the wall, the skill of the architect and the variety (size, color, finish, etc.) of the bricks at his disposal; also whether the apartments are subsidized units for low-income families, or competitive, privately-owned rental units.

For kitchens and bathrooms, glazed brick with thin mortar joints would be preferable to plaster, from the standpoint of appearance and sanitary finish; also it would be lower both in first cost and maintenance cost.

Whether brick or plaster were used in the bedroom hall and in closets would make no significant difference to the tenants. The architect's decision in these cases might depend upon whether such walls were required to be bearing partitions.

We do not know what the reaction of local housing authorities would be to apartment designs using exposed brick for interior walls, in living and bed rooms. But the Chicago Housing Authority, who are interested in this HHFA research project, have indicated that they would accept unplastered brick throughout, if it would reduce construction and maintenance costs.

Fire prevention experts are particularly eager for a surface such as exposed brick which does not require painting; for paint can be the means of spreading flash fires.

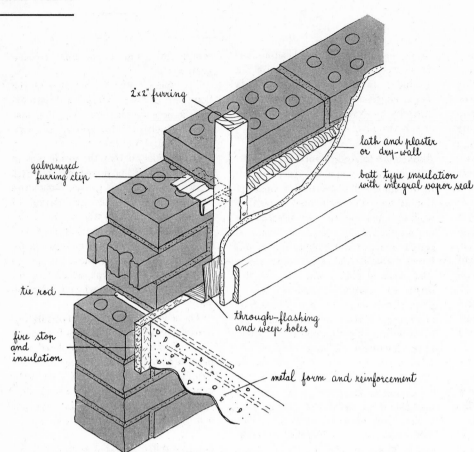

2×2" furring

galvanized
furring clip

tie rod

fire stop
and
insulation

lath and plaster
or dry-wall

batt type insulation
with integral vapor seal

through-flashing
and weep holes

metal form and reinforcement

Suggested construction detail at joint between floor slab and outside wall in the brick wall story construction. Floor and wall are connected at intervals by tie rods, but they are structurally independent and separated one from the other by a layer of insulation. The furred wall shown (U value, including brick, 0.15) is but one of many possibilities

Fire Resistance

Fire tests have not yet been run on a 6 in. brick wall comparable to one made of SCR brick. However, it seems probable, by interpolation of test results gained from 4 in. and 8 in. masonry walls, that the SCR brick wall, unplastered, will have a 2 hour rating, and with furring, lath and plaster on one side a rating of over 4 hours.

Sound Isolation

A high degree of sound isolation is a useful by-product. Theoretical analysis indicates that the 6-in. brick wall without plaster should have a sound attenuation of slightly more than 45 decibels. This is considered satisfactory for dividing walls between one apartment and the next, and it is far above minimum requirements for the partition walls within each apartment.

Construction with SCR Brick

One outstanding advantage possessed by the SCR construction system, when compared with most other new systems, is the immediate and nation-wide availability of the units employed. No special equipment or experience is required for installation; SCR bricks can be laid by any bricklayer.

Resistance to Shock

How would a 10- or 15-story apartment house, built with unreinforced walls of brick behave if subjected to earthquake or atomic blast? Probably the best method of analysis available to the practicing engineer is the use of equivalent static loading, as required by the San Francisco Building Code. Exterior wall bearing masonry buildings at Hiroshima and Nagasaki showed evidence of total collapse. It must be remembered, however, that conventional practice has been primarily to place the major structural masonry on the outside of the building where it is most vulnerable to the bending effects of blasts, wind, or other horizontal loading. Seldom have masonry structures been deliberately engineered to take full advantage of the racking resistance of brick walls in withstanding horizontal loads.

Besides using the dead weight of the brick wall to stabilize the structure and provide useful frictional forces, we position the walls in a multi-story structure so that they will participate in bearing and racking without severe transverse effects.

Conclusion

Before this construction system can be recommended for actual use, certain additional tests must be conducted, and it is assumed that it would be first tried in numerous smaller structures before larger projects are undertaken. The Structural Clay Products Research Foundation intends to continue theoretical and experimental development with the hope that a pilot building can be erected in cooperation with the Housing and Home Finance Agency and one of the municipal housing authorities.

An Architectural Record report on Housing and Home Finance Agency Research Project No. 1-T-99 with Illinois Institute of Technology*

* This article is based on a progress report on Housing and Home Finance Agency's Research Project No. 1-T-99 being conducted under contract by Illinois Institute of Technology, Prof. E. I. Fiesenheiser, Project Director; Howard T. Fisher & Associates, Inc., Architects and Industrial Designers, Subcontractor; Chicago Housing Authority, Collaborator.

The construction system presented here is a development of the Sturctural Clay Products Research Foundation, Robert B. Taylor, Research Director. It is the result of that organization's cooperative participation in advancing the research objectives of HHFA Project No. 1-T-99. The research and development work was performed for, and at the sole expense of, the Structural Clay Products Research Foundation by Howard T. Fisher & Associates, Inc. and Armour Research Foundation of Illinois Institute of Technology. The basic concept was developed by Robert L. Davison in September 1950. Formulation of an engineering philosophy was undertaken by Clarence B. Monk in September 1951, based upon the use of "SCR Brick" (Registered Trademark SCPRF: Patents Pending).

The accuracy of all statement or interpretations is solely the responsibility of the authors. Statements may be altered by further investigation.

PLEATED ASBESTOS ROOF FOR LOW-COST HOUSING

Architect Alvaro Ortega of the UN Technical Assistance Board specializes in developing building techniques that use local materials, labor and manufacturing facilities. In the project shown here, locally-made asbestos-cement pipe is turned into structural channels for low cost housing in Guatemala City

In the investigation carried out by UN expert Ortega in collaboration with the Asbestos-Cement Industry of Guatemala, 12-in. diameter, high pressure asbestos-cement pipe made on the machinery at left is cut in halves which, while still fresh, are pressed into a galvanized metal form (right)

Resulting channels are 21 ft long, 8 in. deep, 15 in. wide at the bottom and 26 in. wide at the top. In the ⅓ in. (8 mm.) thickness selected for production, they weigh slightly less than 15 lb (67 kg), and can easily be handled by two men. They are set in place without cranes— or even stepladders—by resting one end on a wall and lifting the other end onto the wall opposite

Rigid enough to span 20 ft (5 meters) without intermediate support, the channels can also be cantilevered for added protection from sun and rain. (Those shown at left cantilever about 4 ft, those at right about 12 ft). Because the material is produced under high pressure and formed in metal molds, the channels have a dense, smooth surface that needs no interior finish or exterior waterproofing

The final stage of the exploratory project was the load testing of the channels. Under a uniform load imposed by filling the channel trough with water (left), a ½-in. thick test member deflected about 0.8 in. at center-span. Under a concentrated load of 500 lb (right), it deflected about 0.6 in.

Blue Cross-Blue Shield Headquarters Office Building, Boston   **I. B. M. Office Building, Pittsburgh**

THE RETURN OF THE BEARING WALL

by William J. LeMessurier, Structural Engineer   *Wm. J. LeMessurier & Associates, Boston*

A careful observer of the multi-story buildings built in the last five years will have noticed a change in the structure of exterior walls. The new appearance is marked by the deliberate use of closely-spaced columns which give a finely-grained structural scale, and often produce a façade enriched with high relief. In its most developed form, this kind of wall construction becomes a lacework of diagonal columns and horizontal spandrels which simultaneously support vertical and horizontal loads.

The closely tuned ear can detect new phrases in the architectural jargon describing these constructions; "load bearing mullions," "stressed-skin walls," and other descriptions. What is going on? Is this new departure merely an anti-curtain wall reaction, or is there a logic behind this evolving new form? A look at

the operating structural principles may help provide an answer.

Historical Perspective

For several millenia man built the walls of his permanent buildings with masonry—creating a continuous surface interrupted only by those openings necessary for entrance and light. The masonry surface kept out wind, water and fire; supported the floors and roofs; and, last but not least, resisted those forces causing racking and overturning of the whole building. Large openings in masonry walls were only possible when spanned with arches. Even when the metal skeleton frame was first employed in the 19th century, it was used with exterior walls of masonry built in the traditional way. But as the pressure for higher buildings grew, the masonry bearing

wall was abandoned and the complete skeleton frame made its appearance in Chicago, in the late 1800's.

The most characteristic feature of the steel skeleton, as used for multi-story buildings, is its organization into bays of roughly square dimensions which can be added together in a cellular order to produce buildings of any size. Since enclosing vertical surfaces are not an integral part of this skeleton, a secondary structure, the curtain wall, has been used to terminate interior space.

The concept of structural organization by framed bays is so pervasive that architectural form is often strait-jacketed. It may be well to look for other conceptual approaches to structural organization.

In order to clearly understand our terms we shall define two concepts. *A bearing frame* is a vertical plane containing columns and girders which supports loads applied in its own plane and in which the columns have a spacing established by functional requirements. *A bearing wall* is a vertical structure which supports loads applied in its own plane, and in which the elements have a spacing established by structural requirements.

Multi-story buildings may be considered as an assembly of horizontal floor and roof planes combined with vertical bearing frames and/or bearing walls. If we think of the exterior plane as a bearing wall, then what are the structural requirements which establish column spacings? If window openings are variable the determining factor will be structural efficiency.

It will be shown later that the most efficient column spacings for steel within a bearing wall system will range from one-third to one times the story height for usual loads and member proportions. This conclusion may be extended to include reinforced concrete and wood systems as well.

Implications

Considered as bearing wall structures a series of new buildings make very good structural sense. A few examples taken from current practice illustrate the point. The Blue-Cross Blue-Shield building in Boston has exterior columns at alternate spacings of 5 ft and 10 ft. These close spacings eliminate the need for a deep spandrel and allow a total structural floor depth of 17 in. even though the span behind the wall is 34 ft. The new C.B.S. building in New York designed by the late Eero Saarinen has wide exterior columns spaced at 10 ft on center, resulting in alternating 5-ft windows and 5-ft columns. This design is especially well suited to reinforced concrete and makes possible a great height which would be impractical with large exterior bays. The bearing wall appears in its traditional form surrounding the interior core and providing support to the one-way floor systems.

Perhaps one of the clearest illustrations of the modern bearing wall is the 33 Rue Croulebarbe building in Paris, designed by Albert, Boileau, and Henri-Labourdette. The exterior walls are framed by steel pipe columns at 5-ft centers with a wide flange steel spandrel between. The

spandrel, because of its short span, is only 4-in. deep and is encased in the 6-in. cast-in-place floor slab. Two interior bearing walls are similar in construction to the exterior walls, except that diagonal bracing is added. The same bracing appears in the exterior side walls where it becomes an important architectural feature. By including diagonal bracing, the end wall structure of the 33 Rue Croulebarbe building completely satisfies our definition since it can resist loads applied in any direction in its own plane.

Examples

Two American buildings which use bearing walls with great imagination are alike in having diagonal members to carry gravity loads as well as lateral loads. The American Cement building designed by Daniel, Mann, Johnson and Mendenhall uses sculptured precast X units to form a true bearing wall with great rigidity in its own plane. This wall gathers all vertical and lateral loads and carries them down to a deep girder at the base of the tower. Like the C.B.S.

building by Saarinen, the floors have a one-way span back to the interior core. A similar scheme in structural steel is being used in the I.B.M. building in Pittsburgh.

A special problem of the bearing wall arises at the base of the building. Having established a tightly-scaled, highly-efficient system, how can it be designed to provide ground-level openings of monumental scale? That such interruption of the system is indefensible in purely economic terms should be obvious. And Saarinen has eloquently shown that the unbroken structural system can yield a design of great power. But for both esthetic and practical reasons, an open base may be desirable.

Paul Rudolph's Blue-Cross building solves the problem by collecting the column loads in pairs. In principle, this scheme is very simple and efficient. The Brunswick building by Skidmore, Owings and Merrill has a gigantic spandrel girder above the ground floor to carry the loads from a bearing wall.

Further, an economic study of these structures will show that con-

Top photos: American Cement Building, Los Angeles

Bottom photos: 33 Rue Croulebarbe, Paris   *(l'architecture d'aujourd'hui photos)*

C. B. S. Headquarters Building, New York City

Brunswick Building, Chicago

centrating the effort of spanning a large ground floor bay is distinctly advantageous to the spanning that bay in every floor.

The steel structure of the I.B.M. building exploits the modern bearing wall itself to solve the open base problem. By taking advantage of high strength steels the diffused floor and wind loads are gathered to eight points at the ground. The dramatic result shows the design freedom yielded by abandoning the framed bay concept.

To understand the full advantage of its walls, the I.B.M. building must be studied in three dimensions. Since the wall efficiently supports loads applied at any point in its own plane, freedom of floor system design was possible. An optimum floor system of steel beams at 9-ft centers has been used to span 54 ft to the core. The beams support a composite steel and concrete deck which carries lateral loads through diaphragm action to the exterior bearing walls.

Future Potential
What are the future possibilities of the bearing wall? A most likely development, as soon as building codes modernize their treatment of

masonry, will be the resurgence of brick as a structural material. Research progress in high-strength mortars is already at the point where thin, efficient masonry bearing walls may be used for high-rise buildings. In reinforced concrete, greater use of the slip-form method of construction to provide load-bearing exterior walls as well as interior cores can be foreseen.

The practicality of closely spaced steel columns has been greatly increased by the new specification of the American Institute of Steel Construction. In designs where columns are not required to resist lateral loads, the column efficiency factor, K_c, may be reduced up to 75 per cent by providing rigid connections between columns and spandrels. In addition, high-strength steels may be used to keep dimensions more nearly constant as loads accumulate.

Perhaps the most valuable result of reconsidering the structural function of exterior walls will be the restoration of their role as bracing elements for wind and earthquake in tall buildings. Construction in the form of large framed bays with rigid connections is the most inefficient way to resist lateral loads. And since

high efficiency of structural form for purposes of strength is always accompanied by maximum rigidity, the use of rigid bearing walls will improve the structural performance of buildings.

Calculating Column Spacing
Figure 1 shows an idealized bearing wall with story height of h, a column spacing of L, and a uniform load of w/ft applied at each floor. For any given materials, story height h, and load intensity w, there will be an optimum value of L to give the least total material in the wall. As the value of L increases the girder bending moments increase, and the total amount of girder material increases. But an increasing value of L will result in fewer, more heavily loaded columns so that the total amount of column material will decrease. For any situation a minimum value may be found.

Let us see what magnitudes of spacing result in the case of a bearing wall built of steel with typical floor loads. The amount of material per foot in a steel beam designed for 20,000 psi stress may be shown to be:

$$\text{weight/ft} = B = (M)^{2/3} \, 2.42 \times K_b$$

where M is the bending moment

in foot-kips and K_b is a constant depending on the proportions of the beam. For the economical rolled wide flange shapes K_b is about .70. For a solid square $K_b = 3.30$.

The total material in a steel column of height h feet carrying a load of P kips may be shown to be:*

$$C = \frac{P h}{5} + .014 \ K_c \ h^3$$

where K_c is a constant depending on the proportions of the column. For typical wide-flange steel columns $K_c = 12$.

If these two equations are combined, taking $P = wL$ the total material per foot =

$$B + \frac{C}{L} = \left[\frac{wL^2}{8}\right]^{2/3} 2.42 \ K_b$$
$$+ \frac{wL \ h}{5L} + \frac{.014 K_c h^3}{L} = lbs/ft$$

The second term is seen to be independent of L so that the equation may be used to find a minimum value regardless of the number stories. A minimum value exists when

$$L = .097 \left[\frac{K_c}{K_b}\right]^{3/7} h^{9/7} \left[\frac{8}{w}\right]^{2/7}$$

Figure 2 gives values of K_c, K_b, and the ratio K_c/K_b for various shapes. A low value of K_c or K_b indicates high structural efficiency. A low value of K_c/K_b indicates high relative column efficiency. Figure 3 shows curves giving values of L for various values of K_c/K_b and two values of w.

Lateral Loads

Although diagonal bracing is the

* based on allowable axial stress
$= 17,000 \ psi - .485 \left(\frac{L}{r}\right)^2$

I. B. M. BUILDING, PITTSBURGH
Architects: Curtis and Davis
and Associated Architects and Engineers
Structural Engineers:
Worthington, Skilling, Helle & Jackson

BLUE CROSS—BLUE SHIELD
HEADQUARTERS OFFICE BUILDING, BOSTON
Associated Architects: Paul Rudolph;
Anderson, Beckwith and Haible
Structural Engineers:
Goldberg, LeMessurier and Associates

AMERICAN CEMENT BUILDING, LOS ANGELES
Architects and Engineers:
Daniel, Mann, Johnson & Mendenhall

33 RUE CROULEBARBE, PARIS
Architects: E. Albert, R. Boileau,
J. Henri-Labourdette
Structural Engineer: J. L. Sarf

C. B. S. HEADQUARTERS BUILDING, NEW YORK
Architects: Eero Saarinen and Associates
Structural Engineer: Paul Weidlinger

BRUNSWICK BUILDING, CHICAGO
Architects and Engineers:
Skidmore, Owings & Merrill

most efficient way to resist lateral forces, many structures depend on joint rigidity or frame action for lateral strength. In a frame such as Figure 1 the optimum column spacing L for a given story height with a given total lateral force may be determined. Using the approximate portal methods of lateral load analysis and the previous equation for material in members designed for bending, the optimum spacing of verticals is

$$L = \frac{h}{2} \ \frac{K_b \ of \ verticals}{K_b \ of \ horizontals}$$

The factor K_b is the same constant previously used. For beams and columns with similar bending efficiency in the plane of the wall the most logical column spacing lies in the same range determined for gravity loadings.

This discussion is not a plea for mathematical determination of architectural proportions. Optima of any kind are only guides to design. But the understanding that the most efficient scale for the spacing of elements in a wall structure is related to the story height is an important qualitative conclusion. Many structural benefits may follow: Columns at every module avoid awkward projections into office spaces. Closely spaced columns supplement mullions designed only for wind. Deep reveals can provide sun shading.

Perhaps the old fashioned quality of the term bearing wall will disappoint those who favor more romantic terms. But the terminology used here is deliberate. In a rapidly changing world, the constancy of the principles of statics is a comfort to the designer of structures. And it follows that structural form is based on principles which are unchanging. Construction methods, the technology of materials, and the art of analysis are always improving. But the search for structural form is a quest for permanent truth. Therefore, the bearing wall which served well in the past was bound to reappear.

Figure 3 shows the optimum column spacing for steel based on a given load and floor height, as shown in Figure 1, and on a configuration ratio K_c/K_b, Figure 2

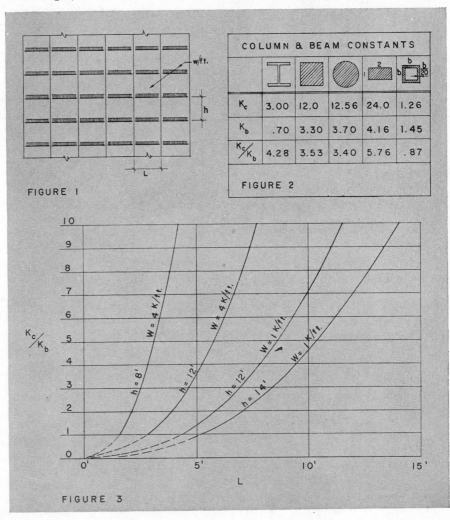

FIGURE I

COLUMN & BEAM CONSTANTS

	I	▨	●	rect	box
K_c	3.00	12.0	12.56	24.0	1.26
K_b	.70	3.30	3.70	4.16	1.45
K_c/K_b	4.28	3.53	3.40	5.76	.87

FIGURE 2

FIGURE 3

APARTMENT FRAMING TO RESIST WIND

Nine systems, both in steel and concrete, designed by Richard M. Gensert, Cleveland engineer, are presented along with his notes and diagrams explaining wind-resistant design

Choice of structural system for high-rise apartment buildings depends on a variety of factors such as: shape of building, degree of flexibility required for locating partitions, availability of new construction techniques, local construction practices and material costs, space required for ductwork and pipes, and fenestration design.

Since bearing loads are light in apartment buildings, this article is devoted to structural techniques to resist wind loads, whether in steel or reinforced concrete.

Notes on Examples:
The multiple rigid-frame steel skeleton in Highland Towers (3) is relatively limber and subject to large deflections. These may be controlled by increasing the moment of inertia of the columns.

Cantilevered concrete walls in Columbus Plaza (4) resist wind forces by a combination of shear and flexural stresses.

The grid wall in Grandview Place (6) combines the rigid-frame action of Highland Towers and the cantilevered action of Columbus Plaza.

Shear walls (4,5,7,8) can be designed so that the lateral movement due to wind loads is much less than that encountered when bending action (of the whole building) predominates.

1. BRACED STEEL SKELETON

Vertical trusses resist wind loads, preventing major bending moments from being introduced into the columns and beams. Columns joined with diagonal web members form these trusses which are located in the planes of the interior walls, thus not interfering with apartment layout. Such braced bents can be located generally every fourth or fifth bay, although they had to be closer in this case. Elimination of major bending moments allows the use of standard beam-to-column connections designed primarily for shear forces. Rigidity of this skeleton minimizes lateral deflections.

This steel frame, although economical, may present overturning problems in the foundations due to its lightness, and the fact that a single bent may be resisting wind forces over several bays. Thus the foundation must be designed to resist overturning moments. *Crystal Towers (25 stories), East Cleveland, Ohio; architect, Bertram S. Koslen.*

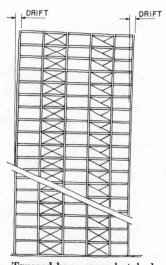

Trussed bays cross-hatched on plan opposite

2. WALL AND SLAB PORTALS

This reinforced concrete frame depends on portal (rigid frame) action for its stability. Closely-spaced exterior columns, corridor walls and floor slabs work together to resist wind moments. If continuous portal action is to be maintained, the exterior of the building should have either bearing walls or relatively close spacing of columns which may become part of the fenestration, as in this example. *Washington Plaza Apartments (23 stories), Pittsburgh, Pa.; architect, I. M. Pei & Associates; associate architects, Deeter & Ritchey.*

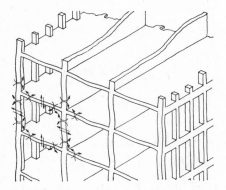

**Rigid-frame action
of continuous slabs, walls and columns**

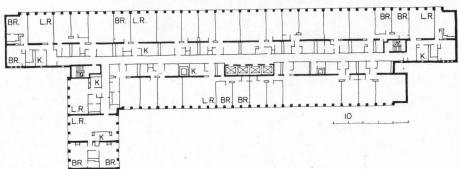

3. CONTINUOUS STEEL FRAME

An open plan along with irregular placing of partitions may not allow braced bents in the steel frame. Continuous steel frames offer more flexibility, but require larger beam and column sections, as well as special moment-resisting connections. If wind moments are taken by each column footing, the foundation design is less critical than for the braced frame. *Highland Towers (22 stories), Pittsburgh, Pa.; architect, Tasso Katselas.*

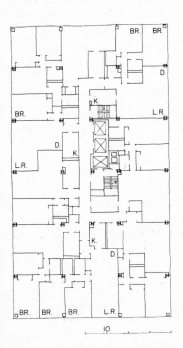

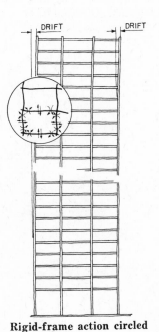

Rigid-frame action circled

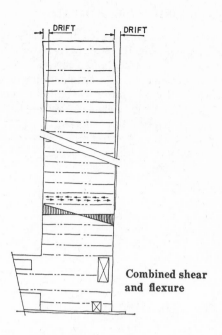

Combined shear
and flexure

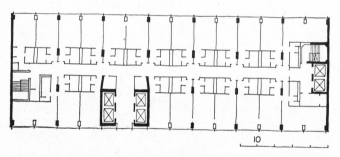

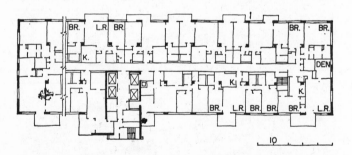

4. and 5. CONCRETE SHEAR WALLS AND FLAT PLATE FLOORS

As the ratio of height to width of a building increases, deflection of portals (rigid frames) becomes critical, and, in addition, wind moments become large. Shear walls solve the deflection problem, and remove bending stresses from column and slab elements. Shear walls are placed perpendicular to the long axis to take the lateral forces; secondarily they provide vertical support for the slabs. If the floor slabs are considered as horizontal girders, transmitting lateral forces to shear walls, the spacing of walls depends mostly on foundation conditions, since the foundation has to resist overturning forces.

Architectural planning may require openings in the shear walls for doors and windows (*see below*). Location of these openings is critical in design of the wall, since shear and tension stresses must be kept within reasonable limits. 4. *Columbus Plaza (24-story hotel), Columbus, Ohio; architects, Kellam & Foley.* 5. *Claridge Towers (31 stories), Cleveland, Ohio; architects, Richard Hawley Cutting and Associates, Inc.*

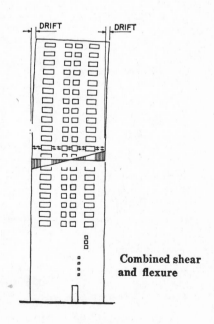

Combined shear
and flexure

6. GRID WALLS WITH MINIMUM DISTORTIONS

Cast-in-place concrete window mullions and spandrels offer a rectangular grid to resist wind loads. This grid is formed of a series of small portals designed for rigid-frame action. The whole wall acts ,in effect, like a vertical girder, lengthening on one side and shortening on the other

The new IBM office building going up in Pittsburgh, designed by Curtis & Davis, has a form of grid wall, but the orientation of its members is diagonal, rather than rectangular. *Grandview Place Apartments (28 stories), Pittsburgh, Pa.; architect, Don M. Hisaka.*

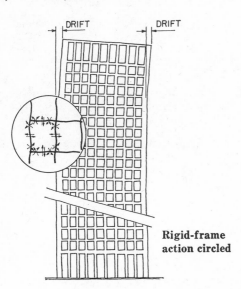

Rigid-frame action circled

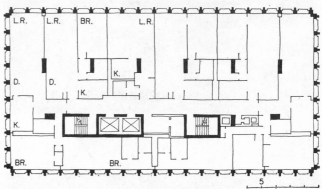

7. PRECAST SHEAR AND BEARING WALLS

Design of this structure contemplates the site precasting of wall and floor panels. The construction process can be likened to that used by children in building structures out of playing cards. A potential economy with this system is the omission of topping over floor slabs. *Allegheny Center Apartments (8 and 10 stories), Pittsburgh, Pa.; architects, Deeter & Ritchey.*

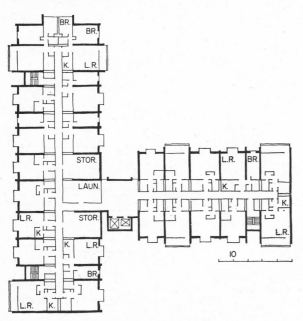

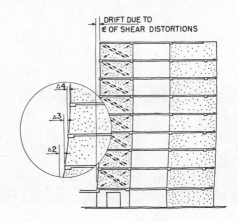

8. POURED CORES SUPPORTING PRECAST SLABS, BEAMS

A judicious arrangement of concrete shear and bearing walls provides structural resistance to horizontal and vertical loads. Slip-form construction offers economies in casting the walls. Beams can be precast and then post-tensioned to avoid expensive moment-resisting connections. *Proposed 18-story apartment; architect, Tasso Katselas.*

9. CANTILEVERED COLUMNS

When depth of shear walls is limited by the plan, and rigid-frame action between columns and floor slabs is not economically feasible, nor visually desired, cantilevered concrete columns may be used.

With only two columns in each cross section, as here, the height to width ratio should be kept under 2.5. The limiting factor in this design is the extent of column rotation at upper floors, inducing moments in the floor and roof slabs. *Neville House (10 stories), Pittsburgh, Pa.; architect, Tasso Katselas.*

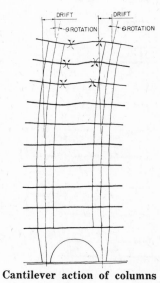

Cantilever action of columns

COMPOSITE CONSTRUCTION IN A NEW LIGHT

by Robert E. Rapp, P. E.

More liberal engineering requirements for composite connectors combined with rigid-frame design make possible application of the method to lightly-loaded buildings such as apartment houses

Elimination of interior columns is a desirable objective when they interfere with the functional layout of space for people and for mechanical equipment. But long-span construction in steel in the past posed two problems: (1) with ordinary beams heavy tonnage of steel was required. Thus the designer was obliged to resort to costly built-up members such as plate girders or to expensive truss framing, (2) relatively deep, heavy members were required to prevent excessive deflection, increasing floor-to-floor height.

Now, however, research into composite construction (steel beams and concrete floor slab working together as a structural unit) has made possible economical long-span construction for many ordinary types of buildings. (It will be shown later how a 60-ft span can be achieved in an apartment structure with a floor-ceiling depth of only 25 in.) At one time composite construction was restricted primarily to bridges and to

heavily loaded building structures.

Composite design was established in a more realistic light when the Joint A.C.I.-A.S.C.E.* Committee on Composite Construction in 1960 issued their report, "Tentative Recommendations for Design and Construction of Composite Beams and Girders for Buildings."

Extensive tests conducted about this time for A.I.S.C.* at Lehigh University showed how shear connectors could be reduced by as much as 50 per cent of that given in the Joint Committee report, while still maintaining a safety factor of 2.5 based on ultimate strength. These findings led to the incorporation of the composite design provisions which appear in the new A.I.S.C. "Specification for the Design, Fabrication & Erection of Structural Steel for Buildings."

Composite design is an ideal method to reduce deflection and, consequently, floor depth. Deflection is inversely proportional to the moment of inertia of the structural section. And since a composite section has a greatly increased moment of inertia over the steel section alone, excessive deflection in long-span construction

is greatly reduced. Also, since shear connectors fasten the concrete slab to the steel beam, lateral stability is increased.

To date, composite design in buildings has generally utilized simple beam-type connections under gravity loadings only. This restricted its economic application to low-rise buildings that were not influenced by wind loading.

But by utilizing the new A.I.S.C. Specification, the Buffalo firm of Backus, Crane and Love, Architects and Engineers, were able to design an 11-story apartment house with a 35-ft clear span and 7-ft cantilever

TYPICAL COMPOSITE SECTION

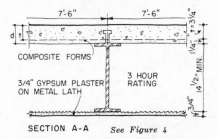

SECTION A-A   *See Figure 4*

Figure 1: Actual beam depth depends on load. Minimum depth of 14½ in. is required for fire-resistance rating

---

*A.C.I.—American Concrete Institute. A.S.C.E.—American Society of Civil Engineers. A.I.S.C.—American Institute of Steel Construction.

Welding of beam composite connectors

In apartment structure they are used on beams and girders, but not on cantilevers

on each side. Shear studs were attached to the girders—with the exception of cantilever ends—and to most of the beams. Formed steel decking was used as a permanent form for the concrete floor.

As a result of all these factors, the designers were able to reduce the weight of steel, and to save 2 to 3 in. in total depth per floor. It took just 17 working days to erect the 775-ton frame, shown in the photos below.

The principles of structural design of this building are the same as will be outlined below: composite design combined with rigid frame analysis.

A Design Example

Design of framing for a hypothetical apartment building which is shown in plan in Figure 2 will be used to exemplify the functional economic and design advantages of composite design. We will examine the framing of a 60- by 60-ft section.

If metal deck forms are used at spans no greater than 7½ ft, all temporary floor shoring and mill-type formwork can be eliminated. This type of construction is illustrated in Figure 1.

If a conventional steel grid pattern had been used, the economical framing plan would be as shown in Figure 3 with girders on 20-ft centers and intermediate beams at 6 ft 8 in. An economical design in concrete flat plate construction, using staggered columns so that they would merge with partitioning, would require even more columns than the steel design.

Figure 4 shows the 60- by 60-ft

module in steel designed with no interior columns; exterior columns are 15 ft on center. This design can be economical when composite construction is employed. The advantages are quickly apparent: (1) the total number of columns per unit area is reduced by one-third, (2) interior columns are completely eliminated, (3) the number of connections has been reduced by 79 per cent, (4) the number of individual pieces of steel to be handled has been reduced by 59 per cent.

By utilizing up-to-date composite design methods, the 60-ft long-span floor system would be approximately 20 per cent heavier in steel weight than the conventional framing shown in Figure 3. However, the functional advantages as well as savings in fabrication and erection costs offset this weight disadvantage. The former A.I.S.C. Specification would have required greater weight for the conventional framing, and if the design had been based on it, the increase in steel tonnage for the long-span frame would have been only 10 per cent.

The economy in long-span construction is achieved by composite design combined with semi-rigid connection theory. Presentation of this technique will take up the balance of this article.

Engineering Calculations

The 60-ft girders are spaced 7 ft 6 in. on center which eliminates shoring of the metal deck floor system. Fire resistance is provided by a vermicu-

lite aggregate, gypsum plaster ceiling on plaster lath which serves as the finished ceiling. A 3-hr rating is obtained if the plaster is ¾ in. thick; 4-hr rating if it is 1 in. thick, providing that a distance of not less than 14½ in. is maintained between the metal lath and the underside of the composite steel form.

The total gravity bending moment for this design amounts to 480 ft-kips. Construction loads were conservatively estimated to be 20 lb per sq ft which were added to the dead load requirements. If the designer does not apply construction loads, then he must be sure to add form loads where applicable. By neglecting construction loads, it would be possible to select a lighter steel member. The engineer, however, must be sure to add loads for partitions if they are required, when calculating live load moments applied to the composite section.

The 480 ft-kip gravity load is divided as follows: dead load moment $(M_D) = 285$ ft-kips; live load moment $(M_L) = 195$ ft-kips. If the engineer designs a fully rigid connection, the dead load moment is distributed as shown in Figure 5a. Deflection of a fully-rigid member is five times less than that for simple beam action; thus this fixed-connection design virtually eliminates deflection problems under dead load conditions. Also, if the end connection is made rigid, cambering of the beam is held to a minimum.

Figure 5b shows the distribution of bending moment under total load (live load plus dead load). This shows that the composite section is called upon to satisfy a positive moment of 290 ft-kips. The greater capacity of the composite member to absorb additional positive moment leads to the economical application of composite design by combining the composite action with semi-rigid connections to take care of the dead load moment only.

This criteria would classify the composite member for Type 3 (semi-rigid) construction under Section 1.2 of the new A.I.S.C. Specification. Connections of beams and girders are assumed to possess a dependable and known moment capacity intermediate in degree between complete rigidity and complete flexibility.

There is no point in extending the shear connectors to the ends of the beam. The Specification (1.11.4)

Clear span is 35 ft; cantilevers, 7 ft

Frame sections are bolted in the field

Backus, Crane and Love, Architects and Engineers

COMPOSITE VS. CONVENTIONAL FRAMING

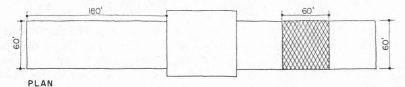

PLAN

Figure 2: Apartment plan of this shape will illustrate the advantages of composite

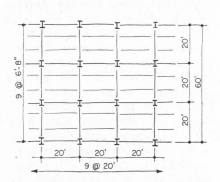

Figure 3: In conventional framing for a 60-ft module, columns are on 20-ft centers; beams are 6 ft 8 in. apart

Figure 4: In composite, girders span 60 ft. Column eccentricity can be eliminated by cantilevering girders

states that shear connectors are to be evenly spaced between the point of maximum moment and a point of contraflexure in continuous beams. The black area in Figure 5b shows the limits of composite action; thus shear connectors should be spaced as required within these limits.

Figure 6 shows the dimensional properties of the composite section to satisfy the gravity loading conditions.

If the steel member is a "compact section" the maximum allowable stress for both the steel alone for dead load moment, and the composite section for total load moment cannot exceed $0.66 F_y$ (F_y is yield strength of steel). For A36 steel this allow-

able stress would be 24,000 psi.

The section modulus of the transformed section is 154 in.³ The required section modulus to satisfy the 290 ft-kip positive moment is 145 in.³ Therefore the gravity loading conditions for the 60-ft span can be satisfied by a 21 WF 55 girder made into a composite beam by means of connecting the girder to the concrete flange with 32 ⅞-in. diameter by 3½-in. studs. Other types of shear connectors are allowed. Their respective values are given in Table 1.11.4 of the new specification for various 28-day compressive strengths of concrete. In the example here the strength is taken as 3,000 psi.

Figure 7 shows a comparison of

available moments for a 21 WF 55 girder in A36 steel using composite and non-composite criteria.

Figure 7a shows the available gravity moment for a steel girder alone with fully-fixed-end conditions conforming to Type 1 (rigid frame) construction. The maximum allowable moment that can be absorbed is equal to 329.1 ft-kips.

Figure 7b shows the maximum available gravity moment for the composite section if the steel connection is designed to its fullest negative moment capacity. The theoretical moment indicated is 527.4 ft-kips. This is an increase of 39 per cent in load carrying capacity of composite over non-composite design.

Figure 7c shows the composite section designed as a semi-rigid connected member. Only a 172 ft-kip negative moment connection would have to be developed. The steel member alone has a capacity of 219.4 ft-kips at $0.66 F_y$; therefore, if the capacity of the semi-rigid joint connection were increased to between 172 and 219 ft-kips, there would be no chance of the member becoming overstressed under static gravity loads. It should be noted that the composite beam has been designed without a cover plate which would raise the cost.

In order to accomplish a satisfactory design using composite design methods with simple beam connections, a 24 WF 84 section would be required.

Application of composite semi-rigid design yields a weight saving of 34.5 per cent over non-composite design and 27.6 per cent over composite design with simple beam connections. This saving was accomplished even

BENDING LOADS

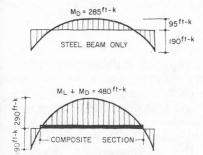

Figure 5a: Bending moment for 60-ft beam due to the dead load

Figure 5b: Bending moment for composite section; live and dead load

COMPOSITE SECTION DESIGN

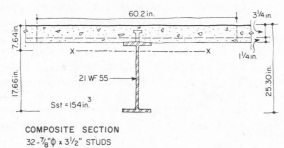

COMPOSITE SECTION
32 - ⅞"ɸ x 3½" STUDS

Figure 6 (above): Design for composite section which will satisfy dead and live load moments

Figure 7 (right): 7a shows load-carrying capacity for non-composite section; 7b shows capacity for composite section with rigid connections; 7c capacity for semi-rigid connection

LOAD-CARRYING CAPACITIES

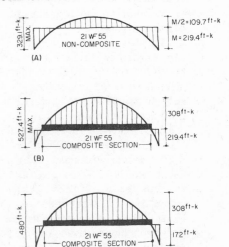

EFFECT OF WIND PLUS GRAVITY LOADS

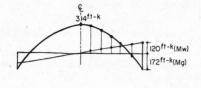

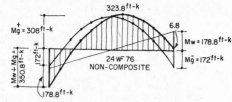

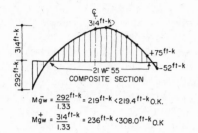

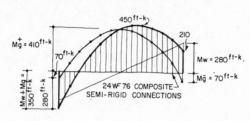

Figure 8a (top): permissible wind load moment. **Figure 8b** (bottom): bending moments due to wind and gravity loads

Figure 9a (top): wind and gravity load moments for a non-composite section. **Figure 9b** (bottom): semi-rigid design

$$\frac{M_w + 172}{1.33} = 219.4 \text{ ft-kips; therefore,}$$

$$M_w = 120 \text{ ft-kips.}$$

These moments are distributed as shown in Figure 8. Under combined wind and gravity loads, the maximum positive moment equals 314 ft-kips; the maximum negative moment equals 292 ft-kips. However, if these respective induced moments were reduced by 33⅓ per cent, or the allowable working stress were increased by this amount, the composite section with an end restraint equal to the capacity of the steel member alone would accommodate a gravity load moment of 480 ft-kips, plus an induced wind moment of 120 ft-kips.

As previously stated, a fully-rigid 24 WF 76 girder would be required to satisfy the gravity loads if composite design were not utilized.

Figure 9 shows a comparison between a fully-rigid, composite and a semi-rigid, composite 24 WF 76 girder subjected to combined gravity and wind loading conditions. By applying the same methods of analysis as in Figure 8 (i.e. equation top of this column) it was found that the non-composite steel member was capable of handling a wind moment of 296 ft-kips (Figure 9a).

Figure 9b shows the same size section designed as a semi-rigid composite member. The allowable wind moment has been increased to 396 ft-kips. This is an increase in moment capacity of 25 per cent. By utilizing composite action, the same size member can be used to satisfy wind-induced moments ranging from 296 ft-kips to 396 ft-kips when combined with a gravity moment of 480.

It should be pointed out that the columns must be made stiff enough, or adjacent bays or cantilevers must be provided to insure that the semi-rigid connection will act between the limits of the design assumptions.

Conclusion

Engineer and architect are seldom faced with the ideal situation when designing a structure. The author selected a problem employing apartment house loading conditions that heretofore had not been considered practical for composite design. This selection was made to emphasize new avenues that have been opened to the designer by utilizing the design techniques presented in this paper. Even greater economies could be achieved under heavier live loading conditions.

with a relatively light live load to dead load ratio. There also is a 12.5 per cent saving in depth.

Deflections. At this point let us make a comparison in the deflections of each of the following designs:

A. *21 WF 55 composite semi-rigid girder:*
deflection, dead load=1.08 in.; deflection, live load=0.31 in.; total deflection=1.39 in.

B. *24 WF 84 composite girder with simple beam connection:*
deflection, dead load=2.60 in.; deflection, live load=0.87 in.; total deflection=3.47 in.

C. *24 WF 76 non-composite rigid connection:*
total deflection=0.99 in.

Total deflection of the 21 WF 55 semi-rigid composite section was figured at a maximum end restraint of 219 ft-kips as shown in Figure 7b. With dead-load deflection of 1.08 in. and live-load deflection of only 0.31 in., it would not be necessary to camber the girder.

Likewise, it would not be necessary to camber the 24 WF 76 girder; however, the 24 WF 84 composite member with no end restraint would require cambering to compensate for dead load deflection.

If the engineer investigates deflection in the semi-rigid composite 21 WF 55 girder with dead load moment equal to 195 ft-kips and live load moment equal to 285 ft-kips, he would find that total deflection would equal 1.17 in., distributed as follows: deflection due to dead load=0.74 in. for steel girder only, rigidly con-

nected; deflection due to live load= 0.43 in. for the transformed section.

The moment distribution, as indicated above, is more in keeping with loading conditions in which composite design has heretofore been utilized. The designer can visualize that deflection is of no consequence regardless how the moment is distributed when semi-rigid design is employed.

In addition to these advantages, the engineer will be able to use the new high-strength steels in this type of design without being limited by deflection.

Composite Design and Wind

Little thought has been given in the past to composite action under wind loading conditions. The reader will note that the available moment capacity for the section covered by figure 7b equals 527.4 ft-kips. This was accomplished, as outlined, by fully fixing the end connection to develop the full negative moment capacity of the 21 WF 55 steel member. If it is assumed that only a 172 ft-kip moment is required to satisfy gravity loads, then the difference between 172 and 219.4 (47.4 ft-kips) is the reserve moment capacity of the composite girder.

According to the A.I.S.C. Specification, the designer can increase the allowable stress for combined loading conditions by 33⅓ per cent; therefore, the induced moment due to wind that would be allowed under combined gravity and wind loads would be:

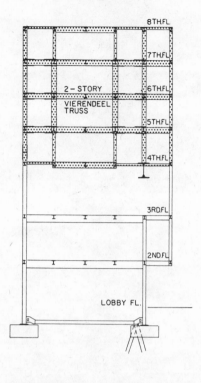

TRIPLE CHORD VIERENDEEL TRUSSES CARRY
FIVE FLOORS

Felix J. Nessikian

Control Tower, Logan International Airport, Boston, Mass. Architects: Samuel Glaser Associates; Structural Engineers: Goldberg, LeMessurier & Associates

BEHIND THE SLEEK GLASS and aluminum face of the recently completed control tower at Boston's Logan International Airport lies a complex structural frame in which triple chord Vierendeel trusses — believed to be the first of their kind — support five of the building's eight floors.

Outward manifestations of the inner workings of the Vierendeel frame include a roadway running directly beneath the building; two floors (the second and third) completely free of columns; and an extra floor squeezed into the total height limitation. Of these, the first two were architectural requirements dictated by the use of the building — and by its location squarely across the main access road to the airport. The third was a bonus made possible by the reduction in floor depth which resulted from the use of a truss frame instead of the clear-span framing scheme first considered.

As finally constructed, the building's 42 ft bays are spanned on the second and third floors by 36 in. wide flange girders, while the upper five floors form an inter-acting structural frame centered in the Vierendeel trusses. The three chord members in each truss are located symmetrically about the sixth floor, with the eighth floor and penthouse supported on columns above and the fourth floor suspended below the truss.

Both floors therefore participate in the frame action, the eighth floor by providing a compression strut at the top, and the fourth floor by acting as a tension tie between the lower extensions of the vertical members of the five trusses.

The trusses themselves are made up of 21-ft center panels flanked by 10 ft-6 in. side panels, plus a 9-ft cantilever at one end. Because of the greater depth given by using the girders in three floors, the trusses could be fabricated from relatively small members. Chord members for the end panels were built up from plates; those for the center panels are 21-in. wide flange sections.

The structure is supported on foundations which were laid when the original passenger facilities at the airport were constructed. Since the existing pile clusters and heavy pile caps were designed to support only vertical loads, with horizontal loads to be taken by an assumed adjoining structure — which did not exist at the time the control tower was built — provision had to be made for carrying lateral wind forces to the ground. This was done by driving seven pairs of battered steel piles between the existing foundations, and using a truss-like subgrade frame to transfer horizontal reactions from the building columns to the new battered-pile foundations.

MORE STRENGTH, LESS WEIGHT
IN PRESTRESSED STEEL

Increased parking at Port of New York Authority Bus Terminal is made possible by 200-ft Warren trusses. Bottom chords are prestressed to minimize their depth. Photos at top show cables before and after prestressing (See also Fig. 8)

by T. R. Higgins
Director of Engineering and Research
American Institute
*of Steel Construction **

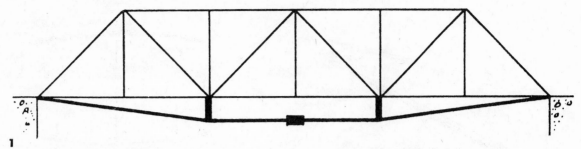

Fig 1. Iron truss rod with turnbuckle, an early application of prestressing

Fig. 2. High strength strand in beam web has effect similar to that of truss rod

Prestressed steel usually consists of high-tensile steel tensioned against an ordinary carbon steel beam, girder, or truss to develop a stronger and more efficient structure. Since steel requires less bracing in tension than in compression, a few highly tensioned bars or cables can be made to take much of the weight, and thus increase load capacity and improve rigidity.

Prestressing was applied to steel long before the availability of today's high strength steels made prestressed concrete possible. Bridges such as Fig. 1 were in common use around the turn of the century. A wrought iron truss rod installed beneath the beam applies tension to the assembly.

While the term *prestress* had not yet come into engineering parlance, this was in fact prestressing even if the stress analysis was sketchy, or even non-existent. The truss rod, when tightened by means of the turnbuckle, not only induced negative moment in the beam to relieve its dead load, it also participated directly in the live load stress by acting as the bottom chord of a truss. But wrought iron or at best mild steel was the only material available for the truss rod. Thus the amount of stress that could be safely applied was limited. Also, as deeper and heavier beams were manufactured, the use of trussed beams declined.

There are several reasons for our current interest in prestressing. The

* This article is based on a talk before the the Industrial Building Congress, New York, September, 1961.

cost of steel, like everything else, has increased. Any method that enables us to get more work out of the same or less steel deserves consideration.

Then, too, the engineer is often called upon to strengthen an existing structure so that it will carry a greater load. In such cases, space limitations often preclude the introduction of additional framing members. Prestressing may offer a solution.

Finally, we are interested in prestressing because the availability of high strength steel rods, wire tendons, and now plates makes the idea of prestressing steel in conventional design an economically intriguing one.

The form in which prestressing has been most often proposed is basically an adaptation of the old trussed beam idea in which the high-strength prestressing strands are installed within the depth of the web as in Fig. 2. They are anchored to the underside of the top flange at the ends of the beam, and pass through saddles in the mid-section. This serves to conceal the cable and to keep the over-all depth of the beam or girder to minimum.

Since steel is equally strong in tension and compression, and it is high in shear strength, there is actually no need to deflect or drape the prestressing strands between top and bottom flanges.

Recently the Iowa Bridge Commission designed a steel I-beam bridge on which the high-strength prestressing rods are installed just below and in contact with the bottom flange, as in Fig. 3. These rods pass

through saddles at 10-ft intervals, and are anchored at each end in steel blocks welded to the bottom flange. The rods are initially anchored at one end and stressed by jacking at the other end, where they are anchored with a conical wedge when the desired level of tension is reached.

This type of construction does not adapt well to continuous beam spans. But for simple spans from 50 ft up and in buildings where exceptional loading occurs and headroom or between-floor space is limited, this application of prestressing offers a logical solution and considerable economy. For example, a 27 WF 94 prestressed in this way, with two 1-in. diameter high strength steel rods would have about the same carrying capacity as a 30 WF 108 with a 1 by 8 in. cover plate on the bottom, such as might be used in composite design on a fairly long, heavily loaded floor span.

We can make our cover plate of high strength steel and prestress the beam by bending it with jacks before welding the cover plate to the flange as shown in Fig. 4. When the jack is released, a negative moment is induced in the beam, maintained by the tension in the plate. To be fully effective, stress should be greater in the cover plate than in the beam. High strength steel is a prerequisite.

Naturally this requires heavy jigs and fixed anchorages capable of taking large jack reactions. Thus the economies of prestressing in the field are dubious except on a volume basis. Where possible, cover plates should be installed in the shop. A bridge using this method is under

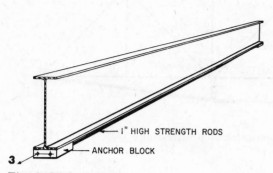

Fig. 3. High strength stressed rods need not be draped in web

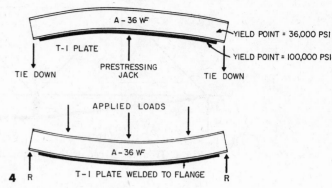

Fig. 4. High strength plate is welded to the beam prestressed by jacking

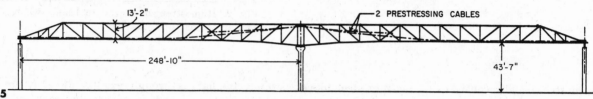

Fig. 5. Magnel's prestressed truss at Melsbrock Airport, Brussels

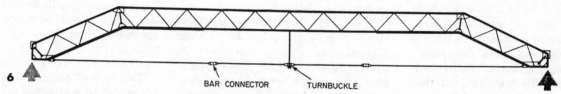

Fig. 6. Prestressed truss at a Harlow, England, plant

construction in Iowa right now.

Prestressing can be applied not only to beams and girders but also to trusses. Actually, the use of prestressed steel was pioneered by the late Professor Gustave Magnel of Belgium, who began his investigations on steel trusses about a dozen years ago. He concluded that "savings in weight up to 33 per cent are available and, assuming the cost of materials and labor for high strength wire units to be three times that of structural steel, a 13 per cent saving in cost is obtainable."

Professor Magnel designed a 47-ft truss for testing. Its bottom chord was pre-compressed by means of eight pairs of high strength wires having a yield strength of 218,000 psi. Based on computations and test measurements, Professor Magnel concluded that stresses in a prestressed steel structure can be calculated with the same accuracy as for conventional steel design. He predicted that prestressed steel trusses 15 ft deep could economically span 500 ft.

Four years later (in 1954) he had his opportunity to put theory into practice. The result is the Melsbrock

Airport building in Brussels, which covers an area 502 by 215 ft using only one centrally located interior column (Fig. 5).

The main truss is prestressed. Its depth at mid-span is 13 ft 9 in., or about one-eighteenth of the span. Four cables, each of which contains 64 wires, accomplish the prestressing. The stresses in these wires vary from 93,000 to 105,000 psi, depending upon wind uplift, snow load, etc. Eight tons of prestressing wires replaced 26 tons of structural steel. The saving in weight as compared with conventional steel design was 12 per cent, and the cost saving was four per cent. Had the wires been prestressed to 130,000 psi, an acceptable figure, the savings would have been about six per cent. A longer span would also result in greater economies. For a span of 300 ft, the weight saved would be about 25 per cent and the money saved about 18 per cent.

Two other significant uses of prestressed steel in buildings took place at about the same time, both of them in England.

In a factory roof at Harlow, the ends of 60-ft trusses were deflected

downward as in Fig. 6, and high tensile bars tightened by turnbuckles were stretched like bowstrings between the truss ends. Although these bars resemble simple tie rods in this application they are pre-tensioned and the truss is prestressed.

The other British example is found at Wigan. Here a space frame roof spans a 90-ft square workshop without internal columns. What would correspond to rafter joists in conventional roofing are here miniature trusses in which the bottom chord is a high strength wire in tension. The resulting roof structure is one of the lightest possible for its span, weighing only 3.72 pounds per square foot.

A recent U. S. example is the United Air Lines hangar at Chicago's O'Hare International Airport where prestressing is used on a 140-ft cantilevered truss as shown in Fig. 7. There are nine such trusses spaced 40 ft on center. Engineer Paul Rogers calculates the saving at $35,000, as compared with conventional cantilever truss design. By using prestressing rods along the upper chord of the truss, Mr. Rogers reduced structural weight from 6.35 to 5.29 pounds per sq ft. In other

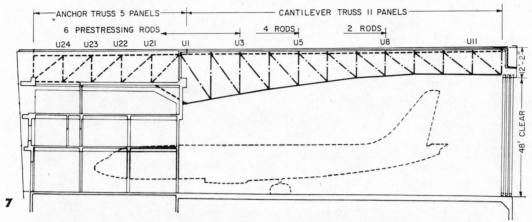

Fig. 7. Cantilevered hangar truss with prestressed steel rods along upper chord

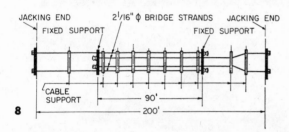

Fig. 8. Arrangement of strands for lower chord of trusses at New York bus terminal. See also photo page 144

words, the conventional truss construction requires approximately 20 per cent more steel than the prestressed space-truss system.

Each truss was prestressed with six 1⅛-in. diameter high strength rods whose minimum yield strength is 130,000 psi. Each rod is anchored in a heavy plate and stiffener assembly welded to the web and inner flange of the 14 in. wide-flange beam comprising the top chord of each truss.

The rods were anchored in pairs at the second, third, and fourth panel points of the anchor trusses. The other ends of the three pairs of rods are anchored at the second, fourth, and seventh panel points of the cantilever trusses.

At a total prestress of 80,000 lbs, per rod, design stresses were reduced 480,000 lbs in the upper chord of panels 5 and 8. These reductions due to prestressing ranged from 25 to 50 per cent of maximum design stresses.

Another airport application of prestressed steel is the Pan American passenger terminal at Idlewild Airport (AR:9/61) in which thirty-two cantilever girders radiate from a central core. Attached to each girder are six 2½ in. cables pretensioned to 600,000 lbs.

In the Port Authority Bus Terminal on New York's west side, expansion plans called for converting the existing roof to parking operations on three new levels. The engineers, Ammann & Whitney, agreed on the construction of fifteen 200-ft Warren trusses, spaced 50 ft on centers. These are carried on new columns and footings outside the existing wall. Because the existing interior columns of the building could not take the increased load of more floors, the new trusses had to span the entire 200 ft. With the heavy traffic planned, the maximum tensile stress in the lower chord came to 5412 kips. A conventional box-section chord would have been very deep and required heavy plates, even with high strength low alloy A-242 steel. A minimum chord depth was important in order that pitch of the ramps within the building be kept to a minimum. Therefore, the engineers decided to prestress the lower chord. The result was a shallower depth and a substantial cost reduction.

After a truss was in place, stressing crews mounted a jacking device at each end of the bottom chord. Four 2¹⁄₁₆-in. diameter steel cables run along both top and bottom of the chord. Pairs of cables are attached to jacking heads, top and bottom at the outer ends of trusses and to welded fixed supports 145 ft from each end. Hence cables overlap 90 ft in the center as shown in Fig. 8. This same scheme occurs on both upper and lower sides of the chord.

There is a total of eight cables at the centers of chords, counting top and bottom cables. Two 300-ton jacks at each truss end were controlled from a single portable console on the roof. These jacks stressed the cables simultaneously to 240,000 lbs each. In addition to meeting space limitations successfully, prestressing also reduced the required steel in each truss from 300 to 240 tons, a 900-ton saving in the building.

Although prestressing has been thought of primarily as a means of renovating a structure so that it will carry increased load, the economies of prestressed steel also warrant its consideration in the design stage on large-span, open buildings.

United Air Lines Hangar, San Francisco. Prismatic concrete columns get their shape by following the stress pattern. Tapered steel girders achieve economy by varying plate thickness and using stiffeners

HANGAR SHOWS ITS STRUCTURAL ECONOMY

Skidmore, Owings & Merrill, Architects, San Francisco; Elliott Brown, Partner-in-charge; Myron Goldsmith, Chief Engineer; Anthony A. Braccia, Chief of Construction.

Choice of structural form for an airplane hangar is based primarily on that shape which allows most efficient use of interior space. At the same time it must be structurally efficient and economical. The once popular barrel vault has given way, at least for the time being, to the cantilever, single and double, self-supporting and cable hung. One reason seems to be that with the jet age, wings are becoming shorter (in scale) and tails taller. (As the height of a barrel increases, so does the span.) Also in the transition period between piston craft and jets, sometimes both —thus different sizes—have to be serviced side by side. This calls for complete flexibility of interior space. A cantilever hangar has unlimited expansibility longitudinally, and the roof can be placed at the proper level to give sufficient clearance for the tail of the largest airplane.

This double-cantilever jet service and maintenance hangar for United Air Lines in San Francisco will accommodate four DC-8 jets, each weighing 300,000 lb and having a wing spread of 150 ft, a length of 150 ft and a tail height of 43 ft. The hangar reflects in its appearance (as a result of its engineering) efficiency not unlike that of the craft it houses.

First, the concrete columns are shaped to follow the stresses corresponding to the moment diagram—of vertical load plus lateral resistance to earthquake forces. Columns are fixed at the base, partially fixed at the second floor and have a point of inflection about 12 ft from the ground; the steel girders are pin-connected to the columns.

Second the tapered, welded steel girders are tailored from end to end in depth, thickness of flange and web, and stiffening—horizontal and vertical—to meet the "real" load requirements. The second floor is hung from

Kurt Bank

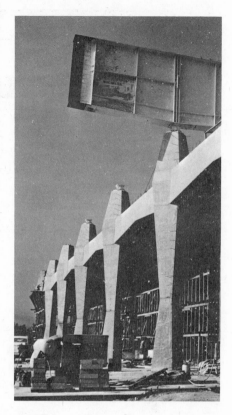

Moulin Studios

Here again, but in more detail, are the three framing elements. Girders cantilever 142 ft; total length of girders is 362 ft. In erection, center sections of two end girders were welded and erected in one piece; center sections of other five girders were spliced and bolted. Cantilever portions (120 ft long) were joined to center sections with high-tensile bolts. Plans and sections across page show nose pockets and relative sizes of DC-7 and DC-8. Note two sets of 3½-in. diameter hangar rods for supporting permanent second floor. Clear height of the hangar door is 50 ft

the girder by means of hangar rods, partially counteracting the tendency of the cantilevers to deflect. The center span is 80 ft and each cantilever is 142 ft, making a total girder length of 362 ft. Maximum depth is 14 ft at the pinned supports, and minimum is 5 ft at the outer edge. Maximum flange size is 2 by 36 in., and minimum is ⅝ by 15 in. Thickest web is ¾ in. and thinnest, ½ in.

Third feature of the structure is a 5-ft-deep triangulated space frame, spanning 51 ft 6 in. between plate girders to support the roof, provide bracing in the horizontal plane and prevent buckling of the compression flange of the girder.

How did it happen that the columns are concrete and the girders steel? In any case the columns had to be fire-protected, and at the time the hangar was being designed, there was a long delivery time for steel. It was decided that the whole core could be completed in concrete by the date the steel arrived. Prestressed concrete, plate girders and steel trusses were included in preliminary design studies, and the costs were found competitive. Plate girders had less depth than trusses, and they formed a partial draft curtain. This and other considerations, including appearance, gave the nod to the steel plate girder design.

To insure a smooth column surface, the forms of 2-in. planking were lined with hardboard. To eliminate bugs in construction and give workmen a picture of what was to be built, a full-scale mock-up of the column and girder intersection was constructed.

SOM's Myron Goldsmith was responsible for the structural design. Objective was to create a structure which would "follow the forces"; which would not be a tour de force, but an economical and esthetically pleasing design. Special consultants on the structure were H. J. Brunnier and Professor Boris Bressler of the University of California.

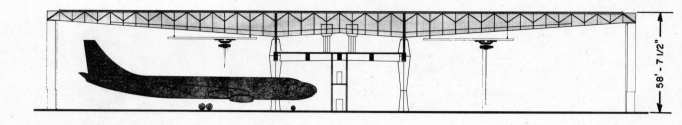

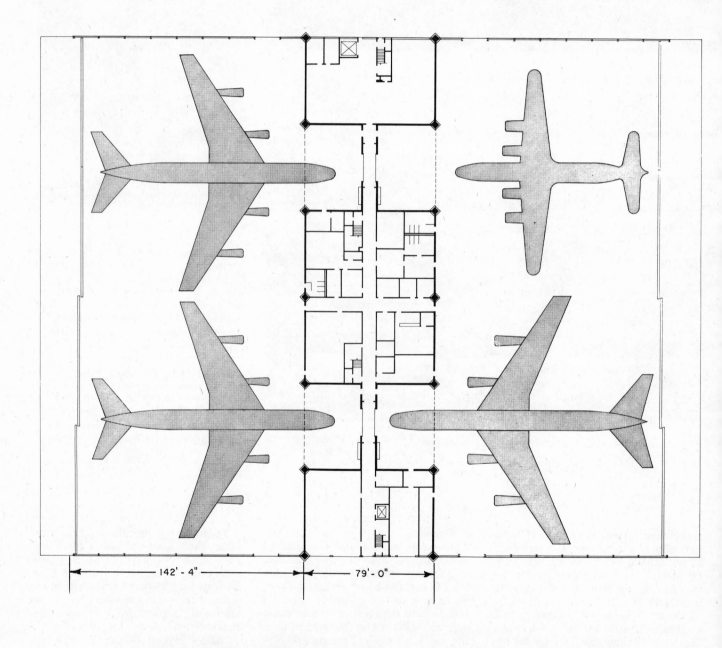

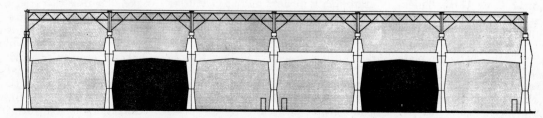

Section **4**

SUSPENSION STRUCTURES

SUSPENSION STRUCTURES

by Seymour Howard, A.I.A., Associate Professor, Pratt Institute

While suspension structures date back to the rope bridge, the principle has seldom been applied to buildings. In single-story structures, where it is most applicable, the hung roof must handle uplift of wind, unbalanced loads such as snow, and, most particularly, the ravages of vibration (flutter). The nature of these forces and methods of stabilizing structures against them are discussed here. The sketches are by the author.

French Pavilion, Zagreb, Yugoslavia, 1935. Single layer of cables; 110-ft diameter, sag/diameter ratio, 1/11. Roof is 14-ga sheet steel hung from steel compression ring. Bernard Lafaille, Engineer

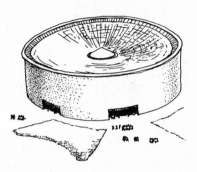

Municipal Stadium, Montevideo, Uruguay, 1957. Single layer of cables; 308-ft diameter, sag/diameter ratio, 1/11. Roof is precast slabs with prestressed grouted joints. Mondino, Viera and Miller, Architects; The Preload Co., Inc., roof consultants

Of the various methods of spanning a space, suspension systems have a special appeal to the imagination because of their potential efficiency in the use of material and the long spans possible. Steel, aluminum or fiber can be used to their maximum advantage in the form of cable or rope. All the loads can be carried in direct tension; there need be no reduction in the allowable stress on account of the danger of buckling. The drawing of steel into wire form increases the proportional limit to stresses in the order of 160,000 psi, instead of 30 to 40,000 psi for structural steel, and the breaking stress to over 220,000 psi*. What economy of material and lightness this seems to promise!

Why, then, apart from the familiar suspension bridge, are so few permanent structures of this type actually built?

The answers to this question constitute the limitations of suspension systems. New buildings will be successfully designed and constructed using tension as the principal type of stress if these limitations are understood and transcended.

MULTI-STORY SYSTEMS
Cables for vertical supports
One of the suspension systems which crops up perennially in architectural projects is shown in Fig. 1. (As far as I know it has never been used in a completed building.) A series of floors are supported by tension cables which are fastened to an overhead truss; a design like this by Amincio Williams of the Argentine received considerable publicity in the late 1930's.

Paul Chelazzi's "Suspen-Arch" system for multi-story buildings is essentially the same, with the substitution of several "Suspen-Arches" at various levels instead of the single truss at the top (see Fig. 2). The principal advantage claimed for this type of construction is that the cross sectional area of vertical elements is reduced to a minimum, and that, as a result, the plan provides maximum flexibility in floor layout.

The Limitations are:

1. Although the area of the tension cables is small, the addition of necessary fireproofing around them must not be forgotten.

2. The spacing of vertical supports is determined by the floor framing system. Therefore the limitations on the layout of offices is essentially the same as if the floor were supported on columns. Neither a column nor a hanger is a welcome obstruction in the middle of a room.

3. Considering the building as a whole, vertical loads must travel a path about three times as far to get to the ground as in normal columnar design. (Any system with trusses or other main transverse supports at intermediate levels will reduce this distance somewhat.)

4. Wind forces must be resisted entirely by the central compression shaft. With conventional columnar framing, on the other hand, the stiffnesses of all of the columns can help resist horizontal forces.

5. The tendency of floors to swing horizontally can be eliminated by correct fastenings to the compression shaft. These must permit relative vertical movement, because the central shaft will shorten under loading while the cables will lengthen.

6. Although methods could be devised to precast the floors on the ground and then raise them by the cables to their final position, the compression shafts and trusses would have to be constructed first. This would be an extra expense as compared with conventional columnar design.

Cables for horizontal supports
These would essentially be adaptations of the single-story systems described below. Not much has yet been done, although Lev Zetlin has been studying some with a 200-ft

* The Modulus of Elasticity (E) for a single wire (29 million psi) is not changed by wire-drawing, but the effective E when the wires are twisted into cable form goes down to 24 million psi for galvanized bridge strand and to 20 million psi for the more flexible galvanized bridge rope. This reduction does not occur in the main cables of suspension bridges, which are spun in place with the wires parallel.

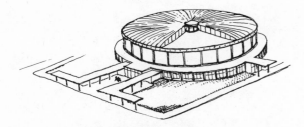

Municipal Auditorium, Utica, N. Y., 1960. Double layer of cables; 240-ft diameter, sag-diameter ratio, 1/12. Prestressed cables hung between concrete compression ring and steel tension ring. Gehron & Seltzer, Architects; Frank Delle Cese, Associated Architect; Lev Zetlin, Structural Engineer

Marie Thumas Pavilion, Brussels Fair, 1958. Steel cables, trussed steel masts, plastic roofing. Plan area 121 by 174 ft. Bottom sketch shows principal supports, guys and boundary cables. Guys are anchored at different levels because of sloping site. Baucher, Blondel, Filippone, Architects; Rene Sarger, Structural Engineer, Batellier, Assistant

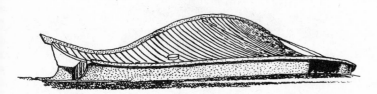

David S. Ingalls Hockey Rink, Yale University, 1958. Concrete spine supports steel cables which are covered by 1 5/8-in. wood planking. Concrete side walls, lyre-shaped in plan, serve as anchorages. Extra guy wires were used to stabilize the spine against unsymmetrical wind and snow loads. Eero Saarinen and Associates, Architects; Douglas Orr, Associated. Severud-Elstad-Krueger, Structural Engineers

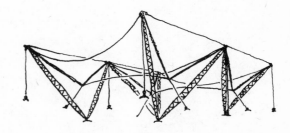

clear span, using his double, prestressed cable system, described later in this article.

SINGLE-STORY SYSTEMS
The hanging roof
If there is one general category for classifying the limitations of hanging roofs, it is MOVEMENT. Under this broad heading can be grouped most of the problems which can be foreseen.

Non-destructive movements
1. Changes in shape due to moving loads. One of the advantages of tension structures is the simplicity with which one can visualize the shape of the tension elements under a load. A perfectly flexible cable or string will take a different shape for every variation in loading; this is the familiar "funicular curve" or "string polygon." Two extreme cases are shown in Fig. 3. On the left is the catenary curve, formed by a cable

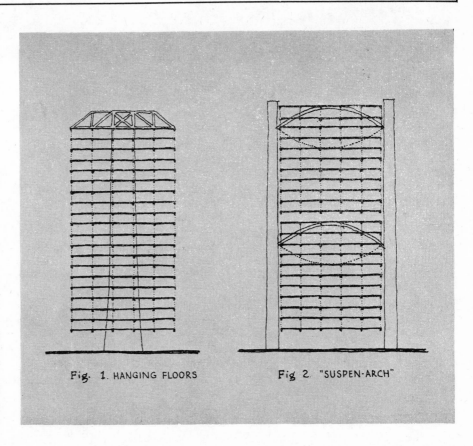

Fig. 1. HANGING FLOORS

Fig 2. "SUSPEN-ARCH"

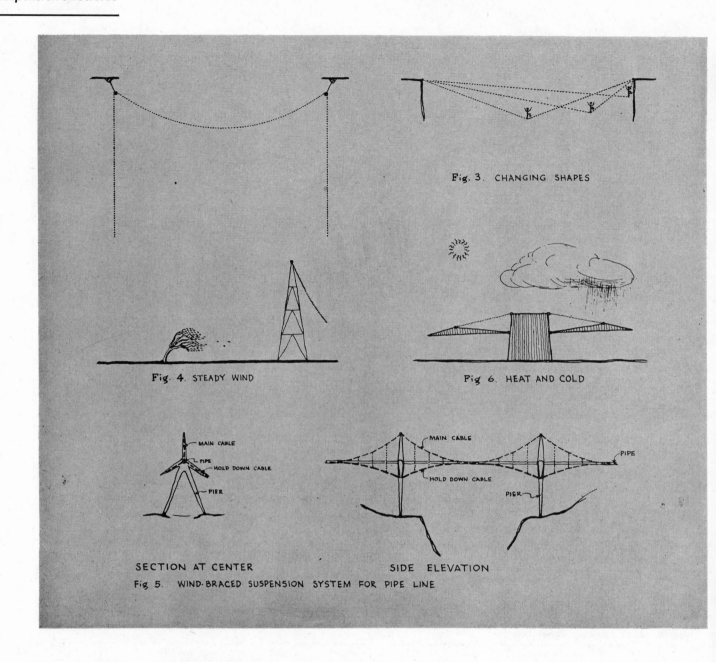

Fig. 3. CHANGING SHAPES

Fig. 4. STEADY WIND

Fig 6. HEAT AND COLD

SECTION AT CENTER

MAIN CABLE
PIPE
HOLD DOWN CABLE
PIER

SIDE ELEVATION

MAIN CABLE
HOLD DOWN CABLE
PIER
PIPE

Fig 5. WIND-BRACED SUSPENSION SYSTEM FOR PIPE LINE

hanging over frictionless pulleys under the influence of its own weight; the weight of the vertical portion is exactly equal to the tension at the supports and the lower end just touches the directrix of the catenary. At right is a cable fastened at each end, and supporting a moving load; cable weight is neglected. Since the length of the cable is fixed, the moving load describes an ellipse with the end fastenings as foci.

The net or membrane in three dimensions corresponds to the cable in two, and gives the picture of a surface which resists forces only by direct tensile stresses. Anyone who has seen acrobats jumping on a circus net or trampoline can understand what is involved.

2. Changes in shape due to unsymetrical loading, such as snow,

over only a portion of the roof are essentially the same as those due to moving loads. In both cases, the greater the live load/dead load ratio, the greater the movement.

Prestressing can be used with the same general effect as an increase in the dead load.

3. Changes in shape due to wind loads. On a single circular cable, a steady wind will act like a statical horizontal load, as in Fig. 4. On a roof surface it will act principally as an upward force (suction), unless the slope is over about 30°. Some means of resisting this must be provided: secondary tie-down cables curving upward (see Fig. 5), tie-down guy wires, an excess of dead weight.

The magnitude of the wind force is not the serious aspect of this prob-

lem. See below for the potentially destructive dynamic effects.

4. Temperature changes must be considered. These can be provided for by hinges which permit rotation as cable lengths change, etc., as in Fig. 6. Particular care is required with structures which are partly outdoors and partly indoors.

Potentially destructive movements
VIBRATION. Flapping, rippling, fluttering and galloping.

Every mass has its own natural period of vibration with its fundamental and higher modes. The period depends on the density of the mass, on its geometrical distribution or shape and on the magnitude of the stresses set up by its own weight and other permanent forces acting on it. The most familiar example is a stretched wire, whose musical note depends on material, length and tension (see Fig. 7).

The number of half-waves formed by the vibrating wire is always a whole number; therefore one of the clues to controlling vibration is an irregular spacing of framing members, ties and supports. In a piano, for example, the hammers strike the strings at the seventh points in order to avoid the seventh harmonic.

When an external pulsating force is applied to such a mass, like a cable, it will be set in motion. This motion can be represented by an infinite number of superimposed modes of vibration. If one of these modes coincides with the natural frequency or fundamental mode of the mass, resonance will ensue. The amplitude or deflection will be increased and the effect of the pulsating force may also be increased. This process may continue until the structure is destroyed.

Types of exciting forces

The general idea of resonant vibration is a familiar one. How may it take place? The possible causes of vibration include:

1. Wind. This is the most usual and the principal danger to suspended structures (see below).

2. Movement of vehicles and the operation of reciprocating and rotating machinery on the structure or on the ground nearby.

3. Sound. Examples: Thin glasses shattered by a musical note; teeth "set on edge"; the vibration of a church interior with the low notes of the organ; pneumatic machinery.

4. Friction may cause squeaks and chattering if part of structure moves due to temperature changes, racking by the wind, etc.

WIND. The flapping of simple suspended elements like a flag, a sail or a canvas awning is very familiar, but how does the wind really act to cause a rhythmic force? A few examples, taken from J. P. DenHartog's "Mechanical Vibrations" (4th Edition, 1956, McGraw-Hill) will help to clarify this:

1. Kármán vortices. If a steady wind blows against a cylinder or other obstruction, the wake is made up of a vortex street (see Fig. 9). The shedding of these vortices on the leeward side causes forces to act on the cylinder at right angles to the direction of the wind, first from one

side and then from the other. The period or frequency: $f = 0.22 \dfrac{V}{D}$ (V is velocity; D is diameter).

This is evidently the cause of the high-pitched hum heard from power lines when a strong wind blows and the cause of fatigue failure when resonance occurs. It is also the cause of vibration failures which often occur in steel industrial smokestacks with winds of about 30 mph. Springs and small shock absorber type dampers have been developed to prevent these failures.

A Kármán vortex about 39-ft long was the cause of the famous Tacoma Bridge collapse, which occurred under a steady 42-mph wind. The deck twisted about 45° from the horizontal in both directions until it broke (see Fig. 10). The deck was rebuilt, using a box section instead of the original H section, thus increasing the resistance to torsion a hundredfold. The new section was made up of open trusses on the sides and an openwork deck to prevent the formation of large eddies or significant pressure differences between the upper and lower surfaces (see Fig. 11).

2. Dynamically Unstable Shapes. The force of the wind on a prismatic shape is usually not in line with the direction of the wind. In analyzing its effect, the force is divided into two components: drag and lift, parallel and perpendicular to the direction of the wind, as shown in Fig. 12. The magnitude of these will vary with changes in the angle of attack and with the section. Thus a cylinder will have no lift, while an oblong

shape will. Some shapes are found to be unstable; this means that if the wind blows at certain angles, the lift force causes them to wobble. A rectangular section is unstable if it is held more or less across the wind as in Fig. 12, a half-cylinder even more so. This effect can be felt by dragging a flat board through water.

The dynamic stability of a given shape can be determined only by experiment. If suspension roof structures are to find more general use, experiments will have to be performed to determine the dynamic stability of various surfaces.

An example of this instability is the galloping transmission line. When a power wire becomes covered with sleet, it loses its symmetrical circular shape and becomes elongated, changing from a stable to an unstable section (see Fig. 13). The wind can now lift it, and a wire of 300-ft span rises about 10 ft, until the stretch of the wire pulls it down again. The frequency is very slow, on the order of once a minute; the wire will gallop up and down for many hours, as long as the wind blows steadily and the sleet remains on the wire. Similar action occurs with a sail turned parallel to the direction of the wind.

DAMPING

A structure or part of a structure which has been set in vibration by a single force will not continue to vibrate forever. Even tuning forks or piano strings will gradually stop due to air resistance and internal friction In a structure it is usually necessary

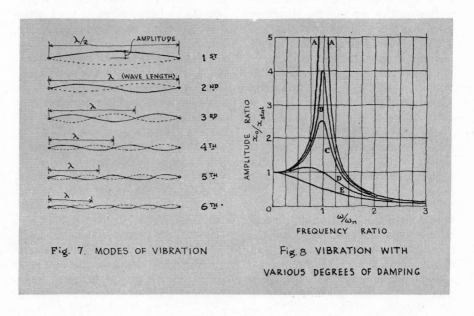

Fig. 7. MODES OF VIBRATION

Fig. 8 VIBRATION WITH VARIOUS DEGREES OF DAMPING

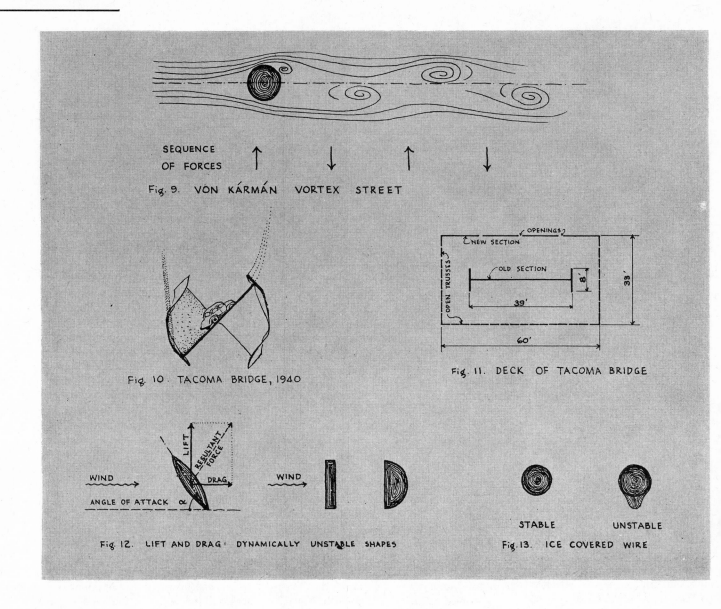

Fig. 9. VON KÁRMÁN VORTEX STREET

SEQUENCE OF FORCES

Fig. 10. TACOMA BRIDGE, 1940

Fig. 11. DECK OF TACOMA BRIDGE

Fig. 12. LIFT AND DRAG· DYNAMICALLY UNSTABLE SHAPES

Fig. 13. ICE COVERED WIRE

to eliminate vibration completely or to have it damped as quickly as possible.

If a damping force can be provided which acts in the opposite direction to that in which the structure is moving when vibration starts, and if that force is proportional to the velocity of the structure (the faster it moves, the greater the damping force), vibration can be prevented or greatly diminished. This is often called viscous damping because a small plunger in a dashpot filled with viscous liquid will provide this type of resisting force. This is similar to the action of the cylinder of a door closer.

A spring alone is not sufficient for viscous damping. Although it may change the period of vibration and prevent or reduce the transmission of vibration from one part of a structure to another, its resisting force does not increase proportionally to

the velocity but only proportionally to the displacement. In other words, the further down the structure is pushed on the spring, the greater the force of the spring pushing it up; but the resisting force of the spring does not increase any more or any less if the structure moves down against it quickly or slowly. Also, during its motion in one direction, the spring stores up energy which is released back into the structure as the spring moves in the opposite direction. With viscous damping on the other hand, the energy is dissipated within the "dashpot".

The diagrams of Fig. 8 show graphically the effect of damping. The abscissas measure the relationship:

$$\frac{\omega}{\omega_n} \quad OR \quad \frac{\text{period (freq.) of exciting force}}{\text{natural frequency of structure}}$$

The period of the exciting force may be the period of the external force (such as machinery) or the period of

vibration of the self-excited force (such as the Kármán vortex street or the changing lift pattern of an airfoil surface).

The ordinates measure the relationship:

$$\frac{x_o}{x_{stat}} \quad OR \quad \frac{\text{amplitude of vibration due to exciting force}}{\text{amplitude of deflection due to a statical force of same magnitude}}$$

The curves plot the effect of various degrees of damping, from none to perfect. Thus, curve A, with no damping ($c/c_o = 0$), shows that the amplitude or deflection goes to infinity at resonance; i.e. the structure would be destroyed. For curve B, with a damping of $\frac{1}{8}$ of critical ($c/c_o = 0.125$), the amplitude at resonance is four times as great as the statical deflection. For curve C, $c/c_o = 0.20$; curve D, $c/c_o = 0.50$. With curve E, showing critical or perfect damping ($c/c_o = 1.0$), the

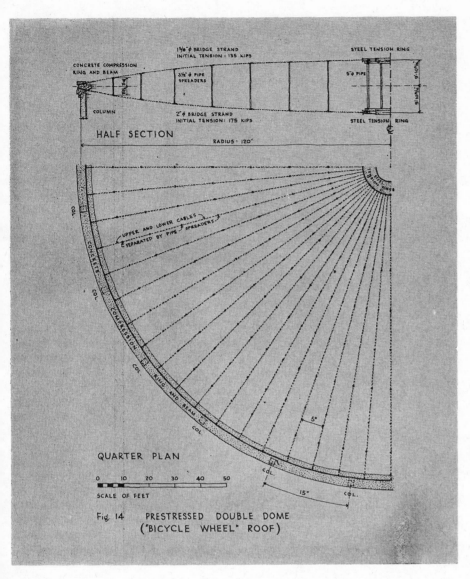

CONCRETE COMPRESSION RING AND BEAM

1⅝"⌀ BRIDGE STRAND INITIAL TENSION: 135 KIPS

3½"⌀ PIPE SPREADERS

STEEL TENSION RING

5"⌀ PIPE

COLUMN

2"⌀ BRIDGE STRAND INITIAL TENSION: 175 KIPS

STEEL TENSION RING

HALF SECTION

RADIUS: 120'

UPPER AND LOWER CABLES SEPARATED BY PIPE SPREADERS

QUARTER PLAN

0 10 20 30 40 50
SCALE OF FEET

Fig. 14 PRESTRESSED DOUBLE DOME
('BICYCLE WHEEL' ROOF)

amplitude is always less than the statical deflection, showing that the damping has no effect if the exciting force is applied very, very slowly, but an ever increasing effect as the period of the exciting force increases.

EXAMPLES OF SUSPENSION STRUCTURES

Apart from the suspension bridge, there is to date no generally accepted body of "good practice". Relatively few buildings have been built. The field is new; experiments and patents are many. Pioneers include such engineers as: Fred Severud and Lev Zetlin in the U.S.; Frei Otto in Germany; Bodiansky, LeRicolais, Bernard Laffaille and René Sarger in France.

Principal elements

1. Compression. Towers, masts.

2. Tension. Main cables and hanger members.

3. Stiffening. For holding down against wind up-lift, for preventing vibration, for maintaining shape under unsymmetrical loading. May be trusses, diagonal tension stays, guy wires, secondary cables with a curvature upward (these may be prestressed) and the dead weight of the structure itself.

4. Anchorage. For vertical components, may be the ground (bedrock), the weight of concrete deadmen or the dead weight of part of the structure such as side walls. For horizontal components, may be bedrock, the resistance to sliding of concrete deadmen, or part of the structure such as a floor, deck or a circumferential ring.

The most promising principles for roof surfaces seem to be:

1. Use two families of cables, one curved downward (concave) and one curved upward (convex).

2. Prestress both families of ca-

bles, so that they will always be in tension and never go slack, no matter what the loading. This will require anchorages or edge supports able to withstand forces at least three times as great as if not prestressed. Force instead of mass is being used to prevent flutter but a good deal of mass reappears in the anchorages.

If followed correctly for every part of a roof surface, these principles will ensure a "rigid" tensile membrane which can carry any vibrations in loading by corresponding variations in the tensile stresses in the surface. They may not by themselves prevent vibration, however. For this further study is required.

Some examples embodying these principles are shown in Figs. 15 through 18.

The Prestressed Double Dome or "Bicycle Wheel" Roof

This roof (Fig. 14) was developed by the engineer Lev Zetlin of New York for the Municipal Auditorium of Utica, N. Y., designed by Gehron and Seltzer, architects, completed this year. (See ARCHITECTURAL RECORD, August, 1959.)

Its main characteristics are: two sets of cables, one curved upward, one downward, both prestressed. This was done by jacking them apart and inserting the pipe spreaders. The compression ring is under a constant radial horizontal load of about 300 kips per pair of cables, which generates a compressive force of about 3500 kips in the ring. The vertical dead load is only about 8 kips per pair of cables or about 13 lb per sq ft (not including the compression ring). The prestressing enables both sets of cables to share in supporting the dead and live loads. Note how the use of intermediate spreaders enables the cables to be attached to the compression ring at relatively steep angles. The cables can thus carry greater vertical forces for a given total tension.

As vertical loads increase, the tension in the upper family of cables will diminish while that in the lower family will increase. As vertical loads decrease due to wind suction, the reverse will occur. As long as the initial prestressing force is not completely cancelled out, neither family will go slack and the horizontal pull on the compression ring will be constant.

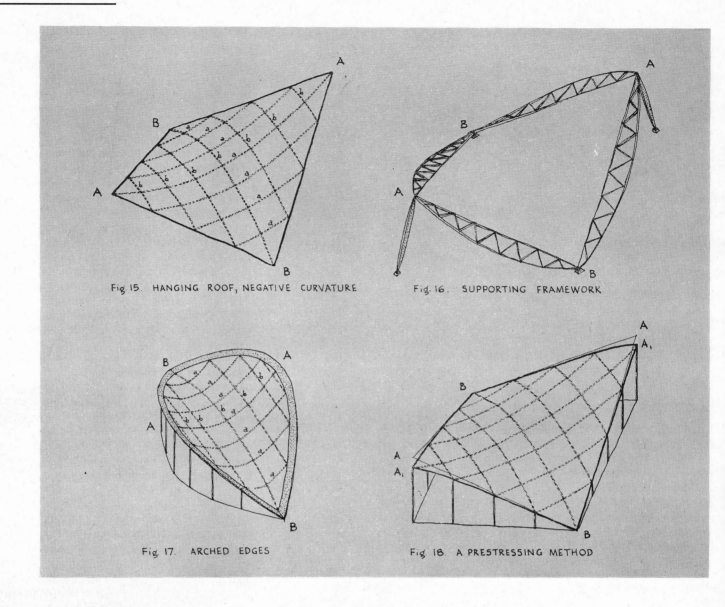

Fig. 15. HANGING ROOF, NEGATIVE CURVATURE

Fig. 16. SUPPORTING FRAMEWORK

Fig. 17. ARCHED EDGES

Fig. 18. A PRESTRESSING METHOD

The greatest advantage of this system is its action as a giant shock absorber. The two sets of cables are of different cross-section, carry different initial tensions and are fastened together by spreaders which are spaced unequally. No matter how the tensions in the two families of cables may vary, their frequencies and wave lengths will differ. Because they are connected by the spreaders, the upper family thus damps any vibration which might start in the lower cables and vice versa. The damping is perfect, corresponding to curve E in Fig. 8.

Although this example shows a 240 ft span, spans up to 1800 ft are possible and would give greater economy per sq ft.

Certain features such as the intermediate spreaders and the use of large prestressing forces are patented (application Serial No. 653,129, April 16, 1957).

Roofs of Negative Curvature

While in the double dome or bicycle wheel roof every point is tied to two systems of cables with opposing curvature, two "surfaces" are needed to accomplish this.

The negative or anticlastic surfaces offer another possibility. Their basic characteristics are shown in Figs. 15 through 18.

Fig. 15 shows a straight-edged surface, with the high points marked A and the low B. The framework necessary to support the surface is indicated in Fig. 16; the struts at A are necessary for the stability of the structure as a whole, the two points of support at B being insufficient unless they were built in as moment connections.

From the edges hang the principal cables, curved downward, which we can call family "a". Hanging under its own weight, each cable will describe a catenary curve. By themselves these cables would be very unstable, moving under the slightest applied load. A second set of cables is therefore added on top to stabilize them and to resist uplift forces due to the wind. These are all curved upward; call them family "b". The points of intersection of the cables all lie on a surface of negative curvature. (Only if all the "a" family cables follow the shape of identical parabolas and if all the "b" family cables follow the shape of identical parabolas would the surface be a true hyperbolic parabola.)

In order to resist the considerable bending set up in the edge beams, structures have been built with the edges curved into arch form so as to resist the pull of the cables by compression alone. Fig. 17 shows this design, which is familiar from the North Carolina State Fair Pavilion (William Dietrich, Architect; Matthew Nowicki, Consultant; Severud-

Elstad-Krueger, Structural Engineers), and which is also familiar from Frei Otto's work in Germany. Note that the edge arches need some vertical support from mullions to assure the stability of the entire structure. In simple hanging roofs of this kind the "b" family of cables is only moderately prestressed and flutter must be prevented by the addition of guy wires attached at critical points and coming off more or less perpendicular to the surface.

The next step is to provide so much prestress in the "b" cables, thus also prestressing the "a" cables (or vice versa), that the surface will be much more resistant to any changes in loading and will act like a rigid membrane.

How to prestress the cables is the difficulty. One solution has been patented by René Sarger and the C.E.T.A.C. (patent No. 1,156,041, Paris, 20 August 1956) and used by him for the French pavilion at the Brussels Fair and other structures. It consists in lowering the points A by pulling down on the edge beam. The inner chord of the edge beam remains in the same vertical plane but is now curved in this plane along the line BA_1, as shown in Fig. 18. The surface remains approximately that of a hyperbolic paraboloid, but not exactly the same one as before. The weight of the side walls plus footing anchorages at the bottom of the mullions are used to hold the edge down.

It is important to distinguish the action of the various roof shapes which follow the hyperbolic paraboloid:

1. The thin-shell surface, acting as a membrane under uniform vertical loads. Tensile forces follow the lines corresponding to the "a" family and compression forces follow the "b" family. The magnitude of these membrane forces is the same at every point and the compression and tensile forces cancel each other out at the edge. This leaves only a shearing force of the same magnitude, which the edge can support as a relatively slender column.

2. The hanging roof, not prestressed. Under uniform vertical loading no forces can be carried by the "b" family. The relatively large horizontal forces needed to support the ends of the cables of the "a" fam-

ily require the edges to be designed as beams, supported at A and B. These horizontal forces will vary considerably with changes in snow and wind loads.

3. The prestressed suspension roof. In order to prestress both families of cables, at least three times as large horizontal reactive forces must be permanently provided by the edges. But, for any variation in loading on the roof due to snow or wind, the prestressed surface will now act similarly to the thin-shell roof, up to the point where the "compressive" force set up in the "b" family cancels out the initial tension.

Weights. Prestressed suspension roofs have been built in this shape and also as conoids (as at the Brussels Fair) with remarkably light dead loads, on the order of 3 lb per sq ft for cables and planking for spans of over 200 ft in both directions. However these light loads were achieved only at the cost of very heavy edge beams and vertical supports which brought the average weight up to about 40 psf.

It would appear therefore that suspension systems for roofs will be most suitable and economical when the edge anchorages do not have to be constructed for that purpose alone but can be provided by some elements of structure which are already necessary for other reasons. These might be stadium seats hanging over their bases, the lean-to shops and maintenance areas of a hanger, floors surrounding a central hall or along two ends of a hall, such as one might find in a museum (see Fig. 19).

REFERENCES:
Das Hangende Dach, Dr. Ing. Frei Otto, Bauwelt Verlag, Berlin 1954

Mechanical Vibrations, J. P. Den Hartog, 4th Ed., McGraw-Hill 1956

Articles by Rene Sarger in *Etudes et Realisations*, January 1959 and in *Acier*, April 1959

Communications from Lev Zetlin (see also ARCHITECTURAL RECORD, Aug. 1959)

Lectures by Lev Zetlin on "Aerodynamics of Structures" at Cornell, Columbia, New York University and Pratt

Lecture by Fred Severud at Pratt Institute, December 1958

Tables and Data from John A. Roebling's Sons Corp., Trenton 2, N. J.

A.S.C.E. Papers:

1709: "Wind Forces on Structures: Fundamental Considerations" by G. B. Woodruff and J. J. Kozak

1718: "Wind Forces on Structures: Structures Subject to Oscillation" by F. B. Farquharson

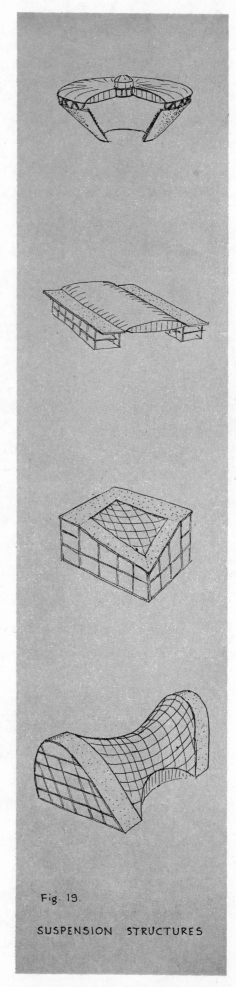

Fig. 19.

SUSPENSION STRUCTURES

Tranquille

All the elements of the roof structure are shown above. Two sets of cables, upper and lower, are attached to an outer concrete compression ring and two inner steel tension rings. When pipe spreaders are inserted between cables, they become prestressed. The diagonal bracing is an added safety factor against large local eccentricities. Horizontal steel angles are for hanging mechanical equipment.

PRESTRESSING PREVENTS FLUTTER OF CABLE ROOF

by Seymour Howard, A.I.A., Associate Professor, Pratt Institute
Municipal Auditorium, City of Utica, New York; Gehron & Seltzer, Architects; Frank Delle Cese, Associate Architect; Lev Zetlin, Structural Engineer; Fred S. Dubin Associates, Mechanical and Electrical Engineer; General Sovereign Construction Co., Ltd., Builder

Steel has remarkable strength in tension so when roof spans must stretch beyond several hundred feet, steel cables surpass other systems in structural efficiency. The thing that has bothered engineers until very recently, however, is flutter. Cables—in contrast to other roof systems—have no inherent rigidity to dynamic loads. So one way or another they have to be stabilized against vibrations or noises caused by wind and other external forces—truck traffic, for example.

So far this has been accomplished by weighting cables down with a heavy roof, by guying them with other cables, and in several cases by partially prestressing a dish-shaped concrete roof. (Suspension bridges are stabilized by means of stiffening trusses.)

The unique method shown here, developed by engineer Dr. Lev Zetlin, builds self-damping right into the cable system. This is done by using two sets of cables, stretched apart by means of spreaders, and thus prestressed by forces of 135,000 lb or more per cable.

Upper cables always have a different tension than the lower cables—first because the prestressing force is applied against cables of different sizes, and second, because any applied load will increase the tension in one set of cables and reduce it in the other. Thus the two sets of cables always have different natural frequencies. No matter what frequency the wind imposes on the roof—even if it happens to be the same as that of one set of cables, the other set will be out of phase and quash the vibration (see diagram p. 181). A much simplified analogy for such a damping system would be the soft pedal on a piano quieting a string.

The cables are anchored to a 240 ft diameter concrete compression ring and to two steel tension rings (see details) and are kept apart by pipe spreaders. The compression ring is supported by 24 rectangular concrete columns spaced 15 degrees apart. Each pair of upper and lower cables is spaced 5 degrees apart, making 72 pairs in all. The distance between upper and lower tension rings is about 20 ft, so the depth/span ratio is 1/12.

How It Was Built

After the concrete columns were completed, the entire compression ring was poured using 5000 psi concrete. Pipe sleeves were cast into the ring to allow cables to pass through. In the meantime the upper and lower welded steel tension rings were fabricated and hoisted to a wooden tower in the center, approximately halfway between the final vertical positions of the two rings.

Now the cables were placed. This was the most critical moment in the erection procedure because the edge compression ring was designed for forces evenly distributed at 5 degrees around the circumference, not for the force of one pair of cables acting alone. Thus a carefully planned sequence for placing cables and pulling them into place was nec-

After the inner steel tension rings were fabricated, cranes hoisted them to a central tower topped with wood blocking.

Then cables were strung between inner and outer rings. Concrete ring is 240 ft in diameter

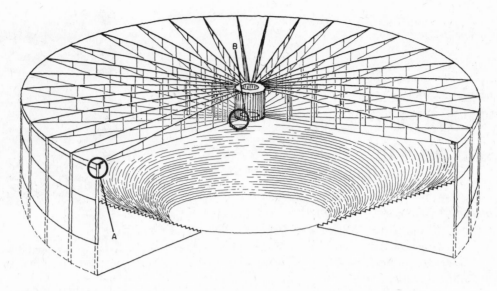

Prestressing of cables plus their curvature both help in resisting deflection due to imposed loads. Predicting the actual curvature was complicated, but had to be done accurately for sizing the spreaders. The details below show how the cables were anchored to the 240-ft concrete compression ring and the steel tension rings. The right-hand detail (b) shows how the tension rings are kept apart. Jacking of these rings was the next step after the cables were strung. Cable work was done by the John R. Roebling & Sons Co.

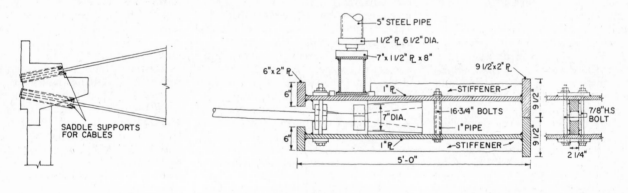

SECTION A

SECTION B

Interstate Photographers

Left: tightening up the bolts on the top tension ring after the cables had been strung. *Center:* to get initial pre-stressing of cables, the two steel tension rings were jacked apart. *Right:* rings are about at their final position and are ready for 5-in. pipe spreaders to be inserted. Detail above indicates how this was done

essary to avoid excessive bending of the ring.

When all of the cables had been fastened, the initial prestressing forces were developed by raising the upper tension ring and lowering the bottom ring, forcing them apart by means of jacks. The spreaders or stanchions were then placed, further increasing the amount of force built into the cable system. The sequence of placing the spreaders was important for the reason already mentioned. This method for introducing prestress by jacking approximately at right angles to the cable is said to be much easier than by applying an axial force using turnbuckles or tightening screws at the end.

Once the initial forces had been achieved, the delicate stage of the construction was passed. Installation of a formed metal roof decking, insulation and roofing is now being completed. The space between the upper and lower cables is used for air conditioning equipment, ducts, lighting, etc. There will be sound absorbing material in the center and around the edge, leaving a wide circular area in between.

How It Works
To get an idea of the relative magnitude of forces, a 20 lb per sq ft dead load would produce 12.6 kips vertical load at each fastening. But the horizontal forces are much greater than this because of the prestressing.

There is no change in the horizontal pull on the compression ring when load is added because the horizontal components cancel out. Roof decking, equipment, snow, etc. decrease the tension in the upper cable and increase the tension in the lower cable. By creating a sufficiently large

initial force in the upper cable, this tension will never be reduced to zero and the cable will never go slack. Wind loads when acting upwards will produce the opposite situation.

The purpose of the prestressing can be summed up as follows:

1. To maintain tension in the cables at all times so there is no sagging.

2. To keep tension at such values as to control natural frequencies of top and bottom cable systems, preventing flutter.

3. To control deflection of the whole cable system under dead and live load. (Worst situation was taken as a downward force on $\frac{1}{8}$ sector and upward force, i.e. wind, on $\frac{1}{8}$ sector diametrically opposite.) Deflection is controlled by the predetermined curvature of the cables as well as by tension of the cables. This was solved in design by trial and error. Deflection due to roof and air conditioning equipment was 4 in.

Damping action at the cables

Tension in the cables was predicted by geometry—i.e., knowing original length of cables, length of spreaders and final length of cables. Final tension was checked by putting a jack on the end of the cables, turning the nuts on the fittings up tight and reading a pressure gage—tension checked out as predicted.

What is the nature of the curves of the upper and lower cables? They will follow the funicular curve for the loadings. Since the loading is complicated, the true shape of the funicular curve is not any simple

mathematical function. We can distinguish three main features:

1. A catenary, due to the dead weight of the cables alone;

2. A polygon, due to the forces generated in the spreaders by the initial prestressing and also due to the partial transfer of loads from the roof deck to the lower cable system by these spreaders;

3. Approximately a third degree parabola, which is the funicular curve for the dead loads acting on the triangular projected area supported by each cable in plan.

The true curve would have as ordinates the algebraic sum of the ordinates of these different curves. This had to be calculated as accurately as possible so that the spreaders could be fabricated to the correct lengths and all of the fittings and sleeves to the correct angles.

Patented Features
The architects, Gehron and Seltzer, decided on a circular building. When they called in Dr. Zetlin, he suggested a cable system as a solution and said he would study the problem of flutter.

Recognizing that he had come up with something new, he and his associate Tyge Hermansen, applied for a patent (Serial No. 653,129, April 16, 1957), covering the main features of the roof system: the large initial tension; the curvature of the cables; and the spreaders required to establish the curvature.

New Applications
Like all suspension systems, this prestressed double cable roof is not particularly appropriate for "small" spans. Dr. Zeltin believes the lower limit of economic applicability to be about a 200 ft span. On the other

Tranquille

Left: key to damping is spreader between two sets of cables. Lower cables have more tension than upper cables; their sizes are 2 in. and 1⅝ in. respectively. Insertion of

the spreaders was a relatively simple way to achieve prestressing. *Right:* walls filled in; roof being covered. Auditorium has 4000 permanent seats, but can hold 6500

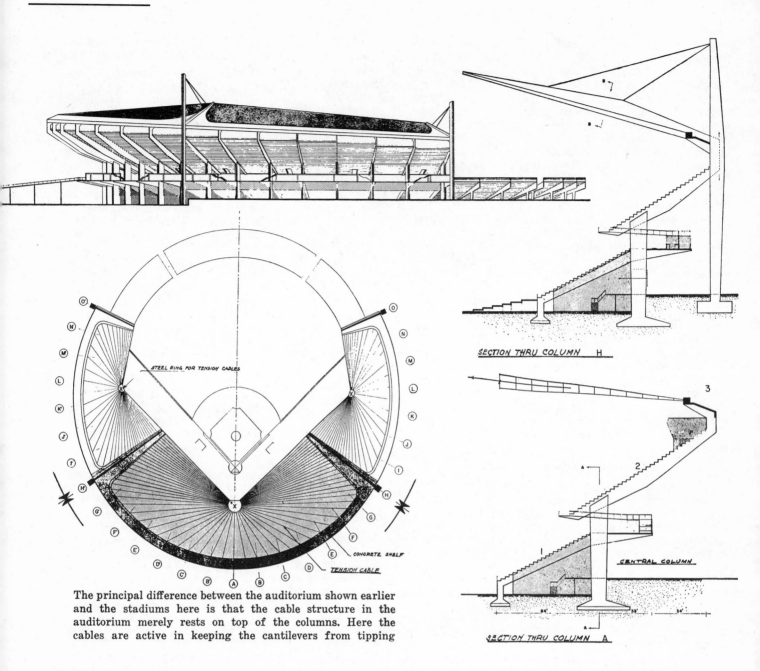

SECTION THRU COLUMN H

SECTION THRU COLUMN A

STEEL RING FOR TENSION CABLES

CONCRETE SHELF

TENSION CABLE

CENTRAL COLUMN

The principal difference between the auditorium shown earlier and the stadiums here is that the cable structure in the auditorium merely rests on top of the columns. Here the cables are active in keeping the cantilevers from tipping

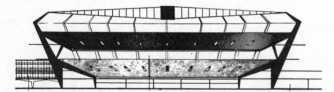

Here is another proposal for a stadium. The plan is a square with rounded corners and cables support cantilevers

hand, the cost per sq ft actually goes down with an increase in span. The upper limit would be about 1800 ft. By increasing the number of cables, their size and initial tension would be kept constant. The spreaders would become heavier to prevent buckling as their length increases. But the cost of fittings and erection would remain more or less constant.

Together with architect Helge Westermann, Dr. Zetlin has drawn up plans for larger buildings, in which he has taken advantage of the constant horizontal force generated by the double cable system to balance cantilevered "C" shaped frames which support grandstands. Two of these are shown here, one a square building with rounded corners, with

an 800 ft span roof, the other an irregular canopy over the seats for a baseball diamond. In this "C" shaped grandstand design, the horizontal forces are distributed in plan in such a way that they resist the tendency of the cantilevers to tip back. This is especially important for the compression member at the top of the cantilevers, which looks like a giant "C" clamp in plan. The cantilevers try to pull it apart; the cables hold it together.

In the Utica Auditorium, the cable system is inert. That is, cables and rings merely sit on top of the columns. In these last two examples, the cables actually support outside cantilevers, permitting their span to be larger and cross-section smaller.

Section 5

COMPONENT SYSTEMS

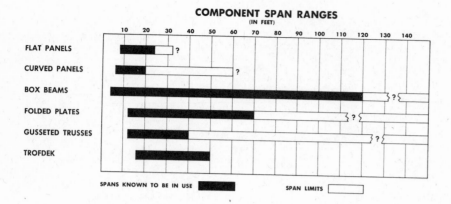

COMPONENT SPAN RANGES
(IN FEET)

| FLAT PANELS |
| CURVED PANELS |
| BOX BEAMS |
| FOLDED PLATES |
| GUSSETED TRUSSES |
| TROFDEK |

SPANS KNOWN TO BE IN USE   SPAN LIMITS

FACTORY-BUILT PLYWOOD COMPONENTS

by Howard P. Vermilya, A.I.A.

Engineered plywood components are a relatively recent addition to the architect's design vocabulary, but the signs point to their becoming a byword. New types of components, improved engineering and fabricating techniques, and an industry-wide quality control program are making plywood structural members as versatile and reliable as other factory-produced structural materials.

The stressed skin panel, the first engineered plywood component to be developed, dates back to the early 'thirties and the Forest Product Laboratory's then-new recognition of the "racking" properties or diaphragm action of plywood. Since then, the Douglas Fir Plywood Association, which began research in the field at about the same time, has developed a wide variety of structural elements designed to take full advantage of plywood's ability to resist flexural and shear forces. Full-size components have been tested to failure. Engineering data and design manuals have been prepared. Techniques of fabrication have been studied, tested and formulated. Specifications have been drawn to control the materials, the production methods and conditions, and the inspection and test procedures.

Much of this specialized information on component fabrication was freely distributed to the construction industry through architects and engineers. But even so, it became increasingly apparent to the plywood association that a critical problem existed involving production facilities, the specialized nature of the

engineering, and the possibility that without proper care in workmanship, fabrication or engineering, the performance of plywood components would be questionable. At the same time, more complicated components, and more sophisticated combinations, were coming into extensive use in constructing floors, walls, roofs and even entire structures, making it vitally important for the architect to be able to rely on the quality of the materials—lumber, plywood and glue, and upon the quality of the workmanship.

For this reason, DFPA two years ago set up Plywood Fabricators Service, Inc., an affiliate whose program is designed to provide a uniform standard of fabrication and the quality controls necessary to encourage the use of engineered plywood components. Before being permitted to use the trademarks indicating compliance with the DFPA's specifications, fabricators licensed by PFS must qualify in general categories based on the quality of fabrication required: Nail-gluing or pressure-gluing; interior or exterior end use; and standard or critical applications. ("Critical" components are

those involving long spans or high design loads: the PFS inspector must examine each lot and himself apply the trademark.) In addition, the fabricator must qualify to produce each type of component, the qualification being controlled by the general categories mentioned. Basic to any qualification at all is a survey of the fabrication facilities and continuing laboratory tests of glue bonds and fabricating techniques.

Box Beams
The box beam, which was developed under the stimulus of the war-time steel shortage, is a typical example of the engineered plywood component. Here plywood and lumber are combined in a lightweight section designed to use each material most effectively. Solid lumber is used for the flanges because of its axial strength, while plywood is used as a web because of its ability to resist shear. The section consists of one or more (usually two or more) vertical plywood webs glued to lumber flanges which are separated along the beam's length by vertical lumber spacers. These spacers function as stiffeners to prevent web buckling and distribute concentrated loads.

The assembly is glued under pressure using clamps or presses, which requires the closely controlled conditions usually found in a factory and not at the site. Nail-gluing is acceptable on only the simplest sections.

Box beams consisting of vertical plywood webs pressure-glued to lumber flanges are capable of spanning distances up to 120 ft. A basic and highly versatile component, they are often used in combination with other plywood components or with plywood panels to form floors and roofs. The nine 36-ft beams shown above were used with plywood deck to roof a small, low cost school. *Murray School, Dublin, Calif.; Architect: Aitken and Collin*

Detail shows typical box beam: vertical plywood webs for shear resistance glued to lumber flanges for axial strength. Flanges are separated at intervals by vertical spaces which function as stiffeners to prevent web buckling and distribute concentrated loads. Details above right indicate various beam sections that may be used. When flange cross section requires lumber with a least dimension greater than 2-in., flanges must be laminated from lumber 2-in. thick or less

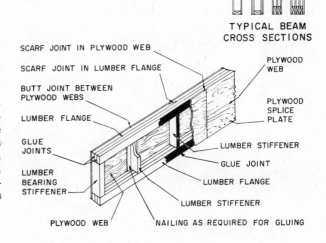

TYPICAL BEAM CROSS SECTIONS

SCARF JOINT IN PLYWOOD WEB
SCARF JOINT IN LUMBER FLANGE
BUTT JOINT BETWEEN PLYWOOD WEBS
LUMBER FLANGE
GLUE JOINTS
LUMBER BEARING STIFFENER
PLYWOOD WEB
PLYWOOD WEB
PLYWOOD SPLICE PLATE
LUMBER STIFFENER
GLUE JOINT
LUMBER FLANGE
LUMBER STIFFENER
NAILING AS REQUIRED FOR GLUING

TYPICAL BOX BEAM

Stressed skin panels, which offer the advantages of economy, strength and fast erection are used as structural coverings for floors, walls and roofs, are probably the most adaptable of the components. For the roof below, 4-ft wide panels laid over box beams serve as both deck and finish ceiling. Typical panels have ½-in. plywood top skins and ⅜-in. bottom skins. Ribs are 2 by 4 and 1 by 4 lumber. *Penn-Jersey Co-op Supermarket Addition, Phillipsburg, N. J. Engineer: Heikki K. Elo*

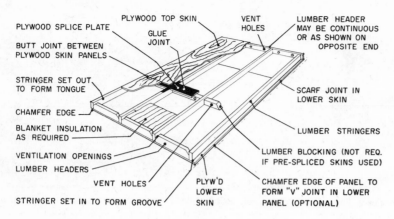

PLYWOOD SPLICE PLATE
BUTT JOINT BETWEEN PLYWOOD SKIN PANELS
STRINGER SET OUT TO FORM TONGUE
CHAMFER EDGE
BLANKET INSULATION AS REQUIRED
VENTILATION OPENINGS
LUMBER HEADERS
VENT HOLES
STRINGER SET IN TO FORM GROOVE

PLYWOOD TOP SKIN
GLUE JOINT
VENT HOLES
LUMBER HEADER MAY BE CONTINUOUS OR AS SHOWN ON OPPOSITE END
SCARF JOINT IN LOWER SKIN
LUMBER STRINGERS
LUMBER BLOCKING (NOT REQ. IF PRE-SPLICED SKINS USED)
CHAMFER EDGE OF PANEL TO FORM "V" JOINT IN LOWER PANEL (OPTIONAL)
PLYW'D LOWER SKIN

TYPICAL STRESSED SKIN PANEL

Essentially a box beam laid flat, the stressed skin panel consists of longitudinal stringers to which a top and bottom skin are bonded so that the whole assembly acts as a unit. The plywood skins then are the flanges for a series of I-beams—or T-beams if only one skin is used—while the stringers carry the shear. The lateral framing members serve only as headers or as blocking

A relatively new version of the stressed-skin panel is the space plane, a folded plate with non-parallel chords. The radial folded plate roof above was erected in less than a day. *AA Headquarters Building, Tucson, Ariz. Architect: Arthur Brown*

In the larger sections the box beam is capable of spanning over 100 feet. It is a basic structural component, for it may be combined with components such as stressed skin panels or with plywood panels to provide floor or roof. It may serve as a rafter or purlin, or it can be formed as a bent. It may also be tapered or curved and cantilevers are routine.

Stressed Skin Panels

In these structural coverings for floors, walls or roofs, longitudinal framing members serve as stringers. The skins are usually bonded one to each side of the stringer to form a series of "I" beams. When only one skin is bonded to the stringer, the skin becomes the flange of a series of "T" beams. (See "Stressed Skin Plywood Panels," by William J. Le-Messurier and Albert G. H. Dietz, *Time-Saver Standards*, ARCHITECT-URAL RECORD, October 1954.)

Stressed skin panels may be fabricated by nail-gluing or pressure-gluing. The latter gives better appearance because of the absence of nail heads and is more efficient when presses or clamps are used in a factory. The panels may also be of sandwich construction, using a honeycomb, foamed plastic or other material as the core between the plywood skins.

The action of the stressed skin panel is similar to that of a box beam laid flat. Where the edges between panels are adequately fastened, these panels can transmit stresses to the walls or ground, greatly increasing the rigidity of the structure. In walls, the skins effectively resist racking, but stressed skin panels in general are designed to resist flexural forces applied perpendicular to whatever shear is involved. They may be used

as a basic element in a folded plate design, but generally are used for floors or roofs, often in conjunction with the box beam or with delta frames.

The panels should be ventilated but may contain insulation, electrical wiring, heating and sprinkler pipes or ducts, often inserted at the time of fabrication. Skins and lumber framing may be scarf jointed or butt joints with splice plates may be used in the skins.

Curved Panels

Curved panels are ideal for roof construction because of their light weight and high strength and because of their design possibilities in single or multiple use. They will span as much as 32 ft or more, but spans up to 24 ft are most practical.

Three different types of curved panels are available:
1. The ribbed, stressed skin panel using a curved stringer usually made from laminated plywood strips;
2. The solid core panel, a plywood sheet lamination; and
3. A sandwich core panel.

They can be designed for use with or without tie-rods, but require the sidewalls or side beam-to-wall connection to be designed for horizontal deflection. A fourth possibility is a curved section, designed as a thin-shelled vault in which the beam action built into the curved section eliminates the need for the usual supporting beam.

Fabrication is simplified by the use of presses: either a chain clamp press using a male form or a curve platen hot press with heating strips in the rib area. The panels are usually 48-inches long and joined with tongue-and-grooved or shiplap connections.

Folded Plates

Folded plate roofs may be conventionally framed and sheathed with plywood, but many are designed to use plywood structural components. These may be divided into two classes:
1. Where box beams are the main supports and the individual folds are designed as stressed skin panels.
2. Where the plates themselves are designed as giant box beams and act as diaphrams, thereby eliminating large valley beams.

The folded plate lends itself to many roof designs, either single bay or multiple bays. It is capable of

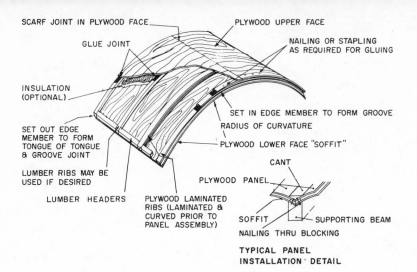

TYPICAL PANEL USING CURVED PLYWOOD RIBS

Labels: SCARF JOINT IN PLYWOOD FACE — PLYWOOD UPPER FACE — GLUE JOINT — NAILING OR STAPLING AS REQUIRED FOR GLUING — INSULATION (OPTIONAL) — SET IN EDGE MEMBER TO FORM GROOVE — RADIUS OF CURVATURE — SET OUT EDGE MEMBER TO FORM TONGUE OF TONGUE & GROOVE JOINT — PLYWOOD LOWER FACE "SOFFIT" — LUMBER RIBS MAY BE USED IF DESIRED — LUMBER HEADERS — PLYWOOD LAMINATED RIBS (LAMINATED & CURVED PRIOR TO PANEL ASSEMBLY) — CANT — PLYWOOD PANEL — SOFFIT — SUPPORTING BEAM — NAILING THRU BLOCKING — TYPICAL PANEL INSTALLATION DETAIL

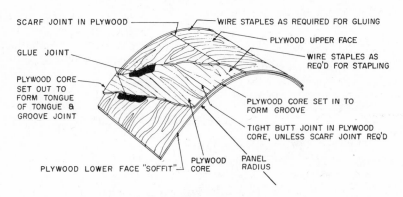

TYPICAL PANEL USING SOLID PLYWOOD CORE

Labels: SCARF JOINT IN PLYWOOD — WIRE STAPLES AS REQUIRED FOR GLUING — GLUE JOINT — PLYWOOD UPPER FACE — WIRE STAPLES AS REQ'D FOR STAPLING — PLYWOOD CORE SET OUT TO FORM TONGUE OF TONGUE & GROOVE JOINT — PLYWOOD CORE SET IN TO FORM GROOVE — TIGHT BUTT JOINT IN PLYWOOD CORE, UNLESS SCARF JOINT REQ'D — PLYWOOD LOWER FACE "SOFFIT" — PLYWOOD CORE — PANEL RADIUS

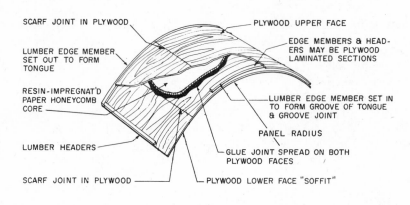

TYPICAL PANEL USING PAPER HONEYCOMB CORE

Labels: SCARF JOINT IN PLYWOOD — PLYWOOD UPPER FACE — LUMBER EDGE MEMBER SET OUT TO FORM TONGUE — EDGE MEMBERS & HEADERS MAY BE PLYWOOD LAMINATED SECTIONS — RESIN-IMPREGNAT'D PAPER HONEYCOMB CORE — LUMBER EDGE MEMBER SET IN TO FORM GROOVE OF TONGUE & GROOVE JOINT — LUMBER HEADERS — PANEL RADIUS — GLUE JOINT SPREAD ON BOTH PLYWOOD FACES — SCARF JOINT IN PLYWOOD — PLYWOOD LOWER FACE "SOFFIT"

Curved stressed skin panels are a natural for roof structures because their arching action permits the spanning of great distances with relatively thin cross sections. Three different panels are available: the ribbed panel (photo right), which is similar to the typical stressed skin panel except that the stringers are curved; the solid core panel, a plywood sheet lamination; and the sandwich core panel. All can be used with or without tie-rods. A fourth possibility, the thin shell vault, has the beam action built into the curved section. The curved panel roof shown in the photo sequence (above right) consists of 4-ft. wide arches with male and female edge joints nailed and glued into beveled ridges in the laminated supporting beams. *Top three photos: Hunt Jr. High School Gymnasium, Tacoma, Wash., Robert Billsborough Price, architect; bottom photo: Greek Orthodox Church, Indianapolis, Ind.*

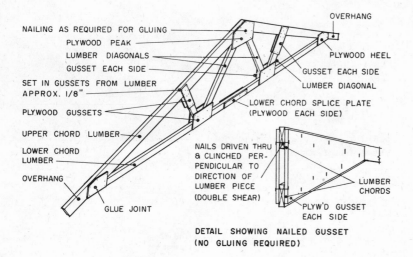

NAILING AS REQUIRED FOR GLUING
PLYWOOD PEAK
LUMBER DIAGONALS
GUSSET EACH SIDE
SET IN GUSSETS FROM LUMBER APPROX. 1/8"
PLYWOOD GUSSETS
UPPER CHORD LUMBER
LOWER CHORD LUMBER
OVERHANG
GLUE JOINT

OVERHANG
PLYWOOD HEEL
GUSSET EACH SIDE
LUMBER DIAGONAL
LOWER CHORD SPLICE PLATE (PLYWOOD EACH SIDE)

NAILS DRIVEN THRU & CLINCHED PERPENDICULAR TO DIRECTION OF LUMBER PIECE (DOUBLE SHEAR)

LUMBER CHORDS

PLYW'D GUSSET EACH SIDE

DETAIL SHOWING NAILED GUSSET (NO GLUING REQUIRED)

TYPICAL NAIL-GLUED TRUSS

When used as truss joint connectors, plywood gusset plates add strength and rigidity, and reduce weight. Used on both sides of a joint, they also eliminate eccentricity, the major cause of twisting. Depending on the roof slope and span, trusses with nail-glued gussets may be of several designs, including the "W" truss shown

spanning large spaces and may be assembled with nails alone.

A recent addition to the language of folded plate roofs is the "space plane." Whereas the ordinary folded plate roof has parallel chords and is composed of rectangular members of regular dimensions, the space plane is characterized by having non-parallel chords that may or may not intersect. The radial folded plate is the simplest illustration of this principle.

Trusses

Trussed rafters with plywood gusset plates may be of several designs, depending upon the roof slope, the ceiling desired and the span. The plywood web roof-frame in which plywood webs replace intermediate supports, is used on low pitches (1/12) for spans from 20 ft-8 in. to 28 ft-8 in. and with sloped ceilings (3/12 pitch on the roof and a 1.5/12 ceiling) for spans from 20 ft-8 in. to 28 ft-8 in. with 2 by 4's and spans up to 32 ft-8 in. with 2 by 6 chords. The king post is used for slopes from 2/12 to 4/12, with 2 by 4 chords for spans of 18 ft to 24 ft-8 in., and with 2 by 6's for spans up to 32 ft-8 in. The nail-glued "W" truss for slopes over 2/12 is designed for spans of from 20 ft-8 in. to 28 ft-8 in. using 2 by 4 chords and up to 40 ft-8 in. using 2 by 6's.

Since these trusses have rigidly connected joints, their design is based upon actual loading tests of full-sized members. All are designed for a load of at least 40 lbs per sq ft of horizontal projection (15 psf dead load and 25 psf live load). The king post and the 2 by 4 "W" trusses are designed for 50 psf with 3/12 pitch and 60 psf with 4/12 pitch. All designs are based on 24 in. o. c. spacing and are nail-glued.

Certain recent technical advances in truss fabrication are making possible economical production of trusses with pressure-glued gusset plates. These appear to be much stronger than nail-glued trusses and are becoming more widely available.

Trofdek

Trofdek, a patented panel developed in England, is a parallel arrangement of "troughs" fabricated from plywood webs and lumber flanges. It resembles a miniature folded plate with troughs that function as sloped-webbed box beams and are designed as such. It can carry design loads ranging from 10 to 20 times its own weight over clear spans up to 50 feet, but its most advantageous spans will range from 28 to 40 feet, which is farther than is usually practical with stressed skin panels. Five standard sections are available, but nonstandard sections can be designed using box beam methods.

The standard sizes are 16, 32 and 48-in. widths with 9.31, 11.62 and 13.5-in. depths, and 19.2 and 38.4-in. widths with 15.6 and 17.10-in.

depths. Standard lengths are in multiples of two feet.

Trofdek may be fabricated by either nail-gluing or pressure-gluing, with the latter preferable for appearance when the deck is left open on the bottom. It can be laid on straight flat supports, pitched supports or curved supports which may be walls, girders, box beams or trusses. It may be used for floors or roofs with the bottom open or surfaced, and the spaces between webs may be used for lighting, as well as for insulation and the usual services.

The panels may also be used for temporary or permanent concrete form work, the reinforcing being laid between the webs forming the upper troughs. When left in place, they provide a finish ceiling and an effective means of fastening. If removed, they give the concrete a striking ribbed design.

Delta Frames

The delta structure uses a number of types of stressed skin panels and box beams in its assembly. Rigid bents composed of two tapered box beams form the predominant delta shape, and additional tapered beams cantilever from each side of this bent, partially balancing moments that would otherwise be quite large. Stressed skin panels, curved panels, *Trofdek* or folded plate roofs may be used to span between the frames.

The delta frame is capable of as many as 608 variations for use in utility structures where economy is desired. The frames also have design potential for use in schools, churches and other structures, and can be used in combination with other components in either square, rectangular or circular buildings. The cantilevered sides may be omitted, used on one side only or propped up to increase their widths.

Delta frames may be of various sizes. An illustration of what is possible would be a structure with the frames resting on 5-ft concrete piers and the bents rising at a slope of 45 degrees, forming a span of 40 ft and a ceiling height of 25 ft as in the prototype shown at right. The sides could then cantilever out another 8 to 28 ft. The bay spacing between frames could be 12 ft, 16 ft, 20 ft or 24 ft, and the structure could consist of any number of bays, thus lending itself to expansion when additional space is required.

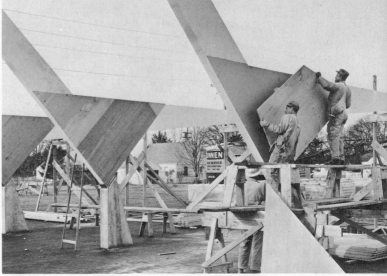

The structure shown above is the DFPA-built prototype of the "delta frame," a rigid bent composed of two tapered box beams with additional tapered box beams cantilevered from each side. The photo above left shows the first of the four 40-ft span A-sections that form the skeleton. At right above, the wing beams are joined to the bent with large plywood gussets. *Play Shelter, Park Lodge Elementary School, Tacoma, Washington*

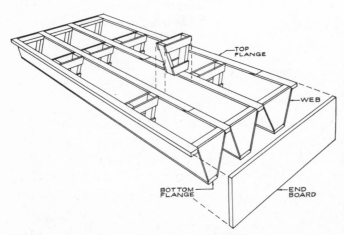

TOP FLANGE

WEB

BOTTOM FLANGE

END BOARD

Trofdek, a miniature version of the folded plate, consists of thin sheets of plywood glued to light lumber stiffeners to form a series of troughs. The resulting roof or floor component is extremely light weight but capable of carrying loads of from 10 to 20 times its own weight over clear spans up to 50 ft. At right, it serves as structural roof and finished ceiling. *Heath Ceramics Company warehouse, Sausalito, California*

MATERIALS, SYSTEMS DIFFER
IN FOUR DEPLOYABLE SCHOOLS

Two Pittsburgh schools, one in steel, the other concrete, come apart in 8-ft sections for portability. The M.I.T. "Instant Schoolhouse" used plastics liberally; it is designed to be expansible and demountable. Portable classrooms in Tacoma employed advanced techniques in plywood

Floor, wall and roof panels and framing were assembled conventionally, but the school comes apart in 8-ft sections

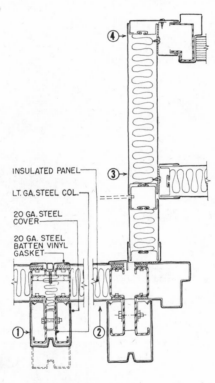

INSULATED PANEL

LT. GA. STEEL COL.

20 GA. STEEL COVER

20 GA. STEEL BATTEN VINYL GASKET

STEEL

An existing *Ambridge** steel component system was adapted to make it portable in 8- by 28-ft sections for an addition to the Phillip Murray Elementary School in Pittsburgh. Light gage mullions are load-bearing and accept both exterior panels and interior partitions. Open web joists are doubled up and bolted together, as are the 8-in. floor channels, to allow disassembly. Heating, plumbing and lighting units stay in place. Site utilities are expendable.

Floor framing sits atop concrete block footings. When the school is to be moved, an 8-ft section is simply jacked up, a low-boy run underneath and the section pulled away.

The school was designed by Pittsburgh architects John Pekruhn, Dahlen Ritchey, and Lawrence and Anthony Wolfe.

*American Bridge Division, United States Steel Corporation

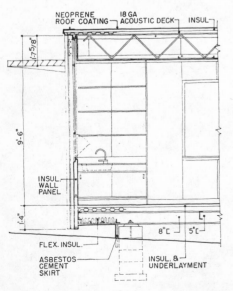

NEOPRENE ROOF COATING — 18 GA ACOUSTIC DECK — INSUL

INSUL. WALL PANEL

FLEX. INSUL.

ASBESTOS CEMENT SKIRT

INSUL. & UNDERLAYMENT

8"C   5"C

9'-6"

1-4"

1-7 5/8"

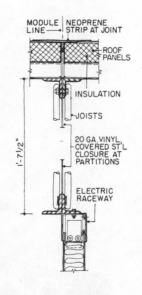

MODULE LINE | NEOPRENE STRIP AT JOINT

ROOF PANELS

INSULATION

JOISTS

20 GA. VINYL COVERED ST'L CLOSURE AT PARTITIONS

ELECTRIC RACEWAY

1'-7 1/2"

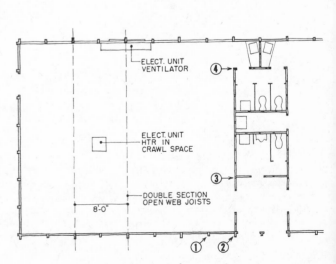

ELECT. UNIT VENTILATOR

ELECT. UNIT HTR IN CRAWL SPACE

DOUBLE SECTION OPEN WEB JOISTS

8'-0"

CONCRETE

Precast concrete units comprising columns, slabs, beams and walls all in an integral piece form the transportable sections for a four classroom addition to Homewood Elementary School in Pittsburgh. It was designed by the same architects as for the steel school opposite. The units are assembled as if a table rightside up were stacked atop another table placed upside down. Main reasons for slicing the school in half were to make construction of steel forms less expensive, precasting more accurate, and handling of units on the job easier. This concept was developed by Albert Henderson of United Precast Structures in Pittsburgh.

The perimeter is windowless to minimize damage from vandalism; windows face into a court.

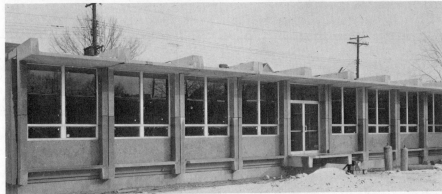

Transportable concrete school in Pittsburgh has precast units to form top and bottom of an 8-ft-wide section. With windows out, it comes apart the same way

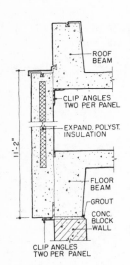

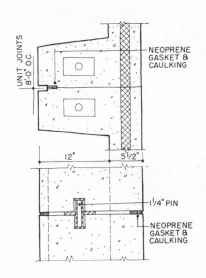

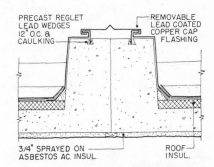

Left: Connection detail for end walls
Center: Detail of column seating
Above: Removable cap flashing detail
Below: Section and part plan

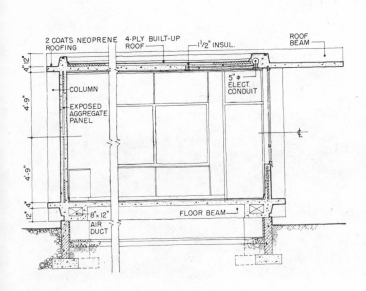

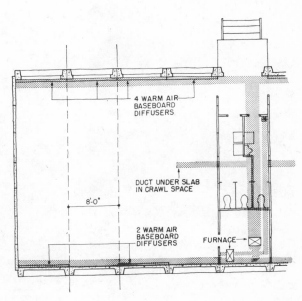

M.I.T.-PLASTIC

This demonstration deployable, expansible schoolroom system was developed jointly by the Departments of Architecture and Civil Engineering at M.I.T., and sponsored by Educational Facilities Laboratories, Inc.

The umbrella-like roof panels were of plastic-plywood sandwich construction, mounted on steel pipe columns. The columns serve additionally as drains and, by virtue of four vertical fins, means for connecting wall components. Various sandwich constructions for the umbrellas are now under investigation by a national firm which intends to manufacture the basic system. Skylight units of translucent plastic were dropped in between column units.

On three of the four walls, aluminum-faced, plastic-core sandwich panels were fitted between columns, underneath a horizontal strip of gray glass. The fourth side had a specially designed storage wall. This wall encloses a self-contained heat pump. Shielded flourescent strips along the walls illuminate room surfaces and desks.

Top: Prototype classroom under construction. Flared column takes roof panels.
Bottom: Model photographs illustrate potential interior and exterior designs

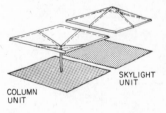

COLUMN UNIT
SKYLIGHT UNIT

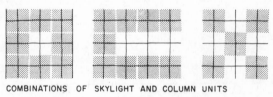

COMBINATIONS OF SKYLIGHT AND COLUMN UNITS

Demonstration model of M.I.T. classroom has exterior walls of glass and aluminum, plastic-core sandwich panels. One of the walls has built-in storage and encloses a self-contained heat pump

PLYWOOD

A portable system for a school district in Tacoma, Washington was developed by the Douglas Fir Plywood Association. Altogether three portable units were built, having almost identical design and floor plans, but varying in the construction techniques employed.

In the first, a 24- by 40-ft floor deck of ⅝-in. tongue-and-groove plywood sheets were laid. Then studs and framing for the wall sections were assembled on the floor deck. With plywood sheets locking the framing into a single, rigid wall, it was possible to erect one side of the building with two jacks. Nailed box beams were then set on the wall framing. A standard joist and plywood panel roof deck completed construction of the structure.

The second unit was constructed of plywood components which included box beams, stressed skin wall and roof panels.

The third unit used component construction, but had several experimental siding and wall panels, finished with factory-applied plastic.

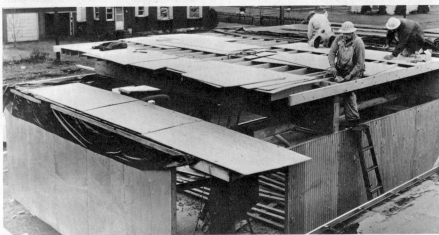

Site-fabricated design had wall framing assembled on top of floor deck. After box beams were placed a conventional plywood and joist roof deck was laid

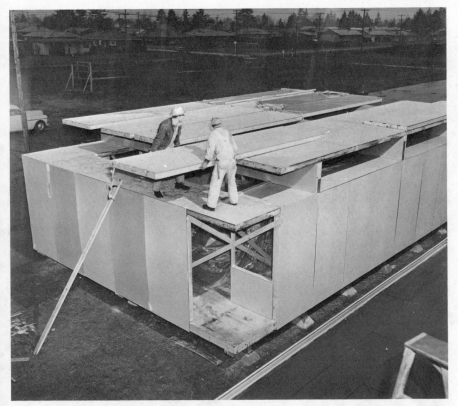

Component-type construction framed a second design. Stressed skin panels formed walls and roof. Translucent plastic panels in clerestory gave spacious feeling

SUPPORT METHOD FOR STRESSED-SKIN PANELS

A two-man crew can precut, assemble and install panel roof on shelter in six days

Research on stressed skin panels by Professor G. L. Nelson of Oklahoma State University indicates a number of advantages for the pre-assembled single-skin type. The panels consist of longitudinal members and a single bonded structural cover (skin) of plywood or asbestos cement. A primary purpose of the research was to develop different methods for supporting the ends of the panels. When the bonding of the panel skins to the stringers is essential to develop stiffness and strength, the gluing must be done under carefully controlled conditions if the glue bond is to remain intact during the full life of the structure.

A two-man crew in about three days can pre-cut and assemble enough panels to cover an average size farm shelter, as shown in the photo. In three additional days, they can install the roof deck system.

In addition to covering, stressed skin panels become an integral part of the structure.

A single-cover stressed skin panel can span from 8 to 12 ft under superimposed loads of 20 lb/sq ft without exceeding normal deflection limitations.

Panels tested at Oklahoma State are supported only by the skin's reinforced lip projecting from panel ends. Panels are fabricated to permit panel-end reaction to be transmitted only through the lip, (Figure 1). The end reactions are transmitted from the main roof frame directly into end lips of plywood covers, rather than through ends of the longitudinals. This allows panels to rest neatly between main frame elements. End headers are not necessary.

Research by Oklahoma State has evaluated stiffness and ultimate strength of stressed-skin panels made with ⅜-in. fir plywood covers placed on 2- by 4-in., S4S, Douglas fir longitudinals and supported on the plywood end lip. Results show panel construction provides a more than adequate margin of safety against peeling failure if the stressed-skin panel ends are reinforced by special nailing.

Addition of stiffener strips (Figure 2) extended 12 in. under panel ends increases the safety factor to approximately eight, based on design load of 20 lb/sq ft. Supporting the panels solely on the projecting lip of the plywood skin produced a safety factor of 6.25 if the ends are reinforced by 10-penny screw-shank nails with 1-in.-sq washers placed under the heads.

Dr. Nelson, Professor of Agricultural Engineering, directs the research which is part of Oklahoma State University's engineering educational program for graduate students.

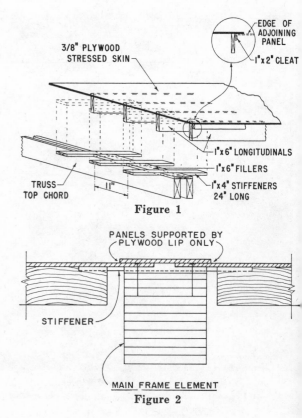

Figure 1

PANELS SUPPORTED BY PLYWOOD LIP ONLY

Figure 2

Stressed-skin roof panels, 4 by 16 ft, of fir plywood pressure-glued to 2x4's, are shop-assembled for installation in Carl Koch's Techbuilt house (left). Note aluminum foil insulation which has been inserted between the plywood skins

Engineering principles are responsible for new structural

systems (such as stressed-skin panels) and for more

efficient use of century-old systems (such as plank

and beam), both of which could be more fully exploited

WOOD STRUCTURES FOR HOUSES

by Albert G. H. Dietz and William J. LeMessurier

Wood, the most traditional material for house construction, is being neglected by today's designers in favor of carefully manufactured materials with engineered design. These new building materials have made possible structural methods adapted to the modern architectural trend toward the use of large glass wall areas, plans with continuous open spaces and unconcealed surfaces. However, wood does not have to be sacrificed in order to have up-to-date house construction. In the discussion that follows several engineered uses of wood will be considered. Detailed designs for many of these applications have appeared as "Time Saver Standards" in October 1954 and later issues of *Architectural Record*.

STRESSED-SKIN CONSTRUCTION

Stressed-skin construction is a method of building walls, roofs and floors in which the surfacing materials are made to act integrally with the studs or joists to which they are attached. In ordinary building methods, flooring, ceilings and wall coverings act structurally only to carry local loads and keep out weather; they are otherwise dead weight. In stressed-skin construction these coverings are continuous skins which are bonded firmly by gluing to the studs or joists. They thus contribute greatly to the strength of the combination. The principal requirement of this skin material is that it be continuous, and in house construction plywood is almost universally used. To achieve proper control and efficiency, stressed-skin construction demands prefabricated assembly.

The principal advantage of stressed-skin construction is its efficient use of materials. Without increasing joist sizes, longer spans can be achieved than are possible with standard procedures. In the usual house construction, for example, 2 x 10 joists of No. 2 Structural Douglas Fir spaced 16 in. on center can span only 16.4 ft with live-load deflection limited to $\frac{1}{360}$ of the span and total deflection limited to $\frac{1}{300}$. The same joists at the same spacing with a glued-on top skin of $\frac{3}{8}$-in. plywood and a

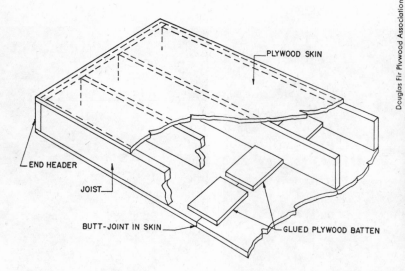

END HEADER

JOIST

BUTT-JOINT IN SKIN

PLYWOOD SKIN

GLUED PLYWOOD BATTEN

Douglas Fir Plywood Association

Left: Typical stressed-skin panel. Right: Stressed-skin wall panel which is hinged to ceiling panel and swings into position as roof section of three wood trusses is hoisted into position for a house designed by John Graham, Seattle architect

bottom skin of ¼-in. plywood can span 22.2 ft with the same deflection limitations, an increase in span of 35 per cent. Expressed as an increase in load-carrying capacity on identical spans, the joists with the glued-on skins will carry 109 per cent more load.

An additional benefit of this method is the labor saving obtained in shop fabrication. For a single building, the labor saved will be little if any; but for a large group of houses, prefabrication will reduce total costs.

To design floor panels with plywood stressed skins, a computational procedure similar to that for steel-plate girders is used. The top plywood skin acts as a compression flange, the joists as webs, and the bottom skin as a tension flange. Only those plies of the plywood having grain parallel to the direction of the span are considered in calculating the moment of inertia. Since the top skin is in a state of almost pure compression, it is subject to buckling and its effectiveness depends on the closeness of joist spacing. In addition to direct tension and compression in the plywood, shearing stresses between plywood and joists are critical. For adequate strength this joint must be glued under pressure. A detailed procedure of gluing is given on p. 225 of the Oct. 1954 issue of *Architectural Record*.

The principal difficulties of using stressed-skin panels occur in the joints between panels and at discontinuities in the skin. At the joint between parallel panels, splines or dowels may be used to prevent differential deflections. If one panel is splined into the adjoining panel, the projecting edges of the plywood must be protected against damage from

handling by a temporary filler strip. To obtain panels longer than 16 ft, the plywood skin must be spliced, since plywood is not readily obtainable in lengths greater than 16 ft. Full continuity may be achieved by gluing a plywood batten over a butt joint in the skin.

To make the most effective use of standard materials, stressed-skin plywood panels may be built of regular 4-ft-wide sheets using four regular 2-in. nominal joists in the cross section. Panels may be made in any length, although the length should be planned to use full plywood sheets where possible in the 8-, 10-, 12- or 16-ft lengths. For the top skin in floor construction, plywood of ¾-in. thickness should be used when it is the only structural material spanning between joists. In all but very thin panels, a full header is required at

each end of the panel to provide lateral rigidity to the joists.

For special uses, such as short spans or light loads, panels may be designed with a skin on one side only. Or when necessary, the plywood skin may be designed to stop short of the ends of the panel to facilitate installation of wiring, piping and ductwork between joists.

PLYWOOD GIRDERS

Girders built with plywood webs and solid or laminated wood flanges are used for very long spans and heavy loads. They are especially useful when incorporated into walls or partitions, as in a spandrel over a large window. Here the structural action of stressed-skin panels is reversed. The plywood becomes the web member and the solid lumber, the flanges. The economy lies

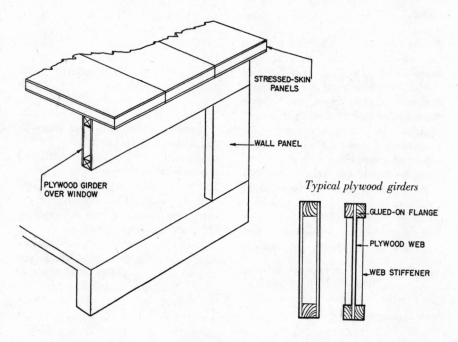

STRESSED-SKIN PANELS

WALL PANEL

PLYWOOD GIRDER OVER WINDOW

Typical plywood girders

GLUED-ON FLANGE

PLYWOOD WEB

WEB STIFFENER

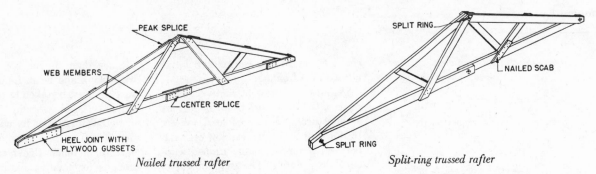

Nailed trussed rafter   **Split-ring trussed rafter**

in using thin material in the lower stressed central portion of the girder and concentrating the lumber at the top and bottom of the section.

The design procedure for such girders consists in proportioning flanges to carry the tensile and compressive stresses set up in bending and in dimensioning the plywood webs to carry shearing stresses. In general, the calculations are similar to those made for a steel-plate girder. They are normally glued together for maximum strength, although they have been successfully built with nails only, the nails being computed for shear as in the design of rivets for a riveted steel-plate girder. In checking deflections for wood girders, the contribution of shear deflection as well as bending deflection should be considered. To prevent local buckling of the plywood, stiffeners are usually necessary. Girders of built-up wood construction will not economically replace the steel or wood girders of normal house construction. Their best use is where a thin, deep girder can serve as structure and wall simultaneously. Detailed discussions of the design procedure for both stressed-skin panels and built-up plywood girders are in "Technical Data on Plywood," published by the Douglas Fir Plywood Association, Tacoma, Wash.

TRUSSED RAFTERS

The trussed rafter is a sophisticated cousin of the standard rafter as used in gable framing. The ordinary pitched roof is built with pairs of fairly deep rafters meeting at a ridge and tied by ceiling joists from plate to plate. This form of construction is the most elementary truss, since it consists of a single triangle. When the width of this triangle becomes large, however, the sizes of the rafters and ceiling joists become excessive. Since these members must carry roof and ceiling loads as beams between the corners of the triangle, their size is primarily determined by beam action. By subdividing the large triangle with additional web members, the spans of each piece between joints are reduced. This in turn reduces the depths of the members needed to resist bending. This more complex construction is commonly called a trussed rafter.

The trussed rafter, by the reduction of bending moments in the individual elements, is capable of spanning much larger distances than simple rafters. Rafters, or chords, as they are called in this case, may be 2 x 4's when trussed instead of 2 x 6's or 2 x 8's. The ability of the trussed rafter to span clear between outside walls eliminates the need for interior bearing partitions. Other partitions installed to subdivide space may be made thinner, and complete flexibility of interior planning is possible. By omitting bearing partitions, foundations are also simplified.

Since the trussed rafter is a rigid, self-contained unit, it may be completely prefabricated. Either in the shop or at the site, a simple jig may be set up and rafters assembled with production-line efficiency.

The chief disadvantage of the trussed rafter results from the elimination of attic space by the presence of web members. Since attic space is lost, roof pitches are ordinarily low. This problem may be overcome with a somewhat modified form of the trussed rafter, utilizing principles of rigid frame design to create an open space in the center of the roof for storage.

The increased complexity of the trussed rafter necessitates careful workmanship and detailing. Each design must be carefully detailed, since the joints between members are critical. The extra labor required may, however, be reduced by well-planned prefabrication.

The connections between individual pieces in trussed rafter construction may be made with nails, bolts, or split-ring connectors. Where spans are small and pitches not too low, nails alone may be used to make connections. With pitches lower than about 4 in 12 and spans greater than 24 ft, bolts or split rings are desirable. The critical joint is at the heel of pitched roof trusses. Here, at the plate, the outward thrust of the rafter must be transmitted to the horizontal bottom tie and the stresses are relatively large. The stresses at this point increase with increasing span or decreasing pitch. It is often impossible to obtain adequate nailing area here, and split-ring connectors are used instead.

In nailed construction the trussed rafter is usually built with the top and bottom chords lying in the same plane. The heel joint is then made with a pair of gussets connecting the bottom chord to the rafter. These gussets may be cut from ½-in. plywood or 1-in. nominal boards. Although twice as many nails are required at this joint compared with a lapped chord connection, the application of the web members is simplified. The web members may simply lap over the chords and be nailed directly to them.

For nailed joints, nailing templates of cardboard or light metal should be prepared. By planning nail placement and spacing carefully, strong joints may be built with little labor. When long spans require bolts or split-ring connectors, the truss assembly is slightly different from the nailed design. To minimize the number of bolts or rings required, the top and bottom chords are lapped at the heel joints. In this way it is usually possible to make a strong joint with a single split ring. Web members will then lap over one chord and be joined to the other with a scab. Assembly with split rings or toothed rings is a new technique for many carpenters, but when a trussed rafter is produced in quantity, the efficiency of these connections will offset time lost in acquiring new skills.

Alternate web systems:

1 Used with light ceiling

2 Used with plaster ceiling

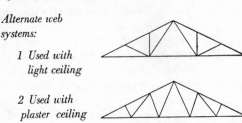

The web system for a trussed rafter may be made in several ways. The simplest and most common is the Pratt truss which uses one diagonal from the middle of the top chord to the third point of the bottom chord, and a second diagonal from the bottom of the first to the peak. This truss then consists of only four different types of pieces, using two of each. For longer spans, diagonals may connect the third points and peak of each rafter to the third or fifth points of the bottom chord.

Trussed rafters with overhangs

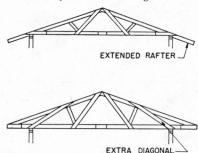

Roof overhangs are detailed most simply with a straight extension of the top chord. *In no case should the heel joint be placed at the edge of the overhang.* If it is desired to extend the bottom chord beyond the plate, a separate web member extending from the middle of the rafter to the plate is necessary.

PLANK AND BEAM CONSTRUCTION

Plank and beam construction as it is used in modern houses is essentially the same as the heavy mill structures which have served industry for over one hundred years. This method is characterized by the use of relatively few, heavy framing members to form a skeleton together with slab-like planking for floors and roofs. The plank and beam system is very close to steel framing in conception. As in any skeleton frame, this method of building achieves structural efficiency by concentrating loads on a few large pieces.

As applied to house building, the plank and beam frame consists of beams at spacings of 4 to 12 or more feet supported on isolated columns of at least 4 x 4 cross section. Tongue and groove planking of 2- or 3-in. nominal thickness spans between beams, forming the complete floor or roof structure.

By comparison with the normal joist floor construction, the most important saving with the plank and beam system results from the reduced number of pieces to handle. The typical joist floor involves setting joists, application of a subfloor, cutting and installing bridging, strapping, lathing and plastering. With the erection of beams and planking, the floor is complete in two operations. In a comparison made by the National Lumber Manufacturers Association, the plank and beam system saved 26 per cent labor and 15 per cent material over normal joist framing.

Perhaps the most attractive advantages of the plank and beam system are architectural. Because of load concentration on posts, large window openings between beams are easily framed without heavy lintels. The requirement of regular beam spacing creates a disciplined structure, ideally suited to modular framing with the resulting elimination of cutting waste. The volume of interior space is increased. With the underside of the planks forming the finish ceiling, the thickness of the actual floor is only 2 or 3 in. The effective floor-to-ceiling height is thereby increased 7 or 10 in. without increased studs or total building height.

In most cases, details are simplified with plank and beam framing. Roof overhangs may be built with short cantilevered beams on side walls and cantilevered planks on the end walls. A narrow fascia board and metal gravel stop and drip complete the eave. Foundations may be built of isolated piers directly supporting the beams in place of continuous foundations under bearing walls.

One of the important reasons for using plank and beam construction for mill buildings is its relative fire safety. It is a fundamental principle of wood construction that the rate of burning depends on the ratio of surface area to volume of timber. Since wood does not lose all of its strength even if its surface is charred, the use of fewer, heavy pieces makes the construction slow-burning. In addition, the lack of concealed spaces through which fire can spread makes the danger more easily detected.

Among the difficulties arising with plank and beam construction, the most important is the need for careful location of partitions over floors. Since the planking is not ordinarily adequate for heavy concentrated loads, partitions should be located over beams. When this is not possible, as with partitions at right angles to beams, extra framing members must be provided. A 4 x 4 or 4 x 6 sole at the base of such partitions may span between beams. Additional light members between main beams may be required beneath bathtubs and other concentrated loads.

Since there are no concealed spaces with plank and beam framing, particular care must be taken to plan electrical wiring. Raceways may be provided along beam bottoms by using cross sections built up from three or four pieces of 2 in. nominal thickness. Concealed troughs for lighting fixtures may also be built in this way.

In building roofs with the plank and beam system, insulation is ordinarily required to prevent undue heat loss and to eliminate condensation. The most effective location for this insulation is above the planks. Since the insulation must be able to support the weight of workmen without crushing, it should be of the rigid type, preferably nailable. A vapor barrier between insulation and planking is essential to prevent condensation, and the thickness of the insulation must be designed to keep the temperature at the vapor barrier above the dew point.

A further requirement of plank and beam construction is the need of materials of good quality and for careful workmanship. If the plank is exposed, lumber of better character than ordinarily used for subflooring is needed. Large knots, streaks, resin ducts and other blemishes will be objectionable even with paint. Carpenters should take particular care to align planking at right angles to beams. In most cases planks must be made continuous over two or more spans to reduce deflections, and careful supervision is necessary to prevent the use of short lengths. Ideally, a drawing showing the exact location and length of all planks should be provided for each case. Careful engineering and architectural design will ordinarily effect sufficient savings to offset the cost of the extra quality.

CONCLUSION

Stressed-skin construction, built-up girders and trussed rafters use wood to build longer, lighter spans. To accomplish this goal, greater complexity and more prefabrication is necessary than is common with traditional methods.

The plank and beam system attains the goal of greater simplicity in construction by using fewer and heavier pieces. But both approaches are valid ways of building better, more economical houses. In all cases the reduction of labor in erection of the individual building is a common denominator. Further progress with wood will increase this saving.

Eave detail

Built-up beam with wiring trough

DESIGN PHILOSOPHY, THEORY

A CHANGE AHEAD FOR STRUCTURAL DESIGN

1. BACKGROUND AND IMPLICATIONS

by Edward Cohen, Associate Partner, Ammann & Whitney, Consulting Engineers, New York

UNTIL MODERN TIMES all structures were built to support the dead weight plus the superimposed live loads without collapse. Factors of safety and stresses, as such, had no meaning to the designer since no rational methods of computation were available. It is interesting to note that the structures of ancient Egypt, Greece, Rome and Renaissance Europe were achieved without the advantage of any reliable scientific theory or mathematical formulas. Structures were built by trial and error. Failures were common and it was not unusual to rebuild structures such as the Roman arches several times before achieving the final results which survive today.

Slowly, rough rules for judging the approximate strength of beams, columns, arches and domes were developed. It was not until the 16th century that Galileo began the solution of the problem of bending and not until the middle of the 17th century that Robert Hooke formulated "Hooke's Law," the proportional relationship of stress and strain in the elastic range. In the following centuries, this law was elaborated to provide rational methods of analysis and design to replace the previous methods based on experience and experiment.

In reinforced concrete design which started at the end of the 19th century, ultimate strength methods based on nonlinear compressive stress-strain diagrams (stress no longer proportional to strain) for concrete were proposed along with the straight-line method. In view of the limited experience and laboratory tests at that time, the straight-line method won acceptance because of its relatively simple mathematics and adequate safety. It was incorporated in the first American code of reinforced concrete in 1909.

However, this was not the end of ultimate strength and in 1937 C. S. Whitney presented a practical, adequately documented method of design based on an inelastic or "plastic" stress-strain relationship. In 1951 the ACI approved an ultimate strength method for the design of reinforced concrete arches, and, this year, has incorporated an *ultimate strength* method as part of the basic building code for all reinforced concrete structures. *Ultimate strength design* has been used for several years in Brazil, Russia and other European countries. Last year an *ultimate strength* code was also adopted in Great Britain.

The first application of limit or *plastic* analysis to structural design was made by G. V. Kazinczy in Hungary in 1914. Later, plastic design for steel structures was proposed by N. C. Kist in Holland in 1920, by J. A. Van den Broek in the United States in 1940, and by J. F. Baker in Great Britain in 1948.

In recent years extensive testing of individual members and full scale structures and research on practical design methods have been conducted at Lehigh University in cooperation with the American Institute of Steel Construction and the Welding Research Council. Although an American code for *plastic* design in steel has not yet been formulated, *plastic* design has been incorporated in the Standard British specifications as an acceptable design method.

One of our oldest building materials, timber, has always been designed on the basis of strength although in recent years the terminology of stress has been adopted. Thus, it appears engineers have been more prone to retain or adopt plastic or ultimate strength methods for the design of those materials which are least amenable to "accurate" analysis.

In discussing ultimate strength today no one proposes returning to the wasteful and often dangerous procedures of previous times. Rather it means carrying forward the analysis of structures into the region where stress is no longer proportional to strain and which the early engineers and mathematicians avoided, partly because either it did not lend itself to the available concepts and methods of analysis, or because many of the common materials of their time were not sufficiently ductile to be trusted far beyond the yield point. It is also true that one phase of ultimate strength methods — redistribution of moments, thrusts, etc., from overstressed points to those originally understressed — is applicable primarily to statically indeterminate structures which have become practical only in recent years with the advent of reinforced concrete and welding.

Although structural engineers have placed great reliance on elastic stress analysis for purposes of analyzing and designing structures, they have not accepted the results without a "grain of salt" based on experience and laboratory tests. For example ductile steel plates with rivet holes are designed for tension on the basis of the average stress on the net section whereas the theoretical elastic stress at the hole may be as high as three times the average. Circular steel sections and pins are allowed higher working stresses in flexure than rectangular or WF members. Continuous WF beams and rigid frame columns are allowed higher working stresses at points of maximum moment than simple beams. Shallow timber beams are allowed higher stresses than deep narrow beams. In those instances where tests and experience showed a flexural strength

BASIC DEFINITIONS

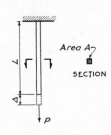

HOOKE'S LAW

Stress is linearly proportional to strain, thus:

$\sigma = E\varepsilon$, *where*

$\sigma = \dfrac{P}{A} =$ *stress or force per unit area*

$E = $ *modulus of elasticity*

$\varepsilon = strain = \dfrac{\Delta}{L}$

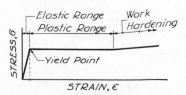

Theoretical Stress-Strain Diagram for Steel in Tension

YIELD POINT

The values of stress and strain after which strain increases without increase in stress

WORK HARDENING

The increase in strength after substantial yielding has taken place

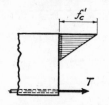

Straight-Line or Elastic Stress Distribution for a Reinforced Concrete Beam

STRAIGHT LINE METHOD

Analysis of reinforced concrete sections on the assumption that stress is proportional to strain. Since concrete has no tensile strength, stress distribution is shown only for the section in compression, for which stresses are assumed to vary from zero at the neutral axis to maximum compression at the top fiber

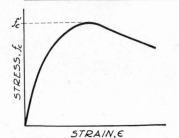

Curve for Concrete Cylinder Under Compression

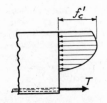

Plastic Stress Distribution for a Reinforced Concrete Beam

PLASTIC THEORY
(Reinforced Concrete)

Application of the actual non-linear stress-strain curve of concrete to design. The stress distribution curve (lower left) more nearly gives the true condition in a concrete beam under load

for columns, the design of such members in both structural steel and reinforced concrete has long been on an ultimate strength basis. Allowances for inelastic action, moment and stress redistribution are not new to building codes.

What is new is the development (and acceptance in reinforced concrete design) of rational and consistent design methods for beams, columns and frames of both reinforced concrete and structural steel which will give a uniformly reliable estimate of their strength. It may come as something of a shock to some that while the present allowable "elastic stress" design methods are adequate and safe, the actual factors of safety are highly variable, though generally on the side of excess safety.

An urgent need for calculating the actual strength of structures beyond the point of initial yield which arose during World War II in the design of shelters, ships, etc., against high explosives brought attention to earlier investigations on the ultimate strength of structures. Further impetus was given this field of research following the war when the government embarked on an extensive program to develop basic data and design methods which could give a reasonably accurate prediction of the effects of atomic bomb blast pressures on structures. In order to make such predictions, an accurate method of strength computation was required and only those methods which considered plasticity and moment redistribution were found adequate. These methods have also been applied to the rational design of structures subjected to other types of dynamic loading such as earthquakes. It is now, partially as a secondary but beneficial result of that program, that the advantages of such methods for normal building design are being presented. Engineers are interested in these methods as new and better tools for proportioning structures to achieve uniformly adequate but not excessive strength.

In general, certain economies can be expected as a result of eliminating excess material required by the methods of elastic stress or frame analysis. These savings are most definite in the case of all-welded, rigid frame structures made of standard rolled steel shapes and reinforced concrete arches and rigid frames. Where controlling design conditions are the result of temperature, shrinkage, settlement, etc. additional economies are possible because the moments and thrusts due to the above are also reduced as the sections become lighter and shallower, thus decreasing the moments of

greater than indicated by elastic theory and the yield stress obtained from simple tension or compression tests on small samples, a new critical value of stress for flexure, the modulus of rupture, was arbitrarily used. This stress, introduced into the equations of elasticity, gives a reliable value of bending strength.

The strengths of tier buildings for lateral loads caused by wind or earthquake are normally computed by limit design. Retaining walls are designed not only to limit the soil bearing stress but also for a given factor of safety against overturning. Although it is only in recent years that a rational theory has been evolved

inertia and increasing the flexibility. Economy is an important by-product of using these new and more reliable and rational methods of design.

Therefore it is not surprising that architects have begun to hear frequent references to *ultimate strength* and *plastic* design from their civil engineering associates, although often without very much explanation and with very little in the way of apparent practical results. To some architects *ultimate strength* design has brought visions of collapsing structures, and plastic design, pictures of tired, sagging beams. Such premonitions have no relationship to actuality. Under working loads, structures which are properly designed by *ultimate strength* or *plastic* methods are still primarily in the elastic range and deflections are kept within allowable limits. It provides a method of keeping factors of safety close to their intended value. It avoids making portions of some structures unnecessarily strong relative to established standards.

Ultimate strength is a term which has come to be most closely identified with reinforced concrete design of sections for flexure and flexure plus direct stress on the basis of a non-linear stress-strain relationship which has been incorporated in the current American Concrete Institute Building Code. Within these terms of reference, ultimate strength design refers to the design of structural members at all sections by plastic theory for thrusts and moments determined from elastic frame analysis for the assumed design loads multiplied by specified load (safety) factors. It is not design for failure but for predetermined factors of safety against the actual ultimate strength of each section. These factors of safety are established on the basis of experience and laboratory tests to avoid excessive cracking of the concrete under working load and allow a margin of safety against overload which is consistent with the intentions of previous practice. Because reinforced concrete structures are designed and detailed for the forces acting on each section, the question of allowing plastic redistribution of moments and thrusts is not important except for special structures or for loads other than considered in the initial design. The retention of elastic frame analysis is the result of such considerations and not because reinforced concrete is not a ductile material. Properly detailed reinforced concrete structures can undergo extremely large plastic deformations without loss of strength. The main differences between

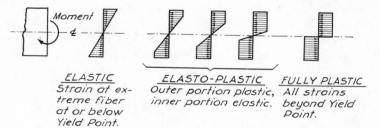

Stages in the Development of Plastic Stress Distribution on a Homogeneous Member

PLASTIC STRESS DISTRIBUTION (Structural Steel)

Distribution of stress over the cross section of a beam when it has reached its full moment capacity and the strains at all locations are past the yield point

PLASTIC HINGE

A section which has reached its full capacity and can continue to rotate without change in moment

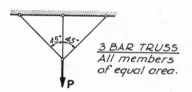

Moment-Rotation Diagram for WF Beam

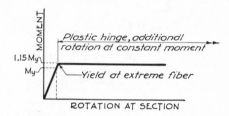

REDISTRIBUTION OF THRUSTS (Limit Analysis)

The process whereby internal forces are transferred from members which are already stressed to their full capacity, to those having reserve strength, as the external load is increased

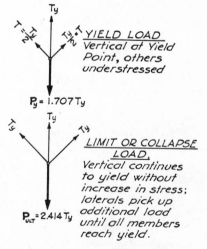

Limit Analysis for a Simple Indeterminate Truss

members designed by *ultimate strength* and those designed by conventional methods come about because these methods greatly underestimate the strength of many commonly used sections.

Although the basic objective of plastic design in steel is the same as in the ultimate strength design of reinforced con-

crete — the achievement of a uniform factor of safety against overload — the approach is quite different in its details. As in the ACI *ultimate strength* code for reinforced concrete there is at present no intention of reducing the minimum factor of safety provided in the present AISC code. On the other hand it could be

BASIC DEFINITIONS

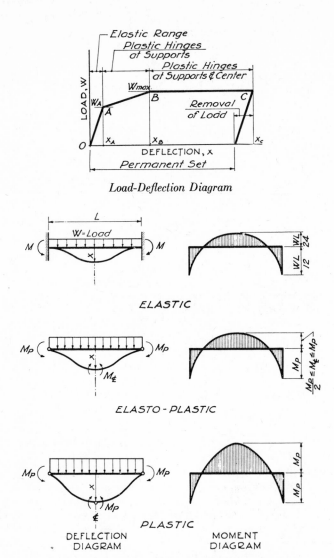

Load-Deflection Diagram

ELASTIC

ELASTO - PLASTIC

PLASTIC

DEFLECTION
DIAGRAM

MOMENT
DIAGRAM

Redistribution of Moments for Fixed End Beams

REDISTRIBUTION OF MOMENTS (Limit Analysis)

The process whereby internal forces are transferred from sections (plastic hinges) already stressed to their full capacity, to those having reserve strength, as the external load is increased. Note what happens in the moment diagrams. In the elastic range the bending moment in the center is half that at the fixed ends; in the elasto-plastic range, the moment may be from over half to nearly equal that at the fixed ends; in the plastic range moments at the center and fixed ends are equal

reworded to state that the factor of safety in flexure could be defined as 1.88 on the plastic strength rather than 1.65 against the yield stress. Thus simple beams, columns and trusses, designed by either present methods or plastic theory would be practically the same.

Flexural members of round or square section for which a plastic stress distribution gives the greatest increase in strength are rare and uneconomical in building construction.

The primary economies possible in the plastic design of structural steel building frames result from the redistribution of moments and thrusts in frames of uniform rolled sections. Because in many

cases economic considerations make the use of uniform rolled sections desirable, greater emphasis has been placed on departure from elastic frame analysis as well as elastic stress analysis by using the plastic moment-thrust capacity in combination with limit design to obtain the true collapse load of the whole structure. Thus, by allowing sections with high elastic moments to be strained beyond yield and develop into plastic hinges, the overload moments are redistributed to sections with low elastic moments until these sections also are brought to their maximum capacity. Final moments at critical sections of a uniform, fixed-end beam under uni-

form load become the same at failure.

Although similar *savings in weight* can be obtained with current design methods by varying the cross-sections, by tapering or haunching members or by the addition of coverplates — that is, designing the members section by section — the fabrication costs are high and, except for long span members, bridges and certain special cases, the final *dollar cost* is increased. For this reason moment redistribution, or limit design plays a role of much greater importance in plastic design of structural steel where uniform sections are desirable, than for reinforced concrete where the reinforcement at each section of a beam is proportioned according to the variations of the moment diagram.

Ultimate strength design in reinforced concrete will soon make its effects known as more designers become familiar with the new appendix to the ACI code and learn to use this simplified but more accurate approach to reduce the computational work of design. It can be expected that as time goes by the tendency will be toward shallower, more heavily reinforced members and slenderer structures in general. At present, plastic design in steel will continue to be used in this country for the design of special structures outside the control of building codes and for investigation of existing structures for unusual loads. When a complete standard specification for plastic design in steel is written and accepted it can be expected that a great impetus will be given to the all-welded rigid frame type of construction where important economies will be possible.

It should not be inferred that the ultimate strength methods will completely replace elastic stress calculations. In many cases the elastic methods are still preferable at present, for example in the design of suspension bridges, thin shells, structures subject to fatigue type loads, brittle materials, etc.

There will not be drastic changes in either steel or reinforced concrete construction as a result of these new design methods. The most glaring deficiencies of elastic stress methods have already been overcome by empirical corrections in current design practice. The appearance of buildings, the methods of framing, etc. will be little affected. These new design methods are new and more effective tools for the structural engineer, but they do not eliminate the fundamental requirements for imagination, good judgment and intelligently evaluated experience on which good and creative design is always based.

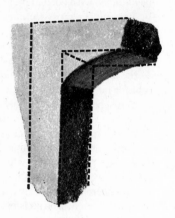

A CHANGE AHEAD FOR STRUCTURAL DESIGN

2. ULTIMATE STRENGTH DESIGN OF CONCRETE

by Edward Cohen, Associate Partner, Ammann & Whitney, Consulting Engineers, New York

AFTER FIFTY YEARS of progress in design, in construction and in the development of a true understanding of the structural mechanics of reinforced concrete, the basic American building code for concrete structures has undergone a fundamental revision. The American Concrete Institute Building Code Requirements of Reinforced Concrete (ACI 318–56) now states that "the ultimate strength method of design may be used for the design of reinforced concrete."

The basic innovations of the ultimate strength method of design consist of (1) using as design loads the actual working loads multiplied by the appropriate load factors or safety factors and (2) proportioning the sections for the resulting ultimate moments and thrusts by the use of a plastic stress distribution. Fundamentally this method affects only the design of column and beam sections for axial load, bending or bending plus axial load. The required strengths are determined from an elastic frame analysis for moments and thrusts and no allowance is made for redistribution of moments (limit design). Under the actual working loads the resulting structures will be primarily in the so-called "elastic range" and the stresses in the steel tension reinforcement will be only slightly higher than those which exist in most current designs for present commonly used grades of steel. However, allowance is made to utilize steels with higher yield points up to 60,000 psi.

Although some additional economy could be obtained, moment redistribution, or limit design, is unnecessary for the design of new structures of reinforced concrete because the reinforcement at each section can be readily proportioned in accordance with the variations of the elastic moment diagram. The use of limit design would involve the use of high stresses under working loads and unnecessary cracking. However, properly designed reinforced concrete has adequate ductility which may be utilized in analyzing existing structures for new overload conditions or in the design of structures for resistance to dynamic loads such as blast or earthquake. Ductility of reinforced concrete has been well demonstrated in the laboratory and in actual structures both under test and in normal use.

The present procedures for the design of reinforced concrete slabs make allowance for some redistribution of moments. In the Scandinavian countries full redistribution of moments has been used as the basic design method for slabs for several years This method, the "yield line" method, is now gaining acceptance in the United States and laboratory studies are under way to refine its use and establish its limitations with respect to cracking and shear strength. Research is also being conducted on the application of plastic methods to the design of thin shells.

It is quite likely that a half century

ago engineers would have been as familiar with some of the general concepts discussed here as they are today. The design theories developed by the early pioneers Ritter 1899, Talbot 1904, Withey 1907, Mensch 1914, although limited in some respects, were based on good agreement with test results. Since then, starting with the first generally accepted code in 1910, design procedures for many years drifted into complete acceptance of the fictitious straight line or elastic stress distribution. However, many engineers were unsatisfied to proportion structures on the basis of methods with important limitations which could not be justified by tests. Starting with the papers by C. S. Whitney in 1937 and 1942 which presented a practical verified design procedure for ultimate strength design, new interest was rapidly developed in this concept.

In 1944 a joint ASCE-ACI Committee on Ultimate Strength Design was formed under the chairmanship of the late A. J. Boase. In 1955 this committee with L. H. Corning as chairman completed its assignment "to evaluate and correlate theories and data bearing on ultimate strength design procedures with a view to establishing them as accepted practice," with publication of its final report.

The 11 years which elapsed between the formation of the committee and its final report have been used to conduct extensive tests and to evaluate carefully

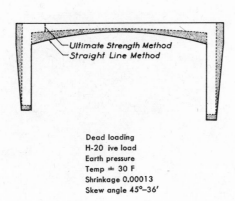

ULTIMATE STRENGTH VS. STRAIGHT LINE METHOD

Sketch shows how size of a reinforced concrete highway bridge can be reduced through use of the ultimate strength theory

Dead loading
H-20 ive load
Earth pressure
Temp ± 30 F
Shrinkage 0.00013
Skew angle 45°–36′

Figure 1

---

the various design methods and load factors. The results of this report have been incorporated in the 1956 ACI Building Code as an acceptable method of design. Previous to this, ultimate strength methods could only be used for the investigation of special structures and for designs either outside the jurisdiction of building codes or with special permission from the supervising authorities. Now, after fifty years of progress, we return to design methods based on the true strength of reinforced concrete sections.

Effects of Ultimate Strength Design Methods

Although present practice already includes many empirical corrections which compensate for some of the more flagrant deviations of the straight line or elastic methods for the design of sections, the application of the new code will give the structural designer new confidence and freedom in proportioning structures. The acknowledgment of the actual strength of flexural members as governed by the compressive strength of the concrete will allow the use of shallower beams and minimize the weight of required compressive reinforcement where the design is governed by the strength requirements. For any given set of load conditions the new provisions will generally result also in smaller columns in rigid frame structures. Additional economies and easier construction will be possible by the use of high strength reinforcement. The revised code now allows the use of steel with a yield point of 60,000 psi, which is equivalent to a maximum working stress

of 33,300 psi as compared with the previously allowed maximum of 20,000 psi, a 65 per cent increase when proper precautions are taken to limit deflections and cracking.

Although it is difficult to define the actual economies in dollars and cents, it is safe to assume that because the designs will be of more uniform strength, savings will be effected by the elimination of excess material from sections where it is not actually needed. Any analysis of savings should consider the savings in formwork, possible reductions of overall story height where beam depths are reduced or haunches eliminated, and savings in foundations where the total weight of materials is reduced.

Structures where obvious major economies are possible are those in which important forces are developed by volumetric changes such as temperature, shrinkage, creep, etc. By reducing the size of members and thus reducing the rigidity of the structure, the stresses caused by the volumetric changes are minimized. Thus, not only are economies possible by using the minimum required material for a given set of moments and thrusts, but the design moments and thrusts are themselves reduced.

Actual comparative studies of fixed concrete arches and rigid frame highway bridges as designed by standard procedures and by ultimate strength methods have indicated that the latter designs result in structures of substantially more slender proportions. The use of such structures has been found to result in (1) economy of concrete in the superstructure and the footings, (2) little if any increases in the total weight of reinforcing steel, (3) a decrease in the centering required for erection and (4) in the case of the bridges, a reduction in earthwork quantities and wingwall heights. For structures founded on piles, the reduction of the total reactions due to the reduced dead load and volumetric effects would mean even greater savings.

However, it is very important to note that the ultimate strength method will not always mean reductions. In some cases it may result in additional tensile reinforcing in order to provide a uniform factor of safety against overload rather than a given allowable stress under working load.

It should be noted that ultimate strength design is only a method of pro-

---

LOAD FACTORS

Effect of load factors and load combinations on the design of sections where the dead load effect is a concentric compression and the live load effect is a moment

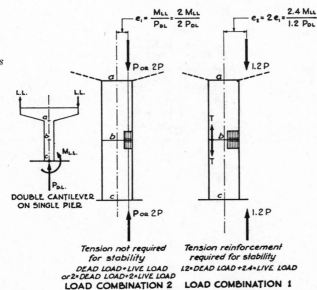

Figure 2

portioning sections based on their actual strength in direct stress, flexure, and combined flexure and direct stress as found by tests. When combined with load factors, it provides a method of obtaining a uniform factor of safety for flexure and thrust, if the field control is adequate to assure the required concrete strength in the structure.

Factors of Safety

The report of the Joint ASCE-ACI Committee on ultimate strength states that members should be proportioned so that:

" (1) They should be capable of carrying without failure the critical load combinations which will insure an ample factor of safety against an increase in live load beyond that assumed in design;

" (2) The strains under working loads should not be so large as to cause excessive cracking."

In order to satisfy these conditions the following load factors are specified where the effects of wind and earthquake can be neglected.

Load Combination (1)
Design Load = 1.2 x Basic Load (Dead Load and Volume Change Effects) plus 2.4 x Live Load

Load Combination (2)
Design Load = K x Basic Load plus Live Load, where K = 1.8 for beams without axial load and 2.0 for columns and members with both bending and axial load.

Based on the above, the minimum factor of safety or load factor for working load (dead plus live) is 1.8. It also provides a factor of safety of almost 2½ against live load. An allowance is made for a 20 per cent increase in dead load above that shown on the construction plans.

Similar formulas have been established where wind and earthquake effects must be considered.

Two conditions are required for the design of reinforced concrete because it is a non-homogeneous material, of which one constituent, the concrete, has adequate compressive strength but so little tensile capacity that it is normally disregarded. The first criterion controls the design when the dead load produces an essentially axial force on the section and

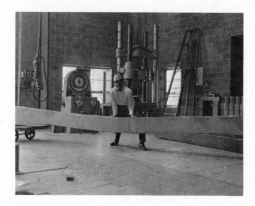

PLASTICITY

A 22-ft clear span concrete haunched beam with fixed ends as it appeared following load test. This member underwent a 7-in. permanent plastic deflection without loss of strength and with little damage

the live load effect has a large eccentricity. For such a case there may be no tensile stress nor requirement for tensile reinforcement under working load or any multiple of working load, but substantial tensile reinforcement may be required when the live load is increased disproportionately to the dead load.

For example, if a member subjected to dead load compression and live load flexure is designed for working loads on the basis of *Load Combination* (2) only or allowable stress, the factor of safety against an increase in live load may be far below the value assumed in selecting the allowable stress or the load factor because the dead load compression is fixed. The effect of increasing the live load moments without changing the dead load compression may be such as to move the resultant from inside the

section to some distance outside the section. If the member were originally designed for compression only, it might have little reserve for the tension stresses produced by the overload condition and failure would follow. The use of *Load Combination* (1) would prevent such failures.

The condition of dead load flexure plus live load tension would be similar.

The load factors recommended for ultimate strength design provide that the maximum internal forces acting on each section of a reinforced concrete structure will bear a uniform ratio to the ultimate strength of that section. It follows that the factors of safety used for the design of the individual sections will be the minimum factors of safety against collapse of the total structure and will be the actual factors

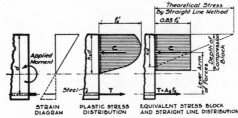

EQUIVALENT STRESS BLOCK

Formulas for proportioning sections to resist moments and thrusts are based on an equivalent rectangular stress block which, for simplicity, replaces the curved, actual stress block

Figure 3

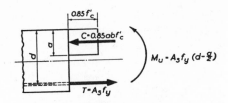

ULTIMATE MOMENT CAPACITY

This sketch shows the magnitude of forces and resisting moment in an under-reinforced concrete beam at the point at which the tension steel is strained beyond the yield point

Figure 4

A_s = Area of tension steel
f_y = Yield point stress of steel reinforcement
b = Width of beam

of safety against collapse only in those structures where moments cannot be redistributed under overload and where no self-relieving stresses are present such as simple beams or columns or rigid frames with single fixed positions of load and free of temperature and other stresses from volumetric changes.

For a rigid frame structure designed for pattern loading or moving loads, the collapse load will be higher than any of the given design loads multiplied by the load factors. This is so because with the present ultimate strength method the design moments and thrusts are computed from elastic frame analyses and generally only one or two sections of the structure are stressed fully by any one position of the design load. Therefore, as the load is increased these sections can yield without loss of strength,

and other sections not fully stressed will be brought to their full capacity. Only then, when plastic hinges are developed will failure take place. Although no allowance is made for such behavior by the ACI Code many tests have indicated that reinforced concrete structures have more than sufficient ductility to allow such redistribution under heavy overload. This characteristic has recently been verified by severe tests of structures subjected to blast pressures of atomic bombs.

An additional factor of safety against collapse due to overload is available in those structures where volumetric effects are present in the final design moments and thrusts. Because the basic design load includes volumetric effects which are self-relieving, that is, reduce and disappear as a result of yielding, and

do not affect the overload capacity, the factor of safety against collapse is increased.

Strength Calculations

The final phase of ultimate strength design involves the proportioning of sections to resist the computed moments and thrusts. For practical purposes the formulas based on an equivalent rectangular stress block given in the ACI Code may be used. (See Fig. 3.)

It should be noted that the depth of the equivalent stress block is not the same as, $k_2 d$, the actual distance to the neutral axis or kd, as computed by the straight line stress distribution method. The essential principles behind the rectangular stress block are that (1) the total compressive force is the same as that for the actual elasto-plastic distribution and (2) the center of the equivalent rectangle is at the same location as the resultant of the actual stress distribution.

In other words the actual irregular stress block is replaced for simplicity with a rectangular stress block of equal total force and an average compressive intensity of $0.85 f'_c$ where f'_c is the crushing strength obtained from a standard test on a 6 x 12 inch plain concrete cylinder at an age of 28 days.

If the beam is under-reinforced so that primary failure will occur in the tensile steel, the concrete will crack as the steel is strained beyond yield and the equivalent depth of the beam in compression, "a", will decrease until the average effective concrete stress reaches the maximum of $0.85 f'_c$. The resisting moment is given by the moment of the force in the tensile reinforcement about the centroid of the compression force. When the section is without compression steel:

$$M_u = A_s f_y \left(d - \frac{a}{2} \right)$$

The moment, M_u, must be equal to the sum of the dead and live load moments times their load factors. If the area of tensile steel is increased to $0.456 \dfrac{f'_c}{f_y}$ the moment capacity of the section will increase until failure occurs by crushing of the concrete at the same time that the stress in the reinforcing steel reaches yield point stress. Any further increases in the area of tension steel will not produce appreciable increases in the moment capacity.

BENDING AND AXIAL LOAD

This is an interaction curve for strength of a reinforced concrete column with both bending moment and axial load. Where strength is controlled by yield of tensile steel, moment capacity increases as axial load is added. Where strength is controlled by crushing of concrete, the moment capacity decreases as axial load is added.

Figure 5

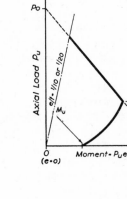

In order to eliminate the possibility of compression failures and maintain ductile sections the new ACI Code limits the maximum ratio of tensile steel for flexural members without compressive reinforcement to

$$\frac{A_s}{bd} = p = 0.40 \frac{f'_c}{f_y} \quad (2)$$

which is slightly less than the true ratio for balanced reinforcement but is about twice that allowed by the straight line method. The ultimate moment corresponding to balanced design by the revised code is

$$M_u = 0.306 \, bd^2 f'_c$$

For the case of a concentric axial load the ultimate capacity of a column is given by:

$$P_o = .85 f'_c \, (A_g - A_{st}) + f_y A_{st},$$
$$A_g = \text{Gross cross-sectional area}$$
$$A_{st} = \text{Total steel area}$$

the direct combination of the strength of the concrete and the reinforcing steel. However, since it is difficult to ensure that the actual loadings will ever be entirely concentric it is required that a minimum eccentricity of $\frac{1}{20}$ the total diameter for round spiral columns and $\frac{1}{10}$ the total thickness of rectangular columns be considered in the design.

The equation for members under combined bending and axial load where the strength is controlled by the tensile reinforcement is derived in a similar manner. Where the compressive strength controls, tests indicate an essentially straight line between the case of pure bending and the case of axial load. It is interesting to note that the moment capacity of a reinforced concrete section increases as axial load is added if it is controlled by yield of the tension reinforcement. Of course, if it is controlled by crushing of the concrete, the effect of axial load is to reduce the moment capacity. This is shown in Fig. 5.

Ultimate strength design of reinforced concrete thus provides one basic method for the design of beams and columns with any amount of eccentricity, from zero to infinity whereas conventional design requires different approaches for axial load, small eccentricity and large eccentricity or pure bending. Adoption of ultimate strength methods will result therefore in considerable simplification of the work of proportioning sections. Design charts are available for flexure of rectangular sections, and for flexure and axial load of rectangular sections, round sections and square sections with round cores. It may be noted that the design formulas contained in the Joint Committee Report and the ACI Code are essentially the same as those proposed by C. S. Whitney 16 years ago.

The ultimate strength method of design requires that the actual concrete strengths and the steel strengths be at least equal to those assumed by the designer. The design formulas provide no factor of safety to cover shortcomings in the materials. For this reason the Code requires use of controlled concrete with not more than one 28-day cylinder test in 10 having an average strength less than that assumed in the design. It is also specified that the average of any three consecutive tests shall not fall below the design value. For the design of the reinforcement the minimum value of the yield stress of the steel is to be used in design. Since the strength of most of the steel and concrete will be higher than the minimum values used for design, most sections will therefore be designed on the safe side; seldom will the factor of safety be less than that intended.

Deflection of Beams and Slabs

Because the ultimate strength method of design will encourage the use of more slender members with steel working at higher stresses, the possibility of increased flexibility makes a careful consideration of deflections more important than ever before. Undesirable deflections have occurred in many structures designed by the straight line method and are not due to the method of design nor, in some cases, to stress conditions caused by dead or live load. It should be noted that the final long time deflections of reinforced concrete members may be 2.5 to 4.0 times those computed by elastic methods based on stress-strain curves which are conventionally used. As a result, the necessity of keeping the deflections within acceptable limits will often determine practical dimensions. With slender compressive members such as arches, the longtime change in shape of the member axis as a result of creep may add substantially to the design moments. The effect of shrinkage on the deflection of thin slabs reinforced on only one face are well known and are best illustrated by the warping which has been reported for precast channel slabs with substantial bottom reinforcement in the stems and light reinforcement in the thin flange slab. Lack of rigidity in formwork supports during the setting period during construction may contribute additional slab deflections, particularly in multi-story buildings.

One of the important ways in which sagging can be limited is by addition of compression steel. This is useful in reducing the effects of creep because the effectiveness of the steel is increased as the effective modulus of elasticity of the concrete is reduced. Compression steel also reduces the effects of shrinkage by bridging and reducing the cracks. Of course, it is well known that the use of good concrete with adequate curing is of prime importance for reducing the effects of shrinkage. Creep is also greatly reduced by postponing the time for removal of forms and supports. Flexural members of minimum depth with heavy reinforcement should be used only where the resulting deflections will not be objectionable. However, it should not be inferred that flexibility properly considered by the designer is objectionable.

Conclusion

The present approved ultimate strength method for reinforced concrete applies primarily to the design of sections for combinations of moment and thrust. The ultimate strength method requires that the structure be detailed to have sufficient shear (diagonal tension) and bond strength to fully develop its moment-thrust capacity. It is also assumed that the control of the concrete production, placing and curing will be adequate to provide the required concrete strength. While designing members for strength the engineer must be careful not to overlook other factors such as deflection, crack resistance, and durability which greatly affect the usefulness and appearance of a structure for its intended purpose.

In designs based on ultimate strength, the engineer can prevent wasting construction material and design time and is allowed more freedom in the selection of sections. With the ultimate strength method as another powerful tool, he can more readily provide a structure which will meet the requirements of architectural design.

A CHANGE AHEAD FOR STRUCTURAL DESIGN

3. PLASTIC-LIMIT DESIGN OF STEEL FRAMES

by Edward Cohen, Associate Partner, Ammann & Whitney, Consulting Engineers, New York

ARCHITECTS AND ENGINEERS throughout this country and abroad are looking toward plastic-limit design of steel structures as a means of obtaining greater elegance and economy in steel construction. Engineers are concerned also with the accurate computation by limit methods of the ultimate load capacity of structures, something which is not possible in conventional design.

In plastic design allowable stresses and elastic stress distributions are disregarded and members are designed at critical sections for their full strength after yielding.

Limit design is the proportioning of structural members such that the entire structure, acting as a unit, is capable of supporting the working load multiplied by a given factor of safety, failure to occur when this load is exceeded. Limit design can be applied to all types of structures — beams, trusses, frames, suspension systems, etc. It gives results different from those found from conventional methods when the structure is statically redundant or indeterminate, as for example, rigid frames, continuous beams, lattice trusses, etc.

Although limit analysis or design does not necessarily require yielding or plastic hinges, present thinking along this line with respect to buildings is concerned primarily with *limit* design of all-welded steel frames making full use of the *plastic* strength of the steel sections and redistribution of moments after the development of plastic hinges. This special case can be called *plastic-limit* design.

Although limit design is a concept that was unconsciously used prior to the development of elastic analysis and design methods, the first rational approach to the subject of *plastic-limit* design was made by Kazinczy in 1914 and followed by Maier-Leibnitz in 1917. In 1936 Professor J. F. Baker of Cambridge University became concerned with the problem and has devoted his efforts almost continuously to its solution. It is he and his associates who are responsible in large measure for the development of a practical *plastic-limit* design method. Important contributions have been made in this country by the research teams at Brown University and Lehigh University.

Intensive research has been conducted in this field for the past 15 years, much of it with the support of the welding industry. Although there is still a great need for additional research on various phases of the subject, sufficient information is available at the present time to allow the practical application of *plastic-limit* design methods. During World War II the design of shelters and later the design of structures to resist atomic explosions were predicated largely on *plastic-limit* methods. Today it is recognized generally that the true resistance of structures to blast and impact loads can be accurately determined only by such methods.

In Great Britain where *plastic-limit* design was recognized as acceptable by the standard specifications (BSS449) in 1948, almost 200 building structures so designed had been built by 1955. Generally great savings in the weight of steel and in cost are possible by this method. The saving in weight is reflected in lighter and more slender members and has caused at least one American Architect, Philip Johnson — *Architectural Review* Vol. 116 (1954) — who viewed a plastically designed British school building to wonder why comparable designs were not being built in the United States. It is hoped that in the near future such designs will be allowed by American codes and that forward looking engineers will use them to full advantage.

It should be noted that *plastic-limit* design is possible, in practical sense, only for welded frames; also, that the maximum benefit may be derived from welding by *plastic-limit* design. The two are interdependent. Increased confidence in the use of welding will tend to bring greater pressure for building code approval of *plastic-limit* design and, vice versa, approval of *plastic-limit* design methods will see a rapid increase in all-welded building construction.

Plastic Strength of Members

Stress concentrations which result in appreciable local yielding are present in most structures designed by current codes. During fabrication and erection, yield is commonly used in cambering or straightening members or forcing them into place. Experience has shown that these strains do not affect the strength of the structure. If steel did not have the ability to yield under high stress without loss of strength, most steel structures would be impossible to construct.

All the standard specifications have long required that steel used for struc-

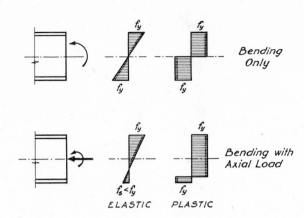

Figure 1. ELASTIC AND PLASTIC STRESS DISTRIBUTIONS

tural purposes be carefully tested to verify its ductility which is often cited as a reason for the reliability of steel structures and the general absence of sudden failures.

Although the actual mechanics of yield and flow of steel are still uncertain and the subject of continued research, the phenomenological or engineering aspects with respect to our present steels have been carefully documented by laboratory tests and experience with full scale structures. At the present time, as a result of research and development work largely over the past 25 years, a rational basis has been established for the use of the plastic strength as a design criteria.

With few exceptions design by the traditional method of allowable elastic stresses is safe and relatively simple. This was the basis of its introduction in the beginning of the 19th Century and its ready and continuous acceptance to the present. However, as early as 1899, the plastic moment capacity of ductile members was discussed in approximately its present form in a British engineering textbook and has never been completely forgotten.

The difference between the flexural strengths obtained by the elastic and plastic methods is a function of the shape of the section as shown in Fig. 2. Thus, a rectangular section has a flexural shape factor of 1.5 as compared to a wide flange member with a shape factor of approximately 1.14. In other words, the plastic moment capacity of the rectangular section is 50 per cent greater than the moment at which yield stress is reached at the extreme fiber while the strength of the WF section is only 14 per cent greater.

This involves no great change in thinking for designers, only a different method of computing the required member size, a method which can be introduced readily into most engineering offices. (For the sake of completeness it may be noted that the shape factors shown in Fig. 2 may be modified by shear and axial load.) Moreover, empirical modifications to the current design specifications have anticipated some of the results of the plastic stress distribution. For example the allowable stress for WF beams is 20,000 psi whereas it has been set at 30,000 psi for circular sections. By plastic analysis it is found that the ratio of the ultimate moment capacity to the allowable elastic moment computed with these stresses is approximately the same for both the rectangular and WF sections.

In the design of beam-columns — members carrying moment and axial load — the demarcation between plastic and conventional methods is vague. Much current practice is empirical and is based on elastic theory as modified by test results and experience. More research in this field is needed and is being continued. It is expected that the end result will be more accurate design methods closely related to the plastic buckling strength of beam-columns as determined from modified plastic theory and laboratory observations. As might be expected, research indicates that the present allowable stress design methods are conservative.

Plastic-Limit Design

The most significant change in thinking required by *plastic-limit* design is that the entire structure must be designed as a unit rather than as the sum of a number of separate individual members or sections. Although it is true that in the elastic analysis of a continuous structure the entire structure must be considered in order to compute the moments, thrusts and shears at each section, all the sections are then designed independently. If each section were made adequate for exactly the required strength and no more, the elastic design would be equivalent to a limit design for the same loads. This, however, would involve the use of members of variable section with haunches and/or cover plates. High fabrication costs

Figure 2. RATIO OF FULL PLASTIC MOMENTS
TO YIELD POINT MOMENTS

SECTION	WF STRONG AXIS	WF WEAK AXIS		
SHAPE FACTOR $\dfrac{M_p}{M_y}$	APPROX. 1.14	APPROX. 1.50	1.50	1.67

M_p = Plastic Moment
M_y = Yield Point Moment
(Yield stress at extreme fiber)

make this approach prohibitive for typical construction. If on the other hand, each member consists of a uniform rolled section, say a WF, then conventional design requires that it be proportioned to limit the maximum stress at the section of highest moment to the allowable value. At all other sections the member is stressed to less than its capacity and some metal is wasted.

In limit design a plastic hinge is allowed to develop at the point of maximum moment and to rotate until all critical sections are fully utilized. (A plastic hinge is formed when a section has reached its full capacity and can continue to rotate without change in moment.) Since the load capacity under this condition is greater than that assumed by an elastic analysis, the size and/or weight of the member can be reduced with considerable savings. It can be seen that by allowing even one plastic hinge to develop, the elastic analysis of moments is invalidated. Also, allowing a plastic hinge to develop at any point of a multiply-redundant structure results in increased moments elsewhere. For this reason it is necessary that the strength of the structure be investigated as a unit. The proportioning of members and the design of the overall structure thus become a single operation.

If the loading is always of the same type and is fixed in position, *plastic-limit* design requires that at ultimate load:

1. The bending moment be adequate to provide equilibrium with the applied load,
2. There be a sufficient number of plastic hinges present to allow formation of a collapse mechanism, and,
3. No computed moments exceed the plastic moment capacity.

From these principles have been developed various methods of computing the actual value of the failure load. In the case of a fixed end member, the mechanism scheme can be obtained by placing hinges at the center and at each end. For more complicated structures considerable calculation may be required. For structures with moving or independently varying loads additional criteria are required. Possible modes of failure for a simple rectangular frame are shown in Fig. 4. It can be seen that adequate, ductile beam to column connections are of major importance.

It may be noted that the three criteria listed above make no reference to temperature stresses or relative settle-

Plastic design for research lab in England permitted wide frame spacing, reducing piling costs. Overall savings totalled 23 per cent

ment of supports. Indeed, these two factors which have played so important a part in elastic design theory can be shown to have no effect on the load carrying capacity of ductile structures. Actually, structural continuity is desirable where poor foundation soils are encountered, because, under working load, it provides a means of shifting part of the load from the weak to the strong points of the foundation.

Plastic-limit design eliminates the need for elastic analysis of continuous structures for the determination of strength. For example, a rigid frame designed by current practice requires a complete elastic analysis for the calculation of moments at critical sections. With *plastic-limit* design, the moments

at critical sections are taken at their ultimate values which are reached when plastic hinges are formed at these points. If necessary, the intermediate moments may then be computed from the principles of statics.

Elastic theory must still be used for the calculation of deflections, the plastic rotations at the hinges being superimposed on the elastic curve. For example, the final deflection of a fixed-end uniform section beam under uniform load may be approximated as the elastic deflection of a fixed-end beam for the load which causes formation of the hinges at the ends plus the elastic deflection of a simple beam for the additional load required to form the hinge at the center.

Plastic-limit design requires that the

Figure 3. COMPARISON OF LOAD CAPACITIES OBTAINED
BY ELASTIC AND LIMIT ANALYSES

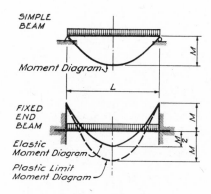

ELASTIC* ANALYSIS LOAD W_e	LIMIT ANALYSIS LOAD W_p	RATIO $W_p:W_e$
$\dfrac{8M}{L}$ **	$\dfrac{8M}{L}$	1.0
$\dfrac{12M}{L}$	$\dfrac{16M}{L}$	1.33

* By Moment Distribution or similar methods.
** M = Moment capacity of the beam section.

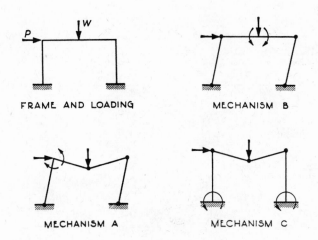

FRAME AND LOADING   MECHANISM B

MECHANISM A   MECHANISM C

Figure 4. POSSIBLE FAILURE MECHANISMS FOR A SIMPLE RECTANGULAR FRAME

load carrying capacity of the structure be limited only by plastic yielding, the failure being preceded by large deformations and deflections. Careful reflection will indicate that in the event of excessive loading this is the most desirable type of failure since it will usually provide adequate warning so that preventive measures can be taken. In order that failure shall be of this type it is necessary to prevent sudden failures such as may be caused by brittle fracture, fatigue failure or plastic buckling. It is obvious that the first two will result in sudden failure. The third, plastic buckling, must also be avoided or its effects carefully considered by the engineer.

In this case, the load capacity does not remain constant or increase with deflection as in the case of simple plastic bending, tension or compression, instead the resistance of the member to load drops off as shown in Fig. 5. Thus, if a member whose resistance to load is limited by plastic buckling is fully loaded, it becomes unstable and any additional accidental deflection will cause a relatively sudden failure. This, of course, assumes that the load cannot be transferred elsewhere. If this is possible, as it is in most complicated continuous frameworks, failure may be prevented or at least retarded. In any case, the designer must consider the maximum deflection or rotation to which the member will be subjected in determining the failure load. It is desir-

able to avoid the inclusion of such weak points in a structure.

The designer must also guard against the possibility of any substantial number of cycles in which the plastic moments reverse direction as a result of alternating loads. Although further study may tend to improve the picture, it appears at present that such reversals may lead to eventual failure after a relatively small number of cycles. It is interesting to note that the most direct *plastic-limit* design approach in such cases is to start the calculation with a complete elastic analysis.

Because of their dramatic nature, brittle failures often make headlines, as for example the World War II Liberty Ships which split open on the high seas and the all welded viaduct which collapsed in Canada in 1951. These failures are attributed to combinations of extremely low temperatures and steel of unsuitable composition particularly with regard to carbon and manganese. However, the standard structural steel, A7, which is in use in the United States for bridges and buildings, has an excellent record. Where temperatures may reach -30 to -40 F., where thick plate material is required and where restraints against ductile behavior cannot be avoided two new steels are now available to provide a greater margin of safety against brittle failures, A373 Structural Steel for Welding and A131 Structural Steel for Ships.

Where fatigue failures due to a large number of repetitions of load are possible, the stress at failure may be far below the yield point, thus precluding the development of the full plastic strength of the section or the formation of plastic hinges as required for *plastic-limit* analysis. For such cases, the allowable stress method combined with elastic analysis appears the most practical method of design.

Load Factors

The criteria for a satisfactory design by elastic theory are that the allowable stresses are not to be exceeded and that the deflections or other deformations shall be within limits which are not objectionable. If the allowable stress is set at $\dfrac{\text{Yield Point}}{\text{Factor of Safety}}$, it may be assumed that the actual factor of safety will never fall below that established unless imperfections are present in the final construction. On the other hand, it is well known that the actual factor of safety may be much higher depending on the shape of the members, the re-

Figure 5. LOAD VERSUS DEFLECTION FOR MEMBERS SUBJECT TO PLASTIC BUCKLING

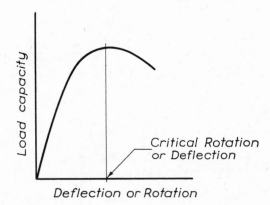

dundancy of the structure and the type of loading.

In the past, the factor of safety has been established primarily on the basis of experience, such that normally well designed, fabricated and erected structures subject to all the normal uncertainties inherent in each step of the construction process would be adequate for their intended usage. It presumes that in a certain number of cases, even where the design load is not exceeded, a combination of faulty material, poor workmanship and careless design will result in failures. The established factor of safety tries to strike a balance such that the losses due to failure will be much less than the cost involved in raising the general factor of safety for all structures.

In proposing a new design method the tendency has been to presume that it would be satisfactory to retain the same actual minimum factor of safety as results from current design methods. However, it must be noted that the factor of safety by *plastic-limit* design becomes uniform for all structures. Although this is desirable, it does mean that the factor of safety of such construction will be in many cases much less than that in construction built from current designs which have factors of safety varying upward from the minimum. In addition, many more points of a structure designed by plastic-limit methods may be stressed beyond yield than are so stressed accidentally at present. Such conditions will affect the resistance of structures to load repetitions and also their resistance to wind and earthquake. In the last two cases, the design loads themselves are the result, to a large extent, of engineering judgment in many cases. This judgment is greatly affected by past experience with structures having variable, usually higher factors of safety.

For these reasons it is desirable to place the selection of loads and load factors on a more scientific basis. Considerable fruitful work has been done in this field in recent years using the theory of probability to determine the expected frequency of live loads, imperfections in material, etc., and adjusting factors of safety accordingly. There is still room for wide improvement in load factors (ratio of collapse load to working load). Unfortunately for designing engineers such improvements are likely to lead to greater complication in design.

It is worth noting that as the variables of doubtful loading, material, workman-

Courtesy American Institute of Steel Construction

Slim, double gable frame for storage building near Andover, England was designed plastically; fabricated by shop welding, field bolting

ship and design are reduced to a minimum by careful control of all operations it becomes possible to reduce the final load factor without impairing the usefulness of the structure. Also, there has been considerable discussion as to the desirability of using different factors for dead load which is a constant known value and for live load which is subject to uncertain variations. Such changes in the controlling specifications are not expected in the near future.

It is expected that when plastic-limit design is included in our building code specifications a load factor of at least 1.88 will be required.

The British Standard Specification adopted in 1948 requires a minimum load factor of 2.00 for *plastic-limit* de-

sign. It states, "[Fully rigid design], as compared with the methods for simple and semi-rigid design, will give the greatest economy in the weight of steel used when applied in appropriate cases. For the purpose of such design, *accurate methods of structural analysis shall be employed leading to a load factor of 2*, based on the calculated or otherwise ascertained failure load of the structure or any of its parts, and due regards shall be paid to the accompanying deformations under working load, so that the deflections and other movements are not in excess of the (normal limits)." Even with these restrictions plastic-limit design has shown substantial economies in material and cost in comparison with conventional design methods.

BIBLIOGRAPHY

GENERAL

1. *Introduction to Plasticity* by A. Phillips, Ronald Press Company, N. Y., N. Y. (1956)
2. *Inelastic Behavior of Engineering Materials and Structures* by A. M. Freudenthal, John Wiley & Sons, Inc., N. Y., N. Y. (1950)
3. *Theory of Limit Design*, by J. A. Van den Broek, John Wiley & Sons, Inc., N. Y., N. Y. (1948)

REINFORCED CONCRETE

1. *Guide to Ultimate Strength Design of Reinforced Concrete* by C. S. Whitney and E. Cohen, *Proceedings*, American Concrete Institute, Vol. 53, November 1956
2. *Final Report of ASCE-ACI Joint Committee on Ultimate Strength Design*, *Proceedings*, American Society of Civil Engineers, Paper No. 809 (1956)

STRUCTURAL STEEL

1. *The Steel Skeleton (Vol. 2 Plastic Behavior and Design)* by J. F. Baker, M. R. Horne and J. Heyman, Cambridge University Press (1956)
2. *Proceedings, National Engineering Conference, 1956*, American Institute of Steel Construction, 101 Park Avenue, N. Y., N. Y. (1956)
3. *Plastic Design in Structural Steel* by L. S. Beedle, B. Thurliman, R. C. Ketter, Lehigh University, Bethlehem, Pennsylvania (1955)
4. *Plastic Strength of Structural Members, a Symposium, Transactions*, American Society of Civil Engineers, Vol. 120, Paper No. 2772 (1955)

Note: The above list of publications is only representative and is not intended as a complete bibliography. Many important works are not included.

HOW STRUCTURAL MODELS ARE USED IN PRACTICE

by Jack R. Janney   *Wiss, Janney and Associates, Consulting Engineers*

Freedom and precision in the design of building structures, particularly indeterminate ones such as shells and space frames, have been handicapped in the past by the available analytical tools. First, it is difficult to visualize and predict the behavior of these structures, and to develop the mathematics that correspond to the presumed behavior. Even then, exact solutions are frequently tedious and time-consuming, so simplifying assumptions are incorporated to make analysis practical; and, naturally, these assumptions tend to be in a conservative direction for safety's sake.

The testing of structural models not only demonstrates structural behavior under load, but, more importantly, provides strain and stress data and deflections for structural design. The classical methods of analysis, adjusted by experience factors (i.e., engineers' intuition and codes) are, nonetheless, requisite so that there is a sound basis for design of the models themselves, and their shape will be headed in the right direction for efficient flow of forces. But because the mathematical analysis only approximates actual behavior, model data will frequently indicate desirable modifications to improve structural efficiency, in addition to providing structural design data that otherwise would be extremely difficult, if not impossible, to determine.

The basic function of structure is to oppose gravity forces. The final criterion which serves engineers in determining the structural adequacy of any configuration is the magnitude of stresses produced by gravity. (Of course wind forces must be considered for tall buildings and seismic forces in earthquake areas.)

How does one establish the magnitude of these all-important stresses? The normal approach involves the use of a drawing which depicts the structure or, most commonly, a part of it. With the aid of mathematics this picture is used to evaluate stresses produced by gravity and in some cases wind or seismic forces.

The picture is usually restricted to a two dimensional configuration for the sake of simplicity.

This method of solving structural problems is sometimes referred to as the "mathematical model." The mathematical model may range in complexity from the solution of stresses produced in a simple beam, to the solution of a highly indeterminate structure such as a complicated shell or space frame.

The Limits of Mathematics

Usefulness of the mathematical model is determined by the following:
1. The ability to express the problem in mathematical terms for which a solution exists or can be obtained.
2. The time, and consequently expense, required to solve the problem after it has been expressed mathematically. The practical limits of mathematics have been extended considerably with the development of electronic computers.
3. The validity of boundary condition assumptions (i.e., where structure is restrained, as by edge beams) which must be made before a solution is feasible.
4. The extreme difficulty encountered in thinking of structural interaction in three dimensions.

In spite of these restrictions many notable structural advancements have taken place in recent years. However, structural designers of buildings do not have to perform their function with the degree of exactitude demanded of aircraft designers.

Such inexactness would be very unsatisfactory in the efforts of space engineers to place a vehicle on the moon. It would also have retarded the development of aircraft technology. In the first place, aircraft engineers have not been constricted by small engineering budgets as have structural engineers. Also because of the limitations of the mathematics, aircraft designers have made extensive use of "physical" models. Use of physical models to assist in the design of structures is not a new

concept in the building field. The idea of employing such a design tool has simply lay more or less dormant for many years in the United States. Structural models have been an important and well accepted part of the design process for complicated structures in Europe. This is especially true in the design of dams.

Some of the early work done by Beggs, Eney and others in the United States is well known to many engineers. Most of their effort as well as most of the work done in photoelastic studies of structures has been confined to investigations of two-dimensional models. The United States Bureau of Reclamation and the University of California have accomplished a great deal in the study of dam structures with small scale models. M.I.T. currently is studying models not only for elastic behavior, but for ultimate strength as well.

Interest has been revitalized in the past three years as a result of: (1) improved technological methods for performing structural model analysis, and (2) increased architectural interest in unconventional structures.

The writer has been involved in about 20 studies which have made use of small scale models during this period. These models have been made of acrylic plastic, and consequently the investigations have been limited to elastic behavior.

Data Provided by Models

Two basic types of measurements are taken on models made of plastic: strains and deflections.

Since models are exact scaled-down versions of actual structures, strain gages can be attached to opposite sides of any surface, and in this way not only can tensions and compressions on the surfaces be determined, but also moments, shears, torsions and reactions at supports.

The strain gages are attached to the models in a rosette pattern, in pairs, or singly depending on the type of structure and information wanted. When stresses occur in several directions, as in thin shells, then

The complete experimental setup for measuring strains (and thus stresses) for a thin shell under uniform loading is shown in Figure 1 (*left*). Strains are measured by means of very small diameter wire gages fastened to the model. Each patch on the model has three gages in a rosette pattern, since the stresses are multi-directional. The model is loaded by evacuating the air from under it with a vacuum pump (note hose lower right). The amount of vacuum is registered on the manometer (upper right). Movement of the shell makes the wires lengthen (tension) or shorten (compression). Lengthening or shortening of the wires changes their resistance which is registered on the electronic meter in the foreground.

This model is of a shell for a physical education building containing field house and swimming pool for Munster, Indiana. The architect is Bachman & Bertram & Associates, and the structural engineer is Kolbjorn Saether & Associates. This "free-form" shaped shell is comprised of a circular dome connected to an elliptical conoid by means of hyperbolic paraboloids. The dome and conoid are prestressed across arcs of their perimeters; prestressing tendons also cross the h.p.'s

Figure 1

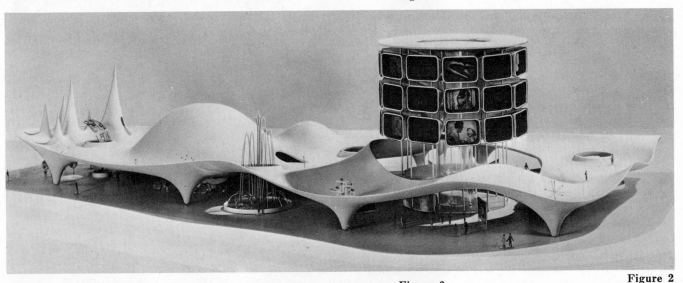

Figure 3

Figure 2

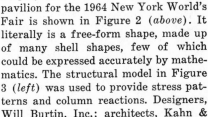

Display model of the Eastman Kodak pavilion for the 1964 New York World's Fair is shown in Figure 2 (*above*). It literally is a free-form shape, made up of many shell shapes, few of which could be expressed accurately by mathematics. The structural model in Figure 3 (*left*) was used to provide stress patterns and column reactions. Designers, Will Burtin, Inc.; architects, Kahn & Jacobs; structural engineers, Lev Zetlin & Associates

three-gage rosettes are installed.

To convert stresses determined from models to stress values for actual structures, they are multiplied by similitude factors (i.e., relationships of moduli of elasticity, sizes and magnitudes of loads for model and actual structure).

A thin shell model is loaded by evacuating the air under it with a vacuum pump. Structures such as beams, frames and arches are loaded by positioning of weights.

Deflections are measured by using dial deflection gages, linear differential transformers or precision levels. A reference grid is used to determine differences between original elevations and elevations under load.

The structural models which we have tested and analyzed as design aids for specific projects have ranged in purpose from providing nearly the complete source of design information to performing simply a check on some structural feature open to question.

Examples of Models

Some example projects are discussed below with respect to purpose and accomplishment, from design as well as economic standpoints.

The model shown in Figure 1 is of a "free-form" thin shell for a high school. The model analysis is being conducted under conditions most effective with respect to the architect-engineer relationship: the two began collaboration at the outset of the preliminary architectural studies. Thus, the architect gained the greatest freedom from structural restriction, and this freedom was further expanded because the structural engineer was fully aware of the value of a structural model analysis. In this case the structural model and a mathematical model are being utilized simultaneously. This gives a check so that the deficiencies of each is being overcome.

The structural model of the complicated thin shell for the Eastman Kodak Pavilion at the New York World's Fair, 1964, is shown in Figures 2 and 3. This model served as a primary source of design data in the structural design process. It also served to establish the space coordinates on which the construction drawings were based.

The interaction of the many shell shapes, few of which could be expressed mathematically, along with the compound system of supporting elements, made it very difficult to develop an accurate mathematical method. Therefore, the structural model was used to provide stress patterns and column reactions. This building is now under construction.

The structural model shown in Figure 4 is of a 29-story apartment using a reinforced concrete flat-plate construction.

A simultaneous study of a mathematical model was made. As a result of comparison between the two methods, the slab steel indicated from the mathematical model was reduced 15 per cent. The shear wall size and disposition was based on the findings of the structural model analysis. The cost of the model was about 15 per cent of the amount of the savings.

The structural model shown in Figure 5 was built and tested as part of a comprehensive development program which was undertaken by Material Service Corporation of Chicago before manufacturing and marketing a precast, prestressed hollow-core floor unit. In addition to tests on a model, a number of load tests were performed on prototype units built under pilot conditions to full scale. The purpose of the model was to learn something about the rather complicated secondary stresses which occur as a result of the Vierendeel-like action in the lateral direction at the end bearing. Also the buckling characteristics of the very thin elements of the concrete cross-section were evaluated.

Obviously, it was much less expensive to perform tests on the small scale model than on full-sized members. However, some testing was done especially to observe behavior throughout all ranges of loading to failure, and enough checking was done during these full scale tests to substantiate the model findings.

The purpose of the model of "wishbone" supports for an access roadway at O'Hare Airport shown in Figure 6 was one of redesign. The original design incorporated large hinges in the supports which were employed to assist in design by mathematics. The structural engineer, in his effort to conserve construction cost, decided to use a structural model analysis and thereby eliminate the costly hinges. Also, his decision was influenced by his knowledge of the probability of other savings through the design refinement resulting from a structural model analysis. The savings resulting from the redesign were about 200 times the cost of the model analysis.

The structure shown in Figure 7 is an open-spandrel arch bridge of five spans which was redesigned before construction in the interest of economy. The original design was based on a conventional mathematical model which presumes the arch to act alone in carrying the loads of the spandrel walls, bridge deck and live load. When bids were received for the structure based on the original design, engineers felt that the cost was too high. A redesign appeared to offer the best remedy for the situation, if advantage could be taken of the strengthening effect of permitting the arch rib, spandrel walls and bridge deck to act together to resist the loads. Such an assumption produces a highly indeterminate structure. Partially in the interest of time, but also in the interest of cost, a structural model was used for the redesign. The redesign was accomplished in a period of a few weeks and resulted in a considerable reduction in cost. It also produced a much more graceful structure. The arch rib was reduced in thickness from 18 in. to 14 in. at the crown, and from 36 in. to 18 in. at the springline. The cost of the model analysis was less than 1 per cent of the savings.

Only those engineers who have firm confidence in their own ability will seriously consider the use of structural models. They are not afraid to ask the architect to approach the owner, who is certainly the principal beneficiary of design refinements, and request special appropriations for the model analysis. This is usually necessary because the fee structure of both architects and engineers seldom contains budget provisions for such effort.

Many engineers are reticent to pose the problem to the architect for fear that it will be construed as an admission of inability. The architect is often hesitant to approach the owner for the same reason. As a consequence, in those areas of doubt, very conservative assumptions are made with the result that the structure is built at greater costs than would otherwise be necessary. In the other extreme the assumptions may be incorrect, with resulting inadequate factors of safety or undesirable behavior.

Figure 4

Tests on the model of a 29-story flat plate structure for Carl Sandburg Housing in Chicago (Figure 4, *left*) indicated that 15 per cent less slab reinforcement was necessary than mathematical analysis showed. Also shear wall size and location was based on the structural model analysis. Cost of the model analysis was about 15 per cent of the savings it made possible.

Although the floor plan has an irregular column spacing, the structure itself contains nothing new. But taking into account the conservatism of conventional design procedures, the engineer turned to structural model analysis to determine slab moments caused by vertical loads and lateral wind forces. Architects, Solomon, Cordwell & Associates; structural engineer, Alfred Benesch.

Hollow-core prestressed floor units manufactured by Material Service Corp. of Chicago (Figure 5, *below, left*) were tested in model form to determine secondary stresses at the bearing point and also buckling characteristics of the thin units.

"Wishbone" supports for access roadway at O'Hare Airport were designed without hinges through model analysis (Figure 6, *below*). Architects, C. F. Murphy Associates; structural engineer, Alfred Benesch

Figure 5

Figure 6

Figure 7

Structural model analysis of this open-spandrel arch bridge for the Illinois Tollway indicated that the arch rib could be reduced considerably in thickness from that indicated by mathematical analysis, cutting cost and producing a more graceful structure (Figure 7). The mathematical analysis presumed the arch to act alone in carrying loads of spandrel wall, bridge deck and live load. In actuality, the elements all work together, and this behavior could easily be determined by testing a model. Structural engineers, Vogt, Ivers & Associates; managing engineers, Knoerle, Bender, Stone Inc.

A NEW LOOK AT FLAT PLATE CONSTRUCTION

by Seymour Howard, A.I.A., Associate Professor, Pratt Institute

A discussion of recent work by Lev Zetlin,
Consulting Engineer, New York

Although flat plate construction—reinforced concrete slabs supported directly on columns without beams—has been on the building scene for some time, its design potential has remained largely unexploited. As reported here, however, structural engineer Lev Zetlin has demonstrated the new architectural possibilities that flat plates offer when their structural advantages are correctly understood and their structural behavior correctly analyzed. Dr. Zetlin has designed economical flat plates with longer-than-customary spans, with openings next to the column, and without spandrel beams.

A "flat plate" is defined as a reinforced concrete floor slab supported directly by columns without beams. Unlike "flat slabs," flat plates have neither capitals nor drop panels over the supporting columns, but rest directly on top of columns which have constant cross section from floor to ceiling.

The expanding practice of using flat plates in multi-story apartment, office and hospital buildings has been brought about largely by the obvious economy effected by the absence of beams: cheaper formwork; elimination of furring and other finishes common to projecting members; flexibility in ductwork and other mechanical fittings; and, finally, reduction of total story height since the entire space between floor and ceiling is utilized. Although flat plate floor slabs are usually thicker than slabs supported by beam grids, the total quantity of concrete in a flat plate is comparable to, or smaller than, that in a beam-and-slab floor.

Flat plates are also gaining favor for their speed and simplicity of erection. Time and again bid prices for flat plates have come in lower than other conventional structural systems. Until recently, a flat plate would prove economical for buildings up to only twelve stories high, but flat plate office buildings and apartment houses are now becoming economical up to 24 stories high due to the longer modern cranes.

One of the other commonly mentioned advantages of flat plates is the flexibility in locating columns in plan, but while this is an advantage for architectural planning, it is not beneficial economically. The design of flat plates with regular column spacing is covered by the ACI building code, but irregular column spacing requires an elaborate design which sometimes results in over-design. Also, irregular bays necessitate variations in size and length of bars, which increases the cost of reinforcement. Regular bay sizes may be monotonous architecturally, but they are more economical.

However, flat plates have a number of other inherent possibilities that do offer further flexibility in architectural design and economy—particularly in mechanical installations, architectural planning and finishing. On the whole, these potentialities of flat plate design have not been explored sufficiently, but Dr. Lev Zetlin's recent practice shows that architects can safely use flat plates to greater advantage, lengthening spans, omitting spandrel beams, and even introducing openings in the slabs next to the columns.

Before discussing these possibilities, however, there is a general question that should be considered.

What is a "Correct Structure"?
This question has preoccupied many architects in recent years as they

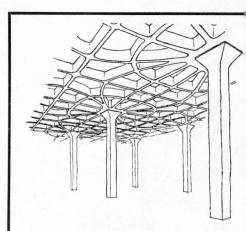

Figure 1

Figure 2

The isostatic ribs of Nervi's Gatti Wool Mill correspond to the natural configuration of the ribs of a leaf in that the forms of both reflect the paths of the forces that act on them

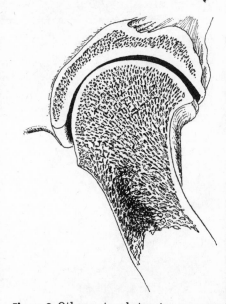

Figure 3. Other natural structures respond to forces with changes in material. In a bone, the wall thickens at the joint, the interior is hollowed out like a sponge

have sought logical shapes for their buildings. The poet-engineers like Maillart and Nervi have been admired for the consistent way they have designed their structures so that the form reflects the path of forces. This might be called the "form follows force" theory and can be substantiated by many examples in nature, particularly in plants.

An esthetic system could be developed as an extension of this theory, using the following argument: From earliest childhood our structural intuition is built up slowly from continually feeling the action of forces on our bodies and from repeatedly seeing natural forms which have received their shape from the forces acting on them. Then, when we are confronted with the isostatic ribs of the Gatti Wool Mill, for example, we are intuitively and consciously aware of the correspondence with the ribs of a leaf. (Figures 1 and 2.) We recognise a principle of design which has general validity. This may be the reason for the almost universal acclaim accorded to the great civil engineering monuments such as bridges and dams whose visible shape is determined by the analysis of forces.

However, we can easily find in nature thousands of examples which are less familiar as structural solutions but which indicate that there are many other aspects to the problem of form and many other answers to our question. Instead of changing the external shape, the material itself may be varied. A section through a bone shows how the solid wall is thickened at the joint and how the structurally less necessary interior is hollowed out like a sponge. The visible shape is determined mainly by mechanical considerations. (See Figure 3.) This might be called the "material follows force" theory of structural design, to distinguish it from the one we have named "form follows force."

Actually the very awkwardness of this terminology reveals the limitations of the theories. The reason is that "structure" by itself is only a concept which is meaningless without reference to some more primary purpose. The objective underlying the form of the leaf is to expose the

maximum number of cells to the sunlight. Its flat shape solves this best and the structure must conform to it, even though ribs subject to bending moments are less efficient than structural elements loaded purely in tension or compression. Even these ribs are given their form as much from their function as food arteries as from structural requirements. An animal must walk or fly or swim. The complicated structure of bones and ligaments and muscles must conform to the mechanical requirements. Similarly the primary forms of ships and airplanes are derived from the requirements of stability and propulsion.

The design of buildings should follow the same principle. The primary form should be given by the need for certain spaces for human activities. In the past we have accepted many limitations on these spaces because of inadequate construction techniques. In fact beauty has been created out of these very limitations. Now that it is technically possible to do almost anything imaginable, we are at a loss. The great architectural problem of our time is to define in human and esthetic terms what the nature of our buildings and cities should be. Every development in technique which frees us from arbitrary limitations should be welcomed, however much it may disorient us when it first appears.

Flat Plates in Reinforced Concrete
An example, though not new, of such a development is the flat plate concrete slab. This consists only of columns and slabs, without drop panels and without capitals for the columns. Here the external form does not follow the distribution of forces as they vary through the slab or column. The building as a whole is primary, with its requirements for mechanical equipment, for the free placement of partitions and for economy. A structurally sensitive design is still possible, however, by varying the nature of the material: the pattern of the steel reinforcement is evidence of this variation.

Flat plate design has been used with increasing frequency in the United States over the past 20 years.

While flat slabs with capitals and drop panels were developed as appropriate for warehouses and factories, flat plates have been found advantageous for the lighter live loads of multi-story apartment houses, offices and hospitals.

The absence of beams and drops simplifies the formwork, permits ductwork and piping to be run without obstructions and usually reduces floor to floor heights. Although flat plate slabs are typically thicker than those supported on beams (usually about $\frac{1}{36}$ of the span), the total quantity of concrete may be less than in a beam and slab floor. The amount of steel is likely to be somewhat greater.

One of the often mentioned advantages of flat plates is the freedom in column location, known by the descriptive term of "spatter column" design. This may help to squeeze low-cost housing plans so that there is no "extravagance" and every room is the exact legal minimum, but it does not save money. Irregular column spacing requires more complicated and hence more expensive structural calculations than regular spacing. Also, irregular bays necessitate variations in sizes and lengths of bars, increasing the cost of reinforcement. Regular bay sizes are definitely more economical and of course can help establish an architectonic rhythm.

Although in general the architect does not personally design the pattern of the reinforcement, it is desirable for him to be aware of the general behavior of a flat plate. A concrete flat slab acts differently from a steel plate of similar span because the stiffness and the strength of the concrete vary with the amount of reinforcement. Given spans, slab thickness and column dimensions, it is mathematically possible and not impractical to calculate accurately the deflections and hence the moments at any point of a steel plate under a given loading, because the material is uniform throughout. The deflections depend on Young's Modulus (E) and on Poisson's ratio, which relates strain in the direction of normal stresses to those at right angles. With steel both of these are constant. For reinforced concrete,

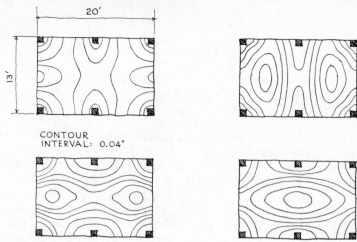

Figure 4. "Contour maps" of the deflections in a flat plate slab show the variations caused by varying the reinforcing steel

both of these vary with the mix of concrete, with the amount and distribution of reinforcement, with the age of the concrete and with the duration of loading.

An interesting illustration of this variation was given by J. Bar of Haifa in the English periodical "Concrete and Constructional Engineering" of November, 1953. A 4-in. slab, freely supported on six 12 by 12-in. columns and loaded only by its own weight, gave four different "contour maps" of deflections merely by varying the steel. These are shown in Figure 4.

It was from studies of this type that Aldo Arcangeli in the office of Nervi and Bartoli devised the concept of isostatic ribs shown in Figure 1, arranging the ribs to intersect each contour line at right angles. Of course, once the ribs are provided, they are bound to carry the maximum share of bending because of their great stiffness. Sensitive structural design is thus a creative act. The magnitude of the stresses will be determined by the variations in form or in material provided by the designer.

Although the most economical spans for flat plates are in the 16 to 24 ft range, Dr. Lev Zetlin, consulting engineer of New York, has recently designed 11-in. thick flat plates spanning 36 ft for the East Branch Public Library in Yonkers, New York (Eli Rabineau, architect). He has also developed an ingenious method for preventing excessive deflections in long spans without using such great thicknesses. For example, a thin slab with a span of 30 ft is calculated with the four corner columns providing necessary moment connections as well as support. Since this will give considerable deflection at the center, another column is introduced as a prop to remove the deflection. This center column can be somewhat slenderer than the corner columns.

This method is illustrated in Figure 5, in which the central prop columns are shown unshaded.

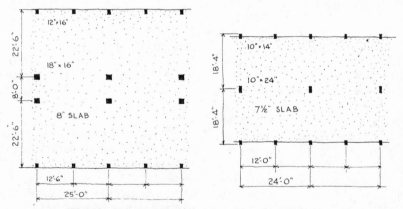

Figure 5. Introducing center "prop" columns prevents excessive deflections in long spans without increasing the thickness of the slab

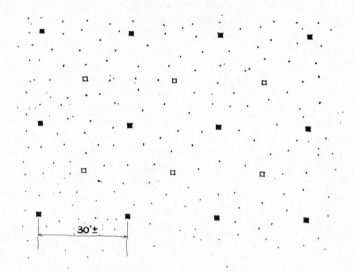

Figure 6. "Half-bay" spacing of exterior columns reduces torsional moments on them, cuts deflection along the edge of the slab

Figure 7. Careful analysis and detailing makes it possible to take advantage of the design implications of column connections like these

Dr. Zetlin has used a somewhat similar device to reduce deflections along the outside edge of a slab and to reduce the torsional moments on the exterior columns. The spacing of the columns along the façade is half that of those on the interior, again minimizing obstructions to free planning. Figure 6 shows two examples, the first for the Cornwall (N.Y.) Hospital, Helge Westermann, architect, and the second for the Sarah Lawrence College Dormitory, Philip Johnson, architect.

Connection between Slab and Column

Much more critical than the general reinforcement of the slab, which is covered adequately by the A.C.I. Code, or the placement of columns is the connection between the slab and column, particularly if the columns are at the edge of the slab.

Many architects are still reluctant to use flat plate design because of the danger of failure when this connection is not properly designed. Unfortunately such failures have occurred. Some engineers refuse to use flat plate design because they

do not believe sufficient stiffness can be provided in the column-slab connection to resist horizontal forces such as wind or earthquake.

This problem has generally been overcome by using spandrel beams, which stiffen the edges of the slab as well as provide an increased area of contact between slab and column. Openings in the slab near the column have been avoided.

Under the pressure of mechanical engineers for duct, pipe and conduit space, and in view of the evident money-saving advantages of simpler formwork, however, Dr. Zetlin has found that the spandrel beam can be omitted and that openings of considerable size can be provided next to the columns. To do this, advantage must be taken of the true shearing strength of concrete and of the great increase in stress resistance achieved by confining the concrete with additional reinforcing around the edges of the section.

The problem can be considered in terms of three possible failures, first imagining the concrete to be unreinforced. Taking the worst possible case, with a large opening next to

the column, Figure 8 indicates the familiar "diagonal tension" failure. Although concrete is strong in shear (about half as strong as in compression), it is weak in tension and cannot resist the tensile stresses which occur along a plane at 45 degrees to the planes of maximum shear. This is easily prevented by diagonal bars or by vertical stirrups.

Figure 9 shows failure in tension due to negative bending. As usual, top steel will prevent this. The region of negative bending will typically extend out about $\frac{1}{5}$ of the span from the column.

In Figure 10 we see the most dangerous possibility and the one most likely to occur—torsion of the slab, which is twisted away from its connection to the column. Just as vertical shear results in a tension failure in concrete, so shearing stresses due to torsion cause tensile stresses to occur along a surface lying at 45 degrees to the surface of maximum shear.

A similar type of failure, with tension along a helicoid surface, can be seen by twisting a piece of

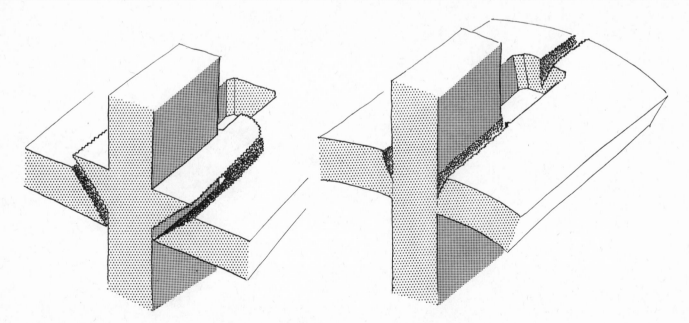

Figure 8. The familiar "diagonal Tension" failure of a flat plate, failure due to tensile stresses along a plane at 45 degrees to the planes of maximum shear, can be prevented by using diagonal reinforcing bars or vertical stirrups

Figure 9. Failure in tension due to negative bending, usually occuring in a region that extends out about two-fifths of the span from the column, can be prevented by careful design and placing of the top reinforcing steel

ordinary chalk or a square eraser until it breaks. The source of the torsion of the slab is found in the rotation of the slab edge as the flat plate is bent or in the bending of the column as it resists the wind.

Analysis of stresses due to torsion arose chiefly in the design of machinery shafting. The French mathematician and physicist Barré de St. Venant published the first complete study of this in 1853. With a circular shaft, the maximum shearing stresses occur along the surface and diminish linearly along radial lines to zero at the center. With non-circular sections, however, warping of the cross-sections occurs. The maximum shearing stresses for a rectangular section will be found at the middle of the long sides, with no shearing stress at the corners.

The column to slab connection shown here is somewhat different because the warping cannot occur immediately adjacent to the face of the column and a greater resistance to torsion is provided. It can also be seen that the tensile stresses due to vertical shear and those due to tor-sion will tend to cancel out, except when torsion occurs in the opposite direction due to the bending of the column under wind loads.

Figure 11 shows a schematic arrangement of the reinforcement as it might be placed to prevent all of these failures. To simplify the drawing, the general reinforcement of the slab is not shown, although it is of course provided.

Analysis by Dr. Zetlin and the engineers in his office have shown theoretically that the stresses in the concrete in such a detail are within the capacities of the material, and experience with constructed buildings has proved the detail to be safe practically. As a result, the architect can add to his vocabulary flat plate floors without spandrel beams and without edge beams around large openings, and can take advantage of the implications for plan and elevation of column connections like those shown in Figure 7.

Of course, it is possible to lay out the floor plan with square bays, and with the columns set in about 2/5 of the bay spacing from the exterior walls, the need for these relatively expensive torsion-resistant connections will be eliminated. The structural solution will be simpler, less expensive and, therefore, "better." However, if this causes awkward planning, the more complicated solution is justified.

References and Credits:

D'Arcy W. Thompson: *On Growth and Form* 2nd edition, Cambridge, 1948

S. P. Timoshenko and S. Woinowsky-Krieger: *Theory of Plates and Shells* 2nd edition, McGraw-Hill, 1959

S. P. Timoshenko: *History of Strength of Materials*, McGraw-Hill, 1953

J. DiStasio and M. P. van Buren: *Flat Plate Floors Designed as Continuous Frames*, Portland Cement Assoc., 1947

American Concrete Institute: *Building Code Requirements for Reinforced Concrete* (ACI 318-56), 1956

Figure 1 redrawn from photograph in: P. L. Nervi, *Structures*, F. W. Dodge, 1956

Figure 3 redrawn from photograph in: Andreas Feininger, *The Anatomy of Nature*, Crown, 1956

Figure 4 redrawn from diagrams in: J. Bar, "A Method of Designing Slabs", *Concrete and Constructional Engineering*, Nov., 1953

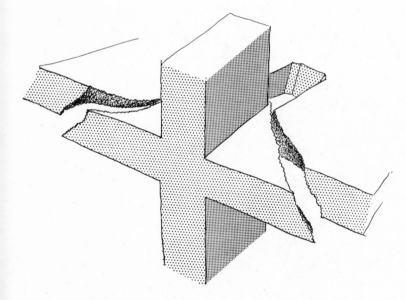

Figure 10. Another common type of tension failure is caused by shearing stresses due to torsion of the slab. However, warping cannot occur adjacent to the column face, which helps the resistance to shear

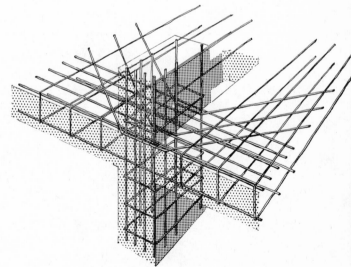

Figure 11. This schematic diagram indicates how reinforcement might be arranged to prevent the failures shown by keeping stresses within the capacity of the concrete. To simplify the drawing, general reinforcement of the slab is not shown

A PHILOSOPHY OF STRUCTURAL DESIGN

by Pier Luigi Nervi

Excerpts from *Structures* by Pier Luigi Nervi, McGraw-Hill Book Company, New York, 1956.

MANY DEBATES about architecture have been heard during the last decades and they continue today. But even if debates led to final conclusions, acceptable to the most severe critics, their practical results would be meager unless the client's judgment, the techniques and economics of building, and the academic preparation of the designer were adequate to the solution of the new architectural, structural and economic problems.

Similarly, the present dynamic development of theoretical research on reinforced concrete will not yield practical results unless we obtain a better knowledge of the actual behavior of this material and learn to relate more strictly the elements of structural intuition, mathematical calculation and construction procedure. Only a perfect synthesis of these factors can realize the unlimited technological and architectural potentialities of reinforced concrete structures.

Construction gathers in a unique synthesis the elements of manual labor, industrial organization, scientific theory, esthetic sensibility, and great economic interests. Construction creates our physical environment, and thus exercises a silent but deep educational influence.

On the other hand, we all help to determine its characteristics and the direction of its development by passing judgments, by expressing preferences or dislikes, or by intervening directly in the construction process.

THE ROLE of the client is as important as it is difficult. In my long life as a designer and builder, I have seldom found clients capable of stating their problem clearly, of choosing the designer and his design wisely, or of accepting the responsibility for a daring structural or esthetic solution.

The designer, after a thorough study of the problem and under the impulse of his creativity, is naturally and understandably daring. The courageous decision of the client is to be admired much more, since it must be unemotional and must weigh, on one hand, his desire to build a structure in which he believes, but which will not necessarily be identified with him, and, on the other, his personal loss if it should fail. The client influences the architectural solution directly. Consciously or unconsciously, by defining the general outline of the structure, by choosing the designer, and by accepting or rejecting the designer's project, he becomes a decisive element of the architectural solution.

The whole structural concept and visual effect of the famed shell for the Turin Exposition Building were made possible through the utilization of a construction material developed by Nervi called Ferro-cemento. It consists of layers of fine wire mesh, and sometimes small bars, embedded in cement mortar to form prefabricated elements. For this shell they are only $1\frac{1}{2}$-in. thick, and thus comparatively lightweight. They are connected at the top and bottom of the undulations by concrete arches

The average quality of the architecture of a nation is more influenced by the tendencies and the cultural level of the clients than by the knowledge and esthetic sensibility of its architects. Any hope that the modern architect, even if exceptionally capable, may win over the unsympathetic client is completely vain: in a coarse society the refined architect will be permanently unemployed.

THE ACADEMIC TRAINING of designers and builders presents a complex and difficult problem. Our universities lack tradition in the scientific approach to building because the theoretical study of structural and construction problems is only about a hundred years old. As far as an artistic approach is concerned, the revolutionary changes in the basic concepts of architectural esthetics, initiated at the beginning of our century and still

in progress, have not given us clearly defined directives, even if they have succeeded in separating our problem from those of the Beaux-Arts academies.

All fields of knowledge play a role in the field of architecture and must find in it a balance capable of expressing values of an artistic, moral and social character which are neither easily definable nor commensurable. Moreover these values are, in a sense, absolute values that truly represent the essential characteristics of all construction — durability in time.

It is my belief that to express an esthetic feeling through the states of static equilibrium, the satisfaction of functional needs and technical and economic requirements — that is, by such

a variety of knowledge — is much more difficult than to express any other kind of feeling by other intellectual means.

The loftiest and most difficult problems arise in architecture from the necessity of realizing a synthesis between opposing sets of factors: the harmony of form and the requirements of technology, the heat of inspiration and the coolness of scientific reason, the freedom of imagination and the iron laws of economy.

DO BUILDING PROBLEMS, even in their most technical aspects (for instance, stability) allow unique and impersonal solutions obtainable by the application of mathematical formulas? Or, on the contrary, can they be solved correctly only through a superior and purely intuitive re-elaboration of the mathematical results, because of the complexity of the inherent deficiency of our theoretical knowledge and, finally, the wide discrepancies between theoretical premises and physical reality?

In this re-elaboration lies the most promising means of penetrating the mysteries of the structural world.

Probably because I have failed to make myself clear, I have often been interpreted as trying to undervalue the results achieved by the mathematical theory of structures. I have thus been both championed and contradicted by people who did not understand my thoughts.

It would be absurd to deny the usefullness of that body of theorems, mathematical developments, and formulas known by the rather inaccurate name of "Theory of Structures." But we must also recognize that these theoretical results are a vague and approximate image of physical reality. We come nearer to this reality only by adding to the mathematical results the results of experiments, by observing the actual phenomena, by establishing a conceptual basis of these phenomena, and above all by understanding intuitively the static behavior of our works.

The fundamental assumption of the theory of structures is that structural materials are isotropic and perfectly elastic. But the most commonly used building materials, like masonry and concrete, are far from being isotropic and elastic.

Theory of structures considers our buildings being out of time, in a kind of eternal stability and invariability. The simple and commonplace fact that all structures decay and, after shorter or longer periods of time, become un-

stable, or at least show excessive displacements and amounts of damage, proves that this second assumption is also unrealistic.

No soil is perfectly stable nor settles uniformly as time goes by. All building materials, but particularly masonry and concrete, flow viscously. The daily and seasonal temperature variations are irregularly distributed in the structure because of prevented displacements, and create stresses of unforeseeable magnitude and direction.

In other words, theory of structures may be compared to a physiology of perfect organisms which are permanently youthful and untouched by disease or functional deficiencies. The programs of our schools of engineering, from which the structural training of our architectural schools are derived, were set up during the second half of the past century. This was a period of great and justified enthusiasm for the developments of mathematical theory of elasticity which clarified the behavior of materials under load and allowed the analysis of statically indeterminate structures. As usual this enthusiasm impaired the objectivity of the engineer, who was led by his mental make-up to believe in the theory even when it was contradicted by facts.

The pre-eminence given to mathematics in our schools of engineering, the purely analytical basis of the theory of elasticity, and its intrinsic difficulties, persuade the young student that there is limitless potency in theoretical calculations, and give him blind faith in their results. Under these conditions neither students nor teachers try to understand and to feel intuitively the physical reality of a structure, how it moves under load, and how the various elements of a statically indeterminate system react among themselves.

We cannot deny that the potentialities of mathematical methods are soon exhausted, even when their application is difficult and complex. Skin-resistant and highly indeterminate structures cannot be analyzed by mathematical theories, although these structures are extremely efficient from a technical, economical and architectural viewpoint.

The formative stage of a design, during which its main characteristics are defined and its qualities and faults are determined once and for all, cannot make use of structural theory and must resort to intuition and schematic simplifications. The essential part of the design of a building consists in conceiving and proportioning its structural system,

Model analysis in design and prefabricated components in construction are two basic elements in the building philosophy of Nervi. His hangars exemplify both. (There were six, all destroyed by war.) The first hangar, (top) built in 1935, was cast in place, and its design was based primarily on model analysis. A major improvement in later hangars was the use of prefabricated trusses to lighten the structure. Trusses were joined by welding of reinforcing bars and filling space with high-strength concrete

in evaluating intuitively the dangerous thermal conditions and support settlements, in choosing materials and construction methods best adapted to the final purpose of the work and to its environment; and, finally, in seeking economy. When all these essential problems have been solved and the structure is thus completely defined, then and only then can we and should we apply the formulas of the mathematical theory of elasticity to specify with greater accuracy its load resisting elements.

The student lacking a thorough knowledge of structures considers an actual building essentially as a form. This attitude fosters solutions which are statically illogical and at times unrealizable, and starts an inner conflict between a desire for structural audacity and the incapacity of its realization, which is common to the great majority of designers today.

Unfortunately, although the present methods of stress analysis are extremely ingenious and one may hope that they will be refined in the near future, their efficiency in solving complicated statically indeterminate systems (particularly three-dimensional systems) is limited in comparison with the creative potentialities of the imaginative designer and the available construction methods. Some of the newer systems cannot be analyzed theoretically, and, therefore, their realization would be impossible without the practically limitless assistance offered by experimental stress analysis.

The only drawback to the experimental procedure is that the preparation of the model, its loading, and the reading of gauges are lengthy and costly operations. Whenever possible, it is therefore more convenient to use a theoretical approach and to limit the use of model analysis to structures of special technical and architectural importance.

WHAT SIGNIFICANCE can we give, and what limits can we assign, to the word *art* in the field of construction? Can we consider as an artistic fact a structure or a building which is strictly defined by the laws of statics and dynamics, independent as they are of the human will and of our esthetic feelings? Are the parabolic profile of a great bridge, the catenary of a suspension bridge, the aerodynamic shape of an airplane to be considered artistic? Doesn't art require a freedom of form and of expression denied to all human products governed by physical laws? And how are we to establish how much freedom is necessary and sufficient to art?

I believe that art gives more than simple esthetic satisfaction. I think art is to be found in that indefinable quality of work to evoke in our minds the feelings and emotions experienced by the artist in the impetus of creation. If this emotional communication be the test of art, to define its characteristics is obviously impossible and to try to teach art would be negative and fruitless.

I believe, therefore, that the most effective artistic training should not go beyond those limits which in the field of literature are represented by grammar and syntax; that is, beyond the mastering of the means of expression. These means allow one to say what is to be said in correct, understandable, and formally satisfying sentences, or at least sentences which are not unpleasant.

The field of architecture presents the same situations. The real danger to architecture, today as always, is not represented by a simple, humble, and correct approach to its problems, but by an emphasis on rhetoric or by a decorative vacuum. These dangers are of a more fundamental character in architecture than in literature, since one cannot ignore an architectural failure, and one cannot forget the economical losses due to architectural rhetoric.

I believe, therefore, that the schools of architecture should above all teach structural correctness, which is identical with functional, technical, and economic truthfulness and is a necessary and sufficient condition of satisfactory esthetic results. The esthetic results achieved by these means usually suffice even if they do not reach superior heights of art.

I believe that even philosophers interested in esthetics find it difficult to explain the origin of our feelings toward forms which are dictated by the laws of statics or dynamics, since these

laws are not intuitively understood, nor are they explainable by the experience of our ancestors. But there is no doubt that any product of high efficiency is always esthetically satisfying.

REINFORCED CONCRETE is truly the most interesting and fertile structural material available to mankind today because of its high compressive strength, its exceptional weather resistance, its constructional simplicity, and its relatively low cost.

As against these and many other positive qualities, reinforced concrete presents some hidden deficiencies and specific characteristics which make its structural behavior difficult, if not altogether impossible, to foresee exactly. Its high thermal sensitivity, its shrinkage, and above all its plasticity, shatter our hopes of investigating or knowing either before or after construction the real conditions of equilibrium of any statically indeterminate structure.

A few days after being poured, a concrete structure, particularly if it is complicated, is strained by internal forces that are independent of the external loads. These forces grow with the shrinkage of concrete and under the influence of thermal variations until the plastic flow of overstressed sections or the development of fine cracks brings about a sufficiently stable condition of equilibrium.

We must frankly confess that neither the designer nor the builder can be entirely satisfied with this final result. Even if the cracks, the excessive stresses, and the plastic flow are not considered dangerous, the solution is obtained at the cost of the structural continuity of the building — that same continuity which was the object of such complicated calculations.

Another factor of great importance to the success of a reinforced concrete structure is good formwork. The lowering of the forms of a concrete structure may well be compared to the critical moment of delivery. Whenever I have witnessed the lowering of the forms of a large structure constituting a single static system, I have noticed the impossibility of lowering all the forms simultaneously and have asked myself with deep anxiety whether the strains and the irregular conditions of loading to which the structure was subjected at the time would not induce stresses far above the allowable limits, or even above the breaking point. The adaptability of concrete structures to unforeseen conditions and their capacity to over-

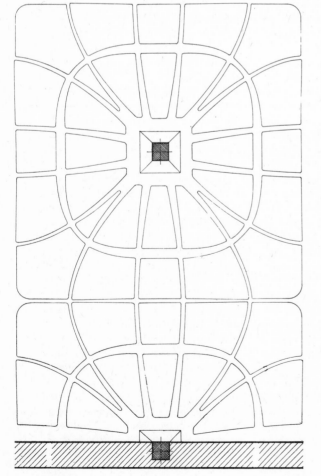

"*The pattern of steel should always have an esthetic quality and give the impression of being a nervous system capable of bringing life to the dead mass of concrete.*" Amazingly, such a design condition may arise out of the structural requirements, as in the Gatti wool plant in Rome. Slab ribs are set along the isostatic lines of principal stress. These lines depend exclusively on the loading of the floor. Movable forms of Ferro-cemento, cast previously in plaster molds, allow complete freedom of form in the ribs

come temporary critical strains always fill me with wonder and admiration.

Although it is difficult to achieve an economical and permanent concrete structure which will remain youthful throughout the years, I shall make a few suggestions on how best to approach the goal.

My first and perhaps most fundamental suggestion is to create structures which are harmonious both in form and in the distribution of steel reinforcement. This quality, which may seem totally abstract and only esthetically important, has a deep correspondence with the physical reality of the structure. As I pointed out above, because of its inherent and unavoidable continuity, a concrete structure is an organism in which stresses spread from one element to another so that all together they withstand the internal or external forces menacing its stability. Almost always these forces are not only those considered as loads in the computations, but also those deriving from shrinkage, thermal variations, and yielding of the supports.

This complicated state of stress in the structure creates singular regions where stress concentrations are bound to arise as soon as the various elements are not well proportioned. Stress concentrations in turn are responsible for both capillary and large cracks. Hence, we must avoid all dimensional discontinuities between adjacent elements and substantial differences in the steel content of the sections of a member or adjacent members.

The steel reinforcement of a com-

plicated structure should be so designed as to form in itself a stable structure capable qualitatively of sustaining the load. The added concrete should then be capable of implementing the equilibrium quantitatively, by connecting the steel bars and by absorbing compressive stresses. The pattern of steel should always have an esthetic quality and give the impression of being a nervous system capable of bringing life to the dead mass of concrete.

THE MOST SPECIFIC characteristic of concrete which usually determines its structural behavior and makes it so difficult to analyze, is the remarkable variability of its stress-strain ratio — that is, its imperfect elastic behavior.

In the first place the elastic modulus of concrete varies due to the problems inherent in mixing, placing and curing. Secondly, the elastic modulus changes due to plastic stresses and the strains or yielding under constant load (viscosity). The structural consequences of these two sets of causes are substantially different.

The first type of variability only gives trouble when it causes the elastic modulus of concrete to differ in two collaborating members of the same structure.

The changes in the elastic modulus due to the second set of causes, including the decrease of the modulus with stress, its increase under repeated loading, and its plastic flow under load, is of greater structural importance.

Due mainly to plastic flow, a concrete structure tries to adapt itself with admirable docility to our calculation schemes, which do not always represent the most logical and spontaneous answer to the requests of the forces at play, and it even tries to correct our deficiencies and errors. Sections and regions too highly stressed yield and channel some of their loads to other sections or regions which accept this additional task with a commendable spirit of collaboration within the limits of their own strength.

What are our present chances of understanding and of mastering such complicated phenomena? At present their qualitative and quantitative determination is out of our grasp. A designer bold enough purposely to increase or decrease the plasticity of certain concrete elements, contributing with others to the strength of the same structure, does not have quantitative data that can lead him to even roughly approximate results. In practice, the importance of this

data would be fundamental. For example, by increasing the plasticity of certain parts of fixed arches the pressure resultant due to the dead load could be centered at all sections, thus resulting in great economy for these structures, in which live load is of minor importance.

THE FUNDAMENTAL IDEA behind the new reinforced concrete material Ferrocemento which I have developed is the well known fact that concrete sustains large strains in the neighborhood of the reinforcement, and that the magnitude of the strains depends on the distribution and subdivision of the reinforcement throughout the mass of concrete. With this principle as a starting point, I asked myself what would be the behavior of thin slabs in which the proportion and subdivision of the reinforcement were increased to a maximum by surrounding layers of fine steel mesh, one on top of the other, with cement mortar.

The square mesh was made out of ductile steel wires 0.02 to 0.06 in. diameter, set 0.4 in. apart. The mortar was made of 0.6 to 0.75 lb of cement to the cubic foot of good quality sand. The slabs were very thin but extremely flexible, elastic, and strong.

Later on, in order to increase the thickness and the strength of the slabs without using more than 10 to 12 layers of mesh, I tried inserting one or more layers of steel bars 0.25 to 0.4 in. in diameter between the middle layers of mesh, thus attaining thicknesses of 2.5 to 4 in.

The material thus obtained did not behave like regular concrete, but presented all the mechanical characteristics of a homogenous material.

Experiments with the new material demonstrated immediately its most important and fruitful properties: absence of cracks in the cement mortar even with a large amount of strain because of the subdivision of the reinforcement; and elimination of forms since the mesh acted as a lath to retain mortar.

During the last few years I have constructed buildings in which Ferrocemento was not only conveniently and interestingly applied, but also was a decisive design factor both technically and architecturally.

The most important of these applications is the large undulated shell of the central hall of the Turin Exposition Building, which spans 300 ft. The shell is built with prefabricated elements of Ferro-cemento, connected by reinforced concrete arches at the top and the bottom of the undulations.

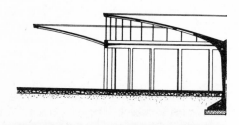

A highly expressive geometric pattern was formed in the ceiling of this restaurant designed by A. La Padula through a refinement in Nervi's prefabrication techniques. Precast, coffered sections, about 1-in. thick were assembled on a platform with spaces left between for reinforcing of the stiffening ribs

REINFORCED CONCRETE is the most revolutionary material of our entire building history. The essence of the revolution consists in the possibility of realizing structures in perfect conformance to statical needs and visually expressive of the play of forces within them.

The most elementary structural elements acquire new and expressive interest. Beams lose the prismatic rigidity of wooden struts and of standard metal sections, and may plastically follow the variations of stress. Columns free themselves from the constant cross-section of stone and masonry pillars. Three-dimensional structures, like domes and barrels, acquire a freedom of form unknown to masonry.

The full development of reinforced concrete depends partly on the mental development of the designer, who must consider the concrete structure as the materialization of the most efficient structural system, but also on the refinement of construction procedures. Through study of these construction methods the rigidity of wooden forms can be eliminated, allowing the economic realization of curved surfaces and elements of variable cross-section, as required by the flow of stress.

Architecturally and structurally, concrete is promising in the field of skin-resistant structures, that is, those structures whose strength is a direct consequence of the curvatures and corrugations of their surfaces.

We cannot deny that the practical realization of large form-resistant structures presents great design difficulties. These theoretical difficulties are, in my opinion, neither unsurmountable nor great. Not only is the theory of struc-

tures being continuously developed, but even today we can solve satisfactorily the most complicated structural problem by experimental stress analysis. The real difficulty to be overcome is the general lack of intuitive understanding about the structural behavior of these resistant systems, and the difficulty of communicating such intuitive knowledge to others.

The many examples of form-resistant structures such as flowers, leaves, sea shells, etc., are either too small in scale to involve the weight of our body or the strength of our muscles, or, being decorative, do not suggest a direct structural experience. Other examples of form-resistant structures, like automobile bodies, airplane wings, and ship hulls, polarize our attention exclusively towards mechanical systems and, hence cannot be translated easily into civil engineering structures. Thus resistance due to form, although the most efficient and the most common type of resistance to be found in nature, has not built yet in our minds those subconscious structural intuitions which are the basis of our structural schemes and realizations. In other words, we are not yet used to thinking structurally in terms of form.

How CAN WE DEFINE and limit the technical potentialities of a material which in fifty short years has conquered the most varied fields of construction? Its structural limitations are hard to foresee. Although our knowledge of concrete is anything but complete, we are already capable of building concrete bridges spanning over 1000 ft (a few years ago Freyssinet designed a bridge spanning over 3000 ft), thin shell barrels and domes spanning over 1000 ft, framed structures for very tall buildings and dams capable of withstanding the pressure of many hundreds of feet of water.

When the actual behavior of concrete under load and in time is better known, when laboratory practices capable of producing 14,000-psi concrete are commonly applied in the field, and when plastic redistribution of stress in complicated structures is foreseeable, the amazing results achieved so far will be easily surpassed.

The shape of things to come is clearly illustrated by the construction of airplane wings of prestressed concrete designed by Freyssinet and built by the Brequet Co. (*See Technique et Science, Aeronautique*, October, 1953). An actual *flying stone* has been realized. What else are we to expect from such a wonderful structural material?

INDEX